Food for the Heart

Food for the Heart

*The Collected Teachings
of Ajahn Chah*

WISDOM PUBLICATIONS • BOSTON

Wisdom Publications
199 Elm Street
Somerville, MA 02144 USA
www.wisdompubs.org

Library of Congress Cataloging-in-Publication Data
Chah, Achaan.
    Food for the Heart / by Ajahn Chah ; foreword by
Jack Kornfield ; introduction by Ajahn Amaro.
        p. cm.
    Includes index.
    ISBN 0-86171-323-0 (alk. paper)
        1. Dharma (Buddhism). 2. Spiritual life—Buddhism.
    3. Buddhism—Doctrines. I. Title.
    BQ4190.C53 2002
    294.3'4—dc21   2002004798

ISBN 0-86171-323-0

First Edition
07 06
6   5   4

Jacket design: Richard Snizik
Interior design: Gopa & Ted2
Back cover photo by Thubten Yeshe

Printed in Canada.

CONTENTS

# FOREWORD

I T'S HARD TO KNOW how to best introduce the wisest man I have ever met. In his presence, there was immediacy and aliveness, simplicity and truth-telling, dignity and intimacy; humor and serious discipline, heart-breaking compassion and spontaneous freedom. Ajahn Amaro's beautiful introduction to this book describes him well.

Most of Ajahn Chah's teaching was done in the reality of the moment, by example, by metaphor, by the aliveness of dialogue. His teaching was direct and honest, with no holds barred. "Look at the cause of suffering in this human realm, it's like this," he would say, pointing our hearts toward the truth. Because he was a consummate performer who taught with a hundred skillful means, because he met each new visitor so directly, adapting his humor and penetrating eye to the circumstances before him, it is hard to wholly capture the vitality of his teaching in words. Fortunately, his legacy also includes nearly two hundred monasteries, many wonderful living and teaching disciples, hundreds of tapes recorded in Thai and some millions of people who have been touched by his wisdom.

On these pages you will find another aspect of Ajahn Chah, the disciplined and somewhat serious side primarily recorded on occasions where he offered longer systematic teachings to groups of monks, nuns, and visitors. In them he invites us all to reflect on the essence of the teachings, to consider them, to take them to heart. In this book he leaps off the page to remind us that, whoever we are, the conditions of life are uncertain: "If death is within you, then where are you going to run to escape it? Whether you are afraid or not, you die just the same. There is nowhere to escape death."

From this ground of truth, he points the way that leads endlessly beyond the changing conditions of birth and death to true freedom. "This is the important thing: you must contemplate until you reach the point where you let go, where there isn't anything left, beyond good and bad, coming and going, birth and death. Train the heart, rest in the unconditioned," he urges. "Liberation is possible."

Those who would follow the teachings of this beloved master must be willing to look into their own heart and mind, to loosen the knots, release the grasping, the fears, the whole false sense of self. "If you really understand, no matter what life you live, you can practice the Dhamma every minute of the day. Why not give it a try?" Ajahn Chah suggests. "It will transform your life!"

May the blessings of the compassionate Buddha be carried by Ajahn Chah's words to feed your heart and benefit all beings everywhere.

With great respect,

Jack Kornfield
Spirit Rock Meditation Center
Woodacre, California, 2002

INTRODUCTION

NIGHT IS FALLING SWIFTLY. The forest reverberates with the undulating buzz of countless crickets and the eerie rising wail of tropical cicadas. A few stars poke dimly through the treetops. Amid the gathering darkness there is a pool of warm light, thrown from a pair of kerosene lanterns, illuminating the open area below a hut raised up on stilts. Beneath it, in the glow, a couple of dozen people are gathered around a small, solidly built monk who is seated cross-legged on a wicker bench. The air is filled with a vibrant peace. Venerable Ajahn Chah is teaching.

In some ways, the group that is gathered here is a motley crew: close beside Ajahn Chah (or *Luang Por*, Venerable Father, as he is affectionately known to his students) are a cluster of *bhikkhus* (monks) and novices; most of them are Thai or Lao, but there are a few pale-skinned figures among them—a Canadian, two Americans, a young Australian, and an Englishman. In front of the Ajahn sits a well-groomed, middle-aged couple—he in a stiff suit, and she coiffed and gold-bedecked—he's a member of parliament from a distant province; they're taking the opportunity while he's in the area on official business to come and pay their respects and make some offerings to the monastery.

A little behind them and to both sides are scattered a sizeable group of local villagers. Their shirts and blouses are worn thin, and the skin on their lean limbs is sun-darkened, wrinkled—baked like the poor earth of the region. A few of those here Luang Por played with as a child—catching frogs and climbing trees—others he helped, and was helped by, in the years before he was a bhikkhu, as they planted out their annual round of rice seedlings and then harvested the fields together at the end of the monsoon. To one side, near the back, is a professor from Freiburg who has come to

Thailand with a friend from her local Dhamma (Skt. *Dharma*) group to study Buddhism; an American nun has come over with her from the women's section of the monastery to guide her through the forest paths and to translate.

Beside them sit three or four other nuns, elder sisters from the nuns' section who decided to take the opportunity to come over as well to ask advice from Luang Por about an issue in the women's community and to request that he come over to their side of the forest and give a Dhamma talk to their whole group—it's been several days now since he last paid them a visit. They've been there for a couple of hours already, so they pay their respects and take their leave, along with the other visitors from the nuns' section—they need to be back before dark and they're already a little late.

Near the back, almost at the edge of the pool of light, sits a stern-faced man in his thirties. He is half turned to one side, as if his presence there is uncomfortable, tentative. He is a local tough guy—a *nak leng.* Deeply disdainful of all things supposedly religious, he nevertheless has a grudging respect for Luang Por; probably stemming as much from the monk's reputation for toughness and his powers of endurance as from the recognition that, as far as religious people go, he might be the real thing—"but he's probably the only one worth bowing to in the whole province."

He's angry and upset, sick at heart. A week ago his beloved younger brother—who ran with his gang and with whom he'd been through a thousand scrapes—came down with cerebral malaria and was dead within days. Since then he has felt as if his heart had a spear through it and that everything in the world had lost its flavor. "If he had been killed in a knife fight at least I could take revenge—what am I going to do: track down the mosquito that bit him and kill it?" "Why not go see Luang Por Chah?" a friend had said. So here he is.

Luang Por smiles broadly as he makes a point, holding up a glass to illustrate his analogy. He has noticed the stark young figure in the shadows. Soon he has somehow managed to coax him to the front, as if he were reeling in a tough and wily fish; next thing, the tough guy has his head in Luang Por's hands and is weeping like a baby; next, he is somehow laughing at his own arrogance and self-obsession—he realizes that he's not the first or only person ever to have lost a dear one—the tears of rage and grief have turned to tears of relief.

All of this happens with twenty total strangers around, yet the atmosphere is one of safety and trust. For although those assembled come from all walks of life and from all around the planet, they are all united at this one moment and place as *saha-dhammika* "fellow Dhamma-farers" or, to use another expression from the Buddhist vernacular, they are all "brothers and sisters in old age, sickness, and death," and thus belong to a single family.

This kind of scenario was played out countless times during the thirty years that Ajahn Chah spent teaching, and it was often at such times that someone had the foresight to bring along a tape recorder (and had managed to find enough batteries to keep it alive) and thus caught some of the talks gathered in this book.

Along with such longer expositions as are printed here, the reader should also know that, more often than not, especially in such informal dialogues, the flow of teaching, and to whom in particular it was directed, was highly spontaneous and unpredictable. In many ways when Ajahn Chah was teaching, he was like a master musician: both leading the flow of harmonious sound and yet producing it entirely in response to the natures and moods of the people he was with; integrating their words, feelings, and questions in the crucible of his heart, and letting the responses flow forth freely.

In any kind of crowd gathered around him, he might use an example of the right and wrong ways to peel a mango one moment, then be describing the nature of ultimate reality the next—with identical matter-of-fact familiarity. In one moment he might be gruff and cold to the inflated, then charming and gentle to the shy; he might crack a joke with an old friend from the village and, with the next turn, look a corrupt police colonel in the eye and speak sincerely of the centrality of honesty on the Path. Within a few minutes he might scold a bhikkhu for being sloppily dressed, then let his own robe slip off his shoulder and allow his rotund belly to show forth. A clever question from an academic type, seeking high-minded philosophical discussion to display his own acumen, might easily find Luang Por's hand moving to remove his false teeth and then handing them to his attendant bhikkhu to be cleaned up a little. His interlocutor would then have to pass the test of the great master, responding to his profound question through broad lips folded in over his gums, before his fresh set of teeth was installed.

Some of the talks in this collection were given in such spontaneous gatherings; others were given on more formal occasions—such as after the recitation of the bhikkhus' rules, or to the whole assembly of laity and monastics on the weekly lunar observance night—however, whether they were of either the former or the latter kind, Ajahn Chah never planned anything. Not one syllable of the Dhamma teachings printed here was plotted out before he started speaking. This was an extremely important principle, he felt, as the job of the teacher was to get out of the way and to let the Dhamma arise according to the needs of the moment—"If it's not alive to the present, it's not Dhamma," he would say.

Once he invited the young Ajahn Sumedho (his first Western student) to give a talk to the assembly at the main monastery, Wat Pah Pong. This was a traumatic test—not only to have to speak to a couple of hundred people who were used to Ajahn Chah's high standard of wit and wisdom, but also to have to do it in Thai, a language he had only started learning three or four years before. His mind teemed with fears and ideas. He had been reading about the Six Realms of Buddhist cosmology and their correlation to psychological states (anger and the hell realms, sensual bliss and the heavenly realms, etc.). He decided that this would be a good theme, and he thought through all his ideas and the right phrases for them. On the big night Ajahn Sumedho gave what he felt was a pretty good exposition, and the next day many members of the Sangha came up and said how much they had appreciated his words. He felt relieved and quite pleased with himself. Sometime later, in a quiet moment, Ajahn Chah caught his attention, fixed him with a direct look, and gently said, "Don't ever do that again."

This style of teaching was not unique to Ajahn Chah but is that espoused throughout what is known as the Thai Forest Tradition. Perhaps it would be helpful at this point to describe the character and origins of this lineage, to give a little more sense of the context from which Ajahn Chah's wisdom has sprung.

THE FOREST TRADITION

In a way, the forest meditation tradition predates even the Buddha. Before his time, in India and the Himalayan region, it was not uncommon for those who sought spiritual liberation to leave the life of the town and village and resort to the mountains and forest wildernesses. As a gesture of leaving worldly values behind it made perfect sense: the forest was a wild, natural place, and the only people who were to be found there were the criminal, the insane, the outcast, and the renunciant religious seekers—it was a sphere outside the influence of materialistic cultural norms and thus ideal for the cultivation of the aspects of the spirit that transcended them.

When the Bodhisattva left the life of the palace at the age of 29, it was to move into the forest and to train in the yogic disciplines that were available in his time. The story is well known, how he became dissatisfied with the teachings of his first instructors and left them to find his own way. He did so, discovering that primal chord of truth he named "the Middle Way" under the shade of the bodhi tree, beside the River Nerañjarā, in what is now Bodh-Gaya, in Bihar State, India.

It is frequently stated that the Buddha was born in a forest, was enlightened in a forest, lived and taught his whole life in a forest, and finally passed away in a forest. When choice was possible, the forest was the environment he opted to live in, since, as he would say: "Tathāgatas delight in secluded places." The lineage now known as the Thai Forest Tradition tries to live in the spirit of the way espoused by the Buddha himself, and to practice according to the same standards he encouraged during his lifetime. It is a branch of the Southern School of Buddhism, more commonly referred to as "Theravāda."

As far as the sketchy historical accounts can tell us, a few months after the Buddha's final passing away a great council of elders was held to formalize and establish the teachings (the discourses and the monastic rules) in a standardized form of the vernacular called *Pālibhasa*—"the language of the texts." The Dhamma teachings formulated in this way over the next hundred years form the core of the Pali canon, the common basis of a range of subsequent Buddhist schools. A hundred years later they had a second council, again to go over all the teachings, in an attempt to keep everyone in accord. However, as it transpired, it was at this time that the first major split in the Sangha occurred. The larger portion of the Sangha wanted to change some of the rules, including allowing the monastics to use money.

The smaller group was cautious about these proposed changes. Rather, they felt: "Well, whether it makes sense or not, we want to do things the way the Buddha and his original disciples did." Those of the small group were known as the *Sthaviras* (in Sanskrit) or *Theras* (in Pali), meaning "Elders." After about another 130 years, they gave rise to the Theravāda school. *Theravāda* literally means "the Way of the Elders," and that has been their abiding theme ever since. The ethos of the tradition can be characterized as something like: "For better or worse, that's the way the Buddha established it so that is the way we'll do it." It has thus always had a particularly conservative quality to it.

As with all religious traditions and human institutions, over time a number of branches sprouted from the Buddha's rootstock. It is said that by about 250 years after the Buddha's time, during the reign of the Emperor Asoka, in India, there were up to eighteen, maybe more, schools and lineages with diverging views of the *Buddha-sāsana,* the Buddha's dispensation. One lineage became established in Sri Lanka, somewhat at a remove from the cultural ferment of India, where a Brahminical revival—and religious influences from West and East—all added to the stirrings of new forms of Buddhist thought. This lineage developed in its own way, with less varied input and stimulation. It formulated its commentaries and interpretations of the Pali scriptures with a view not to developing new forms to meet the challenge of other faiths, but to adding details to the Pali texts. Some of these were of the nature of fables, to catch the hearts of ordinary folk; some were more philosophical and metaphysical, with a scholarly appeal. Out of all this, Theravāda Buddhism crystallized. And despite wars, famines, and other cultural upheavals on the Indian subcontinent, the Theravadins have survived to the present day, largely because of originally having become well established on the island of Sri Lanka—a safer haven than many others. Other Buddhist schools operated there; however, Theravāda Buddhism was continually restored and maintained as the main religion of the island.

The lineage eventually spread throughout Southeast Asia, as at different times missionaries were invited from Sri Lanka and India; they went out to Burma and later on to Thailand, Cambodia, and Laos—later, from these countries to the West. Throughout this period of geographical dispersion of the Theravāda tradition, the theme of a continual looking back to the standards of the Pali canon has been sustained. When being established in new countries, there has always been a strong sense of respectfulness and reverence for the original teachings, and also a respect for the style of life as embodied by the Buddha and the original Sangha, the forest-dwelling monastics of the earliest times. This is the model that was employed then and has thus been carried on.

Obviously, in these many centuries there have been many ups and downs, but this pattern is what has been sustained. Sometimes the religion would die down in Sri Lanka, and then some monks would come from Thailand to lift it up again. Then it would fade out in Thailand, and some monks from Burma would boost it up—supporting each other over the centuries. Thus the religion has managed to keep itself afloat and still largely in its original form.

Another aspect of these cycles, along with degeneration, was the problem of success. Often, when the religion became well developed, the monasteries would get rich; the whole system would then become obese and corrupted and begin to collapse under its own weight. Then a splinter group would say, "Let's get back to basics!" go off into the forest, and would again return to those original standards of keeping the monastic rules, practicing meditation, and studying the original teachings.

It is significant to note that this cycle of progress, overinflation, corruption, and reform has taken place many times in many other Buddhist countries over the ages as well. It is striking how the lives and practices of such luminaries as Venerable Patrul Rinpoche in Tibet and Venerable Master Hsu Yün in China (both of the late nineteenth and early twentieth centuries) are totally in accord with the spirit of the Forest Tradition. Both of these great masters chose to live lives of great simplicity, kept the monastic discipline very strictly, were accomplished meditators and highly gifted teachers. They largely avoided the burdens of rank and official responsibility but inevitably came to positions of great influence through the sheer power of their wisdom and virtue. This is exactly the pattern of life as exemplified by the great forest ajahns of Thailand.

By the mid-nineteenth century, Buddhism in Thailand had a rich variety of regional traditions and practices, but the general field of spiritual life had become somewhat corrupt, with lax monastic discipline, Dhamma teachings mixed up with confused vestiges of tantra and animism, plus the fact that hardly anyone practiced meditation anymore. In addition to this, and perhaps most significantly, the orthodox position held by scholars (not just by lax, unlearned, or confused monks) was that it was not possible to realize *nibbāna* in this age or, in fact, even to attain *jhāna* (meditative absorption).[1]

This was something that the revivers of the Forest Tradition refused to accept. It was also one of the reasons for which they were deemed mavericks and troublemakers by the ecclesiastical hierarchy of the time, and it lies behind the obvious disdain many of them (Ajahn Chah included) had for the majority of study monks of their own Theravāda lineage—as well as their refrain that "you don't get wisdom from books."

It is necessary to elaborate on this point, otherwise the reader may wonder why Ajahn Chah is somewhat down on study—especially as Theravāda is supposed to have great reverence for the word of the Buddha. It is a crucial point that delineates the Thai Forest monastics: the determination to focus on life style, and on personal experience, as opposed to books (especially the commentaries). One might find such sentiments presumptuous or arrogant, or seeming to be expressing the jealousy of an unlearned mind for its betters, unless it is understood that the interpretations of scholars were leading Buddhism into a black hole. In short, it was just the kind of situation that made the spiritual landscape ripe for renewal. And it was out of this fertile ground that the revival of the Forest Tradition emerged.

The Thai Forest Tradition would not exist as it does today were it not for the influence of one particular great master. This was the Venerable Ajahn Mun Bhuridatta. He was born in the 1870s in Ubon Province, where Thailand borders Laos and Cambodia. It was then, and still is, one of the poorer quarters of the country, but it is also one where the harshness of the land and the good-humored character of the people have led to a depth of spirituality rare in the world.

Ajahn Mun was a youth with a lively mind—he excelled at the local art of *mor lam,* spontaneously versified folk-song—and also felt strongly drawn to spiritual practice. Soon after his ordination as a bhikkhu he sought out Venerable Ajahn Sao, one of the rare local forest monks, and asked him to teach him meditation; he also had recognized that a rigorous adherence to the monastic discipline would be crucial to his spiritual progress. He became Ajahn Sao's student and threw himself into the practice with great vigor.

Even though both of these elements (that is, meditation and strict discipline) might seem unremarkable from the vantage point of the present day, at that time monastic discipline had grown extremely lax throughout the region, and meditation was looked upon with great suspicion—probably only those who were interested in the dark arts would be foolish enough to go near it, and it was thought likely to drive one insane or cause possession by spirits.

In time, Ajahn Mun successfully explained and demonstrated the use-fulness of meditation to many people and also became an exemplar of a much higher standard of conduct for the monastic community. Further-more, despite living in the remote provinces, he became the most highly regarded of spiritual teachers in his country. Almost all of the most accom-plished and revered meditation masters of the twentieth century in Thai-land were either his direct disciples or were deeply influenced by him. Ajahn Chah was among these.

AJAHN CHAH

Ajahn Chah was born into a large and comfortable family in a village in Ubon Province, northeast Thailand. On his own initiative, at the tender age of nine, he opted to move out of the family home and went to live in the local monastery. He was ordained as a novice and, still feeling the call of the religious life, on reaching the age of twenty took higher ordination. As a young bhikkhu he studied some basic Dhamma, the discipline, and other scriptures. Later, dissatisfied with the slack standard of discipline in his vil-lage temple and yearning for guidance in meditation, he left these relatively secure confines and undertook the life of a wandering or *tudong* bhikkhu. He sought out several of the local meditation masters and practiced under their guidance. He wandered for a number of years in the style of an asce-tic bhikkhu, sleeping in forests, caves, and cremation grounds, and spent a short but enlightening period with Ajahn Mun himself.

Here is a description of that most significant of encounters, from the forthcoming biography of Luang Por Chah *Uppalamani*—a play on words meaning both "The Jewel of Ubon Province" and "The Jewel in the Lotus"—composed by Phra Ong Neung.

At the end of the retreat, Ajahn Chah, together with three other monks and novices and two laymen, set off on the long walk back to Isahn (the northeast of Thailand). They broke the journey at Bahn Gor, and after a few days rest, began a 250-kilometer hike northward. By the tenth day they had reached the elegant white *stūpa* of Taht Panom, an ancient pilgrimage spot on the banks of the Mekong, and paid homage to the Buddha's relics enshrined there. They continued their walk in stages, by now finding forest monasteries along the way in which to spend the night. Even so, it was an arduous trek, and the novice and a layman asked to turn back. The group consisted of just three monks and a layman when they finally arrived at Wat Peu Nong Nahny, the home of the Venerable Ajahn Mun.

As they walked into the monastery, Ajahn Chah was immediately struck by its tranquil and secluded atmosphere. The central area, in which stood a small meeting hall, was immaculately swept, and the few monks they caught sight of were attending to their daily chores silently, with a measured and composed gracefulness. There was something about the monastery that was like no other that he had been in before—the silence was strangely charged and vibrant. Ajahn Chah and his companions were received politely and after being advised where to put up their *glots* (large umbrellas from which a mosquito net is hung) they took a welcome bath to wash off the grime of the road.

In the evening the three young monks, their double-layered outer robes folded neatly over their left shoulders, minds fluctuating between keen anticipation and cold fear, made their way to the wooden *sālā* (meeting hall) to pay respects to Ajahn Mun. Crawling on his knees toward the great master, flanked on both sides by the resident monks, Ajahn Chah approached a slight and aged figure with an indomitable, diamond-like presence. It is easy to imagine Ajahn Mun's bottomless eyes and his deeply penetrating gaze boring into Ajahn Chah as he bowed three times and sat down at a suitable distance. Most of the monks were sitting with eyes closed in meditation; one sat slightly behind Ajahn Mun, slowly fanning away the evening's mosquitoes. As Ajahn Chah glanced up, he would have noticed how prominently Ajahn Mun's collarbone jutted through the pale skin above his robe and how his thin mouth, stained red with betel juice, formed such an arresting contrast to the strange luminosity of his presence. As is the time-honored custom among Buddhist monks, Ajahn Mun first asked the visitors how long they had been in the robes, the monasteries they had practiced in, and the details of their journey. Did they have any doubts about the practice? Ajahn Chah swallowed. Yes, he did. He had been studying *vinaya* texts with great enthusiasm but had become discouraged. The discipline seemed too detailed to be practical; it didn't seem possible to keep every single rule; what should one's standard be? Ajahn Mun advised Ajahn Chah to take the "Two Guardians of the World," *hiri* (a sense of shame) and *ottappa* (intelligent fear of consequences), as his basic principle. In the presence of those two virtues, he said, everything else would follow. He then began to discourse on the threefold training of *sīla*,[2] *samādhi*,[3] and *paññā*, the four Roads to Success, and the five Spiritual Powers. Eyes half closed, his voice becoming stronger and faster as he proceeded, as if he were moving into a higher and higher gear. With absolute authority he described the "way things truly are" and the path to liberation. Ajahn Chah and his companions sat completely enrapt. Ajahn Chah later said that although he had spent an exhausting day on the road, hearing Ajahn Mun's Dhamma talk made all of his weariness disappear; his mind became peaceful and clear, and he felt as if he were floating in the air above his seat. It was late at night before Ajahn Mun called the meeting to an end and Ajahn Chah returned to his glot, aglow.

On the second night Ajahn Mun gave more teachings, and Ajahn Chah felt that he had come to the end of his doubts about the practice that lay ahead. He felt a joy and rapture in the Dhamma that he had never known before. Now what remained was for him to put his knowledge into practice. Indeed, one of the teachings that had inspired him the most on those two evenings was this injunction to make himself *Sikkhibhūto* (that is, a witness to the truth). But the most clarifying explanation, one that gave him the necessary context or basis for practice that he had hitherto been lacking, was of a distinction between the mind itself and transient states of mind that arose and passed away within it.

"Tan Ajahn Mun said they're merely states. Through not understanding that point we take them to be real, to be the mind itself. In fact they're all just transient states. As soon as he said that, things suddenly became clear. Suppose there's happiness present in the mind— it's a different kind of thing, it's on a different level, to the mind itself. If you see that, then you can stop; you can put things down. When conventional realities are seen for what they are, then it's ultimate truth. Most people lump everything together as the mind itself, but actually there are states of mind together with the knowing of them. If you understand that point then there's not a lot to do."

On the third day Ajahn Chah paid his respects to Ajahn Mun and led his small group off into the lonely forests of Poopahn once more. He left Nong Peu behind him never to return again, but with his heart full of an inspiration that would stay with him for the rest of his life.

In 1954, after many years of travel and practice, he was invited to settle in a dense forest near the village of his birth, Bahn Gor. This grove was uninhabited, known as a place of cobras, tigers, and ghosts, thus being as he said, the perfect location for a forest bhikkhu. A large monastery formed around Ajahn Chah as more and more bhikkhus, nuns, and lay people came to hear his teachings and stay on to practice with him. Now there are disciples living, practicing meditation, and teaching in more than two hundred mountain and forest branch monasteries throughout Thailand and the West.

Although Ajahn Chah passed away in 1992, the training that he established is still carried on at Wat Pah Pong and its branches. There is usually group meditation twice a day and sometimes a talk by the senior teacher, but the heart of the meditation is the way of life. The monastics do manual work, dye and sew their own robes, make most of their own requisites and keep the monastery buildings and grounds in immaculate condition. They live extremely simply, following the ascetic precepts of eating once a day from the alms bowl and limiting their possessions. Scattered throughout the forest are individual huts where bhikkhus and nuns live and meditate in solitude, and where they practice walking meditation on cleared paths under the trees.

In some of the monasteries in the West, and at a few in Thailand, the physical location of the center dictates that there might be some small variations to this style—for instance, the monastery in Switzerland is situated in an old wooden hotel building at the edge of a mountain village—however, regardless of such differences, the exact same spirit of simplicity, quietude, and scrupulosity sets the abiding tone. Discipline is maintained strictly, enabling one to lead a simple and pure life in a harmoniously regulated community where virtue, meditation, and understanding may be skillfully and continuously cultivated.

Along with monastic life as it is lived within the bounds of fixed locations, the practice of tudong—wandering on foot through the countryside, on pilgrimage or in search of quiet places for solitary retreat—is still considered a central part of spiritual training. Even though the forests have been disappearing rapidly throughout Thailand, and the tigers and other wild creatures so often encountered during such tudong journeys in the past have been depleted almost to the point of extinction, it has still been possible for this way of life and practice to continue. Indeed, not only has this practice been maintained by Ajahn Chah, his disciples, and many other forest monastics in Thailand, it has also been sustained by his monks and nuns in many countries of the West and in India. In these situations the strict standards of conduct are still maintained: living only on almsfood freely offered by local people, eating only between dawn and noon, not carrying or using money, sleeping wherever shelter can be found.

Wisdom is a way of living and being, and Ajahn Chah endeavored to preserve the simple monastic lifestyle in all its dimensions in order that people may study and practice Dhamma in the present day.

AJAHN CHAH'S TEACHING OF WESTERNERS

There is a widely circulated and well-attested tale that, shortly before the newly ordained Ajahn Sumedho arrived to request training under Ajahn Chah's guidance in 1967, Ajahn Chah initiated the construction of a new *kuṭī* (meditation cabin) in the forest. As the timbers that formed the corner posts were being put into place, one of the villagers who was helping with the construction asked, "Eh, Luang Por, how come we are building this so tall? The roof is much higher than it needs to be." He was puzzled, as such structures are usually designed to be just enough space for one person to live in comfortably, customarily about eight feet by ten feet with a roof peak at around seven feet.

"Don't worry, it's not being wasteful," he replied. "There will be some *farang* (Western) monks coming here one day; they are a lot bigger than we are."

In the years that followed the arrival of this first student from the West, a gentle but constant stream of them continued to enter through the gates of Ajahn Chah's monasteries. From the very beginning he chose not to give any special treatment to the foreigners, but let them adapt to the climate, food, and culture as best they could, and furthermore to use any discomfort that they might feel as food for the development of wisdom and patient endurance—two of the qualities that he recognized as central to any spiritual progress.

Despite the primary consideration of holding the entire monastic community to a single harmonious standard, and not making the Westerners special in any way, in 1975 circumstances arose whereby Wat Pah Nanachat (the International Forest Monastery) was established near Wat Pah Pong as a place for Westerners to practice. Ajahn Sumedho and a small group of other Western bhikkhus were walking to a branch monastery near the banks of the Muhn River. They stopped overnight in a small forest outside the village of Bung Wai. It so happened that many of the villagers were long-standing disciples of Ajahn Chah, and surprised and delighted to see this group of foreign monks walking together on alms round through their dusty streets, they asked if they would settle in the forest nearby and start a new monastery. The plan received approval from Ajahn Chah, and this special training monastery for the growing numbers of Westerners interested in undertaking monastic practice began.

It wasn't long after this, in 1976, that Ajahn Sumedho was invited by a group in London to come and establish a Theravādan monastery in England. Ajahn Chah came over the following year and left Ajahn Sumedho and a small group of other monastics to reside at the Hampstead Buddhist Vihara, a townhouse on a busy street in north London. Within a few years they had moved to the country and several other branch monasteries had been established.

Since then many of Ajahn Chah's senior Western disciples have been engaged in the work of establishing monasteries and spreading the Dhamma on several different continents. Other monasteries have sprung up in France, Australia, New Zealand, Switzerland, Italy, Canada, and the U.S. Ajahn Chah himself traveled twice to Europe and North America, in 1977 and 1979, and wholeheartedly supported these new foundations. He once said that Buddhism in Thailand was like an old tree that had formerly been vigorous and abundant; now it was so aged that it could only produce a few fruits, and those were small and bitter. Buddhism in the West he likened, in contrast, to a young sapling, full of youthful energy and the potential for growth, but needing proper care and support for its development.

In the same light, on his visit to the U.S. in 1979, he commented, "Britain is a good place for Buddhism to get established in the West, but it too is an old culture. The U.S., however, has the energy and flexibility of a young country—everything is new here—it is here that the Dhamma can really flourish." When speaking to a group of young Americans who had just opened up a Buddhist meditation center, he also added the caveat, "You will succeed in truly spreading the Buddhadhamma here only if you are not afraid to challenge the desires and opinions of your students (literally, "to stab their hearts"). If you do this, you will succeed; if you do not, if you change the teachings and the practice to fit the existent habits and opinions of people out of a misguided sense of wanting to please them, you will have failed in your duty to serve in the best way possible."

THE ESSENTIALS:
VIEW, TEACHING, AND PRACTICE

Even though this book contains many lucid explanations of the Buddha's teachings, it might be helpful, particularly for those unfamiliar with the Theravādan expression of things in general, or with the Thai Forest Tradition in particular, to outline first some of the key terms, attitudes, and concepts that are used throughout this collection

The Four Noble Truths

Although there are numerous volumes of the Buddha's discourses in many traditions, it is also said that the entirety of his teaching was contained in his very first exposition—called *The Setting in Motion of the Wheel of Truth*—which he gave to five monastic companions in the deer park near Benares shortly after his enlightenment. In this brief discourse (it takes only twenty minutes to recite), he expounded on the nature of the Middle Way and the Four Noble Truths. This teaching is common to all Buddhist traditions, and just as an acorn contains within it the genetic coding for what eventually takes shape as a vast oak, so too all the myriad Buddhist teachings can be said to derive from this essential matrix of insight.

The Four Noble Truths are formulated like a medical diagnosis in the ayurvedic tradition: a) the symptoms of the disease, b) the cause, c) the prognosis, and d) the cure. The Buddha was always drawing on structures and forms that were familiar to people in his time, and, in this instance, this is how he laid out the picture.

The First Truth (the "symptom") is that there is *dukkha*—we can experience incompleteness, dissatisfaction, suffering. There might be moments or long periods when we experience happiness, of a coarse or even a transcendent nature; however, there are times when the heart feels discontent. This can vary from extreme anguish at one end of the spectrum to the faintest sense that some blissful feeling we are experiencing will not last— all of this comes under the heading of "dukkha."

Sometimes people read this First Truth and misinterpret it as an absolute statement, that "Reality in every dimension is dukkha." The statement gets taken as a value judgment of all and everything, but that's not what is meant here. If it were, then that would mean that there was no hope of liberation for anyone, and to realize the truth of the way things are, the Dhamma, would not result in an abiding peace and happiness, which, according to the insight of the Buddha, it does.

What is most significant, therefore, is that these are *noble* truths, not *absolute* truths. They are noble in the sense that they are relative truths, but when they are understood, they lead us to a realization of the Absolute or the Ultimate.

The Second Noble Truth is that the cause of this dukkha is self-centered craving, *taṇhā* in Pali (*tṛṣṇā* in Sanskrit), which literally means "thirst." This craving, this grasping, is the cause of dukkha. This can be craving for sense-pleasure; craving to become something, craving to be identified as something; or it can be craving not to be, the desire to disappear, to be annihilated, to get rid of. There are many subtle dimensions of this.

The Third Truth is that of *dukkha-nirodha*—this is the prognosis. *Nirodha* means "cessation." This means that this experience of dukkha, of incompleteness, can fade away, can be transcended. It can end. In other words, dukkha is not an absolute reality. It's just a temporary experience that the heart can be liberated from.

The Fourth Noble Truth is that of the Path, how we get from the Second Truth to the Third, from the causation of dukkha to the ending of it.

The cure is the Eightfold Path, which is, in essence, virtue, concentration, and wisdom.

The Law of Kamma

One of the crucial underpinnings of the Buddhist worldview is that of the inviolability of the law of cause and effect: every action has an equal and opposite reaction. This is seen as not only applying to the realm of physical reality but also, and more importantly, to the psychological and social realms as well. The insight of the Buddha into the nature of reality led him to see that this is a moral universe: good actions reap pleasant results; harmful acts reap painful results—that's the way nature works. It might be that the results come soon after the act or at some very remote time, but the effect that matches the cause will necessarily follow.

The Buddha also made it clear that the key element of kamma (Skt. *karma*) is intention—as it says in the opening words of the *Dhammapada*, the most famous and well loved of all Theravādan scriptures, "Mind is the forerunner of all things: think and act with a corrupt heart and sorrow will follow one as surely as the cart follows the ox that pulls it. Mind is the forerunner of all things: think and act with a pure heart and happiness will follow one as surely as one's never-departing shadow."

This understanding, learned at an early age and taken for granted in much of Asia, will be found to resonate throughout many of the Dhamma talks contained in these pages. However, even though it is something of an article of faith in the Buddhist world, it is also a law that one comes to recognize through experience, rather than being blindly accepted on the assurance of a teacher or because there is some cultural imperative to abide by it. When Ajahn Chah encountered Westerners who said that they didn't believe in kamma as he described it, rather than criticizing them or dismissing them as having "wrong view," or feeling that he had to make them see things his way, he was interested that someone could look at things in such a different manner—he would ask them to describe how they saw things working, and then take the conversation from there.

Everything Is Uncertain

Another of the central teachings, which is oft repeated in the talks gathered in this book, is that of the Three Characteristics of Existence. From the second discourse that the Buddha gave (the *Anattālakkhaṇa Sutta*), and on through the rest of his teaching career, he outlined the fact that all phenomena, internal or external, mental or physical, have three invariable qualities: *anicca, dukkha, anattā*—impermanence, unsatisfactoriness, and "not-self." Everything is changing; nothing can be permanently satisfying or dependable; and nothing can truly be said to be ours, or absolutely who and what we are. And when these three qualities have been seen and known through direct experience, then insight can truly be said to have dawned.

Anicca is the first member of the insight-forming triad, and its contemplation was stressed constantly by Ajahn Chah over the years as being the primary gateway to wisdom. As he says in "Still, Flowing Water"—"What we call 'uncertainty' here is the Buddha. The Buddha is the Dhamma. The Dhamma is the characteristic of uncertainty. Whoever sees the uncertainty of things sees the unchanging reality of them. That's what the Dhamma is like. And that is the Buddha. If you see the Dhamma, you see the Buddha; seeing the Buddha you see the Dhamma. If you know annica, uncertainty, you will let go of things and not grasp on to them."

It is a characteristic of Ajahn Chah's teaching that he habitually used the less familiar rendition of "uncertainty" (*my naer* in Thai) for anicca. Where "impermanence" can have a more abstract or technical tone to it, "uncertainty" better describes the feeling in the heart when that quality of change is met with.

Choice of Expression: "Yes" or "No"

One of the most striking characteristics of the Theravāda teachings, and of many of the ways of speech employed in this anthology, is that the truth and the way leading to it are often indicated by talking about what they are *not* rather than what they *are*. In Christian theological language this is called an "apophatic method"—talking about what God is not—as contrasted with a "kataphatic method"—talking about what God is. This apophatic style of approach, also known as the *via negativa*, was used by a number of eminent

Christians over the centuries; one who immediately springs to mind is the famous mystic and theologian St. John of the Cross. As an example of this style, in his "Ascent of Mount Carmel," his description of the most direct spiritual method (that is, straight up the mountain) runs something like: "Nothing, nothing, nothing, nothing, and even on the mountain, nothing."

The Pali canon possesses much of the same via negativa flavor, which readers have often mistaken for a nihilistic view of life. Nothing could be further from the truth, but it's easy to see how the mistake could be made, particularly if one comes from a culture committed to expressions of life-affirmation.

The story has it that shortly after the Buddha's enlightenment he was walking along a road through the Magadhan countryside, on his way to meet up with the five companions with whom he had practiced austerities before going off alone to seek the truth his own way. Along the road another ascetic wanderer, Upaka by name, saw him approaching and was greatly struck by the Buddha's appearance. Not only was he a warrior-noble prince, with the regal bearing that came from that upbringing, he was also apparently well over six feet tall, extraordinarily handsome, was dressed in the rag robes of the ascetic wanderers, and he shone with a dazzling radiance. Upaka was impressed:

"Who are you, friend? Your face is so clear and bright; your manner is awesome and serene. Surely you must have discovered some great truth— who is your teacher, friend, and what is it that you have discovered?"

The newly awakened Buddha replied: "I am an all-transcender, an all-knower. I have no teacher. In all the world I alone am fully enlightened. There is none who taught me this—I came to it through my own efforts."

"Do you mean to say that you claim to have won victory over birth and death?"

"Indeed, friend, I am a victorious one; and now, in this world of the spiritually blind, I go to Varanasi to beat the drum of Deathlessness."

"Well, good for you, friend," said Upaka, and shaking his head as he went, he left by a different path. (MV 1.6.)

The Buddha realized from this encounter that mere declaration of the truth did not necessarily arouse faith, and might not be effective in communicating it to others either, so by the time he reached the deer park outside Varanasi and had met up with his former companions, he had adopted a much more analytical method (*vibhajjāvada* in Pali) and thus composed the formula of the Four Noble Truths. This reflected the shift of expression from: "I have realized Perfection," to "Let's investigate why anyone experiences imperfection."

In the Buddha's second discourse (again, the *Anattālakkhaṇa Sutta*), which was also given in the deer park at Varanasi and was the teaching that caused the five companions to all realize enlightenment, this via negativa method is most clearly displayed. This is not the place to go into the *sutta* in detail, but in summary, the Buddha uses the search for the self (*atta* in Pali, *atman* in Sanskrit) as his theme, and by using an analytical method he demonstrates that a "self" cannot be found in relation to any of the factors of body or mind; by thus demonstrating he then states: "The wise noble disciple becomes dispassionate toward the body, feelings, perceptions, mental formations, and consciousness." Thus the heart is liberated. Once we let go of what we're not, the nature of what is real becomes apparent. And as that reality is beyond description, it is most appropriate, and least misleading, to leave it undescribed—this is the essence of the "way of negation."

The lion's share of the Buddha's teaching, particularly in the Theravāda tradition, thus addresses the nature of the Path and how best to follow it, rather than waxing lyrically about the goal. This was also true of Ajahn Chah's style for the most part. He avoided talking about levels of attainment and levels of meditative absorption as much as possible, both to counteract spiritual materialism (the gaining mind, competitiveness, and jealousy) as well as to keep people's eyes where they were most needed: on the Path.

Having said that, Ajahn Chah was also notable for the readiness and directness with which he would speak about ultimate reality, should the occasion demand it. The talks "Toward the Unconditioned," "Transcendence," and "No Abiding" being good examples of this. If, however, he thought that a person's understanding was not yet ripe, yet they insisted on asking about transcendent qualities (as in the dialogue "What is Contemplation?") he might well respond, as he does there, "It isn't anything and we don't call it anything—that's all there is to it! Be finished with all of it," (literally: "If there is anything there, then just throw it to the dogs!").

Emphasis on Right View and Virtue

When asked what he considered to be the most essential elements of the teaching, Ajahn Chah frequently responded that his experience had shown him that all spiritual progress depended upon Right View and on purity of conduct. Of Right View the Buddha once said: "Just as the glowing of the dawn sky foretells the rising of the sun, so too is Right View the forerunner of all wholesome states." To establish Right View means firstly that one has a trustworthy map of the terrain of the mind and the world—particularly with respect to an appreciation of the law of kamma—secondly it means that one sees experience in the light of the Four Noble Truths and is thus turning that flow of perceptions, thoughts, and moods into fuel for insight. The four points become the quarters of the compass by which we orient our understanding and thus guide our actions and intentions.

Ajahn Chah saw sīla (virtue) as the great protector of the heart and encouraged a sincere commitment to the precepts by all those who were serious about their search for happiness and a skillfully lived life—whether these were the Five Precepts[4] of the householder or the Eight, Ten, or 227 of the various levels of the monastic community. Virtuous action and speech, sīla, directly brings the heart into accord with Dhamma and thus becomes the foundation for concentration, insight, and finally liberation.

In many ways sīla is the external corollary to the internal quality of Right View, and there is a reciprocal relationship between them: if we understand causality and see the relationship between craving and dukkha, then certainly our actions are more likely to be harmonious and restrained; similarly, if our actions and speech are respectful, honest, and nonviolent, then we create the causes of peace within us, and it will be much easier for us to see the laws governing the mind and its workings, and Right View will develop more easily.

One particular outcome of this relationship, of which Ajahn Chah spoke regularly, as in the talk "Convention and Liberation," is the intrinsic emptiness of all conventions (e.g., money, monasticism, social customs) but the simultaneous need to respect them fully. This might sound somewhat paradoxical, but he saw the Middle Way as synonymous with the resolution of this kind of conundrum. If we cling to conventions we become burdened and limited by them, but if we try to defy them or negate them we find

ourselves lost, conflicted, and bewildered. He saw that, with the right attitude, both aspects could be respected, and in a way that was natural and
freeing, rather than forced or compromised.

It was probably due to his own profound insights in this area that he
was able to be both extraordinarily orthodox and austere as a Buddhist
monk yet utterly relaxed and unfettered by any of the rules he observed. To
many who met him he seemed the happiest man in the world—a fact perhaps ironic about someone who had never had sex in his life, had no money,
never listened to music, was regularly available to people eighteen to twenty
hours a day, slept on a thin grass mat, had a diabetic condition and had had
various forms of malaria, and who was delighted by the fact that Wat Pah
Pong had the reputation for having "the worst food in the world."

METHODS OF TRAINING

There were a multitude of different dimensions to the way that Ajahn Chah
trained his students. Instruction was certainly given verbally, in many of the
ways already described; however, the majority of the learning process
occurred through what might best be described as situational teaching.
Ajahn Chah realized that, in order for the heart to truly learn any aspect of
the teaching and be transformed by it, the lesson had to be absorbed expe-
rientially, not intellectually alone. Thus he employed the 10,000 events and
aspects of the monastic routine, communal living, and the tudong life as
ways to teach and train his disciples: community work projects, learning to
recite the rules, helping with the daily chores, random changes in the schedule—all of these and more were used as a forum in which to investigate the
arising of dukkha and the way leading to its cessation.

He encouraged the attitude of being ready to learn from everything, as
he describes in the talk "Dhamma Nature." He would emphasize over
and over that we are our own teachers: if we are wise, every personal problem, event, and aspect of nature will instruct us; if we are foolish, not even
having the Buddha before us explaining everything would make any real
impression. This insight was also borne out in the way he related to people's questions—he more responded to where someone was coming from
rather than answered their question in their own terms. Often when asked
something, he would appear to receive the question, gently take it to

pieces, and then hand the bits back to the inquirer; they would then see for themselves how it was put together. To their surprise, he had guided them in such a way that they had answered their own question. When asked how it was that he could do this so often, he replied: "If the person did not already know the answer they could not have posed the question in the first place."

Other key attitudes that he encouraged, and which pervade the teachings gathered here, are, firstly, the need to cultivate a profound sense of urgency in meditation practice, and, secondly, to use the training environment to develop patient endurance. This latter quality is not one that has received a great deal of attention in recent times, particularly in spiritual circles in the "quick-fix" culture of the West, but in the forest life it is seen as almost synonymous with spiritual training.

When the Buddha was giving his very first instructions on monastic discipline, and this was to a spontaneous gathering of 1,250 of his enlightened disciples at the Bamboo Grove, his first words were: "Patient endurance is the supreme practice for freeing the heart from unwholesome states."[5] So when someone would come to Ajahn Chah with a tale of woe, of how their husband was drinking and the rice crop looked bad this year, his first response would often be: "Can you endure it?" This was said not as some kind of macho challenge, but more as a way of pointing to the fact that the way beyond suffering is neither to run away from it, wallow in it, or even grit one's teeth and get through on will alone—no—the encouragement of patient endurance is to hold steady in the midst of difficulty, to truly apprehend and digest the experience of dukkha, to understand its causes and let them go.

Teaching the Laity and Teaching Monastics

There were certainly many occasions when Ajahn Chah's teachings were as applicable to lay people as to monastics, but there were also many instances when they were not. This is an important factor for the reader to bear in mind when going through the wide variety of talks contained here, as not to be aware of such differences could be confusing. For example, the talk "Making the Heart Good" is very explicitly aimed at a lay audience—a group of people who have come to visit Wat Pah Pong to *tam boon,* to make offerings to the monastery both to support the community there and to make some good kamma for themselves—whereas a talk like "The Flood of Sensuality" would only be given to the monastics, in that instance just to the monks and male novices.

Such a distinction was not made because of certain teachings being "secret" or higher in some respect; rather, it was through the need to speak in ways that would be appropriate and useful to particular audiences. Lay practitioners would naturally have a different range of concerns and influences on their daily life—e.g., trying to find time for formal meditation practice, maintaining an income, living with a spouse—that a monastic would not. Also, most particularly, the lay community would not have undertaken vows of the renunciate life. An average lay student of Ajahn Chah would commit themselves to a standard of keeping the Five Precepts whereas the monastics would be keeping the Eight, Ten, or 227 Precepts of the various levels of ordination.

When teaching monastics alone, the focus would be much more specifically on using the renunciant way of life as the key methodology of training; the instruction would therefore concern itself with the hurdles, pitfalls, and glories that that way of life might bring. Since the average age of a monk in a monastery in Thailand is usually around 25 to 30, and with the precepts around celibacy being strictly kept, there was also a natural need for Ajahn Chah to guide skillfully the restless and sexual energy that his monks would often experience. When well directed, the individuals would be able to contain and employ that same energy, and transform it to help develop concentration and insight.

The tone of some of the talks to monastics will, in certain instances, also be seen to be considerably more fierce than those given to the lay community; for example, "Dhamma Fighting." This manner of expression represents something of the "take no prisoners" style that is characteristic of many of the teachers of the Thai Forest Tradition. It is a way of speaking that is intended to rouse the "warrior heart"—that attitude toward spiritual practice that enables one to be ready to endure all hardships and to be wise, patient, and faithful, regardless of how difficult things get.

Occasionally such a manner can come across as overly macho or combative in its tone; the reader should therefore bear in mind that the spirit behind such language is the endeavor to encourage the practitioner, to gladden the heart, and provide supportive strength when dealing with the multifarious challenges of freeing the heart from all greed, hatred, and delusion. As Ajahn Chah once said: "All those who seriously engage in spiritual practice should expect to experience a great deal of friction and difficulty." The heart is being trained to go against the current of self-centered habit, so it's quite natural for it to be buffeted around somewhat.

As a final note on this aspect of Ajahn Chah's teachings, particularly with respect to those one might term "higher" or "transcendent," it is significant that he held nothing back to be especially for the monastics. If he felt a group of people was ready for the highest levels of teaching, he would impart that freely and openly, regardless of whether it was to lay people or to monastics; as in, for example, such talks as "Toward the Unconditioned" or "Still, Flowing Water" wherein he states: "People these days study away, looking for good and evil. But that which is beyond good and evil they know nothing of." Like the Buddha, he never employed the "teacher's closed fist," and made his choices of what to teach solely on the basis of what would be useful to his listeners, not on their number of precepts, their religious affiliation or lack of one.

Counteracting Superstition

One of the characteristics that Ajahn Chah was most well known for was his keenness to dispel superstition in relation to Buddhist practice in Thailand. He strongly criticized the magic charms, amulets, and fortune-telling that pervaded so much of the society. He rarely spoke about past or future lives, other realms, visions, or psychic experiences. If anyone came to him asking for a tip about the next winning lottery number (a very common reason why some people go to visit famous ajahns), they would generally get very short shrift. He saw that the Dhamma itself was the most priceless jewel, which could provide genuine protection and security in life, and yet it was continually overlooked for the sake of the promise of minor improvements to *saṁsāra*.

Over and over he emphasized the usefulness and practicality of Buddhist practice—counteracting the common belief that Dhamma was too high or abstruse for the common person—out of a genuine feeling of kindness for others. His criticisms were not just to break down their childish dependencies on good luck and magical charms; rather, he wanted them to invest in something that would truly serve them.

In the light of this lifelong effort, there was also an ironic twist of circumstance that accompanied his funeral in 1993: he passed away on the 16th of January 1992, and they held the funeral exactly a year later; the memorial stupa had 16 pillars, was 32 meters high, and had foundations 16 meters deep—consequently, a huge number of people in Ubon Province bought lottery tickets with ones and sixes together. The next day the headlines in the local paper proclaimed: LUANG POR CHAH'S LAST GIFT TO HIS DISCIPLES—the 16s had cleaned up and a couple of local bookmakers had even gone bankrupt.

Humor

That last story brings us to a final quality of Ajahn Chah's teaching style. He was an amazingly quick-witted man and a natural performer. Although he could be very cool and forbidding, or sensitive and gentle in his way of expression, he also used a high degree of humor in his teaching. He had a way of employing wit to work his way into the hearts of his listeners, not just to amuse, but to help convey truths that would otherwise not be received so easily.

His sense of humor and skillful eye for the tragicomic absurdities of life enabled people to see situations in such a way that they could laugh at themselves and be guided to a wiser outlook. This might be in matters of conduct, such as a famous display he once gave of the many *wrong* ways to carry a monk's bag: slung over the back, looped round the neck, grabbed in the fist, scraped along the ground…. Or it might be in terms of some painful personal struggle. One time a young bhikkhu came to him very downcast. He had seen the sorrows of the world, and the horror of beings' entrapment in birth and death, and had realized that, "I'll never be able to laugh again—it's all so sad and painful." Within 45 minutes, via a graphic tale about a youthful squirrel repeatedly attempting and falling short in its efforts to learn tree climbing, the monk was rolling on the floor clutching his sides, tears pouring down his face as he was convulsed with the laughter that had never been going to return.

Last Years

During the rains retreat of 1981 Ajahn Chah fell seriously ill, with what was apparently some form of stroke. His health had been shaky for the last few years—with dizzy spells and diabetic problems—and now it went down with a crash. Over the next few months he received various kinds of treatment, including a couple of operations, but nothing helped. The slide continued until, by the middle of the following year, he was paralyzed but for some slight movement in one hand, and he had lost the power of speech. He could still blink his eyes.

He remained in this state for the next ten years, his few areas of control diminishing slowly until, by the end, all voluntary movement was lost to him. During this time it was often said that he was still teaching his students: hadn't he reiterated endlessly that the body is of the nature to sicken and decay, and that it is not under personal control? Well, here was a prime object lesson in exactly that—neither a great master, nor even the Buddha himself, could escape the inexorable laws of nature. The task, as always, was to find peace and freedom by not identifying with the changing forms.

During this time, despite his severe limitations, on occasion he still managed to teach in ways other than just being an example of the uncertain processes of life and by giving opportunity for his monks and novices to offer their support through nursing care. The bhikkhus used to work in shifts, three or four at a time, to look after Ajahn Chah's physical needs as he required twenty-four-hour-a-day attention. On one particular shift two monks got into an argument, quite forgetting (as often happens around paralyzed or comatose people) that the other occupant of the room might be fully cognizant of what was going on. Had Ajahn Chah been fully active, it would have been unthinkable that they would have gotten into such a spat in front of him.

As the words got more heated, an agitated movement began in the bed across the room. Suddenly Ajahn Chah coughed violently and, according to reports, sent a sizeable gob of phlegm shooting across the intervening space, passing between the two protagonists and smacking into the wall right beside them. The teaching was duly received, and the argument came to an embarrassed and abrupt conclusion.

During the course of his illness the life of the monasteries continued much as before; the Master being both there yet not there served in a strange way to help the community to adapt to communal decision-making and to the concept of life without their beloved teacher at the center of everything. After such a great elder passes away it is not uncommon for things to dissipate rapidly and for all of their students to go their own way, the teacher's legacy vanishing within a generation or two. It is perhaps a testimony to how well Ajahn Chah trained people to be self-reliant that, whereas at the time of his falling sick there were about seventy-five branch monasteries, this number increased to well over one hundred by the time he passed away, and has now grown to more than two hundred, in Thailand and around the world.

After he passed away, ten years ago, his monastic community set about arranging his funeral. In keeping with the spirit of his life and teachings, the funeral was not to be just a ceremony, but also a time for hearing and practicing Dhamma. It was held over ten days, with several periods of group meditation and instructional talks each day, these being given by many of the most accomplished Dhamma teachers in the country. There were about 6,000 monks, 1,000 nuns, and just over 10,000 lay people camped in the forest for the ten days. Besides these, an estimated 1,000,000 people came through the monastery during the practice period; 400,000, including the king and queen and the prime minister of Thailand, came on the day of the cremation itself.

Again, in the spirit of the standards Ajahn Chah espoused during his entire teaching career, throughout this entire session not one cent was charged for anything: food was supplied for everyone through forty-two free food kitchens, run and stocked by many of the branch monasteries; over $250,000 worth of free Dhamma books were passed out; bottled water was provided by the ton through a local firm; and the local bus company, and other nearby truck owners, ferried out the thousands of monks each morning to go on alms round through villages and towns of the area. It was a grand festival of generosity and a fitting way to bid farewell to the great man.

It is in something of the same spirit of generosity that this present collection of Dhamma talks has been compiled. It is rare for Ajahn Chah's monastic community to allow his teachings to be printed commercially (books are normally sponsored by lay donors and then distributed for free). In fact, this is only the third such book in English to be authorized since Ajahn Chah began teaching.

This collection, *Food for the Heart,* comprises most of Ajahn Chah's talks that have been previously published for free distribution in English. Wisdom Publications requested permission to compile and print these talks as a single volume in order to help bring Ajahn Chah's teachings to an audience wider than that which would normally be reached through monastic channels. This seemed to be a noble intention and thus has been given full support by Ajahn Chah's monastic community. It is also perhaps fitting that this compilation has been made on the tenth anniversary of the great master's passing.

May these teachings provide nourishing contemplation for seekers of the Way and help to establish the heart that is awake, pure, and peaceful.

Amaro Bhikkhu
Abhayagiri Monastery
January the 16th, 2002

Namo Tassa Bhagavato Arahato Sammā-Sambuddhassa

Namo Tassa Bhagavato Arahato Sammā-Sambuddhassa

Namo Tassa Bhagavato Arahato Sammā-Sambuddhassa

CHAPTER I

ABOUT THIS MIND

ABOUT THIS MIND—in truth there is nothing really wrong with it. It is intrinsically pure. Within itself it's already peaceful. If the mind is not peaceful these days, it's because it follows moods. The real mind doesn't have anything to it; it is simply an aspect of nature. It becomes peaceful or agitated because moods deceive it. The untrained mind is stupid. Sense impressions come and trick it into happiness, suffering, gladness, and sorrow, but the mind's true nature is none of those things. That gladness or sadness is not the mind, but only a mood coming to deceive us. The untrained mind gets lost and follows these things; it forgets itself. Then we think that it is we who are upset or at ease or whatever.

But really this mind of ours is already unmoving and peaceful—really peaceful! Just like a leaf which remains still so long as the wind doesn't blow. If a wind comes up, the leaf flutters. The fluttering is due to the wind—the fluttering of the mind is due to those sense impressions; the mind follows them. If it doesn't follow them, it doesn't flutter. If we know fully the true nature of sense impressions, we will be unmoved.

Our practice is simply to see the "Original Mind." We must train the mind to know those sense impressions and not get lost in them, to make it peaceful. Just this is the aim of all this difficult practice we put ourselves through.

CHAPTER 2

FRAGMENTS OF A TEACHING

PEOPLE HEAR ABOUT THE BUDDHIST TEACHINGS from many sources—various teachers or monks, for example. In some cases Dhamma is taught in very broad and vague terms to the point where it is difficult to know how to put it into practice in daily life. In other instances Dhamma is taught in lofty language or special jargon that people find difficult to understand, especially if the teaching is done too literally from the scriptures. Lastly there is Dhamma taught in a balanced way, neither too vague nor too profound, neither too broad nor too esoteric—just right for the listener to understand and practice for personal benefit. Here I would like to share some teachings I have often used to instruct my disciples.

ONE WHO WISHES TO REACH
THE BUDDHADHAMMA

One who wishes to reach the Buddhadhamma must be one who has faith or confidence as a foundation. We must understand the meaning of Buddhadhamma as follows:

> *Buddha:* the "one who knows," the one who has purity, radiance, and peace in the heart.
> *Dhamma:* the characteristics of purity, radiance, and peace, which arise from morality, concentration, and wisdom.

Therefore, one who is to reach the Buddhadhamma is one who cultivates and develops morality, concentration, and wisdom within themselves.

WALKING THE PATH OF BUDDHADHAMMA

People who wish to reach home are not those who merely sit and think of traveling. They must undertake the process of traveling step by step in the right direction. If they take the wrong path they may eventually meet with difficulties such as swamps or similar obstacles. Or they may run into dangerous situations and possibly never reach home. Those who do reach home can relax and sleep comfortably—home is a place of comfort for body and mind. But if travelers instead walk right past their homes or around them, they receive no benefit from having traveled all the way.

In the same way, walking the path to reach the Buddhadhamma is something each one of us must do individually, for no one can do it for us. And we must travel along the proper path of morality, concentration, and wisdom until we attain the blessings of purity, radiance, and peacefulness of mind that are the fruits of traveling the Path.

But if one has knowledge of books and scriptures, sermons, and suttas and only that—that is, only the map or plans for the journey—one will never know purity, radiance, and peacefulness of mind, even if one lives hundreds of lives. Instead one will just waste time and never get to the real benefits of practice. Teachers can only point out the direction of the Path. Whether or not we ourselves walk the Path by practicing, and thereby reap the fruits of practice, is strictly up to each one of us.

Here is another way to look at it. Practice is like the bottles of medicine that doctors give their patients. The bottles have detailed instructions on how to take the medicine. But if the patients only read the directions, even a hundred times, they are bound to die. They will gain no benefit from the medicine. And before they die, they may complain bitterly that the doctor wasn't any good, was a fake, and that the medicine didn't cure them and so was worthless. Yet they spent their time only examining the bottle and reading the instructions. They didn't follow the doctor's advice and take the medicine.

But if patients actually follow a doctor's advice and *take* their medicine regularly as prescribed, they will recover. If they are very ill, they'll have to take a lot of medicine, whereas if they are only mildly ill, only a little medicine will be needed to cure them. That we must use a lot of medicine is a result of the severity of our illness. It's only natural, as you can see for yourself with careful consideration.

Doctors prescribe medicine to eliminate disease from the body. The teachings of the Buddha are prescribed to cure disease of the mind, to bring it back to its natural healthy state. So the Buddha can be considered to be a doctor who prescribes cures for the ills of the mind. He is, in fact, the greatest doctor in the world.

Mental ills are found in each one of us without exception. When you see these mental ills, does it not make sense to look to the Dhamma as support, as medicine to cure you? Traveling the path of the Buddhadhamma is not done with the body. You must travel with the mind or heart. We can divide travelers along the Path into three levels:

The first level comprises those who understand that they themselves must practice and who know how to do so. They take the Buddha, Dhamma, and Sangha as their refuge and have resolved to practice diligently according to the teachings. These persons have discarded the mere following of customs and traditions and instead use reason to examine for themselves the nature of the world. These are the group of "Buddhist practitioners."

The middle level includes those who have practiced until they have an unshakable faith in the teachings of the Buddha, the Dhamma, and the Sangha. They also have penetrated to the understanding of the true nature of all compounded things. These persons gradually reduce clinging and attachment. They do not hold on to things, and their minds reach a deep understanding of the Dhamma. Depending upon the degree of nonattachment and wisdom, they are known as stream-enterers, once-returners, and non-returners, or simply as Noble Ones.

At the highest level are those whose practice has led them to the body, speech, and mind of the Buddha. They are above the world, free of the world, and free of all attachment and clinging. They are known as *arahants* or Perfected Ones, the highest level of the Noble Ones.

HOW TO PURIFY ONE'S MORALITY

Morality is restraint and discipline of body and speech. On the formal level it is divided into classes of precepts for lay people and for monks and nuns. In general terms, however, there is one basic characteristic—which is intention. When we are mindful or self-recollected, we have Right Intention. Practicing mindfulness *(sati)* and self-recollection *(sampajañña)* will generate good morality.

It is only natural that if we put on dirty clothes and our bodies are also dirty, our minds too will be uncomfortable and depressed. But if we keep our bodies clean and wear clean, neat clothes, our minds will be light and cheerful. So too, when morality is not preserved, our bodily actions and speech are soiled, and this makes the mind unhappy, distressed, and heavy. We are separated from the right practice and cannot penetrate to the essence of the Dhamma. Wholesome bodily actions and speech depend on the mind being properly trained, since the mind controls body and speech. Therefore, we must continue practice by training our minds.

THE PRACTICE OF CONCENTRATION

Training in samādhi (concentration) makes the mind firm and steady. This brings about peacefulness of mind. Usually our untrained minds are moving and restless, hard to control and manage. Such a mind follows sense distractions wildly, just like water flowing this way and that, seeking the lowest level. Agriculturalists and engineers know how to control water so that it is of great use to human society; they dam rivers, construct large reservoirs and canals—all of this merely to channel water and make it more useable. The stored water becomes a source of electrical power and light—a further benefit of controlling its flow so that it doesn't run wild or flood lowlands, its usefulness wasted.

So, too, the mind that is dammed and controlled, trained constantly, will be of immeasurable benefit. The Buddha himself taught, "The mind that has been controlled brings true happiness, so train your minds well for the highest of benefits." Similarly, the animals we see around us—elephants, horses, cattle, buffalo—must be trained before they can be useful for work. Only then will their strength benefit us.

The trained mind will bring many more blessings than an untrained mind. The Buddha and his noble disciples all started out the same as we did—with untrained minds. But they later became objects of reverence for us all, and we have gained much benefit from their teachings. Consider how much the entire world has benefited from these beings who have trained their minds and reached the freedom beyond. The mind controlled and trained is better equipped to help us in all professions, in all situations. The disciplined mind will keep our lives balanced, make our work easier, and develop and nurture reason to govern our actions. In the end our happiness will increase accordingly.

The training of the mind can be done in many ways, with many different methods. The most useful method, one that can be practiced by all types of people, is mindfulness of breathing. It is the developing of mindfulness of the in-breath and the out-breath.

In this monastery we concentrate our attention on the tip of the nose and develop awareness of the in- and out-breaths with the mantra *Bud-dho*. If the meditator wishes to use another word, or simply be mindful of the breath moving in and out, this is also fine. Adjust the practice to suit yourself. The essential factor in the meditation is that the noting or awareness of the breath should be kept up in the present moment so that one is mindful of each in-breath and each out-breath just as it occurs. While doing walking meditation we try to be constantly mindful of the sensation of the feet touching the ground.

To bear fruit, the practice of meditation must be pursued as continuously as possible. Don't meditate for a short time one day and then, after a week or two, or even a month, meditate again. This will not yield good results. The Buddha taught us to practice often and to practice diligently, that is, to be as continuous as we can in the practice of mental training. To practice effectively we should find a suitably quiet place, free from distractions. Suitable environments are a garden, in the shade of a tree in our backyard, or anywhere we can be alone. If we are monks or nuns, we should find a hut, a quiet forest, or a cave. The mountains offer exceptionally suitable places for practice.

In any case, wherever we are, we must make an effort to be continuously mindful of breathing in and breathing out. If the attention wanders, pull it back to the object of concentration. Try to put away all other thoughts and cares. Don't think about anything—just watch the breath. If we are mindful of thoughts as soon as they arise, and keep diligently returning to the meditation subject, the mind will become quieter and quieter. When the mind is peaceful and concentrated, release it from the breath as the object of concentration.

Now begin to examine the body and mind composed of the five *khandhas*[6] (groups of existence comprising body and mind): material form, feelings, perceptions, mental formations, and consciousness. Examine these five khandhas as they come and go. You will see clearly that they are impermanent, that this impermanence makes them unsatisfactory and undesirable, and that they come and go of their own: there is no "self" that is running things, but only nature moving according to cause and effect. All things in the world have the characteristics of instability, unsatisfactoriness, and the absence of a permanent ego or soul. If you see all of existence in this light, attachment and clinging to the khandhas will gradually be reduced. This is because you see the true characteristics of the world. We call this the arising of wisdom.

THE ARISING OF WISDOM

Wisdom *(paññā)* is seeing the truth of the various manifestations of body and mind. When we use our trained and concentrated minds to examine the five khandhas, we will see clearly that both body and mind are impermanent, unsatisfactory, and not self. In seeing all compounded things with wisdom we do not cling or grasp. Whatever we receive, we receive mindfully; we do not become excessively happy. When things of ours break up or disappear, we are not unhappy and do not suffer painful feelings—for we see clearly the impermanent nature of all things. When we encounter illness and pain of any sort, we have equanimity because our minds have been well trained. The true refuge is the trained mind.

All of this is known as the wisdom that knows the true characteristics of things as they arise. Wisdom arises from mindfulness and concentration. Concentration arises from a base of morality or virtue. These three—morality, concentration, and wisdom—are so interrelated that it is not really possible to separate them. In practice it works like this. First there is the disciplining of the mind to be attentive to breathing. This is the arising of morality. When mindfulness of breathing is practiced continuously until the mind is quiet, concentration arises. Then examination shows the breath to be impermanent, unsatisfactory, and not self; nonattachment follows, and this is the arising of wisdom. Thus the practice of mindfulness of breathing can be said to be a cause for the development of morality, concentration, and wisdom. They all come together.

When morality, concentration, and wisdom are all developed, we call this practicing the Eightfold Path, which the Buddha taught as our only way out of suffering. The Eightfold Path is supreme because, if properly practiced, it leads directly to nibbāna, to peace.

THE BENEFITS OF PRACTICE

When we have practiced meditation as explained above, the fruits of practice will arise in the following three stages:

First, for those practitioners who are at the level of "Buddhists by faith," there will arise increasing faith in the Buddha, Dhamma, and Sangha. This faith will become their real inner support. They will also understand the cause-and-effect nature of all things: that wholesome action brings wholesome results and that unwholesome action brings unwholesome results. So for such a person there will be a great increase in happiness and mental peace.

Second, those who have reached the noble attainments of stream-enterer, once-returner, or non-returner develop unshakable faith in the Buddha, Dhamma, and Sangha. They are joyful and are pulled toward nibbāna.

Third, for those arahants or Perfected Ones, there will be the happiness free from all suffering. These are the buddhas, free from the world, complete in the practice of the spiritual path.

We have all had the good fortune to be born as human beings and to hear the teaching of the Buddha. This is an opportunity that millions of other beings do not have. Therefore do not be careless or heedless. Hurry and develop wholesomeness, do good, and follow the path of practice in the beginning, middle, and highest levels. Don't let time roll by unused and without purpose. Try to reach the truth of the Buddha's teachings even today. Let me close with a Lao folk-saying: *Many rounds of merriment and pleasure have passed; soon it will be evening. Now, drunk with tears, rest and see. Before long it will be too late to finish the journey.*

PART I

*Conduct—
Virtue and the
World of the Senses*

CHAPTER 3

LIVING IN THE WORLD
WITH DHAMMA

M OST PEOPLE STILL DON'T KNOW the essence of meditation practice. They think that walking meditation, sitting meditation, and listening to Dhamma talks are the practice. That's true too, but these are only the outer forms of practice. The real practice takes place when the mind encounters a sense object. That's the place to practice, where sense contact occurs. When people say things we don't like, there is resentment; if they say things we like, we experience pleasure. Now this is the place to practice. How are we going to practice with these things? This is the crucial point. If we just run around chasing after happiness and running away from suffering, we can practice until the day we die and never see the Dhamma. When pleasure and pain arise how are we going to use the Dhamma to be free of them? This is the point of practice.

Usually when people encounter something disagreeable, they don't open up to it. When people are criticized, for example, they may respond with "Don't bother me! Why blame me?" This is the response of someone who's closed themselves off. Right there is the place to practice. When people criticize us, we should listen. Are they speaking the truth? We should be open and consider what they say. Maybe there is a point to what they say. Perhaps there is something blameworthy within us. They may be right, and yet we immediately take offense. When people point out our faults, we should feel grateful and strive to improve ourselves. This is how intelligent people will practice.

Where there is confusion is where peace can arise. When confusion is penetrated with understanding, what remains is peace. Some people can't accept criticism, they're so arrogant. Instead they turn around and argue. This is especially so when adults deal with children. Actually children may say some intelligent things sometimes, but if you happen to be their mother, for instance, you can't give in to them. If you are a teacher, your students may sometimes tell you something you didn't know. But because you are the teacher you can't listen. This is not Right Thinking.

Venerable Sāriputta, one of the Buddha's disciples, was very astute. Once when the Buddha was expounding the Dhamma he turned to this monk and asked, "Sāriputta, do you believe this?" Sāriputta replied, "No, I don't yet believe it." The Buddha praised his answer. "That's very good, Sāriputta. You are one who is endowed with wisdom. One who is wise doesn't readily believe; they listen with an open mind and then weigh the truth of the matter before believing or disbelieving."

Here the Buddha has set a fine example for a teacher. What Sāriputta said was true. He simply spoke his true feelings. For some people, saying you didn't believe a teaching would amount to questioning the teacher's authority, so they'd be afraid to say such a thing. They'd just go ahead and agree. But the Buddha didn't take offense. He said that you needn't be ashamed of those things that aren't wrong or bad. It's not wrong to say that you don't believe if you don't believe. The Buddha's actions here are a good example for one who is a teacher of others. Sometimes you can learn things even from small children; don't cling blindly to positions of authority.

Whether you are standing, sitting, or walking about, you can always study the things around you. Study in a natural way. Be receptive to all things: sights, sounds, smells, tastes, feelings, or thoughts. The wise person considers them all. In the real practice, we come to the point where there are no longer any concerns weighing on the mind.

If we still don't know likes and dislikes as they arise, there will still be some anxiety in our minds. If we know the truth about them, we reflect, "Oh, there's nothing to this feeling of liking here. It's just a feeling that arises and passes away. Dislike too is just a feeling that arises and passes away. Why make anything out of them?" If we think that pleasure and pain are personal possessions, then we're in for trouble. And these problems feed each other in an endless chain. This is how things are for most people.

But these days teachers don't often talk about the mind when teaching the Dhamma; they don't talk about the truth. If you speak the truth, people even take exception. They say things like "He doesn't know proper time and place. He doesn't know how to speak nicely." But people should listen to the truth. A true teacher doesn't just talk from memory, but speaks the truth. People in society usually speak from memory, and what's more they usually speak in such a way as to exalt themselves. The true monk doesn't talk like that; he speaks the truth, the way things are.

If you understand the Dhamma you should practice accordingly. It isn't necessary to become a monastic, although the monastic life is the ideal form for practice. To really practice, you have to forsake the confusion of the world, give up family and possessions, and take to the forests. That's the ideal way to practice. But if we have a family and responsibilities, how are we to practice? Some people say it's impossible to practice Dhamma as a lay person. But consider, which group is larger, monastics or lay people? There are far more lay people. Now if only the monastics practice and lay people don't, then that means there's going to be a lot of confusion. This understanding is wrong. Becoming a monk or a nun isn't the point! Being a monk doesn't mean anything if you don't practice. If you really understand the practice of Dhamma, then no matter what position or profession you hold in life, be it a teacher, doctor, civil servant, or whatever, you can practice the Dhamma every minute of the day.

To think you can't practice as a lay person is to lose track of the Path completely. Why is it people can find the incentive to do other things? If they feel they are lacking something they make an effort to obtain it. If there is sufficient desire people can do anything. Some say, "I haven't got time to practice the Dhamma." I say, "Then how come you've got time to breathe?" The practice of Dhamma isn't something you have to go running around for or exhaust yourself over. Just look at the feelings that arise in your mind. When the eye sees forms, ear hears sounds, nose smells odors, and so on, they all come to this one mind: "the one who knows." Now when the mind perceives these things, what happens? If we like that object we experience pleasure; if we dislike it we experience displeasure. That's all there is to it.

So where are you going to find happiness in this world? Do you expect everybody to say only pleasant things to you all your life? Is that possible? If it's not possible, then where are you going to go? The world is simply like this; we must know the world—*lokavidū*—know the truth of this world. The world is something we should clearly understand. The Buddha lived in this world. He experienced family life, but he saw its limitations and detached himself from them. Now how are you as lay people going to practice? If you want to practice you must make an effort to follow the Path. If you persevere with the practice you too will see the limitations of this world and be able to let go.

People who drink alcohol sometimes say, "I just can't give it up." Why can't they give it up? Because they don't yet see the liability in it. If you don't see the liability of something, that means you also can't see the benefit of giving it up. Your practice becomes fruitless; you are just playing at practice. But if you clearly see the liability and the benefit of something, you won't have to wait for others to tell you about it. Consider the story of the fisherman who finds something in his fish-trap. He knows something is in there; he can hear it flopping about inside. Thinking it's a fish, he reaches his hand into the trap, only to find a different kind of animal. He can't yet see it, so he's in two minds about it. On one hand it could be an eel,[7] but then again it could be a snake. If he throws it away, he may regret it; it could be an eel. On the other hand, if he holds on to it and it turns out to be a snake, it may bite him. He's caught in a state of doubt. His desire is so strong he holds on, just in case it's an eel, but the minute he brings it out and sees the striped skin he throws it down straight away. He doesn't have to wait for someone to call out, "It's a snake, let it go!" The sight of the snake tells him what to do much more clearly than words could do. Why? Because he sees the danger—snakes can bite! Who has to tell him to let it go? In the same way, if we practice till we see things as they are, we won't meddle with things that are harmful.

People don't usually practice like this. They don't reflect on old age, sickness, and death. They only talk about non-aging and non-death, so they never develop the right feeling for Dhamma practice. They go and listen to Dhamma talks but they don't really listen. Sometimes I get invited to give talks at important functions, but it's a nuisance for me to go. When I look at the people gathered there, I can see that they haven't come to listen to the Dhamma. Some smell of alcohol, some are smoking cigarettes, some are chatting; they don't look at all like people who have come out of faith in the Dhamma. Giving talks at such places yields little fruit. People who are sunk in heedlessness tend to think things like, "When's he ever going to stop talking? 'Can't do this, can't do that...'" and their minds just wander all over the place.

Sometimes they even invite me to give a talk just for the sake of formality: "Please give us just a short Dhamma talk, Venerable Sir." They don't want me to talk too much—it might annoy them! As soon as I hear people say this, I know what they're about. These people don't like listening to Dhamma. It annoys them. If I just give a short talk, they won't understand. If you take only a little food, will it be enough?

Sometimes I'm giving a talk, just warming up to the subject, and some drunkard will call out, "Okay, make way, make way for the Venerable Sir, he's coming out now!"—trying to drive me away! If I meet this kind of person, I get a lot of food for reflection; I get an insight into human nature. It's like a person who has a bottle filled with water and then asks for more. There's nowhere to put it. Pour any more in and it just overflows uselessly. It isn't worth the time and energy to teach such persons, because their minds are already full. I can't put much energy into giving when no one's putting much energy into receiving. If their bottle had some room for more water, both the giver and the receiver would benefit.

These days, giving talks tends to be like this, and it's getting worse all the time. People don't search for truth; they study simply to find the necessary knowledge to make a living, raise families, and look after themselves. They study for a livelihood. There's not much study of Dhamma. Students nowadays have much more knowledge than previous generations. They have all they need at their disposal; everything is more convenient. But they also have a lot more confusion and suffering. Why is this? Because they only look for the kind of knowledge used to make a living.

Even the monks do this. Sometimes I hear them say, "I didn't become a monk to practice the Dhamma! I ordained to study." These are the words of someone who has completely cut off the path of practice. It's a dead end. When these monks teach, it's only from memory. They may teach one thing, but their minds are in a completely different place. Such teachings aren't true.

This is how the world is. If you try to live simply, practicing the Dhamma and living peacefully, they say you are weird and antisocial. They say you're obstructing progress in society. They even intimidate you. Eventually you might even start to believe them and revert to worldly ways, sinking deeper and deeper into the world until it's impossible to get out. Some people say, "I can't get out now, I've gone in too deeply." This is how society tends to be. It doesn't appreciate the value of Dhamma.

The value of Dhamma isn't to be found in books. Those are just the external appearances of Dhamma; they're not the realization of Dhamma as a personal experience. *If you realize the Dhamma, you realize your own mind.* You see the truth there. When the truth becomes apparent it cuts off the stream of delusion.

The teaching of the Buddha is an unchanging truth. The Buddha revealed this truth 2,500 years ago, and it's been the truth ever since. This teaching should not be added to or diminished. The Buddha said, "What the Tathāgata has laid down should not be discarded, and what has not been laid down by the Tathāgata should not be added on." He sealed off the teachings. Why did the Buddha seal them off? Because these teachings are the words of one who has no defilements. No matter how the world may change, these teachings are unaffected, they don't change with it. If something is wrong, does saying it's right make it any less wrong? If something is right, does that change just because people say it's not? Generation after generation may come and go, but these things don't change, because these teachings are the truth.

Now who created this truth? The truth itself created the truth! Did the Buddha create it? No, he didn't. The Buddha only discovered the truth, the way things are, and then he set out to declare it. The truth is constantly true, whether a buddha arises in the world or not. The Buddha only "owns" the Dhamma in this sense; he didn't actually create it. It's been here all the time. Previously, however, no one had searched for and found this truth. The Buddha was the one who searched for and found the deathless and then taught it as the Dhamma. He didn't invent it.

At some point in time the truth is illuminated and the practice of Dhamma flourishes. As time goes on and generations pass away, the practice degenerates until the teachings fade away completely. After a time the teachings are rediscovered and flourish once more. As time goes on, the adherents of the Dhamma multiply, prosperity sets in, and once more the teachings succumb to the darkness of the world. Once more they degenerate until such a time as they can no longer hold ground. Confusion reigns once more. Then it is time to reestablish the truth. In fact the truth doesn't go anywhere. When buddhas pass away, the Dhamma doesn't disappear with them.

The world revolves like this. It's something like a mango tree. The tree matures, puts forth blossoms, and fruits appear and ripen. These become rotten, and the seed goes back into the ground to become a new mango tree. The cycle starts again. This is how the world is. It doesn't go very far; it just revolves around the same old things.

Our lives these days are the same. Today we are simply doing the same old things we've always done. People think too much. There are so many things for them to get interested in, but none of them leads to completion. There are the sciences like mathematics, physics, psychology, and so on. You can delve into any number of them, but you can only finalize things with the realization of the truth.

Picture a cart being pulled by an ox. As the ox walks along, the cart leaves tracks behind it. The cartwheels may not be very big, but the tracks will stretch a long way back. Looking at a cart when it's standing still, you can't see anything long about it, but once the ox starts moving, you see the tracks stretching out behind you. As long as the ox pulls, the wheels keep on turning, but there comes a day when the ox tires and throws off its harness. The ox walks off and leaves the empty cart sitting there. The wheels no longer turn. In time the cart falls apart; its components go back into the four elements—earth, water, wind, and fire.

As you go searching for peace within the world, the wheels of your cart turn ceaselessly and your tracks stretch endlessly behind you. As long as you follow the world, there is no stopping, no rest. But if you simply stop, the cart comes to rest; the wheels no longer turn. Creating bad karma is like this. As long as you follow the old ways, there is no stopping. If you stop, there is stopping. This is how we practice the Dhamma.

CHAPTER 4

MAKING THE HEART GOOD

THESE DAYS people are going all over the place looking for merit.[8] And they always seem to stop over in Wat Pah Pong. If they don't stop over on their way out, they do so on the return trip. Some people are in such a hurry I don't even get a chance to see or speak to them. Most of them are looking for merit. I don't see many looking for a way out of wrongdoing. They're so intent on getting merit they don't know where they're going to put it. It's like trying to dye a dirty, unwashed cloth.

Monks talk straight like this, but it's hard for most people to put this sort of teaching into practice. It's hard because they don't understand. If they understood it would be much easier. Suppose there was a hole, and there was something at the bottom of it. Now anyone who reached into the hole and couldn't touch the bottom would say the hole was too deep. A hundred or a thousand people might put their hands down that hole, and they'd all say the hole was too deep. Not one would say their arm was too short!

Sooner or later all these people looking for merit will have to start looking for a way out of wrongdoing. But not many people are interested in this. The teachings of the Buddha are so brief, but most people just pass them by, just like they pass through Wat Pah Pong. For most people that's what the Dhamma is, a stopover.

Only three lines, hardly anything to it. The first is—*Sabba pāpassa akaraṇaṁ:* refraining from all wrongdoing.[9] That's the teaching of all the buddhas. This is the heart of Buddhism. But people keep jumping over it; they don't want this one. The renunciation of all wrongdoing, great and small, from bodily, verbal, and mental actions—this is the teaching of the buddhas.

If we were to dye a piece of cloth, we'd have to wash it first. But most people don't do that. Without looking at the cloth, they dip it into the dye straight away. If the cloth is dirty, dying it makes it come out even worse than before. Think about it. Dying a dirty old rag, would that look good?

You see? This is how Buddhism teaches, but most people just pass it by. They just want to perform good works, but they don't want to give up wrongdoing. It's just like saying that the hole is too deep when it's the arm that's too short. We have to come back to ourselves. With this teaching you have to take a step back and look at yourself.

Sometimes they go looking for merit by the busload. Maybe they even argue on the bus, or they're drunk. Ask them where they're going and they say they're looking for merit. They want merit but they don't give up vice. They'll never find merit that way.

This is how people are. You have to look at yourself closely. The Buddha taught about having mindfulness and self-awareness in all situations. Wrongdoing arises in bodily, verbal, and mental actions. The source of all good, evil, well-being, and harm lies with actions, speech, and thoughts. This is where you must look, right here. See if your conduct is faulty or not.

People don't really look at these things. Like the housewife washing the dishes with a scowl on her face. She's so intent on cleaning the dishes, she doesn't realize her own mind's unclean! She's looking too far away, isn't she? People concentrate so hard on cleaning the dishes, they let their minds get dirty. This is not good; they're forgetting themselves.

Because they don't see themselves, people can commit all sorts of bad deeds. When people are planning to do something bad, they have to glance around first to see if anyone is looking. Will my mother see me? My husband? The children? My wife? If there's no one watching, they go right ahead and do it. They're insulting themselves: They think no one is watching, so they quickly finish the job before somebody sees. But what about themselves? Aren't they somebody?

You see? Because they overlook themselves like this, people never find what is of real value; they don't find the Dhamma. If you look at yourself, you will see yourself. Whenever you are about to do something bad, if you see yourself in time you can stop. If you want to do something worthwhile, look at your mind. If you know how to look at yourself, you'll know about right and wrong, harm and benefit, vice and virtue.

If I don't speak of these things, you won't know about them. You'll have greed and delusion in the mind, but you won't know it. You won't know anything if you are always looking outside. That's the trouble with people not looking at themselves. Looking inward, you will see good and evil. Seeing goodness, we can take it to heart and practice accordingly.

Giving up the bad, practicing the good—this is the heart of Buddhism. Sabba pāpassa akaraṇaṁ—not committing any wrongdoing, whether through body, speech, or mind. That's the right practice, the teaching of the buddhas. Then our cloth will be clean.

Then we have *kusalassūpasampadā*—making the mind virtuous and skillful.[10] If the mind is virtuous and skillful, we don't have to bus all over the countryside looking for merit. Even sitting at home, we can attain to merit. But most people just go looking for merit all over the countryside without giving up their vices. Returning home empty-handed, they go back to their old sour faces. There they are, scrubbing the dishes with a sour face. Looking inward is just what people don't want to do, so they're far away from merit.

We may know all this, but if we don't really know it within ourselves, Buddhism doesn't enter our heart. If our mind is good and virtuous, it is happy. There's a smile in our heart. But most of us can hardly find time to smile, can we? We can only manage to smile when things go our way. Most people's happiness depends on having everything the way they like it. They have to have everybody in the world say only pleasant things. Is it possible to have everybody in the world say only pleasant things? If that's the way you want it, how will you ever find happiness? How can we ever get others to say things only to our liking every single day? Is that possible? Even your own children, have they ever said things that displease you? Have you ever upset your parents? Not only other people, but even our own minds can upset us. Sometimes the things we think about are unpleasant. What can you do? You might be walking along and suddenly trip on a root. *Thud! Ouch!* Where's the problem? Who tripped who anyway? Who are you going to blame? It's your own fault. Even our own mind can be displeasing to us. If you think about it, you'll see that this is true. Sometimes we do things that even we don't like. All you can say is, "Damn!" There's no one else to blame.

We must use Dhamma to find happiness. Whatever it may be, whether right or wrong, don't blindly cling to it. Just notice it and then lay it down. When the mind is at ease, then you can smile. The minute you become averse to something, the mind goes bad. Then nothing is good at all.

Sacittapariyodapanaṁ: having cleared away impurities, the mind is free of worries—peaceful, kind, and virtuous.[11] When the mind is radiant and has given up evil, there is always ease. The serene and peaceful mind is the true epitome of human achievement.

Merit in Buddhism is giving up that which is wrong. When there is no longer any wrongness, there is no longer any stress. When there is no stress, there is calm. The calm mind is a clean, clear mind, one that harbors no angry thoughts.

How can you make the mind clear? Just by knowing it. For example, you might think, "Today I'm in a really bad mood; everything I look at offends me, even the plates in the cupboard." You might feel like smashing them, every single one of them. Whatever you look at looks bad: the chickens, the ducks, the cats, the dogs—you hate them all. Everything your husband says is offensive. Even looking into your own mind, you're dissatisfied. What can you do in such a situation? Where does this suffering come from? This is called "having no merit." These days in Thailand they have a saying that when someone dies, their merit is finished. But that's not the case. There are plenty of people still alive who've finished their merit already.

Going on these merit-making tours is like building a beautiful house without preparing the area beforehand. It won't be long before the house collapses, right? The foundation was no good. You have to try again, a different way. You have to look into yourself, at the faults in your actions, speech, and thoughts. Where else are you going to practice? People get lost. They want to go and practice Dhamma where it's really peaceful, in the forest or at Wat Pah Pong. Is Wat Pah Pong peaceful? No, it's not really peaceful. Where it's really peaceful is in your own home.

If you have wisdom, wherever you go you will be carefree. The whole world is already just fine as it is. The trees in the forest are fine just as they are: there are tall ones, short ones, hollow ones, all kinds. They are simply the way they are. But we, ignorant of their true nature, go and impose our opinions on them: This tree is too short! This one is hollow! Those trees are simply trees; they're better off than we are.

That's why I've had these little poems put up on the trees here. Let the trees teach you. Have you learned anything from them yet? You should try to learn at least one thing from them. There are so many trees, all with something to teach you. Dhamma is everywhere, in all of nature. You should understand this point. Don't go blaming the hole for being too deep. Turn around and look at your own arm! If you see this, you'll be happy.

If you make merit or virtue, preserve it in your mind. That's the best place to keep it. It's good to make merit the way you did today, but it's not the best way. Contributing to the construction of monastery buildings is meritorious too, but it's not the best thing. Building your own mind into something good is the best way. That way you will find goodness whether you come here or stay at home. Find this excellence within your mind. Outer structures, like this hall, are like the bark of the tree; they're not the heartwood.

If you have wisdom, wherever you look there will be Dhamma. If you lack wisdom, then even the good things turn bad. Where does this badness come from? Just from our own minds, that's where. Look how this mind changes! Husband and wife used to get on all right together; they could talk to each other quite happily. But there comes a day when their mood goes bad; everything the spouse says seems offensive. The mind has gone bad; it's changed again. That's how it is.

So in order to give up evil and cultivate good, you don't have to go looking anywhere else. If your mind has gone bad, don't go looking at others. Just look at your own mind and find out where these thoughts come from. Why does the mind think such things? Understand that all things are transient. Love is transient; hate is transient. Have you loved your children? Of course you have. Have you ever hated them? I'll answer that for you, too. You do sometimes, don't you? You can't throw your children away, can you? Why not? Children aren't like bullets, are they?[12] Bullets are fired outward, but children are fired right back into their parents' hearts. If the children are good it comes back to the parents. If they're bad it comes back to the parents. You could say children are your *kamma*—your kamma. There are good ones and bad ones. Both good and bad are right there in your children. But even the bad ones are precious. One may be born with polio, crippled and deformed, and be even more precious than the others. Whenever you leave home for a while you have to leave a message, "Look after the little one, he's not so strong." You love him even more than the others.

You should, then, set your minds up well—half love, half hate. Don't take only one or the other; always have both sides in mind. Your children are your karma; they are appropriate to their owners. They are your karma, so you must take responsibility for them. If they really give you suffering, just remind yourself, "It's my karma." If they please you, just remind yourself, "It's my karma." Sometimes it gets so frustrating at home, you may just want to run away. It gets so bad some people even contemplate hanging themselves! It's karma. We have to accept the fact. Avoid bad actions, then you will be able to see yourself more clearly.

This is why contemplating things is so important. Usually when one practices meditation, one uses a meditation object, such as *Bud-dho, Dham-mo,* or *San-gho.* But you can make it even shorter than this. Whenever you feel annoyed, whenever your mind goes bad, just say, "So!" When you feel better, just say, "So! It's not a sure thing." If you love someone, just say, "So!" When you feel you're getting angry, just say, "So!" Do you understand? You don't have to go looking into the Tipiṭaka.[13]

Just "So!" This means "it's transient." Love is transient; hate is transient; good is transient; evil is transient. How could they be permanent? Where is there any permanence in them?

You could say that they are permanent insofar as they are invariably impermanent. They are certain in this respect; they never become otherwise. One minute there's love, the next hate. That's how things are. In this sense they are permanent. That's why I say that whenever love arises, just tell it, "So!" It saves a lot of time. You don't have to say, "Anicca, dukkha, anattā." If you don't want a long meditation theme, just take this simple word. If love arises, before you get really lost in it, just tell yourself, "So!" This is enough.

Everything is transient, and it's permanent in that it's invariably transient. Just to see this much is to see the heart of the Dhamma, the True Dhamma.

Now if everybody said, "So!" more often, and applied themselves to training like this, clinging would diminish. People would not be so stuck on love and hate. They would not cling to things. They would put their trust in the truth, not with other things. Just to know this much is enough; what else do you need to know?

Having heard the teaching, you should try to remember it. What should you remember? Meditate. Do you understand? If you understand, and the Dhamma clicks with you, the mind will stop. If there's anger in the mind, just "So!" and that's enough; it stops straightaway. If you don't yet understand then look deeply into the matter. If there is understanding, when anger arises in the mind you can just shut it off with "So! It's impermanent!"

Today you have had a chance to record the Dhamma both inwardly and outwardly. Inwardly, the sound enters through the ears to be recorded in the mind. If you can't do this much, your time at Wat Pah Pong will have been wasted. This tape recorder here is not so important. The really important thing is the "recorder" in the heart. The tape recorder is perishable, but if the Dhamma really reaches the heart, it's imperishable; it's there for good. And you don't have to waste money on batteries.

CHAPTER 5

SENSE CONTACT—
THE FOUNT OF WISDOM

ALL OF US have made up our minds to become bhikkhus and *sāma-ṇera*s, or novices, in the Buddhist dispensation in order to find peace. Now what is true peace? True peace, the Buddha said, is not very far away— it lies right here within us—but we tend to continually overlook it. People long to find peace but still experience confusion and agitation. They remain unsure of themselves and haven't yet found fulfillment in their practice. It's as if we have left home and are traveling to here and there, but as long as we still haven't reached home we don't feel content; we still have some unfinished business to take care of. This is because our journey is unfinished; we haven't yet reached our destination.

All bhikkhus and sāmaṇeras want peace, every one of us. When I was young, I searched all over for it. Wherever I went, I wasn't satisfied. Wandering into forests, visiting various teachers, listening to Dhamma talks, nowhere did I find satisfaction. Why is this? We search for peace in places where there are few sights, sounds, odors, or tastes, believing that living quietly will lead to contentment. But actually, if we live very quietly in places where nothing arises, can wisdom arise? Would we be aware of anything? Think about it. What would it be like if the eye didn't see sights? If the nose didn't experience smells? If the tongue didn't experience flavors? If the body didn't experience feelings? To be like that would be like being a blind and deaf person, one whose nose and tongue had fallen off and who was completely numb with paralysis. Would there be anything there? And yet people tend to think that if they went somewhere where nothing happened, they would find peace.

When I was a young monk just starting to practice, I'd sit in meditation and sounds would disturb me. I'd think to myself, "What can I do to make my mind peaceful?" So I took some beeswax and stuffed my ears with it so that I couldn't hear anything. All that remained was a humming sound. I thought that would be peaceful; but no, all that thinking and confusion didn't arise at the ears after all. It arose at the mind. That is the place to search for peace.

To put it another way, no matter where you stay, you don't want to do anything because it interferes with your practice. You don't want to sweep the grounds or do anything like that; you just want to sit still and find peace that way. The teacher asks you to help out with the chores or any of the daily duties, but you don't put your heart into it because you feel it is only an external concern.

One of my disciples was really eager to "let go" and find peace. I had taught about "letting go," and he thought that by letting go of everything he would become peaceful. Right from the day he came here, he didn't want to do anything. Even when the wind blew half the roof off his kuṭī, he wasn't interested in doing anything about it. He said that that was just an external thing. So he didn't bother fixing it up. When the sunlight or rain came in from one side, he'd move over to the other side. His sole business was to make his mind peaceful. That other stuff was a distraction.

One day I was walking past and saw the collapsed roof. "Hey, whose kuṭī is this?" I wondered. Someone told me whose it was, and I thought, "Hmm, strange." So I had a talk with him, explaining many things, such as *senāsanavatta*—the duties of monks with regard to their dwellings. "We must have a dwelling place, and we must look after it. 'Letting go' isn't like this; it doesn't mean shirking our responsibilities. That's the action of a fool. The rain comes in on one side, so you move over to the other side. Then the sun shines in, so you move back to that side. Why is that? Why don't you bother to let go there?" I gave him a long discourse on this.

When I'd finished, he said, "Oh, Luang Por, sometimes you teach me to cling and sometimes you teach me to let go. I don't know what you want me to do. Even when my roof collapses and I let go to this extent, still you say it's not right. And yet you teach me to let go! I don't know what more you can expect of me."

That's the way some people are. They can be that stupid.

The sense bases of eye, ear, nose, tongue, body, and mind are all things that can facilitate the arising of wisdom, if we know them as they are. If we don't really know them we must deny them, saying we don't want to see sights, hear sounds, and so on, because they disturb us. If we cut off the causal conditions what are we going to contemplate?

This is why we are taught to be restrained. Restraint is sīla. There is the sīla of sense restraint: eyes, ears, nose, tongue, body, and mind: these are our sīla, and they are our samādhi. Reflect on the story of Sāriputta. Once, before he became a bhikkhu, he saw Assaji Thera going on alms round. Seeing him, Sāriputta thought, "This monk is most unusual. He walks neither too fast nor too slow, his robes are neatly worn, his bearing is restrained." Sāriputta found the monk inspiring, so he approached Venerable Assaji, paid his respects, and asked, "Excuse me, sir, who are you?"

"I am a *samaṇa*."

"Who is your teacher?"

"Venerable Gotama is my teacher."

"What does Venerable Gotama teach?"

"He teaches that all things arise because of conditions. When they cease it's because the causal conditions have ceased."

When Sāriputta asked about the Dhamma, Assaji gave this brief explanation of cause and effect. Dhammas arise because of causes. The cause arises first and then the result. If the result is to cease, the cause must first cease. That's all he said, but it was enough for Sāriputta.[14]

Now this was a cause for the arising of Dhamma. At that time Sāriputta had eyes, he had ears, a nose, a tongue, a body, and a mind. All his faculties were intact. If he didn't have his faculties would there have been sufficient causes for wisdom to arise for him? Would he have been aware of anything? But most of us are afraid of contact. Either that or we like to have contact, but we develop no wisdom from it: instead we repeatedly indulge ourselves through eyes, ears, nose, tongue, body, and mind, delighting in sense objects and getting lost in them. These sense bases can entice us into delight and indulgence or they can lead to knowledge and wisdom.

So we should take everything as practice. Even the bad things. When we talk of practice we don't simply mean taking those things that are good and pleasing to us. That's not how it is. In this world some things are to our liking; some are not. Usually whatever we like we want, even with fellow monks and novices. Whatever monk or novice we don't like we don't want to associate with; we only want to be with those we like. You see? This is choosing according to our likes. Usually whatever we don't like, we don't want to see or know about. But the Buddha wanted us to experience these things. Lokavidū—look at this world and know it clearly. If we don't know the truth of the world clearly, then we can't go anywhere. Living in the world, we must understand the world. The Noble Ones of the past, including the Buddha, all lived with these things. They lived in this world, among deluded people, and attained the truth right here, nowhere else. But they had wisdom; they restrained their senses.

Restraint doesn't mean we don't see anything, hear anything, smell, taste, feel, or think anything. If practitioners don't understand this, then as soon as they see or hear something they will cower and run away, thinking that by so doing that thing will eventually lose its power over them, that they will eventually transcend it. But they won't. They won't transcend anything that way. If they run away, not knowing the truth about it, later on the same stuff will pop up and have to be dealt with again.

Consider, for example, those practitioners who are never content, be they in monasteries, forests, or mountains. They wander on a "*dhutanga* pilgrimage"[15] looking at this, that, and the other thing, thinking they'll find contentment that way. They try going to a mountaintop: "Ah! This is the spot, now I'm okay." They feel at peace for a few days and then get tired of it. "Oh, well, off to the seaside." "Ah, here it's nice and cool. This'll do me fine." After a while they get tired of the seaside as well. Tired of the forests, tired of the mountains, tired of the seaside, tired of everything. This is not being tired of things in the right sense,[16] as Right View; it's simply boredom, a kind of wrong view.

When they get back to the monastery: "Now, what will I do? I've been all over and I've come back with nothing." So they throw away their bowls and disrobe. Why do they disrobe? Because they haven't got any grip on the practice, they don't see anything left to do. They go to the south, to the north, to the seaside, to the mountains, into the forests, and still don't see anything. So it's all finished; they "die." This is how it goes. It's because they're continually running away from things. Wisdom doesn't arise.

Now take another example. Suppose there is a monk who resolves to stay with things, not to run away. He looks after himself. He knows himself and others. He's continually dealing with problems. Suppose he's the abbot. An abbot faces a constant stream of things demanding attention. People are always asking questions, so you must be constantly on the alert, constantly awake. Before you can doze off they wake you up again with another problem. This leads you to contemplate and understand things. You become skillful in regard to yourself and others in many, many ways.

This skill arises from contact, from confronting and dealing with things, from not running away. We don't run away physically, but we "run away" in mind, using our wisdom. We understand with wisdom right here; we don't run away from anything.

This is a source of wisdom. One must work, must associate with other things. For instance, living in a big monastery we must all help look after things. Looking at it in one way, you could say that it's all defilement. Living with lots of monks, nuns and novices, with many lay people coming and going, many defilements may arise. But we must live like this, for the development of wisdom and the abandonment of foolishness. Which way are we to go? Are we going to live in order to get rid of our foolishness or to increase it?

We must contemplate. Whenever eyes, ears, nose, tongue, body, or mind make contact, we should be collected and circumspect. When suffering arises, who is suffering? Why did this suffering arise? The abbot of a monastery has to supervise many disciples: this may cause suffering. If we are afraid of suffering and don't want to face it, where are we going to do battle with it? If suffering arises and we don't know it, how are we going to deal with it?

Escaping from suffering means knowing the way out of suffering; it doesn't mean running away from wherever suffering arises. By doing that you just carry your suffering with you.

If you want to understand suffering you must look into the situation at hand. The teachings say that wherever a problem arises, it must be settled right there. Where suffering lies is right where non-suffering will arise; it ceases at the place where it arises. You should settle the issue right there. One who runs away from suffering out of fear is the most foolish person of all. They will simply increase their stupidity endlessly.

Suffering is none other than the First Noble Truth, isn't that so? Are you going to look on it as something bad? *Dukkha sacca, samudaya sacca, nirodha sacca, magga sacca*—the truth of suffering, the truth of its cause, the truth of its cessation, and the truth of the way leading to the cessation of suffering. Running away from these things isn't practicing according to the true Dhamma.

The Buddha taught us to "run away" using wisdom. For instance, suppose you step on a thorn or splinter and it gets embedded in your foot. As you walk, sometimes it hurts, sometimes not. Sometimes when you step on a stone or a stump it really hurts. So you feel around your foot, but, not finding anything, you shrug it off and keep on walking. Eventually you step on something else, and you feel the pain again. This happens repeatedly.

What is the cause of that pain? The cause is that splinter or thorn embedded in your foot. The pain is constantly near. Whenever the pain arises you take a look and feel around a bit, but, not seeing the splinter, you let it go. After a while it hurts again so you take another look.

When suffering arises you must note it; don't just shrug it off. Whenever the pain arises, you note, "Hmm, that splinter is still there." Whenever the pain arises there arises also the thought that that splinter has got to go. If you don't take it out, there will only be more pain later on. The pain recurs again and again, until the desire to take out that thorn is constantly with you. In the end it reaches a point where you make up your mind once and for all to get that splinter out—because it hurts!

Now our effort in the practice must be like this. Wherever it hurts, wherever there's friction, we must investigate. Confront the problem head on. Take that thorn out of your foot; just pull it out. Wherever your mind gets stuck you must take note. As you look into it you will know it, see it, and experience it as it is.

But our practice must be unwavering and persistent. They call it *viriyārambha*—putting forth constant effort. Whenever an unpleasant feeling arises in your foot, for example, you must remind yourself to get that thorn out; you don't give up your resolve. Likewise, when suffering arises in our hearts, we must have the unwavering resolve to try to uproot the defilements, to give them up. This resolve is constantly there, unremitting. Eventually the defilements will fall into our hands, where we can finish them off.

So in regard to happiness and suffering, what are we to do? All *dhammas* arise because of causes. When the result ceases it's because the cause has ceased. Whatever we don't hold fast to, cling to, or fix on to, is as if it weren't there. Suffering doesn't arise. Suffering arises from existence *(bhava)*.[17] If there is existence then there is birth. *Upādāna*—clinging or attachment—is the prerequisite that creates suffering. Wherever suffering arises, look into it. Look right into the present moment. Look at your own mind and body. When suffering arises, ask: Why is there suffering? Look right now. When happiness arises: What is the cause of that happiness? Look right there. Wherever these things arise, be aware. Both happiness and suffering arise from clinging.

The practitioners of old saw their minds in this way. There is only arising and ceasing. There is no abiding entity. They contemplated from all angles and saw that there was nothing much to this mind; nothing is stable. There is only arising and ceasing, ceasing and arising; nothing is of any lasting substance. While walking or sitting, they saw things in this way. Wherever they looked there was only suffering; that's all. It's just like a big iron ball which has just been forged in a furnace. It's hot all over. If you touch the top, it's hot. Touch the sides and they're hot—it's hot all over. There isn't any place on it which is cool.

If we don't consider these things, we know nothing about them. We must see clearly. Don't get "born" into things; don't fall into birth. Know the workings of birth. Such thoughts as, "Oh, I can't stand that person, he does everything wrongly," will no longer arise. Or, "I really like so-and-so." These things don't arise. There remain merely the conventional worldly standards of like and dislike. We must use the conventions of the world to communicate with each other, but inwardly we must be empty. This is the abiding of the Noble Ones. We must all aim for this and practice accordingly. Don't get caught up in doubts.

Before I started to practice, I thought to myself, "The Buddhist religion is here, available for all, and yet why do only some people practice while others don't? Or if they do practice, they do so only for a short while then give it up. Or again, those who don't give it up still don't knuckle down and do the practice? Why is this?" So I resolved, "Okay, I'll give up this body and mind for this lifetime and try to follow the teaching of the Buddha down to the last detail. I'll reach understanding in this very lifetime, because if I don't I'll still be sunk in suffering. I'll let go of everything else and make a determined effort; no matter how much difficulty or suffering I have to endure, I'll persevere. If I don't do this, I'll just keep on doubting."

Thinking like this I got down to practice. No matter how much happiness, suffering, or difficulty I'd have to endure, I would do it. I looked on my whole life as if it were only one day and a night. I gave it up. "I'll follow the teaching of the Buddha; I'll follow the Dhamma to understanding—Why is this world of delusion so wretched?" I wanted to know. I wanted to master the teachings, so I turned to the practice of Dhamma.

How much of the worldly life do we monastics renounce? If we have gone forth for good, it means we renounce it all: We cast off everything that people enjoy—sights, sounds, smells, tastes, and feelings. We throw them all away, and yet we experience them. So Dhamma practitioners must be content with little and remain detached. Whether in regard to speech, in eating, or whatever, we must be easily satisfied: eat simply, sleep simply, live simply. The more you practice like this, the more satisfaction you will find. You will see into your own heart.

The Dhamma is *paccattaṁ*—you know it for yourself. To know for yourself means to practice for yourself. You can depend on a teacher only fifty percent of the way. Even the teaching I have given you today is completely useless in itself. It is worth hearing, but if you were to believe it just because I said so, you wouldn't be using it properly. If you believed me completely, you'd be foolish. Put the teaching into practice for yourself, see it within yourself, do it yourself—this is much more useful. You will then know the taste of Dhamma.

This is why the Buddha didn't talk about the fruits of the practice in much detail, because it's something one can't convey in words. It would be like trying to describe different colors to a person blind from birth: "It's bright yellow." That wouldn't serve much purpose.

The Buddha brings it back down to the individual—you have to see clearly for yourself. If you see clearly for yourself, you'll have clear proof within yourself. Whether standing, walking, sitting, or reclining, you will be free of doubt. Even if someone were to say, "Your practice is all wrong," you'd be unmoved, because you have your own proof.

As a practitioner of the Dhamma, that's the way you must be, wherever you are. Others can't tell you; you must know for yourself. *Sammā diṭṭhi,* Right

View, must be there. But to really practice like this for even one month in five or ten rains retreats would be rare.

Once I went to live up north with some monks who were elderly but newly ordained, with only two or three rains retreats. At the time I had ten rains. Living with those old monks, I decided to perform the various duties that junior monks usually do—receiving their bowls, washing their robes, emptying their spittoons, and so on. I didn't think in terms of doing it for any particular individual; I was simply maintaining my practice. Since others weren't performing these duties, I'd do them myself. I saw it as a good opportunity to gain merit, and it gave me a sense of satisfaction.

On the *uposatha*[18] days, I'd go and clean out the uposatha hall and set out water for washing and drinking. The others didn't know anything about these duties; they just watched. I didn't criticize them, because they didn't know. I did the duties myself, and having done them, I felt pleased with myself. I had inspiration and a lot of energy in my practice.

Whenever I could do something in the monastery, whether in my own kuṭi or others', if it was dirty, I'd clean up. I didn't do it to impress anyone, but simply to maintain a good practice. Cleaning a kuṭi or dwelling place is just like cleaning rubbish out of your own mind.

This is something you should bear in mind. Live together with Dhamma, with peace and restraint, with a trained mind, and you won't have to worry about harmony; it will arise automatically, and there'll be no problems. If there's heavy work to be done, everybody helps out, and in no time at all it gets done. That's the best way.

I have come across some other types of monks, though, and these encounters have been opportunities to grow. For instance, in a big monastery the monks and novices may agree among themselves to wash robes on a certain day. I'd go and boil up the jackfruit wood.[19] Now there'd be some monks who'd wait for someone else to boil up the jackfruit wood and then come along and wash their robes, take them back to their kuṭis, hang them out, and then take a nap. They didn't have to set up the fire, didn't have to clean up afterward. They thought they were on to a good thing, that they were being clever. This is the height of stupidity. These people are just increasing their own foolishness because they don't do anything; they leave all the work up to others.

Therefore, whether speaking, eating, or doing anything whatsoever, reflect on yourself. You may want to live comfortably, eat comfortably, sleep comfortably, but you can't. What have we come here for? If we regularly reflect on this we will be heedful, we won't forget, we will be constantly alert. Being alert like this, we will put forth effort in all postures. If we don't put forth effort, things go quite differently: Sitting, you sit as though you're in the town; walking, you walk as though you're in the town. And then you want to go and fool around in the town with the lay people.

If there is no effort in the practice the mind will tend in that direction. You don't oppose and resist your own mind; you just allow it to waft along on the wind of your moods. This is called following one's moods. Like a child, if we indulge all its wants will it be a good child? If the parents indulge all their child's wishes is that good? Even if they do indulge it somewhat at first, by the time it can speak they may start to occasionally spank it because they're afraid it'll end up stupid. The training of our mind must be like this. You have to know yourself and how to train yourself. If you don't know how to train your own mind, waiting around expecting someone else to train it for you, you'll end up in trouble. Practice has no limits. Whether standing, walking, sitting, or lying down, you can always practice. You can realize the Dhamma while sweeping the monastery grounds or seeing a beam of sunlight. But you must have sati at hand. If you meditate ardently, you can realize the Dhamma at any time, in any place.

Don't be heedless. Be watchful; be alert. While walking on alms round there are all sorts of feelings arising, and it's all good Dhamma. When you get back to the monastery and are eating your food there's plenty of good Dhamma for you to look into. If you have constant effort, all these things will be objects for contemplation; wisdom will arise, and you will see the Dhamma. This is called *Dhamma-vicaya*, reflecting on Dhamma. It's one of the Factors of Enlightenment.[20] If we have mindfulness, we won't simply take it easy, and there will also be inquiry into Dhamma.

If we have reached this stage, our practice will know neither day nor night; it will continue on regardless of the time of day. Nothing will taint the practice, or if something does, we will immediately know it. When our practice enters the flow, there will be Dhamma-vicaya within our minds, constant investigation of the Dhamma. The mind won't go chasing after things: "I think I'll take a trip over there, or perhaps to this other place...but

over there should be interesting." That's the way of the world. Go that way
and the practice will soon die.

Be constantly alert. Study constantly. Seeing a tree or an animal can be
an occasion for study. Bring it all inward. See clearly within your own heart.
When some sensation makes an impact on the heart, witness it clearly for
yourself.

Have you ever seen a kiln for brickmaking? A fire is built about two or
three feet in front of it. If we make a brick kiln in the right way, all the heat
goes into the kiln, and the job gets done quickly. This is the way we
Dhamma practitioners should experience things. All our feelings will be
drawn inward to be turned into Right View. Seeing sights, hearing sounds,
smelling odors, tasting flavors—the mind draws them all inward. Those
feelings can then give rise to wisdom.

CHAPTER 6

UNDERSTANDING VINAYA

THIS PRACTICE OF OURS is not easy. There's still much that we don't know—for example, teachings such as "know the body, then know the body within the body" or "know the mind, then know the mind within the mind." If we haven't yet practiced these things, we may feel baffled. The vinaya is like this. In the past I used to be a teacher,[21] but I was only a "small teacher," not a big one. Why do I say a "small teacher"? Because I didn't practice. I taught the vinaya but I didn't practice it. Such a person I call a small teacher, an inferior teacher. I say an "inferior teacher" because when it came to the practice I was deficient. For the most part my practice was a long way off the mark, just as if I hadn't learned the vinaya at all.

However, I would like to state that in practical terms it's impossible to know the vinaya completely, because some things, whether we know of them or not, are still offenses. This is tricky. Yet it is stressed that if we do not yet understand any particular training rule or teaching, we must study that rule with enthusiasm and respect. If we don't understand it, we should make an effort to learn. If we don't make an effort, that in itself is an offense.

For example, there may be doubt. Suppose there is a woman and, not knowing whether she is a woman or a man, you touch her.[22] You're not sure if this person is a man or woman, but you still go ahead and touch; that's still wrong. I used to wonder why that should be wrong, but when I considered the practice, I realized that a meditator must have sati; they must be circumspect. Whether talking, touching, or holding things, they must first thoroughly consider. The error in this case is that there is no sati, or insufficient sati, or a lack of concern at that time.

Take another example: it's only eleven o'clock in the morning but at the time the sky is cloudy. We can't see the sun, and we have no clock. Now suppose we guess that it is probably afternoon. We really feel that it must be afternoon, and yet we proceed to eat something. We start eating, and then the clouds part and we see from the position of the sun that it's only just past eleven. This is still an offense.[23] I used to wonder, "Huh? It's not yet past midday, so why is this an offense?"

An offense is incurred here because of negligence, carelessness, lack of thorough consideration and restraint. If there is doubt and we act on the doubt, there is a *dukkaṭa*[24] offense just for acting in the face of the doubt. We think that it is afternoon when in fact it isn't. The act of eating is not wrong in itself, but there is an offense here because we are careless and negligent. If it really is afternoon but we think it isn't, then it's the heavier *pācittiya* offense. If we act with doubt, whether the action is wrong or not, we still incur an offense. If the action is not wrong in itself, it's the lesser offense; if it is wrong, then the heavier offense is incurred. The vinaya can get quite bewildering!

Once I went to see Venerable Ajahn Mun. At that time I had just begun to practice. I had read the *Pubbasikkhā*[25] and could understand that fairly well. Then I went on to read the *Visuddhimagga*, where the author writes of the *Sīlanidesa* (Book of Precepts), *Samādhinidesa* (Book of Mind Training), and *Paññānidesa* (Book of Wisdom). My head felt like it was going to burst! After reading that, I felt that it was beyond the ability of a human being to practice. But then I reflected that the Buddha would not teach something that is impossible to practice. He wouldn't teach it and he wouldn't declare it, because those things would be useful neither to himself nor to others. The *Sīlanidesa* is extremely meticulous, the *Samādhinidesa* more so, and the *Paññānidesa* even more so! I sat and thought, "Well, I can't go any further. There's no way ahead." It was as if I'd reached a dead-end.

At this stage I was struggling with my practice. I was stuck. It so happened that I had a chance to go and see Venerable Ajahn Mun, so I asked him: "Venerable Ajahn, what am I to do? I've just begun to practice, but I still don't know the right way. I have so many doubts I can't find any foundation at all in the practice."

He asked, "What's the problem?"

"In the course of my practice I picked up the *Visuddhimagga* and read it, but it seems impossible to put into practice. The contents of the *Sīlanidesa, Samādhinidesa,* and *Paññānidesa* seem to be completely impractical. I don't think there is anybody in the world who could do it, it's so detailed and meticulous. To memorize every single rule would be impossible. It's beyond me."

He said to me: "There's a lot there, it's true, but it's really only a little. If we were to take account of every training rule in the *Sīlanidesa* that would be difficult, true. But actually, what we call the *Sīlanidesa* has evolved from the human mind. If we train this mind to have a sense of shame and a fear of wrongdoing, we will then be restrained, we will be cautious.

"This will condition us to be content with little, with few wishes, because we can't possibly look after a lot. When this happens our sati becomes stronger. We will be able to maintain sati at all times. Wherever we are, we will make the effort to maintain thorough sati. Caution will be developed. Whenever you're in doubt about something, don't say it, don't act on it. If there's anything you don't understand, ask the teacher. Trying to practice every single training rule would indeed be burdensome, but we should examine whether we are prepared to admit our faults or not. Do we accept them?"

This teaching is very important. It's not so much that we must know every single training rule, but that we must know how to train our own minds.

"All that stuff that you've been reading arises from the mind. If you still haven't trained your mind to have sensitivity and clarity, you'll be in doubt all the time. You should try to bring the teachings of the Buddha into your mind. Compose your mind. Whatever arises that you doubt, just give it up. If you don't really know for sure, then don't say it or do it. For instance, if you wonder, "Is this wrong or not?"—but you're not really sure, then don't say it, don't act on it. Don't discard your restraint."

As I sat and listened, I reflected that this teaching conformed with the eight ways for measuring the true teaching of the Buddha. Any teaching that speaks of the diminishing of defilements, leads one out of suffering, and teaches renunciation (of sensual pleasures), contentment with little, humility and disinterest in rank and status, aloofness and seclusion, diligent effort, and ease of maintenance is characteristic of the true *Dhamma-vinaya,* the teaching of the Buddha. Anything in contradiction to these is not.

"If we are genuinely sincere we will have *hiri-ottappa,* a sense of shame and a fear of wrongdoing. We will know that when there is doubt in our mind, we will not act on it nor speak on it. The *Sīlanidesa* is only words. For example, hiri-ottappa in the books is one thing, but in our minds it is another."

Studying the vinaya with Venerable Ajahn Mun, I learned many things. As I sat and listened, understanding arose.

So, when it comes to the vinaya, I've studied it a lot. Some days during the rains retreat I would study from six o'clock in the evening through till dawn. I understand it sufficiently. All the factors of *āpatti*[26] that are covered in the *Pubbasikkhā* I wrote down in a notebook and kept in my bag. I really put effort into it, but later I gradually let go. It was too much. I didn't know which was the essence and which was the trimming; I had just taken all of it. When I understood more fully I let it drop away because it was too heavy. I just put my attention into my own mind and gradually did away with the texts.

However, when I teach the monks here I still take the *Pubbasikkhā* as my standard. For many years here at Wat Pah Pong, I myself read it to the assembly. In those days I would ascend the Dhamma-seat and go on until at least eleven o'clock or midnight, some days even one or two o'clock in the morning. We were interested. And we trained. After listening to the vinaya reading we would go and consider what we'd heard. You can't really understand the vinaya just by listening to it. Having listened to it you must examine it and delve into it further.

Even though I studied these things for many years my knowledge was still not complete, because there were so many ambiguities in the texts. Now that it's been such a long time since I looked at the books, my memory of the various training rules has faded somewhat, but within my mind there is no deficiency or doubt. There is understanding. I put away the books and concentrated on developing my own mind. The mind has an appreciation of virtue; it won't do anything wrong, whether in public or in private. I do not kill animals, even small ones. If someone were to ask me to intentionally kill an ant or a termite, to squash one with my hand, for instance, I couldn't do it, even if they were to offer me a fortune to do so. Even one ant or termite! The ant's life has greater value to me than a pile of money.

However, it may be that I may cause an insect to die, such as when something crawls up my leg and I brush it off. Maybe it dies, but when I look into my mind there is no feeling of guilt. There is no wavering or doubt. Why? Because there was no intention. *Sīlaṁ vadāmi bhikkhave cetanāhaṁ:* "Intention is the essence of moral training." In the past, before I really understood, I would really suffer over things like that. I would think I had committed an offense. "What offense? There was no intention." "No intention, true, but you weren't being careful enough!" I would go on like that, fretting and worrying.

So this vinaya is something that can disturb practitioners of Dhamma, but it also has its value, in keeping with what the teachers say—"Whatever training rules you don't yet know, you should learn. If you don't know, you should question those who do." They really stress this.

Now if we don't know the training rules, we won't be aware of our transgressions against them. Take, for example, a Venerable Thera of the past, Ajahn Pow of Wat Kow Wong Got in Lopburi Province. One day a disciple of his, a *mahā,* was sitting with him, when some women came up and asked Ajahn Pow,

"Luang Por! We want to invite you to go with us on an excursion, will you go?"

Luang Por Pow didn't answer. The Mahā sitting near him thought that Venerable Ajahn Pow hadn't heard, so he said,

"Luang Por, Luang Por! Did you hear? These women invited you to go for a trip."

He said, "I heard."

The women asked again, "Luang Por, are you going or not?"

He just sat there without answering, and so nothing came of the invitation. When they had gone, the Mahā said,

"Luang Por, why didn't you answer those women?"

He said, "Oh, Mahā, don't you know this rule? Those people who were here just now were all women. If women invite you to travel with them, you should not consent. If they make the arrangements themselves, that's fine. Then I can go if I want, because I didn't take part in making the arrangements."

The Mahā sat and thought, "Oh, I've really made a fool of myself."

The vinaya states that to make an arrangement and then travel together

with women, even though you're going as a group not as a couple, is a
pācittiya offense.

Take another case. Lay people would bring money to offer Venerable
Ajahn Pow on a tray. He would extend his receiving cloth,[27] holding it at
one end. But when they brought the tray forward to lay it on the cloth, he
would retract his hand from the cloth. Then he would simply abandon the
money where it lay. He knew it was there, but he would take no interest in
it, just get up and walk away. He did this because in the vinaya it is said that
if one doesn't consent to the money, it isn't necessary to forbid lay people
from offering it. If he had desire for it, he would have to say, "Householder,
this is not allowable for a monk." He would have to tell them that. If you
have desire for something, you must forbid people from offering that which
is unallowable. However, if you really have no desire for it, it isn't necessary.
You just leave it there and go.

Although the Ajahn and his disciples lived together for many years, still
some of his disciples didn't understand Ajahn Pow's practice. This is a poor
state of affairs. As for myself, I looked into and contemplated many of Venerable Ajahn Pow's subtler points of practice.

The vinaya can even cause some people to disrobe. When they study it,
all manner of doubts come up. It extends way back into the past. "My ordination, was it proper?[28] Was my preceptor pure? None of the monks who
sat in on my ordination knew anything about the vinaya, so were they sitting at the proper distance? Was the chanting correct?" The doubts roll on.
"The hall I ordained in, was it proper? It was so small...." They doubt
everything and fall into hell.

So until you know how to ground your mind, it can be really difficult.
You have to be very cool, you can't just jump into things. But being so cool
that you don't bother to look into things is wrong also. I was so confused
I almost disrobed, because I saw so many faults within my own practice and
that of some of my teachers. I was on fire and couldn't sleep because of
those doubts.

The more I doubted, the more I meditated, the more I practiced. Wherever doubt arose, I practiced right at that point. Wisdom arose. Things
began to change. It's hard to describe the change that took place. The mind
changed until there was no more doubt. I don't know how it changed. If I
were to try telling someone, they probably wouldn't understand.

So I reflected on the teaching *Paccattaṁ veditabbo viññūhi*—the wise must know for themselves. It must be a knowing that arises through direct experience. Studying the Dhamma-vinaya is certainly correct; but if it's just study, that's not enough. If you really get down to the practice, you begin to doubt everything. Before I started to practice I wasn't interested in the minor offenses, but when I started practicing, even the dukkaṭa offenses became as important as the *pārājika* offenses. Earlier, the dukkaṭa offenses seemed like nothing, just a trifle. That's how I saw them. In the evening you could confess them and they would be done with. Then you could transgress them again. But this sort of confession is impure, because you don't stop; you don't decide to change. There is no restraint, no perception of the truth, no letting go—you simply do it again and again.

Actually, in terms of ultimate truth, it's not necessary to go through the routine of confessing offenses. If we see that our mind is pure and there is no trace of doubt, then those offenses drop off right there. That we are not yet pure is because we still doubt; we still waver. We are not really pure, so we can't let go. We don't see ourselves—this is the point. This vinaya of ours is like a fence to guard us from making mistakes, so it's something we need to be scrupulous with.

If you don't see the true value of the vinaya for yourself, it's difficult. Many years before I came to Wat Pah Pong I decided I would give up money. For the greater part of a rains retreat I thought about it. In the end I grabbed my wallet and walked over to a certain Mahā who was living with me at the time, and I set the wallet down in front of him.

"Here, Mahā, take this money. From today onward, as long as I'm a monk, I will not receive or hold money. You can be my witness."

"You keep it, friend, you may need it for your studies." The venerable Mahā wasn't keen to take the money. He was embarrassed.

"Why do you want to throw away all this money?" he asked.

"You don't have to worry about me. I've made my decision. I decided last night."

From the day he took that money, it was as if a gap had opened between us. We could no longer understand each other. He's still my witness to this very day. Ever since that day I haven't used money or engaged in any buying or selling. I've been restrained in every way with money. I was constantly wary of wrongdoing, even though I hadn't done anything wrong. Inwardly

I maintained the meditation practice. I no longer needed wealth. I saw it as a poison. Whether you give poison to a human being, a dog, or any other being, it invariably causes death or suffering. If we see this clearly we will be constantly on our guard not to take that "poison." When we clearly see the harm in it, it's not difficult to give up.

Regarding food and meals brought as offerings, if I had doubts about them I wouldn't accept them. No matter how delicious or refined the food might be, I wouldn't eat it. Take a simple example, like raw pickled fish. Suppose you are living in a forest and you go on alms round and receive only rice and some pickled fish wrapped in leaves. When you return to your dwelling and open the packet, you find that it's raw pickled fish—just throw it away![29] Eating plain rice is better than transgressing the precepts. It has to be like this before you can say you really understand. Then the vinaya becomes simpler.

If other monks wanted to give me requisites, such as a bowl, razor, or whatever, I wouldn't accept them unless I knew that the donors were fellow practitioners with a similar standard of vinaya. Why not? How can you trust someone who is unrestrained? They can do all sorts of things. Unrestrained monks don't see the value of the vinaya, so it's possible that they could have obtained those things in improper ways. I was that scrupulous.

As a result, some of my fellow monks would look askance at me. "He doesn't socialize, he won't mix." But I was unmoved. "Well, we can mix with one another when we die," I thought, "for then we're all in the same boat." I lived with forbearance. I was one who spoke little. If others criticized my practice, I was unmoved. Why? Because even if I explained to them they wouldn't understand. They knew nothing about practice. Like those times when I would be invited to a funeral ceremony and somebody would say, "Don't listen to him! Just put the money in his bag and don't say anything about it. Don't let him know."[30] I would say, "Hey, do you think I'm dead or something? Just because one calls alcohol perfume doesn't make it perfume, you know. But you people, when you want to drink alcohol you call it perfume, so go ahead and drink. You must be crazy!"

The vinaya, then, can be difficult. You have to be content with little and stay aloof. You must see things, and see them correctly. Once, when I was traveling through Saraburi, my group went to stay in a village temple for a while. The abbot there had about the same seniority as myself. In the morning, we would all go on alms round together, then come back to the monastery and put down our bowls. Presently the lay people would bring dishes of food into the hall and set them down. Then the monks would go and pick them up, open them, and lay them in a line to be formally offered. One monk would place a finger on the dish at one end of the line, and a layman would place his hand on the dish at the other end. And that was it! With that the monks would bring them over and distribute them to be eaten.

About five monks were traveling with me at the time, but not one of us would touch that food. On alms round all we received was plain rice, so we sat with them and ate plain rice. None of us would dare eat the food from those dishes.

This went on for quite a few days, until I began to sense that the abbot was disturbed by our behavior. One of his monks had probably gone to him and said, "Those visiting monks won't eat any of the food. I don't know what they're up to."

I had to stay there for a few days more, so I went to the abbot to explain.

I said, "Venerable Sir, may I have a moment please? I'm afraid there may be one or two things which you and your fellow monks find puzzling: namely, our not eating the food that has been offered by the lay people. I'd like to clarify this with you, sir. It's really nothing, it's just that I've learned to practice like this—that is, concerning the receiving of the offerings, sir. When the lay people put the food down and then the monks go and open the dishes, sort them out, and then have them formally offered, this is wrong. It's a dukkaṭa offense. Specifically, if a monk handles or touches food that hasn't yet been formally offered into his hands, this ruins the food. According to the vinaya, any monk who eats that food incurs an offense.

"It's simply this one point, sir. It's not that I'm criticizing anybody, or that I'm trying to force you or your monks to stop practicing like this. Not at all. I just wanted to let you know of my good intentions, because it will be necessary for me to stay here for a few more days."

He lifted his hands in *añjali*,[31] "*Sādhu!*[32] Excellent! I've never yet seen a monk who keeps the minor rules in Saraburi. There aren't any to be found these days. If there still are such monks they must live outside of Saraburi. May I commend you. I have no objections at all, that's very good."

The next morning when we came back from alms round, not one of the monks would go near those dishes. The lay people themselves sorted them out and offered them, because they were afraid the monks wouldn't eat. From that day onward the monks and novices there seemed really on edge, so I tried to explain things to them, to put their minds at rest. I think they were afraid of us. They just went into their rooms and closed themselves in silence.

For two or three days I tried to make them feel at ease, because they were so ashamed. I really had nothing against them. I didn't say things like "There's not enough food" or ask them to bring this or that food. I had fasted before, sometimes for seven or eight days. Here I had plain rice; I knew I wouldn't die. I got my strength from the practice, from having studied and practiced accordingly.

I took the Buddha as my example. Wherever I went, whatever others did, I wouldn't involve myself. I devoted myself solely to the practice. Because I cared for myself, I cared for the practice.

Those who don't keep the vinaya or practice meditation and those who do practice can't live together; they must go separate ways. I didn't understand this myself in the past. As a teacher I taught others, but I didn't practice. This is really bad. When I looked deeply into it, my practice and my knowledge were as far apart as earth and sky.

Therefore, I say to those monks who want to establish meditation centers in the forest: don't do it. If you don't really know yet, don't bother trying to teach. You'll only make a mess of it. Some monks think that by going to live in the forest they will find peace, but they still don't understand the essentials of practice. They themselves cut the grass;[33] they do everything themselves. But that won't lead to progress. No matter how peaceful the forest may be, you can't progress if you do it all wrong.

They see the forest monks living in the forest and go to live in the forest like them, but it's not the same. The robes are not the same; eating habits are not the same; everything is different. And they don't train themselves; they don't practice. If living like that works at all, it's only as a venue for showing off or publicizing, just like a medicine show. It goes no further than that. Those who have only practiced a little and then go to teach others are not yet ripe. They don't really understand. In a short time they give up and it all falls apart.

So we must study. Look at the *Navakovāda*,[34] what does it say? Study it, memorize it, until you understand. From time to time ask your teacher about the finer points; he will explain them. Study like this until you really understand the vinaya.

CHAPTER 7

MAINTAINING
THE STANDARD

IN OUR YEARLY MEETING after the annual Dhamma examinations,[35] we reflect on the importance of carrying out the various duties of the monastery, those toward the preceptor and those toward the teachers. These duties hold us together as a single group, enabling us to live in harmony and concord. They also give us respect for one another, which in turn benefits the community.

In all communities, from the time of the Buddha to the present, no matter what form they may take, if the residents have no mutual respect, they cannot succeed. Whether the communities are secular or monastic, if they lack mutual respect they will have no solidarity. Negligence will set in and the practice will eventually degenerate.

Our community of Dhamma practitioners has lived here for about twenty-five years now. It is steadily growing, but it could deteriorate. We must understand this point. But if we are all heedful, have mutual respect, and continue to maintain the standards of practice, I feel that our harmony will be firm. Our practice as a group will support the growth of Buddhism for a long time to come.

Now in regard to study and practice, they form a pair. Buddhism has grown and flourished because study and practice have gone hand in hand. If we simply learn the scriptures in a heedless way, negligence sets in. The first year here, for example, we had seven monks for the rains retreat. At that time I thought to myself, "Whenever monks start studying for Dhamma examinations, the practice seems to degenerate." I tried to discover why. I began to teach the monks who were there for the rains retreat—all seven of them. I taught for about forty days, from after the morning meal till six in the evening, every day. The monks went for the exams, and the results were good: all seven of them passed.

That was good, but there was a certain complication regarding those who were lacking in circumspection. To study, it is necessary to do a lot of reciting and repeating. Very often, those who are unrestrained and unreserved tend to grow lax with their meditation practice and spend all their time studying, repeating, and memorizing. This leads them to abandon their old abiding, their standards of practice.

So it was that when they had finished their studies and taken their exams, I could see a change in the monks' behavior. There was no walking meditation, only a little sitting, and an increase in socializing. There was less restraint and composure.

Actually, in our practice, when you do walking meditation, you should really resolve to walk; when sitting in meditation, you should concentrate on doing just that. Whether you are standing, walking, sitting, or lying down, you should strive to be composed. But when people do a lot of study, their minds are full of words; they get high on the books and forget themselves. This is so only for those who don't have wisdom, who are unrestrained, and whose sati is unsteady. Their minds become more and more distracted. Aimless chatter and socializing become the order of the day. It's not because of the study in itself, but because they don't make the effort, they forget themselves.

Actually, the scriptures are pointers along the path of practice. If we really understand the practice, then reading or studying are both further aspects of meditation. But if we forget ourselves, studying gives rise to a lot of talking and fruitless activity. People throw out the meditation practice and soon want to disrobe. It's not that studying is bad or the practice is wrong, but that people fail to examine themselves.

Seeing this, in the second rains retreat I stopped teaching the scriptures. Many years later more and more young men came to become monks. Some of them knew nothing about the Dhamma-vinaya and were ignorant of the texts, so I decided to rectify the situation, asking those senior monks who had already studied to teach, and they have continued to do so. This is how we came to have studying here.

However, every year when the exams are finished, I ask all the monks to reestablish their practice. All those scriptures that aren't directly concerned with the practice we put away in the cupboard. We reestablish ourselves; we return to the regular standards; we renew our communal practices such as the daily chanting. This is our standard. We do it if only to resist our laziness and aversion.

This is what I tell the monks: Don't discard your basic practices: eating little, speaking little, sleeping little; restraint and composure; aloofness; regular walking and sitting meditation; meeting together regularly at the appropriate times. Please make an effort with these. Don't let this excellent opportunity go to waste. Do the practice. You have this chance to practice here because you live under the guidance of the teacher. He protects you on one level, so you should all devote yourselves to the practice. Walking meditation, sitting meditation, morning and evening chanting—these are your specific duties; please apply yourselves to them.

Those in the robes who simply kill time—who are floundering, homesick, confused—are not strong enough. They don't put their minds on the practice. We can't just lie around here. As Buddhist monks or novices, we live and eat well; we shouldn't take that for granted. *Kāmasukhallikā-nuyoga*—indulgence in sense pleasures and comfort—is a danger. We should strengthen our practice, exhort ourselves to do more, rectify whatever is faulty, and not get lost in externals.

One who has zeal never forgoes walking and sitting meditation, never lets up in the maintenance of restraint and composure. A monk who, having finished the meal, hung out his robes, and attended to any incidental business, then starts to do walking meditation—and when we pass by his kuṭī we see his walking path is well worn—this monk is not bored with the practice. He is one who has effort, who has zeal.

If all of you devote yourselves like this to the practice, then not many problems will arise. If you don't abide with the practice, the walking and sitting meditation, there's nothing more than just traveling around. Not liking it here you go traveling over there; not liking it there you come touring back here. That's all there is to it, following your noses everywhere. You don't have to do a lot of traveling around; just stay here and develop the practice, learn it in detail. Make an effort, all of you.

Progress and decline hinge on this. If you really want to do things properly, then balance your study and practice. When the mind is at ease and the body is healthy, you become composed. When the mind is confused, even if the body is strong, then you experience difficulty.

The study of meditation is the study of cultivation and relinquishment. What I mean by study here is this: Whenever the mind experiences a sensation, do we still cling to it? Do we still create problems around it? Do we still experience enjoyment or aversion over it? To put it simply: Do we still get lost in our thoughts? Most often we do. If we don't like something we react with aversion; if we do like it we react with pleasure; the mind becomes defiled and stained. If that's what we do, then we must recognize that we still have faults, we are still imperfect, and we still have work to do: more relinquishing and persistent cultivation. This is what I mean by studying. If we get stuck on anything, we recognize that we are stuck. We know what state we're in, and we work to correct ourselves.

Living with the teacher or apart from the teacher should be the same. Some people are afraid. They're afraid that if they don't do walking meditation the teacher will upbraid or scold them. This is good in a way, but in the true practice you don't need to be afraid of others; rather, you are wary of faults arising within your own actions, speech, or thoughts. You guard yourself from such faults. *Attano jodayattanaṁ*—"you must exhort yourself." We must quickly improve ourselves, know ourselves. This is what I call studying. Look into this till you see it clearly.

Living in this way we rely on endurance, persevering in the face of all the defilements. Although this is good, it is still on the level of "practicing the Dhamma without having seen it." If we have practiced the Dhamma and seen it, then whatever is wrong we will have already given up; whatever is useful we will have cultivated. Seeing this within ourselves, we experience a sense of well-being. No matter what others say, we know our own mind; we are not moved. We can be at peace anywhere. Now the younger monks and novices who have just begun to practice may think that the senior Ajahn doesn't seem to do much walking or sitting meditation. Don't imitate him in this. You should emulate, but not imitate. To emulate is one thing; to imitate another. The fact is that the senior Ajahn dwells within his own particular contented abiding. Even though he doesn't seem to practice externally, he practices inwardly. Whatever is in his mind cannot be seen by the eye. The practice of Buddhism is the practice of the mind. Even though the practice may not be apparent in his actions or speech, the mind is a different matter.

Thus, a teacher who has practiced for a long time, who is proficient in the practice, may seem to let go of his actions and speech, but he guards his mind. He is composed. Seeing only his outer actions, you may try to imitate him, saying whatever you want; but it's not the same thing. You're not in the same league. You're coming from different places. Although the Ajahn seems to simply sit around, he is not being careless. He lives with things but is not confused by them. We can't see this, so don't judge simply by external appearances. When we speak or act, our state of mind will match that speech or action. But one who has practiced already may do or say things one way yet their state of mind is quite different, because it adheres to Dhamma and the vinaya. For example, sometimes the Ajahn may be severe with his disciples: his speech may appear to be rough and careless, his actions coarse. But all we can see are his bodily and verbal actions; his the mind, which adheres to Dhamma and the vinaya, can't be seen. Stick to the Buddha's instruction, "Heedfulness is the way to the deathless: heedlessness is death" (Dhp, 21). Consider this. Whatever others do is not important, just don't be heedless.

Consider the teaching that says, "A bhikkhu is one who seeks alms." If we define a monk this way, our practice takes on a very coarse form. But if we understand *bhikkhu* the way the Buddha defined it, as "one who sees the danger of saṁsāra," this is much more profound.

One who sees the danger of saṁsāra is one who sees the faults, the liability of this world. In this world there is so much danger, but most people don't see it; they see only the pleasures and happiness. What is saṁsāra? The suffering of saṁsāra is overwhelming; it's intolerable. Happiness is also saṁsāra. If we don't see the danger of saṁsāra, then when there is happiness we cling to the happiness and forget suffering. We are ignorant of it, like a child who doesn't know fire.

If we understand Dhamma practice in this way: "A bhikkhu is one who sees the danger of saṁsāra"—if we have this understanding, this teaching, firmly imbued in our being, whether standing, walking, sitting, or lying down, wherever we may be—we will feel dispassion. We reflect on ourselves; heedfulness is there. Even sitting at ease, we feel this way. Whatever we do we see this danger, so we are in a very different state. This practice is called being "one who sees the danger of saṁsāra."

One who sees the danger of saṁsāra lives within saṁsāra and yet doesn't. That is, they understand concepts and they understand their transcendence. Whatever such a person says is not like what ordinary people say. Whatever they do is not the same; whatever they think is not the same. Their behavior is much wiser.

Therefore it is said: "Emulate but don't imitate." One who is foolish will grab on to everything. You mustn't do that! Don't forget yourselves.

As for me, since my body is not so well, I will leave a few things to the other monks and novices to take care of. Perhaps I will take a rest. From time immemorial it's been this way: as long as the father and mother are still alive, the children are well and prosperous. When the parents die, the children separate. Having been rich, they become poor. This is usually how it is in lay life, and one can see it here as well. For example, while the Ajahn is still alive everybody is well and prosperous. As soon as he passes away decline begins to set in immediately. Why is this? Because while the teacher is still alive people become complacent and forget themselves. They don't really make an effort with the study and the practice. As in lay life, while the mother and father are still alive, the children just leave everything up to them. They lean on their parents and don't know how to look after themselves. When the parents die they become paupers. In the monkhood it's the same. If the Ajahn goes away or dies, almost always the monks tend to socialize, break up into groups, and drift into decline. Living off the merits of the teacher everything runs smoothly. When the teacher passes away, the disciples tend to split up. Their views clash. Those who think wrongly live in one place; those who think rightly live in another. Those who feel uncomfortable leave their old associates and set up new places and start new lineages with their own groups of disciples. This is how it goes. We are at fault. While the teacher is still alive, we live heedlessly; we don't take up the standards of practice taught by the Ajahn and establish them within our own hearts.

Even in the Buddha's time it was the same. Remember that old monk in the scriptures, Subhadda Bhikkhu? When Venerable Mahā Kassapa was returning from Pava he asked an ascetic on the way, "Is the Lord Buddha faring well?" The ascetic answered: "The Lord Buddha entered *Parinibbāna* seven days ago."

Those monks who were still unenlightened were grief-stricken, crying and wailing. Those who had attained the Dhamma reflected to themselves, "Ah, the Buddha has passed away. He has journeyed on." But those who were still thick with defilements, such as Venerable Subhadda, said:

"What are you all crying for? The Buddha has passed away. That's good! Now we can live at ease. When the Buddha was still alive, he was always bothering us with some rule or other; we couldn't do this or say that. Now the Buddha has passed away, that's fine! We can do whatever we want, say what we want. Why should you cry?"

It's been so from way back then till the present day.

However that may be, even though it's impossible to preserve it entirely, suppose we had a glass and we took care to preserve it. Each time we used it we cleaned it and put it away in a safe place. Being very careful with that glass, we can use it for a long time, and then when we've finished with it others can also use it. Now, using glasses carelessly and breaking them every day, and using one glass for ten years before it breaks—which is better?

Our practice is like this. For instance, if out of all of us living here, practicing steadily, only ten of you practice well, then Wat Pah Pong will prosper. Just as in the villages: in a village of one hundred houses, even if there are only fifty good people that village will prosper. Actually, to find even ten would be difficult. Or take a monastery like this one here: it is hard to find even five or six monks who have real commitment, who really do the practice.

In any case, our only responsibility now is to practice well. Think about it; what do we own here? We don't have wealth, possessions, and families anymore. Even food we take only once a day. As monks and novices we give up everything. We own nothing. All those things people really enjoy have been discarded. We go forth as a Buddhist monk in order to practice. Why then should we hanker for other things, indulging in greed, aversion, or delusion?

If we don't practice, we are actually worse off than lay people, for we have no function. If we don't perform any function or accept our responsibilities, it's a waste of the samana's life. It contradicts the aims of a samana.

Being heedless is like being dead. Ask yourself, "Will I have time to practice when I die?" Constantly ask, "When will I die?" If we contemplate in this way, our mind will be alert every second. When there is no heedlessness, sati will automatically follow. Wisdom will be clear, seeing all things as they truly are. Mindfulness will guard the mind, knowing the arising of sensations at all times, day and night. That is to have sati. To have sati is to be composed. To be composed is to be heedful. If one is heedful then one is practicing rightly. This is our responsibility.

CHAPTER 8

WHY ARE WE HERE?

THIS RAINS RETREAT, I don't have much strength, I'm not well, so I've come up to this mountain to get some fresh air. People come to visit, but I can't really receive them like I used to because my voice has just about had it; my breath is just about gone. You can count it a blessing that there's still this body sitting here for you all to see now. Soon you won't see it. The breath will be finished; the voice will be gone. They will fare in accordance with supporting factors, like all compounded things. The Lord Buddha called it *khaya vayaṁ*, the decline and dissolution of all conditioned phenomena.

How do they decline? Consider a lump of ice. Originally it was simply water. You freeze it and it becomes ice. But it doesn't take long before it's melted. Take a big block of ice, and leave it out in the sun. You can see how it dissolves much the same as the body. It will gradually disintegrate. In not many hours or minutes all that's left is a puddle of water. This is called khaya vayaṁ, the decline and dissolution of all compounded things. It's been this way for a long time now, ever since the beginning of time. When we are born we bring this inherent nature into the world with us; we can't avoid it. At birth we bring old age, sickness, and death along with us.

So this is why the Buddha said khaya vayaṁ, the decline and dissolution of all compounded things. All of us sitting here in this hall now, monks, novices, laymen, and laywomen, are without exception lumps of deterioration. Right now the lump is hard, just like the block of ice. It starts out as water, becomes ice for a while, and then melts again. Can you see this decline in yourself? Look at this body. It's aging every day—hair is aging, nails are aging, everything is aging.

You weren't always like this, were you? You were once much smaller than you are now. Now you've grown up and matured. From now on you will decline, following the way of nature. The body declines, just like the block of ice. Soon it'll be gone. All bodies are composed of the four elements of earth, water, wind, and fire—the confluence of which we proceed to call a person. Originally it's hard to say what you could call it, but now we call it a person. We get infatuated with it, saying it's a male, a female, giving it names, Mr., Mrs., and so on, so that we can identify each other more easily. But actually there isn't anybody there. There's earth, water, wind, and fire. When they come together in this form we call the result a person. But don't get excited over it. If you really look into it, there isn't anyone there.

That which is solid in the body, the flesh, skin, bones, and so on, are called the earth element. Those aspects of the body that are liquid are the water element. The faculty of warmth in the body is the fire element, while the winds coursing through the body are the wind element.

At Wat Pah Pong we have a body which seems neither male nor female. It's a skeleton, the one hanging in the main hall. Looking at it, you don't get the feeling that it's a man or a woman. People ask each other whether it's a man or a woman, and all they can do is look blankly at each other. It's only a skeleton; all the skin and flesh are gone.

People are ignorant of these things. Some go to Wat Pah Pong, into the main hall, see the skeleton, and then come running right out again! They can't bear to look. They're afraid of skeletons. I figure these people have never seen themselves before. They ought to reflect on the great value of a skeleton. To get to the monastery they had to ride in a car or walk. If they didn't have bones, how would they get around? Would they be able to walk? But they ride their cars to Wat Pah Pong, walk into the main hall, see the skeleton, and run straight out again! They've never seen such a thing before. They're born with one and yet they've never seen it. It's very fortunate that they have a chance to see it now. Even older people see the skeleton and get scared. What's all the fuss about? This shows that they're not at all in touch with themselves; they don't really know themselves. Maybe they go home and can't sleep for three or four days…and yet they're sleep-

ing with a skeleton! They get dressed with it, eat food with it, do everything
with it, and yet they're scared of it.

How pitiful that people are so out of touch with themselves! They're
always looking outward, at trees, at other people, at external objects, saying,
"This one is big," "that's small," "that's short," "that's long." They're so
busy looking at other things they never see themselves. Honestly, people are
really pitiful. They have no refuge.

In the ordination ceremonies the ordinees must learn the five basic meditation themes: *kesā*, head hair; *lomā*, body hair; *nakhā*, nails; *dantā*, teeth;
taco, skin. Some of the students and educated people snigger to themselves
when they hear this part of the ordination ceremony. "What's the Ajahn trying to teach us here? Teaching us about hair when we've had it for ages. He
doesn't have to teach us about this; we know it already. Why bother teaching us something we already know?" Dim people are like this; they think
they can see the hair already. I tell them that when I say to "see the hair," I
mean to see it as it really is. See body hair as it really is; see nails, teeth, and
skin as they really are. That's what I call "seeing"—not seeing in a superficial way, but seeing in accordance with the truth. We wouldn't be so sunk
up to the ears in things if we could see them as they really are. Hair, nails,
teeth, skin—what are they really like? Are they pretty? Are they clean? Do
they have any real substance? Are they stable? No, there's nothing to them.
They're not pretty, not substantial, but we imagine them to be so.

Hair, nails, teeth, skin—people are really hooked on these things. The
Buddha established these parts of the body as basic themes for meditation;
he taught us to know them. They are transient, imperfect and ownerless;
they are not "me" or "mine." We are born with and are deluded by them,
but really they are foul. Suppose we didn't bathe for a week; could we bear
to be close to each other? We'd really smell bad. When people sweat a lot,
such as when a lot of people are working hard together, the smell is awful.
We go back home and scrub ourselves with soap and water and the smell
abates somewhat. The fragrance of the soap replaces it. Rubbing soap on the
body may make it seem fragrant, but actually the bad smell of the body is
still there, temporarily suppressed. When the smell of the soap is gone, the
smell of the body comes back.

Now we tend to think these bodies are pretty, delightful, long lasting,
and strong. We tend to think that we will never age, sicken, or die. We are

charmed and fooled, and so we are ignorant of the true refuge within ourselves. The true place of refuge is the *mind*. The hall here, where we're sitting, may be pretty big, but it can't be a real refuge. Pigeons take shelter here, and so do geckos and lizards. We may think the hall belongs to us, but it doesn't. We live here together with everything else. This is only a temporary shelter, and sooner or later we must leave it. People mistake these shelters for a true refuge.

So the Buddha said to find your refuge. That means find your real heart. This heart is very important. People don't usually look at important things; they spend most of their time with unimportant things. For example, when they do their housecleaning they may be bent on sweeping the floors, washing the dishes, and so on, but they fail to notice their own hearts. Their heart may be rotten, they may be feeling angry, and they're washing the dishes wearing a sour expression. That their hearts are not very clean they fail to see. This is what I call "taking a temporary shelter for a refuge." They beautify house and home, but they don't think of beautifying their own hearts. They don't examine suffering. The Buddha taught us to find a refuge within our own hearts: *Attāhi attano nātho*—make yourself a refuge unto yourself. Who else can be your refuge? The true refuge is the heart, nothing else. You may try to depend on other things, but they aren't dependable. You can only really depend on other things if you already have a refuge within yourself.

So all of you, both lay people and monastics, who have come to visit today, please consider this teaching. Ask yourselves, "Who am I? Why am I here? Why was I born?" Some people don't know. They want to be happy, but the suffering never stops. Rich or poor, young or old, they suffer just the same. It's all suffering. And why? Because they have no wisdom. The poor are unhappy because they don't have enough, and the rich are unhappy because they have too much.

As a young novice, I once gave a Dhamma discourse about the happiness of wealth and possessions, having servants, and so on—a hundred male servants, a hundred female servants, a hundred elephants, a hundred cows, a hundred buffaloes, a hundred of everything! The lay people really lapped it up. But can you imagine looking after a hundred buffaloes? Or a hundred cows, a hundred male and female servants? Can you imagine having to look after all of that? People don't consider this side of things. They have the desire to have the cows, the buffaloes, the servants…hundreds of them. But I say fifty buffaloes would be too much. Just twining the rope for all those brutes would be too much! But people don't consider this; they only think of the pleasure of acquiring. They don't consider the trouble involved.

If we don't have wisdom, everything round us will be a source of suffering. If we are wise, these things will lead us out of suffering. Eyes, ears, nose, tongue, body, and mind…. Eyes aren't necessarily good things, you know. If you are in a bad mood, just seeing other people can make you angry and make you lose sleep. Or you can fall in love. Love is suffering, too, if you don't get what you want. Love and hate are both suffering, because of desire. Wanting is suffering; wanting not to have is suffering. Wanting to acquire things—even if you get them it's still suffering, because you're afraid you'll lose them. There's only suffering. How are you going to live with that? You may have a large, luxurious house, but if your heart isn't good it never really works out as you expected.

You should take a look at yourself. Why were we born? Do we ever really attain anything in this life? In the countryside people start planting rice right from childhood. When they reach seventeen or eighteen they rush off and get married, afraid they won't have enough time to make their fortunes. They start working from an early age, thinking they'll get rich. They plant rice until they're seventy, eighty, or even ninety. I ask them, "You've been working since you were born. Now it's almost time to go; what are you going to take with you?" They don't know what to say except "Beats me!" We have a saying in these parts, "Don't tarry picking berries along the way. Before you know it, night falls." They're neither here nor there, content with just a "beats me," sitting in the berry bush gorging themselves. "Beats me, beats me…."

When you're still young you think that being single is not so good. You feel a bit lonely. So you find a partner to live with. Put two together and there's friction! Living alone is too quiet, but living with others there's friction.

When children are small the parents think, "When they get bigger we'll be better off." They raise their children, three, four, or five of them, thinking that when the children are grown up their burden will be lighter. But when the children grow up the burden gets even heavier. Like two pieces of wood, one big and one small. You throw away the small one and take the bigger one, thinking it will be lighter, but of course it's not. When children are small they don't bother you very much, just a ball of rice and a banana now and then. When they grow up they want a motorcycle or a car! Well, you love your children; you can't refuse them. So you try to give them what they want. Problems. Sometimes the parents get into arguments over it. "Don't go and buy him a car, we haven't got enough money!" But when you love your children, you go and borrow the money somewhere. Maybe the parents even have to do without to get the things their children want. Then there's education. "When they've finished their studies, we'll be all right." But there's no end to the studying! When are they going to finish? Only in the science of Buddhism is there a point of completion; all the other sciences just go round in circles. In the end it's a real headache. If there's a house with four or five children in it, the parents argue every day.

The suffering that is waiting in the future we fail to see; we think it will never happen. When it happens, we see it. That kind of suffering, the suffering inherent in our bodies, is hard to foresee. When I was a child minding the buffaloes, I'd take charcoal and rub it on my teeth to whiten them. I'd go back home and look in the mirror and see them so nice and white. I was getting fooled by my own bones, that's all. When I reached fifty or sixty my teeth started to get loose. When the teeth start falling out it hurts so much, it feels as if you've been kicked in the mouth. It really hurts when you eat. So I just got the dentist to take them all out. Now I've got false teeth. My real teeth were giving me so much trouble I just had them all taken out, sixteen in one go. The dentist was reluctant to take out sixteen teeth at once, but I said to him, "Just take them out, I'll take the consequences." So he took them all out at once. Some were still good, too, at least five of them. Took them all out. But it was really touch and go. After having them out I couldn't eat for two or three days.

As a young child minding the buffaloes, I thought that polishing my teeth was a great thing to do. I loved my teeth; I thought they were good. But in the end they had to go. The pain almost killed me. I suffered from toothaches for months, years. Sometimes both my gums were swollen at once.

Some of you may get a chance to experience this for yourselves someday. If your teeth are still good and you're brushing them every day to keep them nice and white, watch out! They may start playing tricks with you later on.

Now I'm just letting you know about these things, about the suffering that arises from within our bodies. There's nothing within the body you can depend on. It's not too bad when you're still young, but as you get older things begin to break down. Everything begins to fall apart. Conditions go their natural business. Whether we laugh or cry, whether we're in pain or difficulty, whether we live or die, it makes no difference to them. And there's no knowledge or science that can alter this natural course of things. You may get a dentist to look at your teeth, but even if he can fix them, they'll eventually go their natural way. Eventually even the dentist has the same trouble. Everything falls apart in the end.

These are things that we should contemplate while we still have some vigor; we should practice while we're young. If you want to make merit, hurry up and do so. Don't leave it to the old folks. Most people wait until they get old before they go to a monastery and try to practice Dhamma. Women and men say the same thing. "I'm waiting till I get old first." I don't know why they say that. How much vigor does an old person have? Let them try racing with a young person and see what the difference is. They leave it till they get old as if they're never going to die. When they reach fifty or sixty, it's "Hey, Grandma! Let's go to the monastery!" "You go ahead, dear, my ears aren't so good anymore." You see what I mean? When her ears were good, what was she listening to? "Beats me!" Just dallying with the berries. Finally, when her ears are gone, she goes to the temple. It's hopeless. She listens to the sermon but hasn't a clue what they're saying. People wait till they're all used up before they'll think of practicing the Dhamma.

These are things that you should begin to observe. They are our inheritance. They will gradually get heavier and heavier, a burden for each of us. In the past my legs were strong; I could run. Now just walking around they feel heavy. Before, my legs carried me. Now, I have to carry them. When I was a child I'd see old people getting up from their seat on the floor with a groan. Even when it gets to this stage they still don't learn. Sitting down they moan, "Oh-h!" Getting up they groan, "Oh-h!" There's always this "Oh-h." But they don't know what it is that makes them groan like that. Even then, people don't see the bane of the body. You never know when you're going to be parted from it. What's causing all the pain is simply conditions going about their natural way. People call it arthritis, rheumatism, gout, and so on; the doctor prescribes medicines, but it never completely heals. In the end it all falls apart, even the doctor! This is conditions faring along their natural course. This is their way, their nature.

Now take a look at this. If you see it early, you'll be better off, like seeing a poisonous snake on the path ahead of you. If you see it, you can step aside and not get bitten. If you don't see it, you may step on it.

If suffering arises people don't know what to do. Where to go to treat it? They want to avoid suffering, be free of it, but they don't know how to treat it when it arises. And they live on like this until they get old and sick...and die.

In olden times it was said that if someone was mortally ill, one of the next of kin should whisper *Bud-dho Bud-dho* in their ear. What are they going to do with Buddho? What good is Buddho going to be for them when they're almost on the funeral pyre? Why didn't they learn Buddho when they were young and healthy? Now with the breaths coming fitfully, you go up and say, "Mother! Bud-dho, Bud-dho!" Why waste your time? You'll only confuse her. Let her go peacefully.

When people are newly married they get on together all right, but after age fifty or so they can't understand each other. Whatever the wife says the husband finds intolerable. Whatever the husband says the wife won't listen. They turn their backs on each other.

Now I'm just talking because I've never had a family. Why haven't I had a family? Just looking at this word *household*,[36] I knew what it was all about. What is a "household"? This is a "hold": If somebody were to get some rope and tie us up while we were sitting here, what would that be like? That's called "being held." There is a circle of confinement. The man lives within his circle of confinement, and the woman lives within her circle of confinement.

This word *household* is a heavy one. No trifling matter, it's a real killer. The word *hold* is a symbol of suffering. You can't go anywhere; you've got to stay within your circle of confinement.

Now we come to the word *house.* This means "that which hassles." Have you ever toasted chilies? The whole house chokes and sneezes. This word *household* spells confusion; it's not worth the trouble. Because of this word I was able to be ordained and not disrobe. The household is frightening. You're stuck and can't go anywhere. Problems with the children, with money, and all the rest. Arguments in profusion until your dying day. But where can you go? You're tied down, with nowhere to go, no matter how much suffering it is. The tears pour out and they keep on pouring. If there's no household, you might be able to finish with the tears, but not otherwise.

Consider all this. If you haven't realized it yet, you may later on. Some people have learned it already to some extent. Others have reached the end of their tether. "Will I stay or will I go?" At Wat Pah Pong there are about seventy or eighty huts. When they're almost full I tell the monk in charge to keep a few empty, just in case somebody has an argument with their spouse. And sure enough, in no long time a lady will arrive with her bags. "I'm fed up with the world, Luang Por." "Whoa! Don't say that. Those are heavy words." Then the husband comes and says he's fed up too. After two or three days in the monastery their world-weariness disappears.

They say they're fed up but they're just fooling themselves. When they go off to a kuṭi and sit quietly by themselves, after a while the thoughts start coming: "When's the wife going to come and ask me to come home?" They don't really know what's going on. What is this world-weariness of theirs? They get upset over something and come running to the monastery. At home everything looked wrong: the husband was wrong, the wife was wrong. But after three days' quiet thinking, "Hmm, the wife was right after all, it was I who was wrong." "Hubby was right, I shouldn't have got so upset." They change sides. This is how it is; that's why I don't take the world too seriously. I know its ins and outs already; that's why I've chosen to live as a monk.

Here's your homework. Whether you're in the fields or working in the city, take these words of mine and reflect on them. Ask yourself, "Why was I born? What can I take with me?" Ask yourselves over and over. If you do, you'll become wise. If you don't, you'll remain ignorant. If you don't understand it all right now, maybe you will later. "Oh, that's what Luang Por meant. I couldn't see it before."

I think that's enough for today. If I talk too long this old body gets tired.

CHAPTER 9

THE FLOOD OF SENSUALITY

Kāmogha…the flood of sensuality: sunk in sights, in sounds, in smells, in tastes, in bodily sensations. Sunk because we only look at externals, we don't look inwardly. People don't see themselves, they only look at others. Everybody else they can see, but not themselves. It's not such a difficult thing to do. It's just that people don't really try.

For example, look at a beautiful woman. What does that do to you? Just look within your mind. What is it like to see a woman? As soon as you see the face, you see everything else. Do you see that? The eyes see just a little bit, and then the mind sees all the rest. Why is it so fast?

It's because you have sunk in the flood. You are stuck in your thinking and fantasizing. It's just like being a slave: somebody else has control over you. When they tell you to sit, you've got to sit; when they tell you to walk, you've got to walk. You can't disobey them because you're their slave. Being enslaved by the senses is the same. No matter how hard you try, you can't seem to shake it off. And if you expect others to do it for you, you really get into trouble. You must shake it off for yourself.

Therefore the Buddha left the practice of Dhamma, the transcendence of suffering, up to us. Take nibbāna, for example. The Buddha was thoroughly enlightened, so why didn't he describe nibbāna in detail? Why did he tell us to practice and find out for ourselves? Some people really worry about this. "If the Buddha really knew," they say, "he would have told us. Why should he keep anything hidden?"

This sort of thinking is wrong. We can't see the truth in that way. We must practice, we must cultivate, in order to see. The Buddha only pointed out the way to develop wisdom, that's all. He said that we ourselves must practice. Whoever practices will reach the goal.

But that Path which the Buddha taught goes against our habits. Frugality, restraint—we don't really like that. So we say, "Show us the way, show us the way to nibbāna, so that those of us who like it easy can go there too." It's the same with wisdom. The Buddha can't show you wisdom; it's not something that can be simply handed around. The Buddha can show the way to develop wisdom, but how much of it you develop depends on the individual. Since the merit and accumulated virtues of people naturally differ, the realization of Dhamma is sometimes slow, sometimes fast. The Buddha and his disciples all had to practice for themselves, but even so, they relied on teachers to advise them and give them techniques in the practice.

Now, when we listen to Dhamma we may want to listen until all our doubts are cleared up, but they'll never be cleared up simply by listening. Doubt is not overcome simply by listening or thinking. Listening to the Dhamma alone does not lead to realization. Yet it is beneficial. In the Buddha's time there were those who realized the Dhamma—and reached the highest attainment, arahantship—while listening to a discourse. But those people were already highly developed; they already understood a lot. It's like a football. When a football is pumped up, it expands. Now the air in that football is all pushing to get out, but there's no hole for it to do so. As soon as a needle punctures the football the air comes bursting out.

The mind of those disciples who were enlightened while listening to the Dhamma was like the football. It had this "pressure" within. It was not yet free because of this very small thing concealing the truth. As soon as they heard the Dhamma and it hit the right spot, wisdom arose. They immediately understood, immediately let go and realized the true Dhamma. That's how it was. It was easy. The mind turned itself upright. It changed, or turned, from one view to another. You could say it was far, or you could say it was very near.

This is something we must do for ourselves. The Buddha was only able to give techniques about how to develop wisdom. So why is it that after hearing teachers talk about Dhamma we still can't make that truth our own? Because there's a film obscuring it. You could say that we are sunk. Sunk in kāmogha—the flood of sensuality. Sunk in *bhavogha*—the flood of becoming.

Becoming (bhava) means "the sphere of birth." Sensual desire is born at sights, sounds, tastes, smells, feelings, and thoughts. Identifying with these things, the mind holds fast and is stuck to sensuality.

Some practitioners get bored, fed up, tired of the practice, and lazy. They can't seem to keep the Dhamma in mind. Yet if they get scolded, they'll hold on to the reprimand for ages. They may get scolded at the beginning of the rains retreat, and even after the retreat has ended they haven't forgotten it. As long as they live they won't forget, if it goes deep enough. But when it comes to the Buddha's teaching, telling us to be moderate, to be restrained, to practice conscientiously, why don't people take these things into their hearts? Why do they keep forgetting? Just look at our practice here. For example, establishing standards such as, after the meal while washing your alms bowls, don't chatter! Even this much seems to be beyond people. Even though we know that chattering is not particularly useful and binds us to sensuality, people still like talking. Pretty soon they start to disagree and eventually get into arguments and squabbles.

Now this isn't anything subtle or refined; it's pretty basic. Yet people don't really seem to make much effort with it. They say they want to see the Dhamma, but they want to see it on their own terms; they don't want to follow the path of practice. That's as far as they go. All these standards of practice are skillful means for penetrating to and seeing the Dhamma, but people don't practice accordingly.

"Real practice" or "ardent practice" doesn't necessarily mean you have to expend a whole lot of energy—just put some effort into the mind, making some effort with all the feelings that arise, especially those that are steeped in sensuality. These are our enemies.

But people can't seem to do it. Every year, as the end of the rains retreat approaches, it gets worse and worse. Some of the monks have reached the end of their tether. The closer we get to the end of the rains, the worse they get. They have no consistency in their practice. I speak about this every year, and yet people can't seem to remember it. We establish a certain standard and in not even a year it's fallen apart. The chatter and the socializing start. It all goes to pieces. This is how it tends to be.

Those who are really interested in the practice should consider why this is so. It's because people don't see the adverse results of these things.

When we are accepted into the Buddhist monkhood, we live simply. And yet some monks disrobe to go to the battle front, where the bullets fly every day—they prefer it like that. They really want to go. Danger surrounds them on all sides, and yet they're prepared to go. Why don't they see the danger? They're prepared to die by the gun, but nobody wants to die developing virtue. See this much and you know what it's all about. It's because they're slaves. They don't see the danger.

It's really amazing, isn't it? You'd think they could see it, but they can't. If they can't see it even then, there's no way they can get out. They're determined to whirl around in saṁsāra. This is how things are. Just by talking about simple things like this we can begin to understand.

If you were to ask them, "Why were you born?" they'd probably have a lot of trouble answering, because they can't see it. They're sunk in the world of the senses and sunk in becoming (bhava). Bhava is the sphere of birth, our birthplace. To put it simply, where are beings born from? Bhava is the preliminary condition for birth. Wherever birth takes place, that's bhava.

For example, suppose we have an orchard of apple trees that we're particularly fond of. That's a bhava for us if we don't reflect with wisdom. How so? Suppose our orchard contains a hundred or a thousand apple trees. So long as we consider them to be *our* trees, we are going to be "born" into every single one of them—born as a worm, in a sense, for the becoming mind has wormed its way into every one; or, even though our human body is still back there in the house, it's as if we have sent out "tentacles" into every one of those trees.

Now, how do we know that it's bhava? It's bhava (a sphere of birth) because of our clinging to the idea that those trees are our own. If someone were to take an axe and cut one of them down, we, over here in our house, would "die" along with the tree. We'd get furious and have to set things right. Maybe we'd fight over it. That quarreling is "birth." The "sphere of birth" is the orchard that we cling to as our own. We are "born" right at the point where we consider it to be our own.

Whatever we cling to, we are born right there; we exist right there. We are born as soon as we "know." This is knowing through not-knowing: we know that someone has cut down one of our trees, but we don't know that those trees are not really ours. This is called "knowing through not-knowing." We are bound to be born into that bhava.

Vaṭṭa, the wheel of conditioned existence, turns like this. People cling to bhava; they depend on bhava. If they cherish bhava, this is a birth. And if they fall into suffering over that same thing, this is also a birth. As long as we can't let go we are stuck in the rut of saṁsāra, spinning around like a wheel. Look into this, contemplate it. Whatever we cling to as being us or ours, that is a place for birth.

There must be a bhava, a sphere of birth, before birth can take place. Therefore the Buddha said, "Whatever you have, don't *have* it." Let it be there but don't make it yours. You must understand this having and not-having; know the truth of them. Don't flounder in suffering.

The place that you were born from: do you want to go back there and be born again? Look into this. The nearer monks or meditators get to the end of a retreat, the more they start preparing to go back and be born there.

Really, you'd think that people could appreciate what it would be like, living in a person's belly. How uncomfortable that must be! Just consider, merely staying in your kuṭi for one day is enough. Shut all the doors and windows, and you're suffocating already. So what would it be like to lie in a person's belly for nine or ten months? People don't see the liability of things. Ask them why they are living, or why they are born, and they have no idea. Do you still want to get back in there? What are you stuck on? What are you holding on to?

It's because there is a cause for becoming and birth. In the main hall of this monastery we have a preserved baby, a stillborn child, in a jar. Is anybody alarmed by it? No one. But a baby lying in its mother's belly is just like that preserved fetus. And yet you want to make more of those things, and even want to get back in there yourself and soak. Why don't you see the danger of that, and the benefit of the practice?

That's bhava. The root is right there; everything revolves around that. The Buddha taught us to contemplate this point. People think about it but still don't see. They're all getting ready to go back there again. They know that it wouldn't be very comfortable in there, and yet they want to stick their heads right in, to put their necks in the noose once again. Even though they may know that this noose is really uncomfortable, they still want to lay their heads in there. Why don't they understand this?

When I talk like this people say, "If that's the case then everybody would have to become monastics, and then how would the world function?" You'll never get everybody to become monastics, so don't worry. The world is here because of deluded beings, so this is no trifling matter.

I first became a novice at the age of nine. I started practicing way back then. But in those days I didn't really know what it was all about. I found out when I became a monk. Once I became a monk I became so wary. The sensual pleasures people indulged in didn't seem like so much fun to me. I saw the suffering in them. It was like seeing a delicious banana that I knew was very sweet but which I also knew to be poisoned. No matter how sweet or tempting it was, I knew that if I ate it I would die. I always reflected thus. Every time I wanted to "eat a banana," I would see the "poison" inside, and so eventually I could withdraw my interest from those things. Now, at this age, such things are not at all tempting.

Some people don't see the poison; some see it but still want to try their luck. But as they say, "If you've wounded your hand, don't touch poison."

I, too, used to consider experimenting. When I had lived as a monk for five or six years, I thought of the Buddha. He practiced for five or six years and then was finished with the worldly life, but I was still interested in it and thought of getting back in: "Maybe I should go and 'build the world' for a while. I would gain some experience and learning. Even the Buddha had his son, Rahula. Maybe I'm being too strict?"

I sat and considered this for some time, but then I realized: "Yes, well, that's all very fine, but I'm just afraid that *this* 'buddha' won't be like the last one," a voice in me said, "I'm afraid this 'buddha' will just sink into the mud, not like the last one." And so I resisted those worldly thoughts.

From my sixth or seventh rains retreat up until the twentieth, I really had to put up a fight. These days I seem to have run out of bullets; I've been shooting for a long time. Young monks and novices have still got so much ammunition, they may just want to go and try out their guns. But before they do, they should consider it carefully.

Speaking of sensual desire, it's hard to give up. It's really difficult to see it as it is. We must use skillful means. Think of sensual pleasures as like eating meat that gets stuck between your teeth. Before you finish the meal you have to find a toothpick to pry it out. When the meat comes out, you feel some relief for a while. Maybe you decide not to eat any more meat. But when you see meat again, you can't resist it. You eat some more and then it gets stuck again. Then you have to pick it out again, which gives some relief once more, until you eat meat again. That's all there is to it. There's nothing more to sensual desire than that. The pressure builds up and up until you let a little bit out. That's all there is to it. I don't know what all the fuss is about.

I didn't learn these things from anybody else; they occurred to me in the course of my practice. I would sit in meditation and reflect on sensual pleasure as being like a red ants' nest. A villager takes a piece of wood and pokes the nest until the ants come running out, crawling down the wood and into his face, biting his eyes and ears.[37] And yet he still doesn't see the difficulty he is in.

However it's not beyond our ability. In the teachings of the Buddha it is said that if we've seen the harm of something, no matter how good it may seem to be, we know that it's harmful. Whatever we haven't yet seen the harm of, we just think it's good. If we haven't yet seen the harm of something we can't get out of it.

Have you noticed? No matter how dirty some "work" is, people may like it. This work isn't clean, but you don't have to pay people to do it—they'll gladly volunteer. With other kinds of dirty work, people won't do it even if you pay a good wage. But *this* dirty work they'll submit to gladly; you don't have to pay them. It's not that it's clean work either. So why do people like it? How can you say that people are intelligent when they behave like this?

Look at the dogs on the monastery grounds—there are packs of them. They run around biting each other, some of them even getting maimed. In another month or so they'll be at it. As soon as one of the smaller ones gets into the pack, the bigger ones are after him. Out he comes yelping, dragging a bitten leg behind him. But when the pack runs on, he hobbles on after it. He's only a little one, but he thinks he'll get his chance one day. They bite his leg, and that's all he gets for his trouble. For the whole of the mating season he may not even get a single chance. You can see this for yourself in the monastery here.

These dogs when they run around howling in packs—I figure if they were humans, they'd be singing songs! They think they're having such great fun, they're singing songs, but they don't have a clue what it is that makes them do it—they just blindly follow their instincts.

Think about this carefully. If you really want to practice you should understand your feelings. For example, among the monks, novices, or lay people, who should you socialize with? If you associate with people who talk a lot, they'll lead you to talk a lot too. Your own share is already enough; theirs is even more. Put them together and they explode!

People like to socialize with those who chatter a lot and talk of frivolous things. They can sit and listen to that for hours. But when it comes to listening to Dhamma and talking about practice, not much of it gets through. As soon as I start giving a Dhamma talk— *"Namo Tassa Bhagavato...."*[38]— they're half asleep already. They don't take in the talk at all. When I reach the *"Evaṁ,"* they all open their eyes and wake up. How will they get any benefit? Real Dhamma practitioners will come away from a talk feeling inspired and uplifted. They learn something.

Consider which path you will choose. At each moment you stand at a crossroads between the worldly way and the Dhamma way. Which way will you choose? The choice is yours to make. If you are to be liberated, it is at this point.

CHAPTER 10

THE TWO FACES OF REALITY

IN OUR LIVES we have two possibilities: indulging in the world or going beyond it. The Buddha was someone who was able to free himself from the world and thus he realized spiritual liberation.

In the same way, there are two types of knowledge—knowledge of the worldly realm and knowledge of the spiritual, or true wisdom. If we have not yet practiced and trained ourselves, no matter how much knowledge we have, it is still worldly and thus cannot liberate us.

Think and look closely! The Buddha said that things of the world spin the world around. Following the world, the mind is entangled in the world; it defiles itself whether coming or going, never remaining content. Worldly people are those who are always looking for something—who can never find enough. Worldly knowledge is really ignorance; it isn't knowledge with clear understanding. So there is never an end to it. It revolves around the worldly goals of accumulating things, gaining status, seeking praise and pleasure; it's a mass of delusion which has us stuck fast.

Once we get something, there is jealousy, worry, and selfishness. And when we feel threatened and can't ward it off physically, we use our minds to invent all sorts of devices, right up to weapons and even nuclear bombs, only to blow each other up. Why all this trouble and difficulty?

This is the way of the world. The Buddha said that if one follows it around, there is no reaching an end.

Come to practice for liberation! It isn't easy to live in accordance with true wisdom, but whoever earnestly seeks the Path and fruit and aspires to nibbāna will be able to persevere and endure. Endure being contented and satisfied with little; eating little, sleeping little, speaking little; and living in moderation. By doing this we can put an end to worldliness.

If the seed of worldliness has not yet been uprooted, then we are continually troubled and confused in a never-ending cycle. Even when you are ordained, it continues to pull you away. It creates your views, your opinions; it colors and embellishes all your thoughts—that's the way it is.

People don't realize this. They say that they will get things done in the world. It's always their hope to complete everything. Just like a new government minister who is eager to get started with his new administration. He thinks that he has all the answers, so he carts away everything of the old administration, saying, "Look out! I'll do it all myself." That's all they do, bring things in and throw things out, never getting anything done. They never reach any real completion.

You can never do something that will please everyone—one person likes a little, another likes a lot; one likes short and one likes long; some like salty and some like spicy. To get everyone together and in agreement just cannot be done.

All of us want to accomplish something in our lives. But the world, with all its complexity, makes it almost impossible to bring about any real completion. Even the Buddha, born with all the opportunities of a noble prince, found no completion in the worldly life.

THE TRAP OF THE SENSES

The Buddha talked about desire and the six things by which desire is gratified: sights, sounds, smells, taste, touch, and mind objects. Desire and lust for happiness, for suffering, for good, for evil, and so on pervade everything!

Sights—there isn't any sight that's quite the same as that of a woman. Isn't that so? Doesn't a really attractive woman make you want to look? One with a really attractive figure comes walking along—you can't help but stare! How about sounds? There's no sound that grips you more than that of a woman. It pierces your heart! Smell is the same; a woman's fragrance is the most alluring of all. There's no other smell that's quite the same. Taste—even the taste of the most delicious food cannot compare with that of a woman. Touch is similar; when you caress a woman you are stunned, intoxicated, and sent spinning all around!

There was once a famous master of magical spells from Taxila in ancient India. He taught one of his disciples all he knew about charms and incantations. When the disciple was well versed and ready to fare on his own, he left with this final instruction from his teacher: "I have taught you all that I know of spells, incantations, and protective verses. Creatures with sharp teeth, antlers or horns, and even big tusks, you have no need to fear. You will be guarded from all of these, I can guarantee that. However, there is only one thing that I cannot ensure protection against, and that is the charms of a woman. I cannot help you here. There's no spell for protection against this one; you'll have to look after yourself."

The two sexes—women cause problems for men; men cause problems for women. That's the way it is; they are opposites. If men live together with men, then there's no trouble. If women live together with women, then there's no trouble. When a man sees a woman his heart pounds like a rice pounder: it goes ka-thump, ka-thump, ka-thump. When a woman sees a man, her heart pounds like a rice pounder: ka-thump, ka-thump, ka-thump. What is this? What are these forces? They pull and suck you in—no one realizes that there's a price to pay.

Mental objects arise in the mind. They are born out of desire: a desire for valuable possessions, a wish to be rich, or just a restless seeking after things. This type of greed isn't all that deep or strong; it isn't enough to make you faint or lose control. But when sexual desire arises, you're thrown off balance and lose control. You even forget about those who brought you up— your own parents!

The Buddha taught that the objects of our senses are a trap—a trap of Māra.[39] Māra should be understood as something that harms us. The trap is something that binds us, the same as a snare. It's a trap of Māra's, a hunter's snare, and the hunter is Māra.

When animals get caught in the hunter's trap, they're in a sorrowful predicament. They are caught fast and must wait there for the hunter to kill them. Have you ever snared birds? The snare springs and, "boop"—caught by the neck! A good strong string holds the bird fast. If it tries to escape, it cannot. It flies here and flies there, but it's held tight waiting for the owner of the snare. When the hunter comes along, that's it—there's no escape!

The trap of sights, sounds, smells, tastes, touch, and mind objects is the same. They catch us and bind us fast. If you attach to the senses, you're the same as a fish caught on a hook. When the fisherman comes, struggle all you want, you can't get loose. Actually, you're not caught like a fish; it's more like a frog—a frog gulps the whole hook right down into its guts. A fish just gets it caught in the mouth.

Anyone attached to the senses is the same. They're like a drunk whose liver is not yet destroyed—they don't know when they have had enough. They continue to indulge and drink carelessly. They're caught and later suffer illness and pain.

A man comes walking along a road. He is thirsty from his journey and craves a drink of water. He stops at the roadside and asks for a drink. The person with water says, "You can drink this water if you like; the color is good, the smell is good, the taste is good, but if you drink it you will become ill. I must tell you this beforehand; it'll make you sick enough to die or nearly so." The thirsty man does not listen. He's as thirsty as a person who, because of an operation, has been denied water for seven days—he's crying out for water! It's the same with a person thirsting after the senses. The Buddha taught that they are poisonous—sights, sounds, smells, tastes, touch, and mind objects are poison. They are dangerous traps. But this man is thirsty and doesn't listen. "Give me water, no matter how painful the consequences, let me drink!" So he pours out a bit and swallows it. Finding it tasty, he drinks his fill and gets so sick he almost dies. He didn't listen because of his overpowering desire.

That is how it is for a person caught in the pleasures of the senses. He drinks in sights, sounds, smells, tastes, touch, and mind objects—they are all very delicious! So he drinks without stopping, and there he remains, stuck fast until the day he dies.

THE WORLDLY WAY AND LIBERATION

Some people die because of their desires; others nearly do—that's how it is to be stuck in the way of the world. Worldly wisdom seeks after the senses and their objects. However wise the search may be, it's wise only in a worldly sense. No matter how appealing the object, it's appealing only in a worldly sense. It isn't the happiness of liberation; it won't free you from the world.

We have come to practice as monks in order to penetrate true wisdom, to rid ourselves of attachment. Practice to be free of attachment! Investigate the body; investigate everything around you until you become weary and disenchanted with it all, and then dispassion will set in. Dispassion will not arise easily, however, so long as you still don't see clearly.

We come and receive ordination—we study, we read, we practice, we meditate. We determine to make our minds resolute, but it's hard. We resolve to do a certain practice; we say that we'll practice in this way—but only a day or two goes by, maybe just a few hours, and we forget all about it. Then we remember and try to make our minds firm again. "This time I'll do it right!" Shortly afterward we are pulled away by one of our senses, and it all falls apart again. So we start all over again! This is how it is.

Like a poorly built dam, our practice is weak. We are still unable to see and follow true practice. And it goes on like this until we arrive at true wisdom. Once we penetrate to the truth, we are freed from everything. Only peace remains.

Our minds aren't peaceful because of all our old habits. We inherit these because of our past actions, and thus they follow us around and constantly plague us. We struggle and search for a way out, but we're bound by them and they pull us back. These habits don't forget their old haunts. They grab on to all the old familiar things to use, to admire, and to consume—that's how we live.

No matter how hard you try to free yourself, until you see the value of freedom and the pain of bondage, you won't be able to let go. You usually practice blindly, enduring the hardships, keeping the discipline, just following the form—you don't practice in order to attain freedom or liberation. You must see the value of letting go of your desires before you can really practice; only then is true practice possible.

Everything that you do must be done with clarity and awareness. When you see clearly, there will no longer be any need for endurance or for forcing yourself. You have difficulties and are burdened because you miss this point. Peace comes from doing things completely with your whole body and mind. Whatever is left undone leaves you with a feeling of discontent. These things bind you with worry wherever you go. You want to complete everything, but it's impossible to get it all done.

Take the case of the merchants who often come here to see me. "When my debts are all paid and my property is in order," they say, "I'll come to be ordained." They talk like that, but will they ever get everything in order? There's no end to it. They pay off their debts with another loan, then they pay off that one and do it all again. A merchant thinks that if he frees himself from debt he will be happy, but there's no end to paying things off. That's the way worldliness fools us—we go around and around like this, never realizing our predicament.

CONSTANT PRACTICE

In our practice we just look directly at the mind. Whenever our practice begins to slacken off, we notice this and make it firmer—but then, after awhile, it goes slack again. That's the way the mind pulls us around. But people with good mindfulness take a firm hold and constantly reestablish themselves, pulling themselves back, training, practicing, and developing.

The person with poor mindfulness just lets it all fall apart; they stray off and get sidetracked again and again. They're not strong and firmly rooted in practice, so their worldly desires continuously pull them away—something pulls them here, something else pulls them there. They live following their whims and desires, never putting an end to this worldly cycle.

Being ordained is not so easy. You must resolve to make your mind firm. You should be confident in the practice, confident enough to continue practicing until you become fed up with both your likes and dislikes and then see in accordance with truth. Usually, you are dissatisfied with only your dislikes. If you like something, you aren't ready to give it up. You have to become fed up with your dislikes *and* your likes, your suffering *and* your happiness.

Don't you see that this is the very essence of the Dhamma! The Dhamma of the Buddha is profound and refined. It isn't easy to comprehend. If true wisdom has not yet arisen, you can't see it. You don't look ahead and you don't look backward. When you experience happiness, you think that there will only be happiness. Whenever there is suffering, you think that there will only be suffering. You don't see that wherever there is big, there is small; wherever there is small, there is big. You don't see it that way. You see only one side and thus it's never-ending.

There are two sides to everything; you must see both. Then, when happiness arises, you don't get lost; when suffering arises, you don't get lost. When happiness arises, you don't forget the suffering because you see that they are interdependent.

In a similar way, food is beneficial to all beings for the maintenance of the body. But actually, food can also be harmful, for example, when it causes various stomach upsets. When you see the advantages of something, you must perceive the disadvantages and vice versa. When you feel hatred and aversion, you should contemplate love and understanding. In this way, you become more balanced and your mind becomes more settled.

THE EMPTY FLAG

I once read a book about Zen. In Zen, you know, they teach without giving a lot of explanation. For instance, if a monk is falling asleep during meditation, they come with a stick and *whack!* they give him a hit on the back. When the drowsy student is hit, he shows his gratitude by thanking the attendant. In Zen practice one is taught to be thankful for all the feelings that give one the opportunity to develop.

One day there was an assembly of monks gathered for a meeting. Outside the hall a flag was blowing in the wind. A dispute arose between two monks as to why the flag was blowing. One of the monks claimed that it was because of the wind while the other argued that it was because of the flag. Thus they quarreled because of their narrow views and couldn't come to any kind of agreement. They would have argued like this until the day they died. However, their teacher intervened and said, "Neither one of you is right. The correct understanding is that there is no flag and there is no wind."

This is the practice: not to have anything, not to have the flag and not to have the wind. If there is a flag, then there is a wind; if there is a wind, then there is a flag. You should contemplate and reflect on this thoroughly until you see in accordance with truth. If you consider it well, then nothing will remain. It's all empty—void; empty of flag and empty of wind. In the great emptiness there is no flag and there is no wind. There is no birth, no old age, no sickness or death. Our conventional understanding of flag and wind is only a concept. In reality there is nothing. That's all! There is nothing more than empty labels.

If we practice in this way, we will come to see completeness and all of our problems will come to an end. In the great emptiness the King of Death will never find you. There is nothing for old age, sickness, and death to follow. When we see and understand in accordance with truth, that is, with Right View, then there is only this great emptiness. It's here that there is no more "we," no "they," no "self" at all.

THE FOREST OF THE SENSES

The world with its never-ending ways goes on and on. If we try to understand it all, it leads us only to chaos and confusion. But if we contemplate the world clearly, then true wisdom will arise. The Buddha himself was one well versed in the ways of the world. He had great ability to influence and lead because of his abundant worldly knowledge. By transforming his worldly, mundane wisdom, he penetrated and attained to supramundane wisdom, making him a truly superior being. So, if we work with this teaching, contemplating it inwardly, we will attain an understanding on an entirely new level. When we see an object, there is no object. When we hear a sound, there is no sound. In smelling, we can say that there is no smell. All of the senses are manifest, but they are empty of anything stable. They are just sensations that arise and then pass away.

If we understand according to this reality, then the senses cease to be substantial. They are just sensations that come and go. In truth there isn't any "thing." If there isn't any "thing," then there is no "we" and no "they." If there is no "we," then there is nothing belonging to "us." It's in this way that suffering is extinguished. There isn't anybody to acquire suffering, so who is it that suffers?

When suffering arises, we attach to the suffering and thereby must really suffer. In the same way, when happiness arises, we attach to the happiness and consequently experience pleasure. Attachment to these feelings gives rise to the concept of self or ego, and thoughts of "we" and "they" continually manifest. Here is where it all begins, and then it carries us around in its never-ending cycle.

So we practice meditation and live according to the Dhamma. We leave our homes to come and live in the forest and absorb the peace of mind it gives us. We have fled, not through fear or escapism, but in order to contend with ourselves. However, people who come and live in the forest become attached to living in it, just as people who live in the city become attached to that. They lose their way in the forest and they lose their way in the city. The Buddha praised living in the forest because physical and mental solitude is conducive to the practice for liberation. However, he didn't want us to become dependent upon living in the forest or get stuck in its peace and tranquillity. We come to practice in order for wisdom to arise. Here in the forest we can sow and cultivate the seeds of wisdom. If there is chaos and turmoil, these seeds will have difficulty growing, but once we have learned to live in the forest, we can return and contend with the city and all the stimulation of the senses that it brings us. Learning to live in the forest means allowing wisdom to grow and develop. We can then apply this wisdom no matter where we go.

When our senses are stimulated, we become agitated and the senses become our antagonists. They antagonize us because we are still foolish and don't have the wisdom to deal with them. In reality they are our teachers, but because of our ignorance, we don't see it that way. When we lived in the city we never thought that our senses could teach us anything. As long as true wisdom has not yet manifested, we continue to see the senses and their objects as enemies. Once true wisdom arises, they are no longer our enemies but become the doorway to insight and clear understanding.

Consider the wild chickens here in the forest. Everyone knows how much they are afraid of humans. But living here in the forest, I have been able to teach them and to learn from them as well. I began by throwing out rice for them to eat. At first they were very frightened and wouldn't go near it. After a long time, however, they got used to it and even began to expect it. You see, there is something to be learned here—they originally thought that the rice was dangerous, that it was an enemy. In truth there was no danger in the rice, but they didn't know that the rice was food and so were afraid. When they finally saw for themselves that there was nothing to fear, they could come and eat without any danger.

Chickens learn naturally this way. Living here in the forest, we learn in a similar way. Formerly we thought that our senses were a problem, and because of our ignorance of their proper use, they caused us a lot of trouble. Through experience in practice, however, we learn to see them in accordance with truth. We learn to make use of them, just as the chickens could make use of the rice. Then they are no longer opposed to us, and problems disappear.

As long as we think, investigate, and understand wrongly, these things will oppose us. But as soon as we begin to investigate properly, experience will bring us wisdom and clear understanding. The chickens came to their understanding, and in a sense we can say they practiced *vipassanā*. They knew in accordance with truth; they had their insight.

In our practice we have our senses as tools which, when rightly used, enable us to become enlightened to the Dhamma. This is something that all meditators should contemplate. When we don't see this clearly, we remain in perpetual conflict.

So, as we live in the quietude of the forest, we continue to develop subtle feelings and prepare the ground for cultivating wisdom. But if you've gained some peace of mind living here in the quiet forest, don't think that's enough. Don't settle for just that! Remember that we have come to cultivate and grow the seeds of wisdom.

As wisdom matures and we begin to understand in accordance with the truth, we will no longer be dragged up and down. Usually, if we have a pleasant mood, we behave one way; and if we have an unpleasant mood, we behave another way. We like something and we are up; we dislike something and we are down. In this way we are still in conflict with enemies. When these things no longer oppose us, they become stabilized and balance out. There are no longer ups and downs or highs and lows. We understand these things of the world and know that that's just the way it is. It's just worldly dhamma.

Worldly dhamma changes to become the Path. Worldly dhamma has eight ways; the Path has eight ways. Wherever worldly dhamma exists, the Path is also to be found. When we live with clarity, all of our worldly experience becomes the practicing of the Eightfold Path. Without clarity, worldly dhamma predominates and we are turned away from the Path. When Right Understanding arises, liberation from suffering lies right here before us. You will not find liberation by running around looking elsewhere.

So don't be in a hurry and try to push or rush your practice. Do your meditation gently and gradually, step by step. If you become peaceful, then accept it; if you don't become peaceful, then accept that. That's the nature of the mind. We must find our own practice and keep at it persistently.

Perhaps wisdom does not arise. I used to think about my practice that when I had no wisdom, I could force myself to have it. But it didn't work; things remained the same. Then, after careful consideration, I saw that we can't contemplate things we don't have. So what's the best thing to do? It's better just to practice with equanimity. If nothing causes us concern, there's nothing to remedy. If there's no problem, we don't have to try to solve it. When there is a problem that's when you must solve it, right there! There's no need to go searching for anything special; just live normally. But know where your mind is. Live mindfully and comprehend clearly. Let wisdom be your guide; don't live indulging in your moods. Be heedful and alert. If there is nothing, that's fine; when something arises, then investigate and contemplate it.

COMING TO THE CENTER

Try watching a spider. A spider spins its web in any convenient niche and then sits in the center, still and silent. Sooner or later a fly comes along and lands on the web. As soon as it touches and shakes the web, *boop!*—the spider pounces and winds it up in thread. It stores the insect away and then returns again to collect itself silently in the center of the web.

Watching a spider like this can give rise to wisdom. Our six senses have mind at the center surrounded by eye, ear, nose, tongue, and body. When one of the senses is stimulated—for instance, a form makes contact with the eye—it shakes and reaches the mind. The mind is that which knows, that which knows form. Just this much is enough for wisdom to arise. It's that simple.

Like a spider in its web, we should live keeping to ourselves. As soon as the spider feels an insect contact the web, it quickly grabs it, ties it up, and once again returns to the center. This is not at all different from our own minds. "Coming to the center" means living mindfully with clear comprehension, being always alert, and doing everything with exactness and precision—this is our center. There's really not a lot for us to do; we just live carefully in this way. But that doesn't mean that we live heedlessly and think, "There is no need to do sitting or walking meditation!" and so forget all about our practice. We can't be careless. We must remain alert, just as the spider waits to snatch up insects for its food.

This is all that we have to know—sitting and contemplating that spider. Just this much, and wisdom can arise spontaneously. Just this much, and our practice is complete.

This point is very important! It isn't that we have to do sitting practice or walking meditation all day and all night. If that's our view of practice, we'll really make it difficult for ourselves. We should do what we can according to our strength and energy, using our physical capabilities in the proper amount.

It's very important to know the mind and the other senses well. Know how they come and go, how they arise and pass away. Understand this thoroughly! In the language of Dhamma we can also say that, just as the spider traps the various insects, the mind binds up the senses with anicca, dukkha, anattā. Where can they go? We keep them for food. These things are stored away as our nourishment. That's enough; there's no more to do, just this much. This is the nourishment for our minds, nourishment for one who is aware and who has understanding.

If you know that these things are impermanent, that they are bound up with suffering, and that none of it is you, then you would be crazy to go after them! If you don't see clearly in this way, then you're bound to suffer. When you take a good look and see these things as really impermanent, even though they may seem worth going after, really they are not. Why do you want them when their nature is pain and suffering? They are not ours; there is no self in them; they have nothing in them belonging to us. So why are you seeking after them? All problems are ended right here. Where else will you end them?

Just take a good look at the spider and turn it inward; turn it back onto yourself. You will see that it's all the same. When the mind has seen anicca, dukkha, anattā, it lets go and releases itself. It no longer attaches to suffering or to happiness. This is the nourishment for the mind of one who practices and really trains. It's that simple. You don't have to go searching anywhere. No matter what you are doing, you are there, no need for a lot of fuss and bother. In this way the momentum and energy of your practice will continuously grow and mature.

ESCAPE

This momentum of practice leads toward freedom from the cycle of birth and death. We haven't escaped from that cycle because we still insist on craving and desiring. We don't commit unwholesome or immoral acts, but all that means is that we are living in accordance with the dhamma of morality. For instance, there is a chant in which people ask that all beings not be separated from the things that they love and are fond of. If you think about it, this is very childish. It's the way of people who still can't let go.

This is the nature of human desire—desire for things to be other than the way they are: wishing for longevity, hoping that there will be no death or sickness. Such are people's hopes and desires. So when you tell them that their unfulfilled desires cause them suffering, it clobbers them right over the head. But what can they say in reply? Nothing, because it's the truth! You're pointing right at their desires.

Everyone has desires and wants them fulfilled. Nobody is willing to stop; nobody really wants to escape. So our practice must be patiently refined. Those who practice steadfastly, without deviation or slackness, and have a gentle and restrained manner, always persevering with constancy—those are the ones who will know. No matter what arises, they will remain firm and unshakable.

CHAPTER 11

A GIFT OF DHAMMA

T HE PARENTS OF MONKS HERE at Wat Pah Pong sometimes come to visit their sons. I regret that I have no gifts to offer these visitors. The West already has so many material things, but of Dhamma there's very little. I've been there, and I have seen for myself that there is so little Dhamma there that leads to peace and tranquillity. There are only things that continually make one's mind confused and troubled.

The West is already materially prosperous; it has so many things to offer which are sensually enticing—sights, sounds, smells, tastes, and textures. However, people unaware of Dhamma only become confused by them. So today I will offer you some Dhamma to take back home as a gift from Wat Pah Pong and Wat Pah Nanachat.

What is Dhamma? Dhamma is that which can cut through our problems and difficulties, gradually reducing them to nothing. That's what is called Dhamma and that's what should be studied throughout our daily lives, so that when some mental impression arises in us we'll be able to deal with it.

We all have problems, whether we are living here in Thailand or in other countries. If we don't know how to solve them, we'll always be subject to suffering and distress. That which solves problems is wisdom, and to have wisdom we must develop and train the mind.

The subject of practice isn't far away at all; it's right here in our bodies and minds. Westerners and Thais are the same; they both have a body and mind. A confused body and mind means a confused person, and a peaceful body and mind, a peaceful person.

Actually, the mind, like rain water, is pure in its natural state. But if we drop some green coloring into clear rainwater, it turns green. If we drop yellow coloring, it turns yellow. The mind reacts similarly. When a comfortable mental impression drops into the mind, the mind is comfortable. When an uncomfortable mental impression does so, the mind is uncomfortable. It becomes tinted, just like the water.

When clear water contacts yellow, it turns yellow. When it contacts green, it turns green. It always changes color. Actually, the green or yellow water is naturally clean and clear. This is also the natural state of the mind: clean and pure and unconfused. It becomes confused only because it pursues mental impressions; it gets lost in its moods.

Let me explain more clearly. Imagine you are sitting in a peaceful forest. If there's no wind, the leaves are still. When a wind arises, they flutter. The mind is similar to a leaf. When it contacts a mental impression, it, too, trembles and flutters in a way that depends on the nature of that mental impression. And the less we know of Dhamma, the more the mind will continually pursue mental impressions. Feeling happy, it succumbs to happiness. Feeling suffering, it succumbs to suffering. It's constant confusion!

In the end people become neurotic. Why? Because they don't know. They just follow their moods and don't know how to look after their own minds. When the mind has no one to look after it, it's like a child with no mother or father to take care of it. An orphan has no refuge and because of that feels very insecure. Likewise, if the mind is not looked after, if there is no training or maturation of character with Right Understanding, things can get really troublesome.

The method of training the mind I want to talk about is called *kammaṭṭhāna. Kamma* means "action," and *thāna* means "base." In Buddhism this is the method of making the mind peaceful and tranquil. You use it to train the mind and, once the mind is trained, to investigate the body.

Our being is composed of two parts: one is the body, the other, the mind. There are only these two parts. What is called "the body" is that which can be seen with our physical eyes. The mind, on the other hand, has no physical aspect. The mind can only be seen with the "internal eye" or the "eye of the mind." These two things, body and mind, are in a constant state of turmoil.

What is the mind? The mind isn't really any "thing." Conventionally speaking, it's that which sees or senses. That which senses, receives, and experiences all mental impressions is called "mind." Right at this moment there is mind. When I speak to you, your mind acknowledges what I say. Sounds enter through your ear and you know what is being said. That which experiences this is called "mind."

This mind doesn't have any self or substance. It doesn't have any form. It just experiences mental activities—that's all! If we teach this mind to have Right View, this mind won't have any problems. It will be at ease.

The mind is mind. Mental objects are mental objects. Mental objects are not the mind; the mind is not mental objects. In order to clearly understand our minds and the mental objects in our minds, we say that the mind is that which receives the mental objects which pop into it.

When these two things, mind and its object, come into contact with each other, they give rise to feelings. Some are good, some bad, some cool, some hot—all kinds. Without wisdom to deal with these feelings, however, the mind will be troubled.

Meditation is a way to develop the mind so that it becomes the basis for the arising of wisdom. Here the breath is a physical foundation. We call it *ānāpānasati*, or mindfulness of breathing. We make breathing our mental object. We take this object of meditation because it's the simplest and because it has been the heart of meditation since ancient times.

When we do sitting meditation, we sit cross-legged: right leg on top of the left leg, right hand on top of the left hand. Keep your back straight and erect. Say to yourself, "Now I will let go of all my burdens and concerns." You don't want anything that will cause you worry. Let go of all concerns for the time being.

Now fix your attention on the breath. Then breathe in and breathe out. In developing awareness of breathing, don't intentionally make the breath long or short. Don't make it strong or weak. Just let it flow normally and naturally. Mindfulness and self-awareness, arising from the mind, will know the in-breath and the out-breath.

Be at ease. Don't think about anything. The only thing you have to do is fix your attention on the breathing in and breathing out. You have nothing else to do but that! Keep your mindfulness fixed on the in- and out-breaths as they occur. Be aware of the beginning, middle, and end of each breath. On inhalation, the beginning of the breath is at the nose tip; the middle, at the heart; and the end, in the abdomen. On exhalation, it's just the reverse: the beginning of the breath is in the abdomen; the middle, at the heart; and the end, at the nose tip.

Focusing the attention on these three points will relieve all worries. Don't think of anything else. Keep your attention on the breath. Perhaps other thoughts will enter the mind and distract you. Don't be concerned. Just take up the breathing again as your object of attention. The mind may get caught up in judging and investigating your moods, but continue to practice, being constantly aware of the beginning, middle, and end of each breath.

Eventually, the mind will be aware of the breath at these three points all the time. When you do this practice for some time, the mind and body will get accustomed to the work. Fatigue will disappear. The body will feel lighter and the breath will become more and more refined. Mindfulness and self-awareness will protect the mind and watch over it.

We practice like this until the mind is peaceful and calm, until it is one. "One" means that the mind is completely absorbed in the breathing, that it doesn't separate from the breath. The mind is unconfused and at ease. It knows the beginning, middle, and end of the breath and remains steadily fixed on it.

Then when the mind is peaceful, we fix our attention on the in-breath and out-breath at the nose tip only. We don't have to follow it down to the abdomen and back up. Just concentrate on the tip of the nose where the breath comes in and goes out.

This is called "calming the mind," making it relaxed and peaceful. When tranquillity arises, the mind stops; it stops with its single object, the breath. This is what's known as making the mind peaceful so that wisdom may arise.

This is the beginning, the foundation of our practice. You should try to practice this every single day, wherever you may be. Whether at home, in a car, lying or sitting down, you should be mindfully aware and watch over the mind constantly.

This is called mental training and should be practiced in all the four postures. Not just sitting, but standing, walking, and lying down as well. The point is that we should know what the state of the mind is at each moment, and, to do this, we must be constantly mindful and aware. Is the mind happy or suffering? Is it confused? Is it peaceful? Getting to know the mind in this manner allows it to become tranquil, and when it does become tranquil, wisdom will arise.

With the tranquil mind investigate the meditation subject, the body, from the top of the head down to the soles of the feet, then back up again to the head. Do this over and over. Bring your attention to the hair of the head, hair of the body, the nails, teeth, and skin. In this meditation we will see that this whole body is composed of four elements: earth, water, fire, and air.

The hard and solid parts of our body make up the earth element; the liquid and flowing parts, the water element. Winds that pass up and down our body constitute the air element, and the heat in our body, the fire element.

Taken together, they compose what we call a "human being." When the body is broken down into its component parts, however, only these four elements remain. The Buddha taught that there is no "being" per se, no human, no Thai, no Westerner, no person, but that ultimately there are only these four elements—that's all! We assume that there is a person or a being, but in reality there isn't anything of the sort.

Whether taken separately as earth, water, fire, and air, or taken together, labeled as a "human being," they're all impermanent, subject to suffering, and not self. They are all unstable, uncertain, and in a state of constant change—not stable for a single moment!

Our body is unstable, altering and changing constantly. Hair changes, nails change, teeth change, skin changes—everything changes, completely. Our mind, too, is always changing. It isn't a self or anything substantial. It isn't really "us" or "them," although it may think so. Maybe it will think about killing itself. Maybe it will think of happiness or of suffering—all sorts of things! It's unstable. If we don't have wisdom and we believe this mind of ours, it'll lie to us continually. And we will alternately suffer and be happy.

The mind is an uncertain thing. This body is uncertain. Together they are impermanent. Together they are a source of suffering. Together they are devoid of self. These, the Buddha pointed out, are neither a being, nor a person, nor a self, nor a soul, neither us nor them. They are merely elements: earth, water, fire, and air. Just elements.

When the mind sees this, it will rid itself of the attachment that holds that *I* am beautiful, *I* am good, *I* am evil, *I* am suffering, *I* have, *I* this or *I* that. You will experience a state of unity, for you'll have seen that all of humankind is basically the same. There is no "I." There are only elements.

When you contemplate and see impermanence, suffering, and non-self, there will no longer be clinging to a self, a being, an I, a he or she. The mind that sees this will give rise to *nibbidā*, or disenchantment and dispassion. It will see all things only as impermanent, unsatisfactory, and not self.

The mind then stops. The mind is Dhamma. Greed, hatred, and delusion will then diminish and recede little by little until finally there is only mind—just the pure mind. This is called "practicing meditation."

This gift of Dhamma is for you to study and contemplate in your daily lives. It will show you the way to peace of mind; it will render your mind calm and unconfused. Your body may be in turmoil, but your mind will not. Those in the world may be confused, but you will not be. When you are surrounded by confusion, you will not be confused, because the mind will have seen; the mind is Dhamma. This is the right path, the proper way.

CHAPTER 12

INNER BALANCE

To calm the mind means to find the right balance. If you try to force your mind too much, it goes out too far; if you don't try hard enough, it again misses the point of balance.

Normally the mind isn't still; it's always moving. We must strengthen it. Making the mind strong isn't like making the body strong. To make the body strong we have to exercise it, to push it. To make the mind strong we make it peaceful, not to go thinking of this and that. For most of us, the mind has never been peaceful; it has never had the energy of samādhi, so we must establish it within a boundary. We sit in meditation, staying with the "one who knows."

If we force our breath to be too long or too short, we're not balanced; the mind won't become peaceful. It's like when we first start to use a pedal sewing machine. Before we actually sew something, we practice pedaling the machine to get our coordination right. Following the breath is similar. We don't get concerned over how long or short, weak or strong it is; we just note it. We simply let it be, following the natural breathing.

When it's balanced, we take the breathing as our meditation object. When we breathe in, the beginning of the breath is at the nose tip, the middle at the chest, and the end at the abdomen. When we breathe out, it's the reverse. Simply take note of this path at the nose tip, the chest, and the abdomen. We take note of these three points in order to make the mind firm, to limit mental activity so that mindfulness and self-awareness can easily arise. When our attention can settle on these three points, we let them go and concentrate solely at the nose tip or the upper lip, where the air passes in and out. We don't have to follow the breath, but just establish mindfulness at the nose tip, noting the breath at this one point—entering, leaving, entering, leaving.

There's no need to think of anything special; just concentrate on this simple task for now, having continuous presence of mind. Soon the mind becomes peaceful, the breath refined. The mind and body become light. This is the right state for the work of meditation.

When sitting in meditation the mind becomes refined, but whatever state it's in we should try to be aware of it, to know it. Mental activity is there together with tranquillity. There is *vitakka*. Vitakka is the act of bringing the mind to the theme of contemplation. If there is not much mindfulness, there will not be much vitakka. Then *vicāra,* the contemplation around that theme, follows. Various weak mental impressions may arise from time to time, but our self-awareness is the important thing—whatever may be happening, we know it continuously. As we go deeper we are constantly aware of the state of our meditation, knowing whether or not the mind is firmly established. Thus, both concentration and awareness are present.

Having a peaceful mind does not mean that nothing happens. Mental impressions do arise. For instance, when we talk about the first level of absorption, we say it has five factors. Along with vitakka and vicāra, *pīti* (rapture) arises with the theme of contemplation and then *sukha* (happiness). These four things all lie together in the mind established in tranquillity. They are a single state.

The fifth factor is *ekaggatā,* or one-pointedness. You may wonder how there can be one-pointedness when there are all these other factors as well. This is because they all become unified on that foundation of tranquillity. Together they are called a state of samādhi. They are not everyday states of mind; they are factors of absorption. None of these five characteristics disturb the basic tranquillity. There is vitakka, but it does not disturb the mind; vicāra, rapture, and happiness arise but likewise do not disturb the mind. The mind is therefore one with these factors. This is the first level of absorption.

We don't have to call it jhāna (absorption)—first jhāna, second jhāna, and so on. Let's just call it "a peaceful mind." As the mind becomes progressively calmer it will dispense with vitakka and vicāra, leaving only rapture and happiness. Why does the mind discard vitakka and vicāra? It does so because, as the mind becomes more refined, the activities of vitakka and vicāra are too coarse. At this stage, as the mind leaves off vitakka and vicāra, feelings of great rapture can arise; tears may gush out. But as the samādhi deepens, rapture, too, is discarded, leaving only happiness and one-pointedness, until finally even happiness goes and the mind reaches its greatest refinement. There are only equanimity and one-pointedness; all else has been left behind. The mind stands unmoving.

Once the mind is peaceful this can happen. You don't have to think a lot about it; it just happens by itself when the causal factors are ripe. This is called the energy of a peaceful mind. In this state the mind is not drowsy; the five hindrances—sense desire, aversion, restlessness, dullness, and doubt—have all fled.

But if mental energy is still not strong and mindfulness weak, mental impressions will occasionally intrude. The mind is peaceful but it's as if there's some cloudiness within the calm. It's not a normal sort of drowsiness though; some impressions will manifest—maybe we'll hear a sound or see a dog or something. It's not really clear, but it's not a dream either. This is because these five factors have become unbalanced and weak.

The mind tends to play tricks within these levels of tranquillity. Imagery will sometimes arise when the mind is in this state, through any of the senses, and the meditator may not be able to tell exactly what is happening. "Am I sleeping? No. Is it a dream? No, it's not a dream…." These impressions arise from a middling sort of tranquillity; but if the mind is truly calm and clear, we don't doubt the various mental impressions or images that arise. Questions like, "Did I drift off just then? Was I sleeping? Did I get lost?" don't arise, for they are characteristics of a mind that is still doubting. "Am I asleep or awake?" Here, the mind is fuzzy. This is the mind getting lost in its moods. It's like the moon going behind a cloud. You can still see the moon, but the clouds covering it render it hazy. It's not like the clear, bright moon that has emerged from behind the clouds.

When the mind is peaceful and established firmly in mindfulness and self-awareness, we will have no doubt about the various phenomena that we encounter. The mind will truly be beyond the hindrances. We will clearly know everything that arises in the mind, just as it is. We do not fall into doubt because the mind is clear and bright. The mind in samādhi is like this.

Some people find it hard to enter samādhi because they don't have the right tendencies. There is some samādhi, but it's not strong or firm. Such people can, however, attain peace through the use of wisdom, through contemplating and seeing the truth of things, and solve their problems that way. This is using wisdom rather than the power of samādhi. To attain calm in practice, it's not necessary to be sitting in meditation. Just ask yourself, "Hey, what is that?" and solve your problem right there! A person with wisdom can do this. Perhaps they can't really attain high levels of samādhi, but they do have enough to cultivate wisdom. It's like the difference between farming rice and farming corn. One can depend on rice more than corn for one's livelihood. Our practice can be like this; we depend more on wisdom to solve problems. When we see the truth, peace arises.

The ways of wisdom and concentration are not the same. Some people have insight and are strong in wisdom but do not have much samādhi. When they sit in meditation they aren't very peaceful. They tend to think a lot, contemplating this and that, until eventually they contemplate happiness and suffering and see the truth of them. Whether standing, walking, sitting, or lying, enlightenment of the Dhamma can take place. They attain peace through seeing, through relinquishing, through knowing the truth and going beyond doubt, because they have seen it for themselves.

Other people have only a little wisdom but their samādhi is very strong. They can enter very deep samādhi quickly, but, not having much wisdom, they cannot catch their defilements; they don't know them. They can't solve their problems.

But regardless of the approach, we must do away with wrong thinking, leaving only Right View. We must get rid of confusion, leaving only peace.

Either way we end up at the same place. These two sides to practice, calm and insight, go together. We can't do away with either of them.

That which "looks over" the various factors that arise in meditation is sati, mindfulness. This sati is a condition that, through practice, can help other factors to arise. Sati is life. Whenever we don't have sati, when we are heedless, it's as if we are dead. If we have no sati, then our speech and actions have no meaning. Sati is simply mindfulness. It's a cause for the arising of self-awareness and wisdom. Whatever virtues we have cultivated

are imperfect if they lack sati. Sati is that which watches over us while standing, walking, sitting, and lying. Even when we are no longer in samādhi, sati
should be present throughout.

Whatever we do, we take care. A sense of shame[40] will arise. We will feel
ashamed about the things we do that aren't correct. As shame increases,
our collectedness will increase as well. When collectedness increases, heedlessness will disappear. Even if we don't sit in meditation, these factors will
be present in the mind.

And this arises because of cultivating sati. Develop sati! It has real value.
This is the quality that looks over the work we are doing in the present. If
we know ourselves like this, right will distinguish itself from wrong, the Path
will become clear, and cause for all shame will dissolve. Wisdom will arise.

We can sum up the practice as morality, concentration, and wisdom.
To be collected, to be controlled, this is morality. The firm establishing of
the mind within that control is concentration. Complete, overall knowledge
within the activity in which we are engaged is wisdom. The practice, in
brief, is just morality, concentration, and wisdom, or in other words, the
Path. There is no other way.

CHAPTER 13

THE PATH IN HARMONY

How CONFIDENT, how certain, are you in your meditation practice? It's reasonable to ask because these days many people, both monks and lay people, teach meditation, so you may be caused to experience wavering and doubt. But if you have a clear understanding, you will be able to make your mind peaceful and firm.

You should understand the Eightfold Path as morality, concentration, and wisdom. The Path comes together as simply this. Our practice is to make this Path arise within us.

When sitting in meditation we are told to close the eyes, not to look at anything else, because now we are going to look directly at the mind. When we close our eyes, our attention comes inward. We establish our attention on the breath, center our feelings there, put our mindfulness there. When the factors of the Path are in harmony, we will be able to see the breath, the feelings, the mind, and mental objects for what they are. Here we will see the "focus point," where samādhi and the other factors of the Path converge in harmony.

When you are sitting in meditation along with other people, imagine that you are sitting by yourself. Develop this feeling that you are sitting alone until the mind lets go of all externals, concentrating solely on the breath. If you keep thinking, "This person is sitting over here, that person is sitting over there," there'll be no peace, for the mind won't come inward. Just cast all that aside until you feel there is no one sitting around you, until there is nothing at all, until you have no wavering, no interest in your surroundings.

Let the breath go naturally; don't force it to be short or long; just sit and watch it going in and out. When the mind lets go of all external impressions, the sounds of cars and the like won't disturb you. Nothing, whether sights or sounds, will disturb you, because the mind doesn't receive them. Your attention will come together on the breath.

If the mind is confused and won't concentrate on the breath, take a full, deep breath, as deep as you can, and then let it all out till there is nothing left. Do this three times and then reestablish your attention. The mind will become calm.

It's natural for the mind to stay calm for a while, and then restlessness and confusion arises again. When this happens, concentrate, breathe deeply again, and then reestablish your attention on the breath. Just keep going like this. When this has happened many times you will become adept at it; the mind will let go of all external manifestations. Sati will be firmly established.

As the mind becomes more refined, so does the breath. Feelings will become finer and finer, and the body and mind will be light. Our attention is fixed solely on the inner: we see the in-breaths and out-breaths clearly, we see all impressions clearly. Here we will see the coming together of morality, concentration, and wisdom. This is called the Path in harmony. When there is this harmony our mind will be free of confusion; it will come together as one. This is called samādhi.

After watching the breath for a long time, it may become very refined; the awareness of the breath will gradually cease, leaving only bare awareness. What will we take as our object of meditation now? We take just this knowledge as our object, that is, the awareness that there's no breath. Unexpected things may happen at this time; some people experience them, some don't. If they do arise, we should be firm and have strong mindfulness. Some people see that the breath has disappeared and get a fright; they're afraid they'll die. Here we should know the situation just as it is. We simply notice that there's no breath and take that as our object of awareness.

This, we can say, is the firmest type of samādhi: an unmoving state of mind. Perhaps the body will become so light it's as if there is no body at all. We feel like we're sitting in empty space, completely empty. Although this may seem very unusual, you should understand that there's nothing to worry about. Firmly establish your mind like this.

When the mind is firmly unified, having no sense impressions to disturb it, one can remain in that state for any length of time. There will be no painful feelings to disturb us. When samādhi has reached this level, we can leave it whenever we choose; but when we come out of this samādhi, we do so comfortably, not because we've become bored with it or tired. We come out because we've had enough for now, we feel at ease, we have no problems at all.

If we can develop this type of samādhi, then if we sit, say, thirty minutes or an hour, the mind will remain cool and calm for many days. When the mind is cool and calm like this, it is clean. Whatever we experience, the mind will take up and investigate. This is a fruit of samādhi.

Morality has one function, concentration has another function, and wisdom yet another. These factors are like a cycle. We can see them all within the peaceful mind. When the mind is calm, it has collectedness and restraint because of wisdom and the energy of concentration. As it becomes more collected, it becomes more refined, which in turn increases moral purity. As our morality becomes purer, this will help in the development of concentration. Concentration, when firmly established, helps wisdom arise. Morality, concentration, and wisdom are interrelated like this.

In the end the Path becomes one and functions at all times. We should nurture the strength that arises from the Path, for it leads to insight and wisdom.

ON THE DANGERS OF SAMĀDHI

Samādhi is capable of bringing much benefit or much harm to the meditator. For one who has no wisdom it is harmful, but for one who has wisdom it can bring real benefit, for it can lead to insight.

That which can possibly be harmful to the meditator is absorption samādhi (jhāna): samādhi with deep, sustained calm. Such samādhi brings great peace. Where there is peace, there is happiness. When there is happiness, attachment and clinging to that happiness arise. The meditator doesn't want to contemplate anything else; they just want to indulge in that pleasant feeling. When we have been practicing for a long time we may become adept at entering this samādhi very quickly. As soon as we start to note our meditation object, the mind becomes calm, and we don't want to come out to investigate anything. We just get stuck on that happiness. This is a danger.

We must use *upacāra samādhi*. Here, we enter calm and then, when the mind is sufficiently calm, we come out and look at outer activity.[41] Looking at the outside with a calm mind gives rise to wisdom. This is hard to understand, because it's almost like ordinary thinking and imagining. When thinking is present, we may assume the mind isn't peaceful; but actually the thinking is taking place within the calm. There is contemplation, but it doesn't disturb the calm. We may bring thinking up in order to contemplate it, to investigate it. It's not that we are aimlessly thinking or speculating away; the contemplation arises from a peaceful mind. This is called "awareness within calm and calm within awareness." If it's simply ordinary thinking and imagining, the mind won't be peaceful; it will be disturbed. But I am not talking about ordinary thinking. It's contemplation. Wisdom is born right here.

So, there can be right samādhi and wrong samādhi. Wrong samādhi is where the mind enters calm and there's no awareness at all. You can sit for two hours or even all day, but the mind doesn't know where it's been or what's happened. There is calm, but that's all. It's like a sharp knife that we don't bother to put to any use. This is a deluded type of calm, because there is not much awareness. The meditator may think they have reached the ultimate already, so they don't bother to look for anything else. Samādhi can be an enemy at this level. Wisdom cannot arise because there is no awareness of right and wrong.

With right samādhi, no matter what level of calm is reached, there is awareness. There is full mindfulness and clear comprehension. This is the samādhi that gives rise to wisdom; one cannot get lost in it. Meditators should understand this. You can't do without this awareness; it must be present from beginning to end. This kind of samādhi has no danger.

You may wonder how wisdom arises from samādhi. When right samādhi has been developed, wisdom has an opportunity to arise at any time—in all postures. When the eye sees a form, the ear hears a sound, the nose smells an odor, the tongue experiences a taste, the body experiences a touch, or the mind experiences a mental impression, the mind stays with full knowledge of the true nature of those sense impressions; it doesn't follow them.

When the mind has wisdom it doesn't pick and choose. In any posture we are fully aware of the birth of happiness and unhappiness. We let go of both of these things; we don't cling. This is right practice, which we do in all postures. *All postures* does not refer only to bodily postures; it also refers to the mind, which has mindfulness and clear comprehension of the truth at all times. When samādhi has been rightly developed, wisdom arises like this. This is insight, knowledge of the truth.

There are two kinds of peace—the coarse and the refined. The peace that comes from samādhi is the coarse type. When the mind is peaceful there is happiness. The mind then takes this happiness to be peace. But happiness and unhappiness lie within the realm of becoming and birth. There is no escape from saṁsāra so long as we still cling to happiness. So happiness is not peace; peace is not happiness.

The other type of peace is that which comes from wisdom. Here we don't confuse peace with happiness; we see that the mind of wisdom—which contemplates and knows happiness *and* unhappiness—is peace. The peace that arises from wisdom sees the truth of both happiness and unhappiness. Clinging to those states does not arise; the mind rises above them. This is the true goal of all Buddhist practice.

CHAPTER 14

THE TRAINING
OF THE HEART

I N THE TIME of Ajahn Mun and Ajahn Sao, life was a lot simpler, a lot less complicated than it is today. In those days monks had few duties and ceremonies to perform. They lived in forests without permanent resting places. There they could devote themselves entirely to the practice of meditation. They rarely encountered the luxuries that are so commonplace today. They made their drinking cups and spittoons out of bamboo. Lay people seldom came to visit. Monks didn't want or expect much and had to be content with what they had. They lived and breathed meditation!

The monks suffered many privations living like this. If someone caught malaria and went to ask for medicine, the teacher would say, "You don't need medicine! Keep practicing." Besides, there simply weren't all the drugs that are available now. All one had were the herbs and roots that grew in the forest. The environment was such that monks had to have a great deal of patience and endurance; they didn't bother over minor ailments. Nowadays you get a bit of an ache and you're off to the hospital!

Sometimes you had to walk ten to twelve kilometers on alms round. You would leave as soon as it was light and maybe return around ten or eleven o'clock. You didn't get very much either, perhaps some glutinous rice, salt, or a few chilies. Whether you got anything to eat with the rice or not didn't matter. That's the way it was. No one dared complain of hunger or fatigue; they were just not inclined to complain but learned to take care of themselves. They practiced in the forest with patience and endurance alongside the many dangers that lurked in the surroundings. Many fierce wild animals lived in the jungles, and there were many hardships, both physical and mental, in the ascetic dhutanga practice of the forest-dwelling monk. Indeed, the patience and endurance of the monks in those days was excellent because the circumstances compelled it.

Today circumstances push us in the opposite direction. In ancient times, one had to travel by foot; then came the oxcart and then the automobile. Aspiration and ambition grew, so that now, if a car is not air-conditioned, you won't even sit in it—impossible to go if there is no air-conditioning! The virtues of patience and endurance are growing weaker and weaker. The standards for meditation and practice are lax and getting laxer. Meditators these days like to follow their own opinions and desires. When the old folks talk about the old days, it's like listening to a myth or a legend. You just listen indifferently, but you don't understand. It just doesn't reach you.

According to our ancient monastic tradition, as a monk you should spend at least five years with your teacher. Some days you should avoid speaking to anyone. Don't allow yourself to talk very much. Don't read books. Read your own heart instead.[42] Take Wat Pah Pong for example. These days many university graduates are coming to be ordained. I try to stop them from spending their time reading books about Dhamma, because these people are always reading books. They have so many opportunities for reading books, but opportunities for reading their own hearts are rare. So, when they come to be ordained for three months following the Thai custom, I try to get them to close their books and manuals. While they are ordained they have this splendid opportunity to read their own hearts.

Listening to your own heart is really very interesting. This untrained heart races around following its own habits. It jumps about excitedly, randomly, because it has never been trained. Train your heart! Buddhist meditation is about the heart; it's about developing the heart or mind, about developing your own heart. This is very, very important. Buddhism is the religion of the heart. Only this. One who practices to develop the heart is one who practices Buddhism.

This heart of ours lives in a cage, and what's more, there's a raging tiger in that cage. If this maverick heart of ours doesn't get what it wants, it makes trouble. You must discipline it with meditation, with samādhi. This is called "training the heart." At the very beginning, the foundation of practice is the establishment of moral discipline (sīla). Sīla is the training of the body and speech. Training in moral discipline can lead to conflict and confusion. When you don't let yourself do what you want to do, there is conflict. The conflict here is that between wisdom and the defilements, and it is also known as "the suffering that leads to the end of suffering."

Eat little. Sleep little. Speak little. Whatever your worldly habits may be, lessen them; go against their power. Don't just do as you like; don't indulge in your thoughts. Stop this slavish adherence. You must constantly go against the stream of ignorance. This is called discipline. When you discipline your heart, it becomes very dissatisfied and begins to struggle. It becomes restricted and oppressed. When the heart is prevented from doing what it wants to do, it starts wandering and struggling. Suffering becomes apparent to us.

This suffering is the first of the Four Noble Truths. Most people want to get away from it. They don't want to have any kind of suffering at all. Actually, this suffering is what brings us wisdom; it makes us contemplate dukkha. Happiness (sukha) tends to make us close our eyes and ears. It never allows us to develop patience. Comfort and happiness make us careless. Of these two defilements, dukkha is the easiest to see. Therefore we must bring up suffering in order to put an end to our suffering. We must first know what dukkha is before we can know how to practice meditation.

In the beginning you have to train your heart like this. You may not understand what is happening or what the point of it is, but when the teacher tells you to do something, then you must do it. You will develop the virtues of patience and endurance. Whatever happens, you endure, because that's the way it is. For example, when you begin to practice samādhi you want peace and tranquillity. But you don't get any. You don't get any because you have never practiced this way. Your heart says, "I'll sit until I attain tranquillity." But when tranquillity doesn't arise, you suffer. And when there is suffering, you get up and run away! To practice like this cannot be called developing the heart. It's called desertion.

Instead of indulging in your moods, you train yourself with the Dhamma of the Buddha. Lazy or diligent, you just keep on practicing. Don't you think that this is a better way? The other way, the way of following your moods, will never lead you to the Dhamma. If you practice the Dhamma, then whatever the mood may be, you keep on practicing, constantly practicing. The way of self-indulgence is not the way of the Buddha. When we follow our own views on practice, our own opinions about the Dhamma, we never see clearly what is right and what is wrong. We don't know our own heart. We don't know ourselves.

Therefore, to practice while following your own teachings is the slow way. To practice while following the Dhamma is the direct way. Lazy, you practice; diligent, you practice. You are aware of time and place. This is called developing the heart.

If you indulge in following your own views and practice accordingly, you will start thinking and doubting a lot. You'll think to yourself, "I don't have very much merit. I don't have any luck. I've been practicing meditation for years now and I'm still unenlightened. I still haven't seen the Dhamma." To practice with this kind of attitude cannot be called developing the heart. It's called developing disaster.[43]

If that's what you are doing—if you are a meditator who still doesn't know, who doesn't see, if you haven't renewed yourself yet—it's because you've been practicing wrongly. You haven't been following the teachings of the Buddha. The Buddha taught like this: "Ānanda, practice a lot! Develop your practice constantly. Then all your doubts, all your uncertainties, will vanish." Your doubts will never vanish through thinking, theorizing, speculating, or discussing. Nor will your doubts disappear by not doing anything. All defilements will vanish only through developing the heart, through right practice.

The way of developing the heart as taught by the Buddha is the exact opposite of the way of the world, because his teachings come from a pure heart. A pure heart, unattached to defilements, is the way of the Buddha and his disciples.

If you practice the Dhamma, you must bow your heart to the Dhamma. You must not make the Dhamma bow to you—when you practice like that, suffering arises. There isn't a single person who can escape this suffering. So when you commence your practice suffering is right there.

The duties of meditators are mindfulness, collectedness, and contentment. These things stop us. They stop the habits of the hearts of those who have never trained. And why should we bother to do this? If you don't train your heart, it remains wild; it follows the ways of nature. It's possible to train that nature so that it can be used to advantage. You can compare it to using a tree. If we just left trees in their natural state, then we would never be able to build a house with them. We couldn't make planks or anything of use in building a house. But if a carpenter wants to build a house, he will go looking for trees. He will take this raw material and use it to advantage. In a short time he will have a house built.

Meditation and developing the heart are similar to this. You must take this untrained heart, just as you would take a tree in the forest, and train it so that it is more refined, more aware of itself, more sensitive. Everything is in its natural state. When we understand nature, we can change it. We can detach from it and let go. Then we won't suffer anymore.

The nature of our heart is such that whenever it clings and grasps there is agitation and confusion. First it might wander over there, then it might wander over here. When we come to observe this agitation, we might think that it's impossible to train the heart, and so we suffer accordingly. We don't understand that this is the way the heart is. There will be thoughts and feelings moving about like this even though we are practicing, trying to attain peace. That's the way it is.

When we have contemplated the nature of the heart again and again, we will come to understand that this heart is just as it is and can't be otherwise. We will know that the heart's ways are just as they are. That's its nature. If we see this clearly, then we can detach from thoughts and feelings. And we don't have to add on anything more by constantly having to tell ourselves that "that's just the way it is." When the heart truly understands, it lets go of everything. Thinking and feeling will still be there, but that very thinking and feeling will be deprived of power.

This is similar to a child who likes to play and frolic in ways that annoy us, to the extent that we scold or spank them. We should understand that it's natural for a child to act that way. Then we can let go and leave them to play in their own way. So our troubles are over. How are they over? Because we accept the ways of children. Our outlook changes and we accept the true nature of things. We let go and our heart becomes more peaceful. We have Right Understanding.

If we have a wrong understanding, then even living in a deep, dark cave will be chaos; living high up in the mountains will also be chaos. The heart can only be at peace when there is Right Understanding. Then there are no more riddles to solve and no more problems arise.

This is the way it is. You detach. You let go. Whenever there is any feeling of clinging, we detach from it, because we know that that very feeling is just as it is. It didn't come along especially to annoy us. We might imagine that it does, but in fact that's just the way it is. If we start to think and consider it further, that, too, is just as it is. If we let go, then form is merely form, sound is merely sound, odor is merely odor, taste is merely taste, touch is merely touch, and the heart is merely the heart. It's similar to oil and water. If you put the two together in a bottle, they won't mix because of the difference of their nature.

Oil and water are different in the same way that a wise person and an ignorant person are different. The Buddha lived with form, sound, odor, taste, touch, and thought. He was an arahant, an Enlightened One, so he turned away from rather than toward these things. He turned away and detached, little by little, since he understood that the heart is just the heart and thought is just thought. He didn't confuse and mix them together.

The heart is just the heart; thoughts and feelings are just thoughts and feelings. Let things be just as they are. Let form be just form; let sound be just sound; let thought be just thought. Why should we bother to attach to them? If we think and feel in this way, then there is detachment and separateness. Our thoughts and feelings will be on one side and our heart will be on the other. Just like oil and water, they are in the same bottle but they are separate.

The Buddha and his enlightened disciples lived with ordinary, unenlightened people. They not only lived with these people, but they taught these ordinary, unenlightened, unaware ones how to be noble, enlightened, wise ones. They could do this because they knew how to practice. They knew that it's a matter of the heart, just as I have explained.

So, as far as your practice of meditation goes, don't go and cast doubt on it. If we run away from home to be ordained, we're not running away to get lost in delusion. Nor are we doing so out of cowardice or fear. We're running away in order to train ourselves, in order to master ourselves. If we understand this, then we can follow the Dhamma. The Dhamma will become clearer and clearer. Those who understand the Dhamma understand themselves, and those who understand themselves understand the Dhamma. Nowadays, only the sterile remains of the Dhamma have become the accepted order. In reality, the true Dhamma is everywhere. There is no need to escape to somewhere else. Instead escape through wisdom. Escape through intelligence. Escape through skill. Don't escape through ignorance. If you want peace, then let it be the peace of wisdom. That's enough.

Whenever we see the Dhamma, then there is the right way, the right path. Defilements are just defilements; the heart is just the heart. Whenever we detach and separate so that there are just these things as they really are, then they are merely objects to us. When we are on the right path, then we are impeccable. When we are impeccable, there is openness and freedom all the time.

The Buddha said, "Listen to me, monks. You must not cling to any dhammas." What are these dhammas? They are everything; there isn't anything that is not. Love and hate are dhammas, happiness and suffering are dhammas, like and dislike are dhammas; all of these things, no matter how insignificant, are dhammas. When we practice the Dhamma, when we understand, then we can let go. And thus we can comply with the Buddha's teaching of not clinging to any dhammas.

All conditions that are born in our heart, all conditions of our mind, all conditions of our body, are always in a state of change. The Buddha taught us not to cling to any of them. He taught his disciples to practice in order to detach from all conditions, and not to practice in order to acquire any more.

If we follow the teachings of the Buddha, then we are right. We are right, but it is also troublesome. It's not that the teachings are troublesome, but it's our defilements that are troublesome. Wrongly comprehended, our defilements obstruct us and cause us trouble. There isn't really anything troublesome with following the Buddha's teaching. In fact we can say that clinging to the Path of the Buddha doesn't bring suffering, because the Path is simply to let go of every single dhamma.

As the ultimate practice of Buddhist meditation, the Buddha taught *letting go*. Don't carry anything around. Detach. If you see goodness, let it go. If you see rightness, let it go. The words *let go* do not mean that we don't have to practice. It means that we have to practice following the method of letting go itself. The Buddha taught us to contemplate all dhammas, to develop the Path through contemplating our own body and heart. The Dhamma isn't anywhere else. It's right here. Not some place far away. It's right here in this very body and heart of ours.

Therefore a meditator must practice with energy. Make the heart grander and brighter. Make it free and independent. Having done a good deed, don't carry it around in your heart; let it go. Having refrained from doing an evil deed, let it go. The Buddha taught us to live in the immediacy of the present, in the here and now. Don't lose yourself in the past or the future.

The teaching that people least understand, and which conflicts most with their own opinions, is this teaching of letting go, or of working with an empty mind. This way of talking is called "Dhamma language." When we conceive this in worldly terms, we become confused and think that we can do anything we want. It can be interpreted this way, but its real meaning is closer to this: It's as if we are carrying a heavy rock—after a while we begin to feel its weight, but we don't know how to let it go. So we endure this heavy burden all the time. If someone tells us to throw it away, we say, "If I throw it away, I won't have anything left." If we hear of all the benefits to be gained from throwing it away, we don't believe them but keep thinking, "If I throw it away, I will have nothing." So we keep on carrying this heavy rock until we become so weak and exhausted that we can no longer endure. Then we drop it.

Having dropped it, we suddenly experience the benefits of letting go. We immediately feel better and lighter, and we know for ourselves how much of a burden carrying a rock can be. Before we let go of the rock, we couldn't possibly know the benefits of letting go. So if someone tells us to let go, an unenlightened person wouldn't see the point of it. They would just blindly clutch at the rock and refuse to let go until it became so unbearably heavy that they just had to let go. Then they could feel for themselves the lightness and relief and thus know the benefits of letting go. Later on we may start carrying burdens again, but now we know what the results will be, so we can let go more easily. This understanding, that it's useless to carry burdens around and that letting go brings ease and lightness, is an example of knowing ourselves.

Our pride, our sense of self that we depend on, is the same as that heavy rock. When we imagine letting go of self-conceit, we become fearful that without it there would be nothing left. But if we can finally let it go, we'll realize for ourselves the ease and comfort of not clinging.

In the training of the heart, you mustn't cling to either praise or blame. To want just praise and not blame is the way of the world. The way of the Buddha is to accept praise when it is appropriate and to accept blame when it is appropriate. For example, in raising a child it is very good not to scold all the time. Some people scold too much. A wise person knows the proper time to scold and the proper time to praise. Our heart is the same. Use intelligence to know the heart. Use skill in taking care of your heart. Then you will be one who is clever in the training of the heart. And when the heart is skilled, it can rid us of our suffering. Suffering exists right here in our hearts. It's always complicating things, making the heart heavy. It's born here. It also dies here.

The way of the heart is like this. Sometimes there are good thoughts, sometimes bad thoughts. The heart is deceitful. Don't trust it! Instead look straight at the conditions of the heart itself. Accept them as they are. They're just as they are. Whether it's good or evil or whatever, that's the way it is. If you don't grab hold of these conditions, then they don't become anything more or less than what they already are. If we grab hold, we'll get bitten and will suffer.

With Right Understanding there's only peace. Samādhi is born and wisdom takes over. Wherever you sit or lie down, there is peace. There is peace everywhere, no matter where you may go.

So today you listen to the Dhamma. Some of it you may understand; some of it you may not. In order for you to understand more easily, I've talked about the practice of meditation. Whether you think it is right or not, you should take it and contemplate it.

As a teacher myself, I've been in a similar predicament. I, too, have longed to listen to Dhamma talks because, wherever I went, I was always giving talks to others but never had a chance to listen. So you really appreciate listening to a talk from a teacher. Time passes by so quickly when you're sitting and listening quietly. You're hungry for Dhamma, so you really want to listen. At first, giving talks to others is a pleasure, but after a while the pleasure goes. You feel bored and tired. Then you want to listen. So when you listen to a talk from a teacher, you feel much inspiration and you understand easily. When you're getting old and there's hunger for Dhamma, its flavor is especially delicious.

Being a teacher of others, you are an example to them; you're a model for other bhikkhus. You're an example to everybody, so don't forget yourself. But don't think about yourself either. If such thoughts do arise, get rid of them. If you do this, you will be one who knows yourself.

There are a million ways to practice Dhamma. There's no end to the things that can be said about meditation. There are so many things that can make us doubt. Just keep sweeping them out; then there's no more doubt! When we have Right Understanding like this, no matter where we sit or walk, there is peace and ease. Wherever we may meditate, that's the place you bring your awareness. Don't hold that one meditates only while sitting or walking. Everything and everywhere is our practice. There's awareness all the time. There is mindfulness all the time. We can see the birth and death of mind and body all the time. Don't let it clutter your heart. Let it go constantly. If love comes, let it go back to its home. If greed comes, let it go home. If anger comes, let it go home. Where do they live? Find out, and then escort them there. Don't keep anything. If you practice like this then you are like an empty house. Or, put another way, this is an empty heart, a heart empty and free of all evil. We call it an "empty heart"; but it isn't empty as if there was nothing; it's empty of evil but filled with wisdom. Then whatever you do, you'll do with wisdom. You'll think with wisdom. You'll eat with wisdom. There will only be wisdom.

This is the teaching for today and I offer it to you. It was recorded on tape. If listening to Dhamma makes your heart at peace, that's good enough. You don't need to remember anything. Some may not believe this. If we make our heart peaceful and just listen, letting it pass by but contemplating continuously like this, then we're like a tape recorder. When we turn it on sometime later, everything is still there. Have no fear that there won't be anything. As soon as you turn on your tape recorder, everything is there.

I wish to offer this to every bhikkhu and to everyone. Some of you probably know only a little Thai, but that doesn't matter. May you learn the language of the Dhamma. That's good enough!

CHAPTER 15

READING
THE NATURAL MIND

O̲UR WAY OF PRACTICE involves looking closely at things and making them clear. We're persistent and constant, yet not rushed or hurried. Neither are we too slow. It's a matter of gradually feeling our way and bringing things together. All this bringing together leads toward something, however. There is a point to our practice.

For most of us, when we first start to practice, there's just nothing other than desire. We start to practice because of wanting. At this stage our wanting is wanting in the wrong way. That is, it's deluded. It's wanting mixed with wrong understanding.

If wanting is not mixed with wrong understanding like this, we say that it's wanting with wisdom. It's not deluded—it's wanting with Right Understanding. In a case like this we say that it's due to a person's *pāramis*,[44] or past accumulations of spiritual qualities. This isn't the case with everyone, however.

Some people don't want to have desires, or they want not to have desires, because they think that our practice is directed at not wanting. But if there is no desire, then there's no way of practice.

We can see this for ourselves. The Buddha and all his disciples practiced to put an end to defilements. We must want to practice and must want to put an end to defilements. We must want to have peace of mind and want not to have confusion. If this wanting is mixed with wrong understanding, however, then it will only create more difficulties for us. If we are honest about it, we really know nothing at all. Or, what we do know is of no consequence, since we are unable to use it properly.

Everybody, including the Buddha, started out like this, with the desire to practice—wanting to have peace of mind and wanting not to have confusion and suffering. These two kinds of desire have exactly the same value. If not understood, then both wanting to be free from confusion and not wanting to have suffering are defilements. They're a foolish way of wanting—desire without wisdom.

In our practice we see this desire as either sensual indulgence or self-mortification. It's in this very conflict, just this dilemma, that our teacher, the Buddha, was caught. He followed many methods of practice that merely ended up in these two extremes. And these days we are exactly the same. We are still afflicted by this duality, and because of it we keep falling from the Way.

However, this is how we must start out. We start out as worldly beings, as beings with defilements, with wanting devoid of wisdom, desire without Right Understanding. If we lack proper understanding, then both kinds of desire work against us. Whether it's wanting or not wanting, it's still craving (taṇhā). If we don't understand these two things, we won't know how to deal with them when they arise. We will feel that to go forward is wrong and to go backward is wrong, and yet we can't stop. Whatever we do we just find more wanting. This is because of the lack of wisdom and because of craving.

It's right here, with this wanting and not wanting, that we can understand the Dhamma. The Dhamma for which we are looking exists right here, but we don't see it. Rather, we persist in our efforts to stop wanting. We want things to be a certain way and not any other way. Or we want them not to be a certain way but to be another way. Really these two things are the same. They are part of the same duality.

Perhaps we may not realize that the Buddha and all of his disciples had this kind of wanting. The Buddha, however, reached an understanding of wanting and not wanting. He understood that they are simply the activity of mind, that such things merely appear in a flash and then disappear. These kinds of desires are going on all the time. When there is wisdom, we don't identify with them—we are free from clinging. Whether it's wanting or not wanting, we simply see it as such, as merely the activity of the natural mind. When we take a close look, we see clearly that this is how it is.

THE WISDOM OF EVERYDAY EXPERIENCE

So it's here that our practice of contemplation will lead us to understanding. Let us take an example, the example of a fisherman pulling in his net with a big fish in it. How do you think he feels about pulling it in? If he's afraid that the fish will escape, he'll be rushed and start to struggle with the net, grabbing and tugging at it. Before he knows it, the big fish has escaped—he was trying too hard.

In the olden days they would talk like this. They taught that we should do it gradually, carefully gathering it in without losing it. This is how it is in our practice; we gradually feel our way with it, carefully gathering it in without losing it. Sometimes it happens that we don't feel like doing it. Maybe we don't want to look or maybe we don't want to know, but we keep on with it. We continue feeling for it. This is practice: if we feel like doing it, we do it, and if we don't feel like doing it, we do it just the same. We just keep on doing it.

If we are enthusiastic about our practice, the power of our faith will give energy to what we are doing. But at this stage we are still without wisdom. Even though we are very energetic, we will not derive much benefit from our practice. We may continue with it for a long time, and a feeling will arise that we aren't going to find the way. We may feel that we cannot find peace and tranquillity, or that we aren't sufficiently equipped to do the practice. Or maybe we feel that this Way just isn't possible anymore. So we give up.

At this point we must be very, very careful. We must use great patience and endurance. It's just like pulling in the big fish—we gradually feel our way with it. We carefully pull it in. The struggle won't be too difficult; so without stopping we continue pulling it in. Eventually, after some time, the fish becomes tired and stops fighting and we're able to catch it easily. Usually this is how it happens; we practice gradually gathering it together.

This is how we do our contemplation. If we don't have any particular knowledge or learning in the theoretical aspects of the teaching, we contemplate according to our everyday experience. We use the knowledge we already have, the knowledge derived from our everyday experience. This kind of knowledge is natural to the mind. Actually, whether we study about it or not, we have the reality of the mind right here already. The mind is the mind whether we have learned about it or not. This is why we say that whether the Buddha is born in the world or not, everything is the way it is. Everything already exists according to its own nature. This natural condition doesn't change, nor does it go anywhere. It just is that way. This is the *sacca-dhamma,* or the truth. If we don't understand about this sacca-dhamma, however, we won't be able to recognize it.

CONSTANT EFFORT

Until we are able to stop our mind, until we reach tranquillity, the mind will just continue as before. It's for this reason that the teacher says, "Just keep on doing it, keep on with the practice." Maybe we think, "If I don't yet understand, how can I do it?" But until we are able to practice properly, wisdom doesn't arise. So we say, "Just keep on with it." If we practice without stopping, we'll begin to think about what we are doing. We'll start to consider our practice.

Nothing happens immediately, so in the beginning we can't see any results from our practice. This is like the example of the man who tries to make fire by rubbing two sticks of wood together. He says to himself, "They say there's fire here," and he begins rubbing energetically. He's very impetuous. He rubs on and on but he's very impatient. He wants to have that fire, but the fire doesn't come. So he gets discouraged and stops to rest for a while. Then he starts again, but the going is slow, so he rests again. By then the heat has disappeared; he didn't keep at it long enough. He rubs and rubs until he tires and then he stops altogether. Not only is he tired, but he becomes more and more discouraged until he gives up completely, "There's no fire here." Actually, he was doing the work, but there wasn't enough heat to start a fire. The fire was there all the time, but he didn't carry on to the end.

This sort of experience causes meditators to get discouraged in their practice, and so they restlessly change from one practice to another. It's the same for everybody. Why? Because we are still grounded in defilements. The Buddha had defilements too, but he had a lot of wisdom. When they were still worldlings, the Buddha and the arahants were just the same as us. If we are worldlings, we don't think rightly. When wanting arises, we don't see it, and when not wanting arises, we don't see it. Sometimes we feel stirred up, and sometimes we feel contented. When we have not-wanting, we have a kind of contentment, but we also have a kind of confusion. When we have wanting, this can be contentment and confusion of another kind. It's all intermixed in this way.

KNOWING ONESELF AND KNOWING OTHERS

The Buddha taught us to contemplate our body. For example: hair of the head, hair of the body, nails, teeth, skin—it's all body. Take a look. We are told to investigate right here. If we don't see these things clearly as they are in ourselves, we won't have any understanding about other people. We won't see others clearly, nor will we see ourselves. If we do understand and see clearly the nature of our own bodies, however, our doubts and wonderings regarding others will disappear. This is because body and mind are the same for everybody. It isn't necessary to go and examine all the bodies in the world, since we know that they are the same as us. If we have this kind of understanding then our burden becomes lighter. Without this kind of understanding, all we do is develop a heavier burden.

Our vinaya, our code of monks' discipline, is similar to this. When we look at our vinaya, we feel that it's very difficult. We must keep every rule, study every rule, review our practice with every rule. We may think, "Oh, it's impossible!" We read the literal meaning of all the numerous rules and, if we merely follow our thinking, we could well decide that it's beyond our ability to keep them all. There are a lot of rules.

The scriptures tell us that we must examine ourselves regarding each and every rule and keep them all strictly. We must know them all and observe them perfectly. This is the same as saying that to understand about others we must go and examine absolutely everybody. This is a very heavy attitude. And it's heavy because we take what is said literally. If we follow the textbooks, this is the way we must go. Some teachers teach in this manner— strict adherence to what the textbooks say. It just can't work that way. If we know how to guard our own minds, then it is the same as observing all of the numerous rules of the vinaya.

Actually, if we study theory like this, our practice won't develop at all. Our faith in the Way will disappear. This is because we haven't yet understood. When there is wisdom we will understand that all the people in the entire world really amount to just this one person. They are the same as this very being. So we study and contemplate our own body and mind. With the seeing and understanding of the nature of our body and mind comes an understanding of the bodies and minds of everyone. And so, in this way, our practice becomes lighter.

The Buddha said we must teach and instruct ourselves—nobody else can do it for us. When we study and understand the nature of our own existence, we will understand the nature of all existence. Everyone is really the same. We are all the same "make" and come from the same company—our skins are just different shades, that's all! Just like two brands of painkiller: both do the same thing, but one brand is called one thing, and the other, something else. But really, there's no difference.

You will find that this way of seeing things gets easier and easier as you gradually bring it all together. We call this "feeling our way," and this is how we begin to practice. We become skilled at doing it. We keep on with it until we arrive at understanding, and when this understanding arises, we see reality clearly.

THEORY AND PRACTICE

So we continue this practice until we have a feeling for it. After a time, depending on our particular tendencies and abilities, a new kind of understanding arises. This we call investigation of Dhamma (Dhamma-vicaya), and this is how the seven Factors of Enlightenment arise in the mind. Investigation of Dhamma is one of them. The others are mindfulness, energy, rapture, tranquillity, concentration, and equanimity.

If we have studied about the seven Factors of Enlightenment, then we'll know what the books say, but we won't have seen the real Factors of Enlightenment. The real Factors of Enlightenment arise in the mind. Thus the Buddha came to give us all the various teachings. All the Enlightened Ones have taught the way out of suffering, and their recorded teachings we call the theoretical teachings. This theory originally came from the practice, but it has become merely book learning or words.

The real Factors of Enlightenment have disappeared because we don't know them within ourselves; we don't see them within our own minds. If they arise, they arise out of practice and lead to insight into the Dhamma.

This means that we can use their arising as an indication that our practice is correct. If we are not practicing rightly, such things will not appear.

If we practice in the right way, then we can see Dhamma. So we say to keep on practicing, feeling your way gradually and continually investigating. Don't think that what you are looking for can be found anywhere other than right here. One of my senior disciples had been learning Pali at a study temple before he came here. He hadn't been very successful with his studies, so he thought that, since monks who practice meditation are able to see and understand everything just by sitting, he would come and try this way. He came here to Wat Pah Pong with the intention of sitting in meditation so he would be able to translate Pali scriptures. That was his understanding of the practice. So I explained to him about our way. He had misunderstood completely. He had thought it an easy matter just to sit and make everything clear.

When they talk about understanding Dhamma, both study monks and practice monks use the same words. But the actual understanding that comes from studying theory and that which comes from practicing Dhamma are not quite the same. The two may seem to be the same, but one is more profound, deeper. The kind of understanding that comes from practice leads to surrender, to giving up. Until there is complete surrender we persevere—we persist in our contemplation. If desires or anger and dislike arise in our mind, we aren't indifferent to them. We don't just leave them but rather take them and investigate to see how and from where they arise. If such moods are already in our mind, then we contemplate and see how they work against us. We see them clearly and understand the difficulties that we cause ourselves by believing and following them. This kind of understanding is not found anywhere other than in our own pure mind.

It's because of this that those who study theory and those who practice meditation misunderstand each other. Usually those who emphasize study say things like "Monks who only practice meditation just follow their own opinions. They have no basis for their teaching." Actually, in a sense, these ways of study and practice are exactly the same thing. They are like the front and back of our hand. If we put our hand out, it seems as if the back of the hand has disappeared. But it's just hidden underneath. When we turn our hand over, the same thing happens to the palm of the hand. It doesn't go anywhere; it's merely hidden underneath.

We should keep this in mind when we consider practice. If we think that our practice has disappeared, we'll decide to go off and study in hopes of getting results. But it doesn't matter how much you study about Dhamma, you'll never understand, because you won't know in accordance with truth. If we do understand the real nature of Dhamma, then it becomes letting go. This is surrender—removing attachment, not clinging anymore. Or if there's still clinging, it becomes less and less.

When we talk about study, we can understand it like this: our eye is a subject of study, our ear is a subject of study—everything is a subject of study. We may know that form is like this or like that, but we become attached to form and don't know the way out. We can distinguish sounds, but then we get attached to them. Forms, sounds, smells, tastes, bodily feelings, and mental impressions are like snares that entrap all beings.

Investigating these things is our way of practicing Dhamma. When a feeling arises we turn to our understanding to appreciate it. If we are knowledgeable regarding theory, we will immediately turn to that and see how such and such a thing happens like this and then becomes that, and so on. If we haven't learned theory in this way, then we have just the natural state of our mind to work with. This is our Dhamma. If we have wisdom then we'll be able to examine this natural mind of ours and use this as our subject of study. It's exactly the same thing. Our natural mind is theory. The Buddha said to take whatever thoughts and feelings arise and investigate them. Use the reality of our natural mind as our theory. We rely on this reality.

INSIGHT MEDITATION (VIPASSANĀ)

If you have faith it doesn't matter whether you have studied theory or not. If our believing mind leads us to develop practice, if it leads us to constantly develop energy and patience, then study doesn't matter. We have mindfulness as a foundation for our practice. We are mindful in all bodily postures, whether sitting, standing, walking, or lying down. And if there is mindfulness there will be clear comprehension to accompany it. Mindfulness and clear comprehension will arise together. They may arise so rapidly, however, that we can't tell them apart. But, when there is mindfulness, there will also be clear comprehension.

When our mind is firm and stable, mindfulness will arise quickly and easily, and this is also where we have wisdom. Sometimes, though, wisdom is insufficient or doesn't arise at the right time. There may be mindfulness and clear comprehension, but these alone are not enough to deal with the situation. Generally, if mindfulness and clear comprehension are a foundation of mind, then wisdom will be there to assist. However, we must constantly develop this wisdom through the practice of insight meditation. This means that whatever arises in the mind can be the object of mindfulness and clear comprehension. But we must see according to anicca, dukkha, and anattā. *Anicca* is the basis. *Dukkha* refers to the quality of unsatisfactoriness, and *anattā* says that the object is not an individual entity. We see that it's simply a sensation that has arisen, that it has no self, that it is not an entity, and that it disappears of its own accord. Just that! Someone who is deluded, someone who doesn't have wisdom, will miss this occasion. They won't be able to use these things to advantage.

If wisdom is present then mindfulness and clear comprehension will be right there with it. At this initial stage, however, the wisdom may not be perfectly clear. Thus mindfulness and clear comprehension aren't able to catch every object, but wisdom comes to help. It can see what quality of mindfulness there is and what kind of sensation has arisen. Or, in its most general aspect, whatever mindfulness there is or whatever sensation there is, it's all Dhamma.

The Buddha took the practice of insight meditation as his foundation. He saw that this mindfulness and clear comprehension were both uncertain and unstable. Anything that's unstable, and that we want to be stable, causes us to suffer. We want things to be according to our desires, but we suffer because things just aren't that way. This is the influence of a tainted mind, the influence of a mind that is lacking wisdom.

When we practice we tend to become caught up in wanting it easy, wanting it to be the way we like. We don't have to go very far to understand about such an attitude. Merely look at this body. Is it ever really the way we want it? One minute we want it to be one way and the next minute we want it to be another way. Have we ever really had it the way we liked? The nature of our bodies and minds is exactly the same. It simply is the way it is.

This point in our practice can be easily missed. Usually, whatever we feel doesn't agree with us, we throw out; whatever doesn't please us, we get rid of. We don't stop to think whether the way we like and dislike things is really the correct way or not. We merely think that the things we find disagreeable must be wrong, and those that we find agreeable must be right.

This is where craving comes from. When we receive stimuli by way of eye, ear, nose, tongue, body, or mind, a feeling of liking or disliking arises. This shows that the mind is full of attachment. So the Buddha gave us this teaching of impermanence. He gave us a way to contemplate things. If we cling to something that isn't permanent, then we'll experience suffering. There's no reason why we should want to have these things in accordance with our likes and dislikes. It isn't possible for us to make things be that way. We don't have that kind of authority or power. Regardless of how we want things to be, everything is already the way it is. Wanting like this is not the way out of suffering.

Here we can see how the mind that is deluded understands one way, and the mind that is not deluded understands another way. When the mind with wisdom receives some sensation, for example, it sees it as something not to be clung to or identified with. This is what indicates wisdom. If there isn't any wisdom then we merely follow our stupidity. This stupidity is not seeing impermanence, unsatisfactoriness, and not-self. That which we like we see as good and right. That which we don't like we see as not good. We can't arrive at Dhamma this way—wisdom cannot arise.

The Buddha firmly established the practice of insight meditation in his mind and used it to investigate all the various mental impressions. Whatever arose in his mind he investigated like this: even though we like it, it's uncertain. And it's unsatisfactory, because these things which are constantly rising and falling don't follow the influence of our minds. All these things are not a being or a self; they don't belong to us. The Buddha taught us to see them just as they are. It is this principle on which we stand in practice.

We understand, then, that we aren't able to just bring about various moods as we wish. Both good moods and bad moods are going to come up. Some of them are helpful and some of them are not. If we don't understand these things rightly, we won't be able to judge correctly. Instead we will go running after craving—running off following our desires.

Sometimes we feel happy and sometimes we feel sad, but this is natural. Sometimes we'll feel pleased and at other times disappointed. What we like we hold as good, and what we don't like we hold as bad. In this way we separate ourselves further and further from Dhamma. When this happens, we aren't able to understand or recognize Dhamma, and thus we are confused. Desires increase because our minds have nothing but delusion.

This is how we talk about the mind. It isn't necessary to go far away from ourselves to find understanding. We simply see that these states of mind aren't permanent. We see that they are unsatisfactory and that they aren't a permanent self. If we continue to develop our practice in this way, we call it the practice of vipassanā, or insight meditation. We say that it is recognizing the contents of our mind, and in this way we develop wisdom.

SAMATHA MEDITATION

Our practice of *samatha* (calm) is like this: We establish the practice of mindfulness on the in- and out-breath, for example, as a foundation or means of steadying the mind. By having the mind follow the flow of the breath it becomes steadfast, calm and still. This practice of calming the mind is called samatha meditation. We need to do a lot of this practice because the mind is full of many disturbances. It's very confused. We can't say how many years or how many lives it's been this way. If we sit and contemplate, we'll see that there's a lot that doesn't conduce to peace and calm and a lot that leads to confusion.

The Buddha taught that we must find a meditation subject that is suitable to our particular tendencies, a way of practice that is right for our character. For example, going over and over the parts of the body—hair of the head, hair of the body, nails, teeth, and skin—can be very calming. The mind can become very peaceful from this practice. If contemplating these five things leads to calm, it's because they are appropriate objects for contemplation according to our tendencies. Whatever we find to be appropriate in this way, we can consider to be our practice and use it to subdue the defilements.

Another example is recollection of death. For those who still have strong greed, aversion, and delusion and find them difficult to contain, it's useful to take one's own death as a meditation subject. We'll come to see that everybody, whether rich or poor, good or evil, has to die. Developing this practice we find that an attitude of dispassion arises. The more we practice, the more calm our sitting produces. This is because it's a suitable and appropriate practice for us. But if this practice of calm meditation isn't agreeable to our particular tendencies, it won't produce this attitude of dispassion. Only if the object is truly suited to us will we find it arising regularly, without great difficulty, and find ourselves thinking about it often.

We can see an example in our everyday lives. When lay people bring trays of many different types of food to offer us monks, we taste them to see which we like. When we've tried each one we can tell which is most agreeable to us. This is just an example. That which we find agreeable to our taste, we'll eat; we won't bother with the other dishes.

The practice of concentrating our attention on the in- and out-breath is an example of a type of meditation that is suitable for us all. It seems that when we go around doing various different practices, we don't feel so good. But as soon as we sit and observe our breath, we have a good feeling; we can see it clearly. There's no need to go looking far away; we can use what is close to us. Just watch the breath. It goes out and comes in, out and in— we watch it like this. For a long time we keep watching our breathing in and out and slowly our mind settles. Other activity will arise but we feel like it is distant from us. Just like when we live apart from each other and don't feel so close anymore. We don't have the same strong contact anymore or perhaps no contact at all.

When we have a feeling for this practice of mindfulness of breathing, it becomes easier. If we keep on with this practice we gain experience and become skilled at knowing the nature of the breath. We'll know what it's like when it's long and what it's like when it's short.

Looking at it one way, the breath is like food. If we think about it we see that we exist only with the help of food. If we don't eat ordinary food for ten minutes, an hour, or even a day, it doesn't matter. So this is a coarse kind of food. But if we don't breathe for even a short time, we'll die. While sitting or walking we breathe, while sleeping we breathe, while awake we breathe. If we don't breathe for five or ten minutes we would be dead.

One who is practicing mindfulness of breathing should have this kind of understanding. The knowledge that comes from this practice is indeed wonderful. If we don't contemplate then we won't see the breath as food, but actually we are "eating" air all the time—in, out, in, out…all the time. Also you'll find that the more you contemplate in this way, the greater the benefits derived from the practice and the more delicate the breath becomes. It may even happen that the breath stops. It appears as if we aren't breathing at all. Actually, the breath is passing through the pores of the skin. This is called the "delicate breath." When our mind is perfectly calm, normal breathing can cease in this way. We need not be at all startled or afraid. If there's no breathing, what should we do? Just know it. Know that there is no breathing, that's all. This is the right practice.

Here we are talking about the way of samatha practice, the practice of developing calm. There is enough in this practice to take us all the way, or at least to where we can see our way clearly and proceed with strong faith. If we keep on with contemplation in this manner, energy will come to us. It's like water in an urn. We pour in water and keep it topped up. We keep on filling the urn with water, and thereby the insects living in the water don't die. Making effort and doing our everyday practice is just like this. It all comes back to practice. We feel very good and peaceful.

This peacefulness comes from our one-pointed state of mind. This one-pointedness can be very troublesome, however, since we don't want other mental states to disturb us. Actually, other mental states do come, and if we think about it, that in itself can be the one-pointed state of mind. It's like when we see various men and women, but we don't have the same feeling about them as we do about our mother and father. In reality all men are males just like our father and all women are females just like our mother, but we don't have the same feeling about them. We feel that our parents are more important. They hold greater value for us.

This is how it should be with our one-pointed state of mind. We should have the same attitude toward it as we would have toward our own mother and father. All other activities that arise we appreciate in much the same way that we feel about men and women in general. We don't stop seeing them; we simply acknowledge their presence and don't ascribe to them the same value as our parents.

UNTYING THE KNOT

When our practice of samatha arrives at calm, the mind will be clear and bright. There will be less mental activity; fewer impressions will arise. When this happens great peace and happiness may arise. But we may attach to that happiness, so we should contemplate that happiness as uncertain. We should also contemplate unhappiness as impermanent. We'll understand that all the various feelings are not lasting and not to be clung to. We'll see things thus if there's wisdom. We'll understand that things are this way according to their nature.

It's like taking hold of a strand of knotted rope. If we pull it in the right direction, the knot will loosen and begin to untangle. It'll no longer be so tight or so tense. This is similar to understanding that it doesn't always have to be this way. Before, we felt that things would always be the way they were and, in so doing, we pulled the knot even tighter. This tightness is suffering. Living that way is very tense. So we loosen the knot a little and relax. Why do we loosen it? Because it's tight! If we don't cling to it then we can loosen it. Tightness is not a permanent condition.

We use the teaching of impermanence as our basis. We see that both happiness and unhappiness are impermanent. We see them as undependable. There is absolutely nothing that's permanent. With this kind of understanding we gradually stop believing in our various moods and feelings. Wrong understanding will decrease to the same degree that we stop believing in it. This is what is meant by untying the knot. It continues to loosen. Attachment will be gradually uprooted.

DISENCHANTMENT

When we come to see impermanence, unsatisfactoriness, and not-self in ourselves, in this body and mind, in this world, then we'll find that a kind of boredom will arise. This isn't the everyday boredom that makes us feel like not wanting to know or see or say anything, or not wanting to have anything to do with anybody at all. That isn't real boredom; it still has attachment; we still don't understand. We still have feelings of envy and resentment and are still clinging to the things that cause us suffering.

The boredom, or world-weariness, that the Buddha talked about is without aversion or attraction. It arises out of seeing everything as impermanent. When pleasant feeling arises in our mind, we see that it isn't lasting. This is the kind of boredom we have. We call it *nibbidā*, or disenchantment. It's the opposite of sensual craving and passion. We see nothing as being worthy of desire. Whether or not things accord with our likes and dislikes, it doesn't matter to us. We don't identify with them or give them any special value.

Practicing like this, we don't give things reason to cause us difficulty. We've seen that identifying with moods cannot give rise to any real happiness: clinging to happiness and unhappiness, and to liking and disliking, causes suffering. If we are still clinging like this, we don't have an even-minded attitude toward things. Such attachment causes suffering. As the Buddha taught, whatever causes suffering is in itself unsatisfactory.

THE FOUR NOBLE TRUTHS

Hence we understand that the Buddha teaches us to know four things: suffering, the cause of suffering, freedom from suffering, and the practice leading to freedom. He taught us to know just these four things. When we understand them, we'll be able to recognize suffering when it arises and will know that it has a cause. We'll know that it didn't just drift in. When we wish to be free from this suffering, we'll be able to eliminate its cause.

Why do we have this feeling of suffering, this feeling of unsatisfactoriness? We'll see that it's because we are clinging to our various likes and dislikes. We come to know that we are suffering because of our own actions. We suffer because we ascribe value to things. So we say, "Know suffering, know the cause of suffering, know freedom from suffering, and know the Way to this freedom." When we know about suffering, we untangle the knot. But we must be sure to untangle it by pulling in the right direction. That is to say, we must know that this is how things are. Attachment will be uprooted. This is the practice that puts an end to our suffering.

Know suffering, know the cause of suffering, know freedom from suffering, and know the Path (magga) that leads out of suffering. The Path goes like this: Right View, Right Intention, Right Speech, Right Action, Right Livelihood, Right Effort, Right Mindfulness, Right Concentration. When we have the Right Understanding regarding these things, then we have the Path. These things can put an end to suffering. They lead us to morality, concentration, and wisdom.

We must clearly understand these four things. We must want to understand. We must want to see these things in terms of reality. When we see these four things we call this sacca-dhamma, or truth. Whether we look inside or in front, or to the right or left, all we see is sacca-dhamma. We simply see that everything is the way it is. For someone who has arrived at

Dhamma, someone who really understands Dhamma, wherever they go, everything will be Dhamma.

CHAPTER 16

THE KEY TO LIBERATION

The whole reason for studying the Dhamma, the teachings of the Buddha, is to search for a way to transcend suffering and attain peace and happiness. Whether we study physical or mental phenomena, the mind *(citta)* or its psychological factors *(cetasikas)*, it's only when we make liberation from suffering our ultimate goal that we're on the right path: nothing less. Suffering has a cause and conditions for its existence.

Please clearly understand that when the mind is still, it's in its natural, unadulterated state. As soon as the mind moves, it becomes conditioned *(saṅkhāra)*. When the mind is attracted to something, it becomes conditioned. When aversion arises, it becomes conditioned. The desire to move here and there arises from conditioning. If our awareness doesn't keep pace with these mental proliferations as they occur, the mind will chase after them and be conditioned by them. Whenever the mind moves, at that moment, it becomes a conventional reality.

So the Buddha taught us to contemplate these wavering conditions of the mind. Whenever the mind moves, it becomes unstable and impermanent (anicca), and unsatisfactory (dukkha) and cannot be taken as a self (anattā). These are the three universal characteristics of all conditioned phenomena. The Buddha taught us to observe and contemplate these movements of the mind.

It's likewise with the teaching of dependent origination *(paṭicca-samuppāda)*: deluded understanding *(avijjā)* is the cause and condition for the arising of volitional kammic formations (saṅkhāra); which is the cause and condition for the arising of consciousness *(viññāna)*, which is the cause and condition for the arising of mentality and materiality *(nāma-rūpa)*, and so on, just as we've studied in the scriptures. The Buddha separated each link of the chain to make it easier to study. This is an accurate description of reality, but when this process actually occurs in real life the scholars aren't able to keep up with what's happening. It's like falling from the top of a tree to come crashing down to the ground below. We have no idea how many branches we've passed on the way down. Similarly, when the mind is suddenly hit by a mental impression, if it delights in it, then it flies off into a good mood. It considers it good without being aware of the chain of conditions that led there. The process takes place in accordance with what is outlined in the theory, but simultaneously it goes beyond the limits of that theory.

There's nothing that announces, "This is delusion. This is volitional kammic formations, and that is consciousness." The process doesn't give the scholars a chance to read out the list as it's happening. Although the Buddha analyzed and explained the sequence of mind moments in minute detail, to me it's more like falling out of a tree. As we come crashing down there's no opportunity to estimate how many feet and inches we've fallen. What we do know is that we've hit the ground with a thud and it hurts!

The mind is the same. When it falls for something, what we're aware of is the pain. Where has all this suffering, pain, grief, and despair come from? It didn't come from theory in a book. There isn't anywhere where the details of our suffering are written down. Our pain won't correspond exactly with the theory, but the two travel along the same road. So scholarship alone can't keep pace with the reality. That's why the Buddha taught to cultivate clear knowing for ourselves. Whatever arises, arises in this knowing. When that which knows, knows in accordance with the truth, then the mind and its psychological factors are recognized as not ours. Ultimately all these phenomena are to be discarded and thrown away as if they were rubbish. We shouldn't cling or give them any meaning.

THEORY AND REALITY

The Buddha did not teach about the mind and its psychological factors so that we'd get attached to the concepts. His sole intention was that we would recognize them as impermanent, unsatisfactory, and not-self. Then let go.

Lay them aside. Be aware and know them as they arise. This mind has already been conditioned. It's been trained and conditioned to turn away and spin out from a state of pure awareness. As it spins it creates conditioned phenomena that further influence the mind, and the proliferation carries on. The process gives birth to the good, the evil, and everything else under the sun. The Buddha taught to abandon it all. Initially, however, you have to familiarize yourself with the theory in order that you'll be able to abandon it all at the later stage. This is a natural process. The mind is just this way. Psychological factors are just this way.

Take the Noble Eightfold Path, for example. When wisdom (paññā) views things correctly with insight, this Right View then leads to Right Intention, Right Speech, Right Action, and so on. This all involves psychological conditions that have arisen from that pure knowing awareness. This knowing is like a lantern shedding light on the path ahead on a dark night. If the knowing is right, is in accordance with truth, it will pervade and illuminate each of the other steps on the path in turn.

Whatever we experience, it all arises from within this knowing. If this mind did not exist, the knowing would not exist either. All this is phenomena of the mind. As the Buddha said, the mind is merely the mind. It's not a being, a person, a self, or yourself. It's neither us nor them. The Dhamma is simply the Dhamma. This natural process is not oneself. It does not belong to us or anyone else. It's not any thing. Whatever an individual experiences it all falls within five fundamental categories (khandhas): body, feeling, memory/perception, thoughts, and consciousness. The Buddha said to let it all go.

Meditation is like a single stick of wood. Insight *(vipassanā)* is one end of the stick and serenity *(samatha)* the other. If we pick it up, does only one end come up or do both? When anyone picks up a stick both ends rise together. Which part then is vipassanā, and which is samatha? Where does one end and the other begin? They are both the mind. As the mind becomes peaceful, initially the peace will arise from the serenity of samatha. We focus and unify the mind in states of meditative peace *(samādhi)*. However, if the peace and stillness of samādhi fades away, suffering arises in its place. Why is that? Because the peace afforded by samatha meditation alone is still based on attachment. This attachment can then be a cause of suffering. Serenity is not the end of the Path. The Buddha saw from his own experience that such peace of mind was not the ultimate. The causes underlying the process of existence had not yet been brought to cessation. The conditions for rebirth still existed. His spiritual work had not yet attained perfection. Why? Because there was still suffering. So based on that serenity of samatha he proceeded to contemplate, investigate, and analyze the conditioned nature of reality until he was free of all attachments, even the attachment to serenity. Serenity is still part of the world of conditioned existence and conventional reality. Clinging to this type of peace is clinging to conventional reality, and as long as we cling, we will be mired in existence and rebirth. Delighting in the peace of samatha still leads to further existence and rebirth. Once the mind's restlessness and agitation calms down, one clings to the resultant peace.

So the Buddha examined the causes and conditions underlying existence and rebirth. As long as he had not yet fully penetrated the matter and understood the truth, he continued to probe deeper and deeper with a peaceful mind, reflecting on how all things, peaceful or not, come into existence. His investigation forged ahead until it was clear to him that everything that comes into existence is like a lump of red-hot iron. The five categories of a being's experience are all a lump of red-hot iron. When a lump of iron is glowing red hot, is there anywhere it can be touched without getting burnt? Is there anywhere at all that is cool? Try touching it on the top, the sides, or underneath. Is there a single spot that can be found that's cool? Impossible. This searing lump of iron is entirely red-hot. We can't even attach to serenity. If we identify with that peace, assuming that there is someone who is calm and serene, this reinforces the sense that there is an independent self or soul. This sense of self is part of conventional reality. Thinking, "I'm peaceful," "I'm agitated," "I'm good," "I'm bad," "I'm happy," or "I'm unhappy," we are caught in more existence and birth. It's more suffering. If our happiness vanishes, then we're unhappy instead. When our sorrow vanishes, then we're happy again. Caught in this endless cycle, we revolve repeatedly through heaven and hell.

Before his enlightenment, the Buddha recognized this pattern in his own heart. He knew that the conditions for existence and rebirth had not yet ceased. His work was not yet finished. Focusing on life's conditionality, he contemplated in accordance with nature: "Due to this cause there is birth, due to birth there is death, and all this movement of coming and going."

So the Buddha took up these themes for contemplation in order to understand the truth about the five khandhas. Everything mental and physical, everything conceived and thought about without exception, is conditioned. Once he knew this, he taught us to set it down. Once he knew this, he taught to abandon it all. He encouraged others to understand in accordance with this truth. If we don't, we'll suffer. We won't be able to let go of these things. However, once we do see the truth of the matter, we'll recognize how these things delude us. As the Buddha taught, "The mind has no substance; it's not any thing."

The mind isn't born belonging to anyone. It doesn't die as anyone's. This mind is free, brilliantly radiant, and unentangled with any problem or issues. The reason problems arise is because the mind is deluded by conditioned things, deluded by this misperception of self. So the Buddha taught to observe this mind. In the beginning what is there? There is truly nothing there. It doesn't arise with conditioned things, and it doesn't die with them. When the mind encounters something good, it doesn't change to become good. When the mind encounters something bad, it doesn't become bad as well. That's how it is when there is clear insight into one's nature. There is understanding that this is essentially a substanceless state of affairs.

The Buddha's insight saw it all as impermanent, unsatisfactory, and not-self. He wants us to fully comprehend in the same way. The "knowing" then knows in accordance with truth. When it knows happiness or sorrow, it remains unmoved. The emotion of happiness is a form of birth. The tendency to become sad is a form of death. When there's death there is birth, and what is born has to die. That which arises and passes away is caught in this unremitting cycle of becoming. Once the meditator's mind comes to this state of understanding, no doubt remains about whether there is further becoming and rebirth. There's no need to ask anyone else.

The Buddha comprehensively investigated conditioned phenomena and so was able to let it all go. The five khandhas were let go of, and the knowing carried on merely as an impartial observer of the process. If he experienced something positive, he didn't become positive along with it. He simply observed and remained aware. If he experienced something negative, he didn't become negative. And why was that? Because his mind had been cut free from such causes and conditions. He'd penetrated the truth. The

FOOD FOR THE HEART

conditions leading to rebirth no longer existed. This is the knowing that is certain and reliable. This is a mind that is truly at peace. This is what is not born, doesn't age, doesn't get sick, and doesn't die. This is neither cause nor effect, nor dependent on cause and effect. It is independent of the process of causal conditioning. The causes then cease with no conditioning remaining. This mind is above and beyond birth and death, above and beyond happiness and sorrow, above and beyond both good and evil. What can you say? It's beyond the limitations of language to describe it. All supporting conditions have ceased and any attempt to describe it will merely lead to attachment. The words then become the theory of the mind.

Theoretical descriptions of the mind and its workings are accurate, but the Buddha realized that this type of knowledge was relatively useless. You understand something intellectually and then believe it, but it's of no real benefit. It doesn't lead to peace of mind. The knowing of the Buddha leads to letting go. It results in abandoning and renunciation. Because it's precisely this mind that leads us to get involved with both what's right and what's wrong. If we're smart we get involved with those things that are right. If we're stupid we get involved with those things that are wrong. Such a mind is the world, and the Blessed One took the things of this world to examine this very world. Having come to know the world as it actually was, he was then known as the "one who clearly comprehends the world."

So to come back to this issue of samatha and vipassanā, the important thing is to develop these states in our own hearts. Only when we genuinely cultivate them ourselves will we know what they actually are. We can go and study what all the books say about psychological factors of the mind, but that kind of intellectual understanding is useless for actually cutting off selfish desire, anger, and delusion. We only study the theory about selfish desire, anger, and delusion, merely describing the various characteristics of these mental defilements: "Selfish desire has this meaning; anger means that; delusion is defined as this." Only knowing their theoretical qualities, we can talk about them only on that level. We know and we are intelligent, but when these defilements actually appear in our minds, do they correspond with the theory or not? When, for instance, we experience something undesirable do we react and get into a bad mood? Do we attach? Can we let it go? If aversion comes up and we recognize it, do we still hang on to it? Or once we have seen it, do we let it go? If we find that we see something we don't like and retain that aversion in our hearts, we'd better go back and start studying again. Because it's still not right. The practice is not yet perfect. When it reaches perfection, letting go happens. Look at it in this light.

We truly have to look deeply into our own hearts if we want to experience the fruits of this practice. Attempting to describe the psychology of the mind in terms of the numerous separate moments of consciousness and their different characteristics is, in my opinion, not taking the practice far enough. There's still a lot more to it. If we are going to study these things, then know them absolutely, with clarity and penetrative understanding. Without clarity of insight, how will we ever be finished with them? There's no end to it. We'll never complete our studies.

Practicing Dhamma is thus extremely important. When I practiced, that's how I studied. I didn't know anything about mind moments or psychological factors. I just observed the quality of knowing. If a thought of hate arose, I asked myself why. If a thought of love arose, I asked myself why. This is the way. Whether it's labeled thoughts or called psychological factors, so what? Just penetrate this one point until you're able to resolve these feelings of love and hate, until they completely vanish from the heart. When I was able to stop loving and hating under any circumstance, I was able to transcend suffering. Then it doesn't matter what happens, the heart and mind are released and at ease. Nothing remains. It has all stopped.

Practice like this. If people want to talk a lot about theory that's their business. But no matter how much it's debated, the practice always comes down to this single point right here. When something arises, it arises right here. Whether a lot or a little, it originates right here. When it ceases, the cessation is right here. Where else? The Buddha called this point the "knowing." When it knows the way things are accurately, in line with the truth, we'll understand the meaning of mind. They incessantly deceive. As you study them, they're simultaneously deceiving you. How else can I put it? Even though you know about them, you are still being deluded by them precisely where you know them. That's the situation. The issue is this: It's my opinion that the Buddha didn't intend that we only know what these things are called. The aim of the Buddha's teachings is to figure out the way to liberate ourselves from these things through searching for the underlying causes.

SĪLA, SAMĀDHI, AND PAÑÑĀ

I practiced Dhamma without knowing a great deal. I just knew that the path to liberation began with virtue (sīla). Virtue is the beautiful beginning of the Path. The deep peace of samādhi is the beautiful middle. Wisdom (paññā) is the beautiful end. Although they can be separated as three unique aspects of the training, as we look into them more and more deeply, these three qualities converge as one. To uphold virtue, you have to be wise. We usually advise people to develop ethical standards first by keeping the Five Precepts so that their virtue will become solid. However, the perfection of virtue takes a lot of wisdom. We have to consider our speech and actions, and analyze their consequences. This is all the work of wisdom. We have to rely on our wisdom in order to cultivate virtue.

According to the theory, virtue comes first, then samādhi, and then wisdom, but when I examined it I found that wisdom is the foundation stone for every other aspect of the practice. In order to fully comprehend the consequences of what you say and do—especially the harmful consequences—you need to use wisdom to guide and supervise, to scrutinize the workings of cause and effect. This will purify our actions and speech. Once we become familiar with ethical and unethical behavior, we see the place to practice. We then abandon what's bad and cultivate what's good. We abandon what's wrong and cultivate what's right. This is virtue. As we do this, the heart becomes increasingly firm and steadfast. A steadfast and unwavering heart is free of apprehension, remorse, and confusion concerning our actions and speech. This is samādhi.

This stable unification of mind forms a secondary and more powerful source of energy in our Dhamma practice, allowing a deeper contemplation of the sights, sounds, etc., that we experience. Once the mind is established with firm and unwavering mindfulness and peace, we can engage in sustained inquiry into the reality of the body, feeling, perception, thought, consciousness, sights, sounds, smells, tastes, bodily sensations, and objects of mind. As they continually arise, we continually investigate with a sincere determination not to lose our mindfulness. Then we'll know what these things actually are. They come into existence following their own natural truth. As our understanding steadily grows, wisdom is born. Once there's clear comprehension of the way things truly are, our old perceptions are uprooted and our conceptual knowledge transforms into wisdom. That's how virtue, samādhi, and wisdom merge and function as one.

As wisdom increases in strength and intrepidity, samādhi evolves to become increasingly firm. The more unshakable samādhi is, the more unshakable and all-encompassing virtue becomes. As virtue is perfected, it nurtures samādhi, and the additional strengthening of samādhi leads to a maturing of wisdom. These three aspects of the training mesh and intertwine. United, they form the Noble Eightfold Path, the way of the Buddha. Once virtue, samādhi, and wisdom reach their peak, this Path has the power to eradicate those things which defile the mind's purity.[45] When sensual desire comes up, when anger and delusion show their face, this Path is the only thing capable of cutting them down in their tracks.

The framework for Dhamma practice is the Four Noble Truths: suffering *(dukkha)*, the origin of suffering *(samudaya)*, the cessation of suffering *(nirodha)*, and the Path leading to the cessation of suffering *(magga)*. This Path consists of virtue, samādhi, and wisdom, the framework for training the heart. Their true meaning is not to be found in these words but dwells in the depth of your heart. That's what virtue, samādhi, and wisdom are like. They revolve continually. The Noble Eightfold Path will envelop any sight, sound, smell, taste, bodily sensation, or object of mind that arises. However, if the factors of the Eightfold Path are weak and timid, the defilements will possess your mind. If the Noble Path is strong and courageous, it will conquer and slay the defilements. If it's the defilements that are powerful and brave while the Path is feeble and frail, the defilements will conquer the Path. They conquer our hearts. If the knowing isn't quick and nimble enough as forms, feelings, perceptions, and thoughts are experienced, they possess and devastate us. The Path and the defilements proceed in tandem. As Dhamma practice develops in the heart, these two forces have to battle it out every step of the way. It's like there are two people arguing inside the mind, but it's just the Path of Dhamma and the defilements struggling to win the dominion of the heart. The Path guides and fosters our ability to contemplate. As long as we are able to contemplate accurately, the defilements will be losing ground. But if we are shaky, whenever defilements regroup and regain their strength, the Path will be routed as defilements take its place. The two sides will continue to fight it out until eventually there is a victor and the whole affair is settled.

If we focus our endeavor on developing the way of Dhamma, defilements will be gradually and persistently eradicated. Once fully cultivated, the Four Noble Truths reside in our hearts. In whatever form suffering takes, it always exists due to a cause. That's the Second Noble Truth. And what is the cause? Weak virtue. Weak samādhi. Weak wisdom. When the Path isn't durable, the defilements dominate the mind. When they dominate, the Second Noble Truth comes into play, and it gives rise to all sorts of suffering. Once we are suffering, those qualities that are able to quell the suffering disappear. The conditions that give rise to the Path are virtue, samādhi, and wisdom. When they have attained full strength, the Path of Dhamma is unstoppable, advancing inexorably to conquer the attachment and clinging that bring us so much agony. Suffering can't arise because the Path is destroying the defilements. It's at this point that cessation of suffering occurs. Why is the Path able to bring about the cessation of suffering? Because virtue, samādhi, and wisdom are attaining their peak of perfection, and the Path has gathered an unstoppable momentum. It all comes together right here. I would say for anyone who practices like this, theoretical ideas about the mind don't come into the picture. If the mind is liberated from these, then it is utterly dependable and certain. Now whatever path it takes, we don't have to goad it much to keep it going straight.

Consider the leaves of a mango tree. What are they like? By examining just a single leaf we know. Even if there are ten thousand of them we know what all those leaves are like. Just look at one leaf. The others are essentially the same. Similarly with the trunk. We only have to see the trunk of one mango tree to know the characteristics of them all. Just look at one tree. All the other mango trees will be essentially no different. Even if there were one hundred thousand of them, if I knew one I'd know them all. This is what the Buddha taught.

Virtue, samādhi, and wisdom constitute the Path of the Buddha. But the Way is not the essence of the Dhamma. The Path isn't an end in itself, not the ultimate aim of the Blessed One. But it's the way leading inward. It's just like how you traveled from Bangkok to my monastery, Wat Nong Pah Pong. It's not the road you were after. What you wanted was to reach the monastery, but you needed the road for the journey. The road you traveled on is not the monastery. It's just the way to get here. But if you want to arrive at the monastery, you have to follow the road. It's the same with virtue, samādhi and wisdom. We could say they are not the essence of the Dhamma, but they are the road to arrive there. When virtue, samādhi, and wisdom have been mastered, the result is profound peace of mind. That's the destination. Once we've arrived at this peace, even if we hear a noise, the mind remains unruffled. Once we've reached this peace, there's nothing remaining to do. The Buddha taught to give it all up. Whatever happens, there's nothing to worry about. Then we truly, unquestionably, know for ourselves. We no longer simply believe what other people say.

The essential principle of Buddhism is empty of any phenomena. It's not contingent upon miraculous displays of psychic powers, paranormal abilities, or anything else mystical or bizarre. The Buddha did not emphasize the importance of these things. Such powers, however, do exist and may be possible to develop, but this facet of Dhamma is deluding, so the Buddha did not advocate or encourage it. The only people he praised were the ones who were able to liberate themselves from suffering. To accomplish this requires training, and the tools and equipment to get the job done are generosity, virtue, samādhi, and wisdom. We have to take them up and train with them. Together they form a Path inclining inward, and wisdom is the first step. This Path cannot mature if the mind is encrusted with defilements, but if we are stout-hearted and strong, the Path will exterminate these impurities. However, if it's the defilements that are stout-hearted and strong they will obliterate the Path. Dhamma practice simply involves these two forces battling it out incessantly until the end of the road is reached. They engage in unremitting combat until the very end.

THE DANGERS OF ATTACHMENT

Using the tools of practice entails hardship and arduous challenges. We rely on patience, endurance, and going without. We have to do it ourselves, experience it for ourselves, realize it ourselves. Scholars, however, tend to get confused a lot. For example, when they sit in meditation, as soon as their minds experience a teeny bit of tranquillity they start to think, "Hey, this must be first jhāna." This is how their minds work. And once those thoughts arise the tranquillity they'd experienced is shattered. Soon they start to think that it must have been the second jhāna they'd attained. Don't think and speculate about it. There aren't any billboards that announce which level of samādhi we're experiencing. The reality is completely different. There aren't any signs like the road signs that tell you, "This way to Wat Nong Pah Pong." That's not how I read the mind. It doesn't announce.

Although a number of highly esteemed scholars have written descriptions of the first, second, third, and fourth jhānas, what's written is merely external information. If the mind actually enters these states of profound peace, it doesn't know anything about those written descriptions. It knows, but what it knows isn't the same as the theory we study. If the scholars try to clutch their theory and drag it into their meditation, sitting and pondering, "Hmmm...what could this be? Is this first jhāna yet?" There! The peace is shattered, and they don't experience anything of real substance. And why is that? Because there is desire, and once there's craving what happens? The mind simultaneously withdraws out of the meditation. So it's necessary for all of us to relinquish thinking and speculation. Abandon them completely. Just take up the body, speech, and mind and delve entirely into the practice. Observe the workings of the mind, but don't lug the Dhamma books in there with you. Otherwise everything becomes a big mess, because nothing in those books corresponds precisely to the reality of the way things truly are.

People who study a lot, who are full of theoretical knowledge, usually don't succeed in Dhamma practice. They get bogged down at the information level. The truth is, the heart and mind can't be measured by external standards. If the mind is getting peaceful, just allow it to be peaceful. The most profound levels of deep peace do exist. Personally, I didn't know much about the theory of practice. I'd been a monk for three years and still had a lot of questions about what samādhi actually was. I kept trying to think about it and figure it out as I meditated, but my mind became even more restless and distracted than it had been before! The amount of thinking actually increased. When I wasn't meditating it was more peaceful. Boy, was it difficult, so exasperating, but even though I encountered so many obstacles, I never threw in the towel. I just kept on doing it. When I wasn't trying to do anything in particular, my mind was relatively at ease. But whenever I determined to make the mind unify in samādhi, it went out of control. "What's going on here," I wondered. "Why is this happening?"

Later on I began to realize that meditation was comparable to the process of breathing. If we're determined to force the breath to be shallow, deep, or just right, it's very difficult to do. However, if we go for a stroll and we're not even aware of when we're breathing in or out, it's extremely relaxing. So I reflected, *"Aha!* Maybe that's the way it works." When a person is normally walking around in the course of the day, not focusing attention on their breath, does their breathing cause them suffering? No, they just feel relaxed. But when I'd sit down and vow with determination that I was going to make my mind peaceful, clinging and attachment set in. When I tried to control the breath to be shallow or deep, it just brought on more stress than I had before. Why? Because the willpower I was using was tainted with clinging and attachment. I didn't know *what* was going on. All that frustration and hardship was coming up because I was bringing craving into the meditation.

"SPONTANEOUS COMBUSTION"

I once stayed in a forest monastery that was half a mile from a village. One night the villagers were celebrating with a loud party as I was practicing walking meditation. It must have been after 11:00 and I was feeling a bit peculiar. I'd been feeling strange like this since midday. My mind was quiet. There were hardly any thoughts. I felt very relaxed and at ease. I did walking meditation until I was tired and then went to sit in my grass-roofed hut. As I sat down I barely had time to cross my legs before, amazingly, my mind just wanted to delve into a profound state of peace. It happened all by itself. As soon as I sat down, the mind became truly peaceful. It was rock solid. It wasn't as if I couldn't hear the noise of the villagers singing and dancing—I still could—but I could also shut the sound out entirely.

Strange. When I didn't pay attention to the sound, it was perfectly quiet—didn't hear a thing. But if I wanted to hear, I could, without it being a disturbance. It was like there were two objects in my mind that were placed side by side but not touching. I could see that the mind and its object of awareness were separate and distinct, just like this spittoon and water kettle here. Then I understood: When the mind unifies in samādhi, if you direct your attention outward you can hear, but if you let it dwell in its emptiness then it's perfectly silent. When sound was perceived, I could see that the knowing and the sound were distinctly different. I contemplated:

"If this isn't the way it is, how else could it be?" That's the way it was. These two things were totally separate. I continued on investigating like this until my understanding deepened even further: "Ah, this is important. When the perceived continuity of phenomena is cut, the result is peace." The previous illusion of continuity *(santati)* transformed into peace of mind *(santi)*. So I continued to sit, putting effort into the meditation. The mind at that time was focused solely on the meditation, indifferent to everything else. Had I stopped meditating at this point it would have been merely because it was complete. I could have taken it easy, but it wouldn't have been because of laziness, tiredness, or feeling annoyed. Not at all. These were absent from the heart. There was only perfect inner balance and equipoise— just right.

Eventually I did take a break, but it was only the posture of sitting that changed. My heart remained constant, unwavering and unflagging. I pulled a pillow over, intending to take a rest. As I reclined, the mind remained just as peaceful as it had been before. Then, just before my head hit the pillow, the mind's awareness began flowing inward; I didn't know where it was headed, but it kept flowing deeper and deeper within. It was like a current of electricity flowing down a cable to a switch. When it hit the switch my body exploded with a deafening bang. The knowing during that time was extremely lucid and subtle. Once past that point the mind was released to penetrate deeply inside. It went inside to the point where there wasn't anything at all. Absolutely nothing from the outside world could come into that place. Nothing at all could reach it. Having dwelt internally for some time, the mind then retreated to flow back out. However, when I say it retreated, I don't mean to imply that I made it flow back out. I was simply an observer, only knowing and witnessing. The mind came out more and more until it finally returned to "normal."

Once my normal state of consciousness returned, the question arose, "What was that?!" The answer came immediately, "These things happen of their own accord. You don't have to search for an explanation." This answer was enough to satisfy my mind.

After a short time my mind again began flowing inward. I wasn't making any conscious effort to direct the mind. It took off by itself. As I moved deeper and deeper inside, it again hit that same switch. This time my body shattered into the most minute particles and fragments. Again the mind was released to penetrate deeply inside itself. Utter silence. It was even more profound than the first time. Absolutely nothing external could reach it. The mind abided here for some time, for as long as it wished, and then retreated to flow outward. At that time it was following its own momentum and happening all by itself. I wasn't influencing or directing my mind to be in any particular way, to flow inward or retreat outward. I was merely the one knowing and watching.

My mind again returned to its normal state of consciousness, and I didn't wonder or speculate about what was happening. As I meditated, the mind once again inclined inward. This time the entire cosmos shattered and disintegrated into minute particles. The earth, ground, mountains, fields, and forests—the whole world—disintegrated into the space element. People had vanished. Everything had disappeared. On this third occasion absolutely nothing remained.

The mind, having inclined inward, settled down there for as long as it wished. I can't say I understand exactly how it remained there. It's difficult to describe what happened. There's nothing I can compare it to. No simile is apt. This time the mind remained inside far longer than it had previously, and only after an extended period did it come out of that state. When I say it came out, I don't mean to imply that I made it come out or that I was controlling what was happening. The mind did it all by itself. I was merely an observer. Eventually it again returned to its normal state of consciousness. How could you put a name on what happened during these three times? Who knows? What term are you going to use to label it?

THE POWER OF SAMĀDHI

Everything I've been relating to you concerns the mind following the way of nature. This was no theoretical description of the mind or psychological states. There's no need for that. When there's faith or confidence you get in there and really do it. Not just playing around, you put your life on the line. And when your practice reaches the stage that I've been describing, afterward the whole world is turned upside down. Your understanding of reality is completely different. Your view is utterly transformed. If someone saw you at that moment, they might think you were insane. If this experience happened to someone who didn't have a thorough grip on themselves, they might actually go crazy, because nothing is the same as it was before. The people of the world appear differently than they used to. But you're the only one who sees this. Absolutely everything changes. Your thoughts are transmuted: other people now think in one way, while you think in another. They think about things in one way, while you think in another. They're descending one path while you're climbing another. You're no longer the same as other human beings. This way of experiencing things doesn't deteriorate. It persists and carries on. Give it a try. If it really is as I describe, you won't have to go searching very far. Just look into your own heart. This heart is staunchly courageous, unshakably valiant. This is the heart's power, it's source of strength and energy. The heart has this potential strength. This is the power and force of samādhi.

At this point it's still just the power and purity that the mind derives from samādhi. This level of is samādhi at its ultimate. The mind has attained the summit of samādhi; it's not mere momentary concentration. If you were to switch to vipassanā meditation at this point, the contemplation would be uninterrupted and insightful. Or you could take that focused energy and use it in other ways. From this point on you could develop psychic powers, perform miraculous feats, or use it any way you wanted. Ascetics and hermits have used samādhi energy for making holy water, talismans, or casting spells. These things are all possible at this stage, and may be of some benefit in their own way; but it's like the benefit of alcohol. You drink it and then you get drunk.

This level of samādhi is a rest stop. The Buddha stopped and rested here. It forms the foundation for contemplation and vipassanā. However, it's not necessary to have such profound samādhi as this in order to observe the conditions around us, so keep on steadily contemplating the process of cause and effect. To do this we focus the peace and clarity of our mind to analyze the sights, sounds, smells, tastes, physical sensations, thoughts, and mental states we experience. Examine moods and emotions, whether positive or negative, happy or unhappy. Examine everything. It's just like someone else has climbed up a mango tree and is shaking down the fruit while we wait underneath to gather them up. The ones that are rotten, we don't pick up. Just gather the good mangoes. It's not exhausting, because we don't have to climb up the tree. We simply wait underneath to reap the fruit.

Do you get the meaning of this simile? Everything experienced with a peaceful mind confers greater understanding. No longer do we create proliferating interpretations around what is experienced. Wealth, fame, blame, praise, happiness, and unhappiness come of their own accord. And we're at peace. We're wise. It's actually fun. It becomes fun to sift through and sort out these things. What other people call good, bad, evil, here, there, happiness, unhappiness, or whatever—it all gets taken in for our own profit. Someone else has climbed up the mango tree and is shaking the branches to make the mangoes fall down to us. We simply enjoy ourselves gathering the fruit without fear. What's there to be afraid of anyway? It's someone else who's shaking the mangoes down to us. Wealth, fame, praise, criticism, happiness, unhappiness, and all the rest are no more than mangoes falling down, and we examine them with a serene heart. Then we'll know which ones are good and which are rotten.

WORKING IN ACCORD WITH NATURE

When we begin to wield the peace and serenity we've been developing in meditation to contemplate these things, wisdom arises. This is what I call wisdom. This is vipassanā. It's not something fabricated and construed. If we're wise, vipassanā will develop naturally. We don't have to label what's happening. If there's only a little clarity of insight, we call this "little vipassanā." When clear seeing increases a bit, we call that "moderate vipassanā." If knowing is fully in accordance with the truth, you call that "ultimate vipassanā." Personally I prefer to use the word *wisdom* (paññā) than "vipassanā." If we think we are going to sit down from time to time and practice "vipassanā meditation," we're going to have a very difficult time of it. Insight has to proceed from peace and tranquillity. The entire process will happen naturally of its own accord. We can't force it.

The Buddha taught that this process matures at its own rate. Having reached this level of practice, we allow it to develop according to our innate capabilities, spiritual aptitude, and the merit we've accumulated in the past. But we never stop putting effort into the practice. Whether the progress is swift or slow is out of our control. It's just like planting a tree. The tree knows how fast it should grow. If we want it to grow more quickly than it is, this is pure delusion. If we want it to grow more slowly, recognize this as delusion as well. If we do the work, the results will be forthcoming—just like planting a tree. For example, say we wanted to plant a chili bush. Our responsibility is to dig a hole, plant the seedling, water it, fertilize it, and protect it from insects. This is our job, our end of the bargain. This is where faith then comes in. Whether the chili plant grows or not is up to it. It's not our business. We can't go tugging on the plant, trying to stretch it and make it grow faster. That's not how nature works. Our responsibility is to water and fertilize it. Practicing Dhamma in the same way puts our heart at ease.

If we realize enlightenment in this lifetime, that's fine. If we have to wait until our next life, no matter. We have faith and unfaltering conviction in the Dhamma. Whether we progress quickly or slowly is up to our innate capabilities, spiritual aptitude, and the merit we've accumulated so far. Practicing like this puts the heart at ease. It's like we're riding in a horse cart. We don't put the cart before the horse. Or it's like trying to plow a rice paddy while walking in front of our water buffalo rather than behind. What I'm saying here is that the mind is getting ahead of itself. It's impatient to get quick results. That's not the way to do it. Don't walk in front of your water buffalo. You have to walk *behind* the water buffalo.

It's just like that chili plant we are nurturing. Give it water and fertilizer, and it will do the job of absorbing the nutrients. When ants or termites come to infest it, we chase them away. Doing just this much is enough for the chili to grow beautifully on its own, and once it is growing beautifully, don't try to force it to flower when we think it should flower. It's none of our business. It will just create useless suffering. Allow it to bloom on its own. And once the flowers do bloom don't demand that it immediately produce chili peppers. Don't rely on coercion. That really causes suffering! Once we figure this out, we understand what our responsibilities are and are not. Each has their specific duty to fulfill. The mind knows its role in the work to be done. If the mind doesn't understand its role, it will try to force the chili plant to produce peppers on the very day we plant it. The mind will insist that it grow, flower, and produce peppers all in one day.

This is nothing but the Second Noble Truth: craving causes suffering to arise. If we are aware of this Truth and ponder it, we'll understand that trying to force results in our Dhamma practice is pure delusion. It's wrong. Understanding how it works, we let go and allow things to mature according to our innate capabilities, spiritual aptitude, and the merit we've accumulated. We keep doing our part. Don't worry that it might take a long time. Even if it takes a hundred or a thousand lifetimes to get enlightened, so what? However many lifetimes it takes we just keep practicing with a heart at ease, comfortable with our pace. Once our mind has entered the stream, there's nothing to fear. It will have gone beyond even the smallest evil action. The Buddha said that the mind of a *sotāpanna,* someone who has attained the first stage of enlightenment, has entered the stream of Dhamma that flows to enlightenment. These people will never again have to experience the grim lower realms of existence, never again fall into hell. How could they possibly fall into hell when their minds have abandoned evil? They've seen the danger in making bad kamma. Even if you tried to force them to do or say something evil, they would be incapable of it, so there's no chance of ever again descending into hell or the lower realms of existence. Their minds are flowing with the current of Dhamma.

Once you're in the stream, you know what your responsibilities are. You comprehend the work ahead. You understand how to practice Dhamma. You know when to strive hard and when to relax. You comprehend your body and mind, this physical and mental process, and you renounce the things that should be renounced, continually abandoning without a shred of doubt.

CHANGING OUR VISION

In my life of practicing Dhamma, I didn't attempt to master a wide range of subjects. Just one. I refined this heart. Say we look at a body. If we find that we're attracted to a body then analyze it. Have a good look: head hair, body hair, nails, teeth, and skin.[46] The Buddha taught us to thoroughly and repeatedly contemplate these parts of the body. Visualize them separately, pull them apart, burn them up, and peel off the skin. This is how to do it. Stick with this meditation until it's firmly established and unwavering. See everyone the same. For example, when the monks and novices go into the village on alms round in the morning, whoever they see—whether it's another monk or a villager—they imagine him or her as a dead body, a walking corpse staggering along on the road ahead of them. Remain focused on this perception. This is how to put forth effort. It leads to maturity and development. When you see a young woman whom you find attractive, imagine her as a walking corpse, her body putrid and reeking from decomposition. See everyone like that. And don't let them get too close! Don't allow the infatuation to persist in your heart. If you perceive others as putrid and reeking, I can assure you the infatuation won't persist. Contemplate until you're sure about what you're seeing, until it's definite, until you're proficient. Whatever path you then wander down you won't go astray. Put your whole heart into it. Whenever you see someone it's no different to looking at a corpse. Whether male or female, look at that person as a dead body. And don't forget to see yourself as a dead body! Eventually this is all that's left. Try to develop this way of seeing as thoroughly as you can. Train with it until it increasingly becomes part and parcel of your mind. I promise it's great fun—if you actually do it. But if you are preoccupied with reading about it in books, you'll have a difficult time of it. You've got to *do* it. And do it with utmost sincerity. Do it until this meditation becomes a part of you. Make realization of truth your aim. If you're motivated by the desire to transcend suffering, then you'll be on the right path.

These days there are many people teaching vipassanā and a wide range of meditation techniques. I'll say this: doing vipassanā is not easy. We can't just jump straight into it. It won't work if it's not proceeding from a high standard of morality. Find out for yourself. Moral discipline and training precepts are necessary, because if our behavior, actions, and speech aren't impeccable we'll never be able to stand on our own two feet. Meditation without virtue is like trying to skip over an essential section of the Path. Similarly, occasionally you hear people say, "You don't need to develop tranquillity. Skip over it and go straight into the insight meditation of vipassanā." Sloppy people who like to cut corners say things like this. They say you don't have to bother with moral discipline. Upholding and refining your virtue is challenging, not just playing around. If we could skip over all the teachings on ethical behavior, we'd have it pretty easy, wouldn't we? Whenever we'd encounter a difficulty, we just avoid it by skipping over it. Of course, we'd all like to skip over the difficult bits.

There was once a monk I met who told me he was a real meditator. He asked for permission to stay with me here and inquired about the schedule and standard of monastic discipline. I explained to him that in this monastery we live according to the vinaya, the Buddha's code of monastic discipline, and if he wanted to come and train with me he'd have to

renounce his money and private stores of robes and medicines. He told me
his practice was "nonattachment to all conventions." I told him I didn't
know what he was talking about. "How about if I stay here," he asked, "and
keep all my money but don't attach to it. Money's just a convention." I said,
"Sure, no problem. If you can eat salt and not find it salty, then you can use
money and not be attached it." He was just speaking gibberish. Actually, he
was just too lazy to follow the details of the vinaya. I'm telling you, it's
difficult. "When you can eat salt and honestly assure me it's not salty, then
I'll take you seriously. And if you tell me it's not salty then I'll give you a
whole sack to eat. Just try it. Will it really not taste salty? Nonattachment
to conventions isn't just a matter of clever speech. If you're going to talk like
this, you can't stay with me." So he left.

We have to try and maintain the practice of virtue. Monastics should
train by experimenting with the ascetic practices, while lay people practicing at home should keep the Five Precepts. Attempt to attain impeccabil-
ity in everything said and done. We should cultivate goodness to the best
of our ability, and keep on gradually doing it.

When starting to cultivate the serenity of samatha meditation, don't make
the mistake of trying once or twice and then giving up because the mind is
not peaceful. That's not the right way. You have to cultivate meditation
over a long period of time. Why does it have to take so long? Think about
it. How many years have we allowed our minds to wander astray? How
many years have we not been doing samatha meditation? Whenever the
mind has ordered us to follow it down a particular path, we've rushed after
it. To calm that wandering mind, to bring it to a stop, to make it still, a couple of months of meditation won't be enough. Consider this. When we
undertake to train the mind to be at peace with every situation, please understand that in the beginning when a defiled emotion comes up, the mind
won't be peaceful. It's going be distracted and out of control. Why? Because
there's craving. We don't want our mind to think. We don't want to experience any distracting moods or emotions. Not wanting is craving, the craving for non-existence. The more we crave not to experience certain things,
the more we invite and usher them in. "I don't want these things, so why
do they keep coming to me? I wish it wasn't this way, so why is it this way?"

There we go! We crave for things to exist in a particular way, because we
don't understand our own mind. It can take an incredibly long time before

we realize that playing around with these things is a mistake. Finally, when we consider it clearly, we see, "Oh, these things come because I call them."

Craving not to experience something, craving to be at peace, craving not to be distracted and agitated—it's all craving. It's all a red-hot chunk of iron. But never mind. Just get on with the practice. Whenever we experience a mood or emotion, examine it in terms of its impermanence, unsatisfactoriness, and selfless qualities, and toss it into one of these three categories. Then reflect and investigate: These defiled emotions are almost always accompanied by excessive thinking. Wherever a mood leads, thinking straggles along behind. Thinking and wisdom are two very different things. Thinking merely reacts to and follows our moods, and they carry on with no end in sight. But if wisdom is operating, it will bring the mind to stillness. The mind stops and doesn't go anywhere. There's simply knowing and acknowledging what's being experienced: when this emotion comes, the mind's like this; when that mood comes, it's like that. We sustain the "knowing." Eventually it occurs to us, "Hey, all this thinking, this aimless mental chatter, this worrying and judging—it's all insubstantial nonsense. It's all impermanent, unsatisfactory, and not me or mine." Toss it into one of these three all-encompassing categories, and quell the uprising. You cut it off at its source. Later when we again sit meditation, it will come up again. Keep a close watch on it. Spy on it.

It's just like raising water buffaloes. You've got the farmer, some rice plants, and the water buffalo. Now the water buffalo, it wants to eat those rice plants. Rice plants are what water buffaloes like to eat, right? Your mind is a water buffalo. Defiled emotions are like the rice plants. The knowing is the farmer. Dhamma practice is just like this. No different. Compare it for yourself. When tending a water buffalo, what do you do? You release it, allowing it to wander freely, but you keep a close eye on it. If it strays too close to the rice plants, you yell out. When the buffalo hears, it backs away. But don't be inattentive, oblivious to what the buffalo is doing. If you've got a stubborn water buffalo that won't heed your warning, take a stick and give it a stout whack on the backside. Then it won't dare go near the rice plants. But don't get caught taking a siesta. If you lie down and doze off, those rice plants will be history. Dhamma practice is the same: you watch over your mind; the knowing tends the mind.

"Those people who keep a close watch over their minds will be liberated from Māra's snare." And yet this knowing mind is also the mind, so who's the one observing the mind? Such ideas can make you extremely confused. The mind is one thing, the knowing another; and yet the knowing originates in this very same mind. What does it mean to know the mind? What's it like to encounter moods and emotions? What's it like to be without any defiled emotions whatsoever? That which knows what these things are like is what is meant by the "knowing." The knowing observantly follows the mind, and it's from this knowing that wisdom is born. The mind is that which thinks and gets entangled in emotions, one after another—precisely like our water buffalo. Whatever directions it strays in, maintain a watchful eye. How could it get away? If it mosies over to the rice plants, yell out. If it won't listen, pick up a stick and stride over to it. *"Whack!"* This is how you frustrate its craving.

Training the mind is no different. When the mind experiences an emotion and instantly grabs it, it's the job of the knowing to teach. Examine the mood to see if it's good or bad. Explain to the mind how cause and effect function. And when it again grabs onto something that it thinks is adorable, the knowing has to again teach the mind, again explain cause and effect, until the mind is able to cast that thing aside. This leads to peace of mind. After finding out that whatever it grabs and grasps is inherently undesirable, the mind simply stops. It can't be bothered with those things anymore, because it's come under a constant barrage of rebukes and reprimands. Thwart the craving of the mind with determination. Challenge it to its core, until the teachings penetrate to the heart. That's how you train the mind.

Since the time when I withdrew to the forest to practice meditation, I've been practicing like this. When I train my disciples, I train them to practice like this. Because I want them to see the truth, rather than just read what's in the scriptures; I want them to see if their hearts have been liberated from conceptual thinking. When liberation occurs, you know; and when liberation has not yet happened, then contemplate the process of how one thing causes and leads to another. Contemplate until you know and understand it through and through. Once it's been penetrated with insight, it will fall away on its own. When something comes your way and gets stuck, then investigate. Don't give up until it has released its grip. Repeatedly investigate right here. Personally, this is how I approached the training, because the Buddha taught that you have to know for yourself. All sages know the truth for themselves. You've got to discover it in the depths of your own heart. Know yourself.

If you are confident in what you know and trust yourself, you will feel relaxed whether others criticize or praise you. Whatever other people say, you're at ease. Why? Because you know yourself. If someone bolsters you with praise, but you're not actually worthy of it, are you really going to believe them? Of course not. You just carry on with your Dhamma practice. When people who aren't confident in what they know get praised by others, they get sucked into believing it and it warps their perception. Likewise when someone criticizes you, take a look at and examine yourself. "No, what they say isn't true. They accuse me of being wrong, but actually I'm not. Their accusation isn't valid." If that's the case, what would be the point of getting angry with them? Their words aren't true. If, however, we are at fault just as they accuse, then their criticism is correct. If that's the case, what would be the point of getting angry with them? When you're able to think like this, life is truly untroubled and comfortable. Nothing that then happens is wrong. Then everything is Dhamma. That is how I practiced.

FOLLOWING THE MIDDLE PATH

It's the shortest and most direct path. You can come and argue with me on points of Dhamma, but I won't join in. Rather than argue back, I'd just offer some reflections for you to consider. Please understand what the Buddha taught: let go of everything. Let go with knowing and awareness. Without knowing and awareness, the letting go is no different than that of cows and water buffaloes. Without putting your heart into it, the letting go isn't correct. You let go because you understand conventional reality. This is nonattachment. The Buddha taught that in the beginning stages of Dhamma practice you should work very hard, develop things thoroughly, and attach a lot. Attach to the Buddha. Attach to the Dhamma. Attach to the Sangha. Attach firmly and deeply. That's what the Buddha taught. Attach with sincerity and persistence and hold on tight.

In my own search I tried nearly every possible means of contemplation. I sacrificed my life for the Dhamma, because I had faith in the reality of enlightenment and the Path to get there. These things actually do exist, just like the Buddha said they did. But to realize them takes practice, right practice. It takes pushing yourself to the limit. It takes the courage to train, to reflect, and to fundamentally change. It takes the courage to actually do what it takes. And how do you do it? Train the heart. The thoughts in our heads tell us to go in one direction, but the Buddha tells us to go in another. Why is it necessary to train? Because the heart is totally encrusted with and plastered over with defilements. That's what a heart is like that has not yet been transformed through the training. It's unreliable, so don't believe it. It's not yet virtuous. How can we trust a heart that lacks purity and clarity? Therefore the Buddha warned us not to put our trust in a defiled heart. Initially the heart is only the hired hand of defilement, but if they associate together for an extended period of time, the heart perverts to become defilement itself. That's why the Buddha taught us not to trust our hearts.

If we take a good look at our monastic discipline, we'll see that the whole thing is about training the heart. And whenever we train the heart we feel hot and bothered. As soon as we're hot and bothered we start to complain, "Boy, this practice is incredibly difficult! It's impossible." But the Buddha didn't think like that. He considered that when the training was causing us heat and friction, that meant we're on the right track. We don't think that way. We think it's a sign that something is wrong. This misunderstanding is what makes the practice seem so arduous. In the beginning we feel hot and bothered, so we think we're off track. Everyone wants to feel good, but they're less concerned about whether it's right or not. When we go against the grain of the defilements and challenge our cravings, of course we feel suffering. We get hot, upset, and bothered and then quit. We think we're on the wrong path. The Buddha, however, would say we're getting it right. We're confronting our defilements, and they are what is getting hot and bothered. But we think it's us who are hot and bothered.

The Buddha taught that it's the defilements that get stirred up and upset. It's the same for everyone. That's why Dhamma practice is so demanding. People don't examine things clearly. Generally, they lose the Path on either the side of sensual indulgence or self-torment. They get stuck in these two extremes. On one hand they like to indulge their heart's desires. Whatever they feel like doing they just do it. They like to sit in comfort. They love to lie down and stretch out in comfort. Whatever they do, they seek to do it in comfort. This is what I mean by sensual indulgence: clinging to feeling good. With such indulgence how could Dhamma practice possibly progress?

If we can no longer indulge in comfort, sensuality, and feeling good, we become irritated. We get upset and angry and suffer because of it. This is falling off the Path on the side of self-torment. This is not the path of a peaceful sage, not the way of someone who's still. The Buddha warned not to stray down these two sidetracks of sensual indulgence and self-torment. When experiencing happiness, just know that with awareness. When experiencing anger, ill will, and irritation, understand that you are not following in the footsteps of the Buddha. Those aren't the paths of people seeking peace, but the roads of common people. A monk at peace doesn't walk down those roads. He strides straight down the middle with sensual indulgence on the left and self-torment on the right. This is correct Dhamma practice.

If you're going to take up this monastic training, you have to walk this Middle Way, not getting worked up about either happiness or unhappiness. Set them down. But it feels like they're kicking us around. First they kick us from one side, *"Ow!"* then they kick us from the other, *"Ow!"* We feel like the clapper in our wooden bell, knocked back and forth from side to side. The Middle Way is all about letting go of happiness and unhappiness, and the right practice is the practice in the middle. When the craving for happiness hits and we don't satisfy it, we feel the pain.

Walking down the Middle Path of the Buddha is arduous and challenging. There are just these two extremes of good and bad. If we believe what they tell us, we have to follow their orders. If we become enraged at someone, we immediately go searching for a stick to attack them. No patient endurance. If we love someone we want to caress them from head to toe. Am I right? These two sidetracks completely miss the middle. This is not what the Buddha recommended. His teaching was to gradually put these things down. His practice was a path leading out of existence, away from rebirth—a path free of becoming, birth, happiness, unhappiness, good, and evil.

Those people who crave existence are blind to what's in the middle. They fall off the Path on the side of happiness and then completely pass over the middle on their way to the other side of dissatisfaction and irritation. They continually skip over the center. This sacred place is invisible to them as they rush back and forth. They don't stay in that place where there is no existence and no birth. They don't like it, so they don't stay. Either they go down out of their home and get bitten by a dog or fly up to get pecked by a vulture. This is existence.

Humanity is blind to that which is free from existence with no rebirth. The human heart is blind to it, so it repeatedly passes it by and skips over it. The Middle Way walked by the Buddha, the path of correct Dhamma practice, transcends existence and rebirth. The mind that is beyond both the wholesome and the unwholesome is released. This is the path of a peaceful sage. If we don't walk it we'll never be a sage at peace. That peace will never have a chance to bloom. Why? Because of existence and rebirth. Because there's birth and death. The Path of the Buddha is without birth or death. There's no low and no high. There's no happiness and no suffering. There's no good and no evil. This is the straight path. This is the path of peace and stillness. It's peacefully free of pleasure and pain, happiness and sorrow. This is how to practice Dhamma. Experiencing this, the mind can stop. It can stop asking questions. There's no longer any need to search for answers. There! That's why the Buddha said that the Dhamma is something that the wise know directly for themselves. No need to ask anybody. We understand clearly for ourselves without a shred of doubt that things are exactly as the Buddha said they were.

DEDICATION TO THE PRACTICE

So I've told you a few brief stories about how I practiced. I didn't have a lot of knowledge. I didn't study much. What I did study was this heart and mind of mine, and I learned in a natural way through experimentation, trial and error. When I liked something, then I examined what was going on and where it would lead. Inevitably, it would drag me to some distant suffering. My practice was to observe myself. As understanding and insight deepened, gradually I came to know myself.

Practice with unflinching dedication! If you want to practice Dhamma, then please try not to think too much. If you're meditating and you find yourself trying to force specific results, then it's better to stop. When your mind settles down to become peaceful and then you think, "That's it! That's it, isn't it? Is this it?" then stop. Take all your analytical and theoretical knowledge, wrap it up, and store it away in a chest. And don't drag it out for discussion or to teach. That's not the type of knowledge that penetrates inside. They are different types of knowledge.

When the reality of something is seen, it's not the same as the written descriptions. For example, let's say we write down the words "sensual desire." When sensual desire actually overwhelms the heart, it's impossible that the written words can convey the same meaning as the reality. It's the same with "anger." We can write the letters on a blackboard, but when we're actually angry the experience is not the same. We can't read those letters fast enough, and the heart is engulfed by rage.

This is an extremely important point. The theoretical teachings are accurate, but it's essential to bring them into our hearts. They must be internalized. If the Dhamma isn't brought into the heart, it's not truly known. It's not actually seen. I was no different. I didn't study extensively, but I did do enough to pass some of the exams on Buddhist theory. One day I had the opportunity to listen to a Dhamma talk from a meditation master. As I listened, some disrespectful thoughts came up. I didn't know how to listen to a real Dhamma talk. I couldn't figure out what this wandering meditation monk was talking about. He was teaching as though it was coming from his own direct experience, as if he was after the truth.

As time went on and I gained some firsthand experience in the practice, I saw for myself the truth of what that monk taught. I understood how to understand. Insight then followed in its wake. Dhamma was taking root in my own heart and mind. It was a long, long time before I realized that everything that that wandering monk had taught came from what he'd seen for himself. The Dhamma he taught came directly from his own experience, not from a book. He spoke according to his understanding and insight. When I walked the Path myself, I came across every detail he'd described and had to admit he was right. So I continued on.

Try to take every opportunity you can to put effort into Dhamma practice. Whether it's peaceful or not, don't worry about it at this point. The highest priority is to set the wheels of practice in motion and create the causes for future liberation. If you've done the work, there's no need to worry about the results. Don't be anxious that you won't gain results. Anxiety is not peaceful. If, however, you don't do the work, how can you expect results? How can you ever hope to see? It's the one who searches who discovers. It's the one who eats who's full. Everything around us lies to us. Recognizing this even ten times is still pretty good. But the same old coot keeps telling us the same old lies and stories. If we know he's lying, it's not so bad, but it can be an exceedingly long time before we know.

The old fellow comes and tries to hoodwink us with his lies time and time again.

Practicing Dhamma means upholding virtue, developing samādhi, and cultivating wisdom in our hearts. Remember and reflect on the Triple Gem: the Buddha, the Dhamma, and the Sangha. Abandon absolutely everything without exception. Our own actions are the causes and conditions that will ripen in this very life. So strive on with sincerity.

Even if we have to sit in a chair to meditate, it's still possible to focus our attention. In the beginning we don't have to focus on many things—just our breath. If we prefer, we can mentally repeat the words "Buddha, Dhamma, or Sangha" in conjunction with each breath. While focusing attention, resolve not to control the breath. If breathing seems laborious or uncomfortable, this indicates we're not approaching it right. As long as we're not yet at ease with the breath, it will seem too shallow or too deep, too subtle or too rough. However, once we relax with our breath, finding it pleasant and comfortable, clearly aware of each inhalation and exhalation, then we're getting the hang of it. If we're not doing it properly we will lose the breath. If this happens then it's better to stop for a moment and refocus the mindfulness.

If while meditating you get the urge to experience psychic phenomena or the mind becomes luminous and radiant or you have visions of celestial palaces, etc., there's no need to fear. Simply be aware of whatever you're experiencing, and continue on meditating. Occasionally, after some time, the breath may appear to slow to a halt. The sensation of the breath seems to vanish and you become alarmed. Don't worry; there's nothing to be afraid of. You only think your breathing has stopped. Actually, the breath is still there, but it's functioning on a much more subtle level than usual. With time the breath will return to normal by itself.

In the beginning, just concentrate on making the mind calm and peaceful. Whether sitting in a chair, riding in a car, taking a boat ride, or wherever you happen to be, you should be proficient enough in your meditation that you can enter a state of peace at will. When you get on a train and sit down, quickly bring your mind to a state of peace. Wherever you are, you can always sit. This level of proficiency indicates that you're becoming familiar with the Path. You then investigate. Utilize the power of this peaceful mind to investigate what you experience—at times it's what you see; at times what you hear, smell, taste, feel with your body, or think and feel in your heart. Whatever sensory experience presents itself—like it or not—take that up for contemplation. Simply know what you are experiencing. Don't project meaning or interpretations onto those objects of sensory awareness. If it's good, just know that it's good. If it's bad, just know that it's bad. This is conventional reality. Good or evil, it's all impermanent, unsatisfying, and not-self. It's all undependable. None of it is worthy of being grasped or clung to. If you can maintain this practice of peace and inquiry, wisdom will automatically be generated. Everything sensed and experienced then falls into these three pits of impermanence, unsatisfactoriness, and not-self. This is vipassanā meditation. The mind is already peaceful, and whenever impure states of mind surface, throw them away into one of these three rubbish pits. This is the essence of vipassanā: discarding everything down into impermanence, unsatisfactoriness, and not-self. Good, bad, horrible, or whatever, toss it down. In a short time, understanding and insight will blossom forth in the midst of the three universal characteristics—feeble insight, that is. At this beginning stage the wisdom is still weak and feeble, but try to maintain this practice with consistency.

DO IT!

It's high time we started to meditate. Meditate to understand, to abandon, to relinquish, and to be at peace. It's difficult to put into words, but it's as if somebody wanted to get to know me, they'd have to come and live here. Eventually with daily contact we would get to know each other.

I used to be a wandering monk. I'd travel by foot to visit teachers and seek solitude. I didn't go around giving Dhamma talks. I went to listen to the Dhamma talks of the great Buddhist masters of the time. I didn't go to teach them. I listened to whatever advice they had to offer. Even when young or junior monks tried to tell me what the Dhamma was, I listened patiently. However, I rarely got into discussions about the Dhamma. I couldn't see the point in getting involved in lengthy discussions. Whatever teachings I accepted I took on board straight away, directly where they pointed to renunciation and letting go. What I did, I did for renunciation and letting go. We don't have to become experts in the scriptures. We're getting older with every day that passes, and every day we pounce on a mirage, missing the real thing. Practicing the Dhamma is something quite different than studying it.

I don't criticize any of the wide variety of meditation styles and techniques. As long as we understand their true purpose and meaning, they're not wrong. However, calling ourselves Buddhist meditators, but not strictly follow the monastic code of discipline (vinaya) will, in my opinion, never meet with success. Why? Because we try to bypass a vital section of the Path, skipping over virtue, samādhi, or wisdom. Some people may tell you not to get attached to the serenity of samatha meditation: "Don't bother with samatha; advance straight to the wisdom and insight practices of vipassanā." As I see it, if we attempt to detour straight to vipassanā, we'll find it impossible to successfully complete the journey.

Don't forsake the style of practice and meditation techniques of the eminent Forest Masters, such as the Venerable Ajahns Sao, Mun, Taungrut, and Upali. The path they taught is utterly reliable and true—if we do it the way they did. If we follow in their footsteps we'll gain true insight into ourselves. Ajahn Sao cared for his virtue impeccably. He didn't say we should bypass it. If these great masters of the Forest Tradition recommended practicing meditation and monastic etiquette in a particular way, then out of deep respect for them we should follow what they taught. If they said to do it, then do it. If they said to stop because it's wrong, then stop. We do it out of faith. We do it with unwavering sincerity and determination. We do it until we see the Dhamma in our own hearts, until we *are* the Dhamma. This is what the Forest Masters taught. Their disciples consequently developed profound respect, awe, and affection for them, because it was through following their path that they saw what their teachers saw.

Give it a try. Do it just like I say. If you actually do it, you'll see the Dhamma, be the Dhamma. If you actually undertake the search, what would stop you? The defilements of the mind will be vanquished if you approach them with the right strategy: be someone who renounces, one who is frugal with words, who is content with little, and who abandons all views and opinions stemming from self-importance and conceit. You will then be able to listen to anyone patiently, even if what they're saying is wrong. You will also be able to listen patiently to people when they're right. Examine yourself in this way. I assure you, it's possible, if you try. Scholars however, rarely come and put the Dhamma into practice. There are some, but they are few. It's a shame. The fact that you've made it this far and have come to visit is already worthy of praise. It shows inner strength. Some monasteries only encourage studying. The monks study and study, on and on, with no end in sight, and never cut that which needs to be cut. They only study the word "peace." But if you can stop still, then you'll discover something of real value. This is how you do research. This research is truly valuable and completely immobile. It goes straight to what you've been reading about. If scholars don't practice meditation, however, their knowledge has little understanding. Once they put the teachings into practice, those things that they have studied about then become vivid and clear.

So start practicing! Develop this type of understanding. Give living in the forest a try and come stay in one of these tiny huts. Trying out this training for a while and testing it for yourself would be of far greater value than just reading books. Then you can have discussions with yourself. While observing the mind it's as if it lets go and rests in its natural state. When it ripples and wavers from this still, natural state in the form of thoughts and concepts, the conditioning process of saṅkhāra is set in motion. Be very careful and keep a watchful eye on this process of conditioning. Once it moves and is dislodged from this natural state, Dhamma practice is no longer on the right track. It steps off into either sensual indulgence or self-torment. Right there. That's what gives rise to this web of mental conditioning. If the state of mind is a good one, this creates positive conditioning. If it's bad, the conditioning is negative. These originate in your own mind.

I'm telling you, it's great fun to closely observe how the mind works. I could happily talk about this one subject the whole day. When you get to know the ways of the mind, you'll see how this process functions and how it's kept going through being brainwashed by the mind's impurities. I see the mind as merely a single point. Psychological states are guests who come to visit this spot. Sometimes this person comes to call; sometimes that person pays a visit. They come to the visitor center. Train the mind to watch and know them all with the eyes of alert awareness. This is how you care for your heart and mind. Whenever a visitor approaches you wave them away. If you forbid them to enter, where are they going to sit down? There's only one seat, and you're sitting in it. Spend the whole day in this one spot.

This is the Buddha's firm and unshakable awareness; it watches over and protects the mind. You're sitting right here. Since the moment you emerged from the womb, every visitor that's ever come to call has arrived right here. No matter how often they come, they always come to this same spot, right here. Knowing them all, the Buddha's awareness sits alone, firm and unshakable. Those visitors journey here seeking to exert influence to condition and sway your mind in various ways. When they succeed in getting the mind entangled in their issues, psychological states arise. Whatever the issue is, wherever it seems to be leading, just forget it—it doesn't matter. Simply know who the guests are as they arrive. Once they've dropped by they will find that there's only one chair, and as long as you're occupying it they will have no place to sit down. They come thinking to fill your ear with gossip, but this time there's no room for them to sit. Next time they come there will also be no chair free. No matter how many times these chattering visitors show up, they always meet the same fellow sitting in the same spot. You haven't budged from that chair. How long do you think they will continue to put up with this situation? In just speaking to them you get to know them thoroughly. Everyone and everything you've ever known since you began to experience the world will come for a visit. Simply observing and being aware right here is enough to see the Dhamma entirely. You discuss, observe, and contemplate by yourself.

This is how to discuss Dhamma. I don't know how to talk about anything else. I can continue on speaking in this fashion, but in the end it's nothing but talking and listening. I'd recommend you actually go and do the practice. If you have a look for yourself, you'll encounter certain experiences. There's a Path to guide you and offer directions. As you carry on, the situation changes and you have to adjust your approach to remedy the problems that come up. It can be a long time before you see a clear signpost. If you're going to walk the same path as I did, the journey definitely has to take place in your own heart. If not, you'll encounter numerous obstacles.

It's just like hearing a sound. The hearing is one thing, the sound another, and we are consciously aware of both without compounding the event. We rely on nature to provide the raw material for the investigation in search of truth. Eventually the mind dissects and separates phenomena on its own. Simply put, the mind doesn't get involved. When the ears pick up a sound, observe what happens in the heart and mind. Do they get bound up, entangled, and carried away by it? Do they get irritated? At least know this much. When a sound then registers, it won't disturb the mind.

Being here, we take up those things close at hand rather than those far away. Even if we'd like to flee from sound, there's no escape. The only escape possible is through training the mind to be unwavering in the face of sound. Set sound down. The sounds we let go of, we can still hear. We hear but we let sound go, because we've already set it down. It's not that we have to forcefully separate the hearing and the sound. It separates automatically due to abandoning and letting go. Even if we then wanted to cling to a sound, the mind wouldn't cling. Because once we understand the true nature of sights, sounds, smells, tastes, and all the rest, and the heart sees with clear insight, everything sensed without exception falls within the domain of the universal characteristics of impermanence, unsatisfactoriness, and non-self.

Any time we hear a sound it's understood in terms of these universal characteristics. Whenever there's sense contact with the ear, we hear, but it's as if we didn't hear. This doesn't mean the mind no longer functions. Mindfulness and the mind intertwine and merge to monitor each other at all times without a lapse. When the mind is trained to this level, no matter what path we then choose to walk we will be doing research. We will be cultivating the analysis of phenomena, one of the essential factors of enlightenment, and this analysis will keep rolling on with its own momentum.

Discuss Dhamma with yourself. Unravel and release feeling, memory, perception, thinking, intentions, and consciousness. Nothing will be able to touch them as they continue to perform their functions on their own. For people who have mastered their minds, this process of reflection and investigation flows along automatically. It's no longer necessary to direct it intentionally. Whatever sphere the mind inclines toward, the contemplation is immediately appropriate.

ESTABLISHING THE BASIS OF MEDITATION

If Dhamma practice reaches this level, there's another interesting side benefit. While asleep: snoring, talking in our sleep, gnashing our teeth, and tossing and turning will all stop. Even if we've been resting in deep sleep, when we wake up we won't be drowsy. We'll feel energized and alert as if we'd been awake the whole time. I used to snore, but once the mind remained awake at all times, snoring stopped. How can you snore when you're awake? It's only the body that stops and sleeps. The mind is wide awake day and night, around the clock. This is the pure and heightened awareness of the Buddha: the one who knows, the awakened one, the joyous one, the brilliantly radiant one. This clear awareness never sleeps. Its energy is self-sustaining, and it never gets dull or sleepy. At this stage we can go without rest for two or three days. When the body begins to show signs of exhaustion, we sit down to meditate, immediately enter deep samādhi for five or ten minutes, and when we come out of that state, we feel fresh and invigorated as if we've had a full night's sleep. If we're beyond concern for the body, sleep is of minimal importance. We take appropriate measures to care for the body, but we aren't anxious about its physical condition. Let it follow its natural laws. We don't have to tell the body what to do. It tells itself. It's as if someone is prodding us, urging us to strive on in our efforts. Even if we feel lazy, there's a voice inside that constantly rouses our diligence. Stagnation at this point is impossible, because effort and progress have gathered an unstoppable momentum. Please check this out for yourself. You've been studying and learning a long time. Now it's time to study and learn about yourself.

In the beginning stages of Dhamma practice, physical seclusion is of vital importance. When you live alone in isolation you will recall the words of Venerable Sāriputta: "Physical seclusion is a cause and condition for the arising of mental seclusion, states of profound samādhi free from external sense contact. The seclusion of the mind is in turn a cause and condition for seclusion from mental defilements, enlightenment." And yet some people still say that seclusion is not important: "If your heart is peaceful, it doesn't matter where you are." It's true, but in the beginning stages we should remember that physical seclusion in a suitable environment comes first. Today or sometime soon, seek out a lonely cremation ground in a remote forest far from any habitation. Experiment with living all alone. Or seek out a fear-inspiring mountain peak. Go live alone, okay? You'll have lots of fun all night long. Only then will you know for yourself. Even I once thought that physical seclusion wasn't particularly important. That's what I thought, but once I actually got out there and did it, I reflected on what the Buddha taught. The Blessed One encouraged his disciples to practice in remote locations far removed from society. In the beginning this builds a foundation for internal seclusion of the mind which then supports the unshakable seclusion from defilements.

For example, say you're a lay person with a home and a family. What seclusion do you get? When you return home, as soon as you step inside the front door you get hit with chaos and complication. There's no physical seclusion. So you slip away for a retreat in a remote environment and the atmosphere is completely different. It's necessary to comprehend the importance of physical isolation and solitude in the initial stages of Dhamma practice. You then seek out a meditation master for instruction. He or she guides, advises, and points out those areas where your understanding is wrong, because it's precisely where you misunderstand that you think you are right. Right where you're wrong, you're sure you're right. Once the teacher explains, you understand what is wrong, and right where the teacher says you're wrong is precisely where you thought you were right.

From what I've heard, there are a number of Buddhist scholar monks who search and research in accordance with the scriptures. There's no reason why we shouldn't experiment. When it's time to open our books and study, we learn in that style. But when it's time to take up arms and engage in combat, we have to fight in a style that may not correspond with the theory. If a warrior enters battle and fights according to what he's read, he'll be no match for his opponent. When the warrior is sincere and the fight is real, he has to battle in a style that goes beyond theory. That's how it is. The Buddha's words in the scriptures are only guidelines and examples to follow, and studying can sometimes lead to carelessness.

The way of the Forest Masters is the way of renunciation. On this Path there's only abandoning. We uproot views stemming from self-importance. We uproot the very essence of our sense of self. I assure you, this practice will challenge you to the core, but no matter how difficult it is don't discard the Forest Masters and their teachings. Without proper guidance the mind and samādhi are potentially very deluding. Things that shouldn't be possible begin to happen. I've always approached such phenomena with caution and care. When I was a young monk, just starting out in practice during my first few years, I couldn't yet trust my mind. However, once I'd gained considerable experience and could fully trust the workings of my mind, nothing could pose a problem. Even if unusual phenomena manifested, I'd just leave it at that. If we are clued in to how these things work, they cease by themselves. It's all fuel for wisdom. As time goes by we find ourselves completely at ease.

In meditation, things that usually aren't wrong can be wrong. For example, we sit down cross-legged with determination and resolve: "Alright! No pussy-footing around this time. I will concentrate the mind. Just watch me!" No way that approach will work! Every time I tried that my meditation got nowhere. But we love the bravado. From what I've observed, meditation will develop at its own rate. Many evenings as I sat down to meditate I thought to myself, "Alright! Tonight I won't budge from this spot until at least 1:00 A.M." Even with this thought I was already making some bad kamma, because it wasn't long before the pain in my body attacked from all sides, overwhelming me until it felt like I was going to die. However, those occasions when the meditation went well, were times when I didn't place any limits on the sitting. I didn't set a goal of 7:00, 8:00, 9:00, or whatever, but simply kept sitting, steadily carrying on, letting go with equanimity. Don't force the meditation. Don't attempt to interpret what's happening. Don't coerce your heart with unrealistic demands that it enter a state of samādhi— or else you'll find it even more agitated and unpredictable than normal. Just allow the heart and mind to relax, to be comfortable and at ease.

Allow the breathing to flow easily at just the right pace, neither too short nor too long. Don't try to make it into anything special. Let the body relax, comfortable and at ease. Then keep doing it. Your mind will ask you, "How late are we going to meditate tonight? What time are we going to quit?" It incessantly nags, so you have to bellow out a reprimand, "Listen, buddy, just leave me alone." This inquisitive busybody needs to be regularly subdued, because it's nothing other than defilement coming to annoy you. Don't pay it any mind whatsoever. You have to be tough with it. "Whether I call it quits early or have a late night, it's none of your damn business! If I want to sit all night, it doesn't make any difference to anyone, so why do you come and stick your nose into my meditation?" You have to cut the nosy fellow off like that. You can then carry on meditating for as long as you wish, according to what feels right.

As you allow the mind to relax and be at ease, it becomes peaceful. Experiencing this, you'll recognize and appreciate the power of clinging. When you can sit on and on, for a very long time, going past midnight, comfortable and relaxed, you'll know you're getting the hang of meditation. You'll understand how attachment and clinging really do defile the mind.

When some people sit down to meditate they light a stick of incense in front of them and vow, "I won't get up until this stick of incense has burned down." Then they sit. After what seems like an hour they open their eyes and realize only five minutes have gone by. They stare at the incense, disappointed at how exceedingly long the stick still is. They close their eyes again and continue. Soon their eyes are open once more to check that stick of incense. These people don't get anywhere in meditation. Don't do it like that. Just sitting and dreaming about that stick of incense, "I wonder if it's almost finished burning," the meditation gets nowhere. Don't give importance to such things. The mind doesn't have to do anything special.

If we are going to undertake the task of developing the mind in meditation, don't let the defilement of craving know the ground rules or the goal. "How will you meditate, venerable?" it inquires. "How much will you do? How late are you thinking of going?" Craving keeps pestering until we submit to an agreement. Once we declare we're going to sit until midnight, it immediately begins to hassle us. Before even an hour has passed we're feeling so restless and impatient that we can't continue. Then more hindrances attack as we berate ourselves, "Hopeless! What, is sitting going to kill you? You said you were going to make your mind unshakable in samādhi, but it's still unreliable and all over the place. You made a vow and you didn't keep it." Thoughts of self-depreciation and dejection assail our minds, and we sink into self-hatred. There's no one else to blame or get angry at, and that makes it all the worse. Once we make a vow we have to keep it. We either fulfill it or die in the process. If we do vow to sit for a certain length of time, then we shouldn't break that vow and stop. In the meantime, however, just gradually practice and develop. There's no need for making dramatic vows. Try steadily and persistently to train the mind. Occasionally, the meditation will be peaceful, and all the aches and discomfort in the body will vanish. The pain in the ankles and knees will cease by itself.

Once we try our hand at cultivating meditation, if strange images, visions, or sensory perceptions start coming up, the first thing to do is to check our state of mind. Don't discard this basic principle. For such images to arise the mind has to be relatively peaceful. Don't crave for them to appear, and don't crave for them not to appear. If they do arise then examine them, but don't allow them to delude. Just remember they're not ours.

They are impermanent, unsatisfying, and not-self, just like everything else. Even if they are real, don't dwell on or pay much attention to them. If they stubbornly refuse to fade, then refocus your awareness on your breath with increased vigor. Take at least three long, deep breaths and each time slowly exhale completely. This may do the trick. Keep refocusing the attention.

Don't become possessive of such phenomena. They are nothing more than what they are, and what they are is potentially deluding. Either we like them and fall in love with them or the mind becomes poisoned with fear. They're unreliable: they may not be true or what they appear to be. If you experience them, don't try to interpret their meaning or project meaning onto them. Remember they're not ours, so don't run after these visions or sensations. Instead, immediately go back and check the present state of mind. This is our rule of thumb. If we abandon this basic principle and become drawn into what we believe we are seeing, we can forget ourselves and start babbling—or even go insane. We may lose our marbles to the point where we can't even relate to other people on a normal level. Place your trust in your own heart. Whatever happens, simply carry on observing the heart and mind. Strange meditative experiences can be beneficial for people with wisdom, but dangerous for those without. Whatever occurs don't become elated or alarmed. If experiences happen, they happen.

CONTEMPLATION

Another way to approach Dhamma practice is to contemplate and examine everything we see, do, and experience. Don't discard meditation. When some people finish sitting or walking meditation they think it's time to stop and rest. They stop focusing their minds on their object of meditation or theme of contemplation. They completely drop it. Don't practice like that. Whatever you see, inquire into what it really is. Contemplate the good people in the world. Contemplate the evil ones too. Take a penetrating look at the rich and powerful; the destitute and poverty-stricken. When you see a child, an elderly person, or a young man or woman, investigate the meaning of age. Everything is fuel for inquiry. This is how you cultivate the mind.

The contemplation that leads to the Dhamma is the contemplation of conditionality, the process of cause and effect, in all its various manifestations: both major and minor, black and white, good and bad. In short, everything. When you think, recognize it as a thought and contemplate that it's merely that, nothing more. All these things wind up in the graveyard of impermanence, unsatisfactoriness, and not-self, so don't possessively cling to any of them. This is the cremation ground of all phenomena. Bury and cremate them in order to experience the truth.

Having insight into impermanence means not allowing ourselves to suffer. It's a matter of investigating with wisdom. For example, we obtain something we consider good or pleasurable, and so we're happy. Take a close and sustained look at this goodness and pleasure. Sometimes after having it for a long time we get fed up with it. We want to give it away or sell it. If there's nobody who wants to buy it, we're ready to throw it away. Why? What are the reasons underlying this dynamic? Everything is impermanent, inconstant, and changing, that's why. If we can't sell it or even throw it away, we start to suffer. This entire issue is just like that, and once one incident is fully understood, no matter how many more similar situations arise, they are all understood to be just the same. That's simply the way things are. As the saying goes, "If you've seen one, you've seen them all."

Occasionally we see things we don't like. At times we hear annoying or unpleasant noises and get irritated. Examine this and remember it. Because some time in the future we might like those noises. We might actually delight in those very same things we once detested. It's possible! Then it occurs to us with clarity and insight, *"Aha!* All things are impermanent, unable to fully satisfy, and not-self." Throw them into the mass grave of these universal characteristics. The clinging to the likeable things we think we get, have, and are will then cease. We come to see everything as essentially the same. Everything we then experience generates insight into the Dhamma.

Everything I've said so far is simply for you to listen to and think about. It's just talk, that's all. When people come to see me, I speak. These sorts of subjects aren't the things we should sit around and gab about for hours. Just do it. Get in there and do it. It's like when we call a friend to go somewhere. We invite them. We get an answer. Then we're off, without a big fuss. We say just the right amount and leave it at that. I can tell you a thing or two about meditation, because I've done the work. But you know, maybe I'm wrong. Your job is to investigate and find out for yourself if what I say is true.

CHAPTER 17

MEDITATION
(SAMĀDHI BHĀVANA)

WHY DO YOU PRACTICE MEDITATION? It is because your hearts and minds do not understand what should be understood. In other words, you don't truly know how things are, or what is what. You don't know what is wrong and what is right, what it is that brings you suffering and causes you to doubt. The reason that you have come here to develop calm and restraint is that your hearts and minds are not at ease. They are swayed by doubting and agitation.

Although there may appear to be many ways to practice, really there is only one. As with fruit trees, it is possible to get fruit quickly by planting a cutting, but the tree will not be resilient and hardy. Another way is to cultivate a tree right from the seed, which produces a strong and resilient tree. Practice is the same.

When I first began to practice I had problems understanding this. As long as I still didn't know what's what, sitting meditation was a real chore, even bringing me to tears on occasion. Sometimes I would be aiming too high, at other times not high enough, never finding the point of balance. To practice in a way that's peaceful means to place the mind neither too high nor too low, but at the point of balance.

Practicing in different ways with different teachers can be very confusing. One teacher says you must practice one way; another says you should practice another way. You wonder which method to use, unsure of the essence of the practice. The result is confusion, doubt, and uncertainty. Nobody knows how to harmonize their practice.

So you must try not to think too much. If you do think, then do so with awareness. First, you must make your mind calm. Where there is knowing, there is no need to think. Awareness will arise in its place, and this will in turn become wisdom (paññā). The ordinary kind of thinking is not wisdom, but simply the aimless and unaware wandering of the mind, which inevitably results in agitation.

So at this stage you don't need to think. It just stirs up the heart. Obsessive thinking can even bring you to tears. The Buddha was a very wise person: he learned how to stop thinking. To meditate, you have to resolve that now is the time for training the mind and nothing else. Don't let the mind shoot off to the left or to the right, to the front or behind, above or below. At that time our only duty is to practice mindfulness of breathing. Fix your attention at the crown of the head and move it down through the body to the tips of the feet, and then back up to the head. Pass your awareness down through the body, observing with wisdom. We do this to gain an initial understanding of the way the body is. Then begin the meditation, remembering that your sole duty is to observe the inhalations and exhalations. Don't force the breath to be any longer or shorter than normal, just allow it to continue easily. Let it flow evenly, letting go with each in-breath and out-breath.

Although you are letting go, there should still be awareness. You must maintain this awareness, allowing the breath to enter and leave comfortably. Maintain the resolve that at this time you have no other duties or responsibilities. Thoughts about what will happen or what you will see during meditation may arise from time to time, but once they arise just let them cease by themselves; don't be unduly concerned with them.

During the meditation there is no need to pay attention to sense impressions. Whenever the mind is affected by sense contact, wherever there is a feeling or sensation in the mind, just let it go. Whether those sensations are good or bad is unimportant. Don't make something out of those sensations, just let them pass away and return your attention to the breath. Maintain the awareness of the breath entering and leaving. Don't create suffering over the breath being too long or too short, but simply observe it without trying to control or suppress it in any way. In other words, don't attach. As you continue, the mind will gradually lay things down and come to rest, the breath becoming lighter and lighter until it becomes so faint that it seems like it's not there at all. Both the body and the mind will feel light and energized. All that will remain will be a one-pointed knowing. The mind has reached a state of calm.

If the mind is agitated, set up mindfulness and inhale deeply till there is no space left for more air, then release it all completely until none remains. Follow this with another deep inhalation and exhalation. Do this two or three times, then reestablish concentration. The mind should be calmer. Each time sense impressions agitate the mind, repeat the process. Similarly with walking meditation. If, while walking, the mind becomes agitated, stop, calm the mind, reestablish the awareness with the meditation object, and then continue walking. Sitting and walking meditation are in essence the same, differing only in terms of the physical posture used.

Sometimes there may be doubt, so you must have sati. Be one who knows, who continually follows and examines the agitated mind in whatever form it takes. This is to have sati. Sati watches over and takes care of the mind. You must maintain this knowing and not be careless or wander astray, no matter what condition the mind takes on.

The trick is to have sati take control and supervise the mind. Once the mind is unified with sati, a new kind of awareness will emerge. The mind that has developed calm is held in check by that calm, just like a chicken held in a coop: the chicken is unable to wander outside, but it can still move around within the coop. Its walking to and fro doesn't get it into trouble because it is restrained by the coop. Likewise the awareness that takes place when the mind has sati and is calm does not cause trouble. None of the thinking or sensations that take place within the calm mind cause harm or disturbance.

Some people don't want to experience any thoughts or feelings at all, but this is going too far. Feelings arise within the state of calm. The mind is both experiencing feelings and calm at the same time, without being disturbed. When there is calm like this, there are no harmful consequences. Problems occur when the chicken gets out of the coop. For instance, you may be watching the breath entering and leaving and then forget yourself, allowing the mind to wander away from the breath, back home, off to the shops, or to any number of different places. Perhaps even half an hour may pass before you suddenly realize you're supposed to be practicing meditation and reprimand yourself for your lack of sati. This is where you have to be really careful, because this is where the chicken gets out of the coop—the mind leaves its base of calm.

You must take care to maintain the awareness with sati and try to pull the mind back. Although I use the words "pull the mind back," in fact the mind doesn't really go anywhere, only the object of awareness has changed. You must make the mind stay right here and now. As long as there is sati there will be presence of mind. It seems like you are pulling the mind back, but really it hasn't gone anywhere; it has simply changed a little. When sati is regained, in a flash you are back with the mind, without it having to be brought from anywhere.

When there is total knowing, a continuous and unbroken awareness at each and every moment, this is called presence of mind. If your attention drifts from the breath to other places, then the knowing is broken. Whenever there is awareness of the breath, the mind is there.

There must be both sati and sampajañña. Sati is mindfulness and sampajañña is self-awareness. Right now you are clearly aware of the breath. This exercise of watching the breath helps sati and sampajañña develop together. They share the work. Having both sati and sampajañña is like having two workers to lift a heavy plank of wood. Suppose these two workers try to lift some heavy planks, but the weight is so great it's almost unendurable. Then a third worker, imbued with goodwill, sees them and rushes in to help. In the same way, when there is sati and sampajañña, then paññā (wisdom) will arise at the same place to help out. Then all three of them support each other.

With paññā there will be an understanding of sense objects. For instance, during meditation you may start to think of a friend, but then paññā should immediately counter with "It doesn't matter," "Stop," or "Forget it." Or if there are thoughts about where you will go tomorrow, then the response of paññā will be "I'm not interested, I don't want to concern myself with such things." If you start thinking about other people, you should think, "No, I don't want to get involved," "Just let go," or "It's all uncertain." This is how you should deal with sense objects in meditation, recognizing them as "not sure, not sure," and maintaining this kind of awareness.

You must give up all the thinking, the inner dialogue, and the doubting. Don't get caught up in these things during the meditation. In the end all that will remain in the mind in its purest form are sati, sampajañña, and paññā. Whenever these weaken, doubts will arise; but try to abandon those doubts immediately, leaving only sati, sampajañña, and paññā. Try to develop sati like this until it can be maintained at all times. Then you will understand sati, sampajañña, and paññā thoroughly.

Focusing the attention at this point you will see sati, sampajañña, samādhi, and paññā together. Whether you are attracted to or repelled by external sense objects, you will be able to tell yourself, "It's not sure." Either way they are just hindrances to be swept away till the mind is clean. All that should remain is sati, mindfulness; sampajañña, clear awareness; samādhi, the firm and unwavering mind; and paññā, or consummate wisdom.

Now about the tools or aids to meditation practice—there should be *mettā* (goodwill) in your heart; in other words, the qualities of generosity, kindness, and helpfulness. These should be maintained as the foundation for mental purity. For example, begin doing away with *lobha,* or greed, through giving. When people are selfish they aren't happy. Selfishness leads to a sense of discontent, and yet people tend to be very selfish without realizing how it affects them.

You can experience this at any time, especially when you are hungry. Suppose you get some apples and you have the opportunity to share them with a friend; you think it over for a while, and, sure, the intention to give is there all right, but you want to give the smaller one. To give the big one would be...well, such a shame. It's hard to think straight. You tell them to go ahead and pick one, but then you say, "Take this one!" and give them the smaller apple! This is a form of selfishness that people usually don't notice.

You really have to go against the grain to give. Even though you may really only want to give the smaller apple, you must force yourself to give away the bigger one. Of course, once you have given it to your friend you feel good inside. Training the mind by going against the grain requires self-discipline—you must know how to give and how to give up, not allowing selfishness to stick. Once you learn how to give to others, your mind will be joyful. If you hesitate over which fruit to give, then while you deliberate you will be troubled, and even if you give a bigger one, there will still be a sense of reluctance. But as soon as you firmly decide to give the bigger one, the matter is over and done with. This is going against the grain in the right way.

Doing this, you win mastery over yourself. If you can't do it, you'll be a victim of yourself and continue to be selfish. All of us have been selfish— it's a defilement that has to be cut off. In the Pali scriptures, giving is called *dāna,* which results in happiness for others and helps to cleanse the mind from defilement. You should reflect on this and develop it in your practice.

You may think that practicing like this involves hounding yourself, but it doesn't really. Actually it's hounding craving and the defilements. If defilements arise within you, you have to do something to remedy them. Defilements are like a stray cat. If you give it as much food as it wants, it will always be coming around looking for more; but if you stop feeding it, after a couple of days it'll stop coming around. It's the same with the defilements. If you stop feeding them, they won't come to disturb you; they'll leave your mind in peace. So rather than being afraid of defilements, make them afraid of you. You do that by seeing the Dhamma within your minds.

Where does the Dhamma arise? It arises with our knowing and understanding in this way. Everyone is able to know and understand the Dhamma. It's not something that has to be researched in books or studied a lot. Just reflect right now, and you can see what I am talking about. Everybody has defilements, don't they? In the past you've pampered your defilements, but now you must know their nature and not allow them to bother you.

The next constituent of practice is moral restraint (sīla). Sīla watches over and nurtures the practice in the same way as parents look after their children. Maintaining moral restraint means not only to avoid harming others but also to help and encourage them. At the very least you should maintain the Five Precepts, which are:

Not only not killing or deliberately harming others, but also spreading goodwill toward all beings.

Being honest, refraining from infringing on the rights of others—in other words, not stealing.

Knowing moderation in sexual relations. The family structure is based on the husband and wife. A husband or wife should know each other's disposition, needs, and wishes, observe moderation, and know the proper bounds of sexual activity. Some people don't know the limits. Having a husband or wife isn't enough; they have to have a second or third partner. The way I see it, you can't consume even one partner completely, so to have two or three is just plain indulgence. You must try to cleanse the mind and train it to know moderation. Knowing moderation is true purity. Without it there are no limits to your behavior. When eating delicious food don't dwell too much on how it tastes; think of your stomach and consider how much is appropriate to its needs. If you eat too much, there'll be trouble. Moderation is the best way. Just one partner is enough. Two or three is an indulgence and will only cause problems.

Being honest in speech—this is also a tool for eradicating defilements. You must be honest and straight, truthful and upright.

Refraining from taking intoxicants. You must know restraint and preferably give these things up altogether. People are already intoxicated enough with their families, relatives and friends, material possessions, wealth, and all the rest of it. That's quite enough already without making things worse by taking intoxicants as well. These things just create darkness in the mind. Those who take large amounts should try to gradually cut down and eventually give it up altogether. You need to know what is what. What are the things that are oppressing you in your everyday lives? What are the actions that cause this oppression? Good actions bring good results and bad actions bring bad results. These are the causes.

Once moral restraint is pure there will be a sense of honesty and kindness toward others. This will bring about contentment and freedom from worries and remorse. Freedom from remorse is a form of happiness. It's almost like a heavenly state. You eat and sleep in comfort with the happiness arising from moral restraint. This is a principle of Dhamma practice— refraining from bad actions so that goodness can arise. If moral restraint is maintained in this way, evil will disappear and good will arise in its place.

But this isn't the end of the story. Once people have attained some happiness they tend to be heedless and not go any further in the practice. They get stuck on happiness. They don't want to progress any further; they prefer the happiness of "heaven." It's comfortable, but there's no real understanding. You must keep reflecting to avoid being deluded. Reflect again and again on the disadvantages of this happiness. It's transient; it doesn't last forever. Soon you are separated from it. It's not a sure thing. Once happiness disappears, suffering arises in its place and the tears come again. Even heavenly beings end up crying and suffering.

So the Lord Buddha taught us that there is an unsatisfactory side to happiness. Usually when this kind of happiness is experienced, there is no real understanding of it. The peace that is truly certain and lasting is masked by this deceptive happiness. This happiness is a refined form of defilement to which we attach. Everybody likes to be happy. Happiness arises because of our liking for something. But as soon as that liking changes to dislike, suffering arises. We must reflect on this happiness to see its uncertainty and limitation. Once things change, suffering arises. This suffering is also uncertain; don't think that it is fixed or absolute. This kind of reflection is called *ādinavakathā,* or reflection on the inadequacy and limitation of the conditioned world. This means to reflect on happiness rather than accepting it at face value. Seeing that it is uncertain, you shouldn't cling fast to it. You should take hold of it but then let it go, seeing both the benefit and the harm of happiness.

When you see that things are imperfect, your heart will come to understand *nekkhammakathā,* or reflection on renunciation. The mind will become disenchanted and seek for a way out. Disenchantment comes from having seen the way forms really are, the way tastes really are, the way love and hatred really are. By disenchantment we mean that there is no longer the desire to cling to or attach to things. There is a withdrawal from clinging, to a point where you can abide comfortably, observing with an equanimity that is free of attachment. This is the peace that arises from practice.

CHAPTER 18

DHAMMA FIGHTING

FIGHT AGAINST GREED, against aversion, against delusion—they are the enemies. In the practice of Buddhism, the path of the Buddha, we fight with the help of Dhamma and with patient endurance. We fight by resisting our countless moods.

Dhamma and the world are interrelated. Where there is Dhamma, there is the world; where there is the world, there is Dhamma. Where there are defilements, there are those who conquer defilements, those who do battle with them. This is called fighting inwardly. To fight outwardly, people drop bombs and shoot guns; they conquer others or are conquered by them. Conquering others is the way of the world. In the practice of Dhamma we don't fight others but instead conquer our own minds, patiently enduring and resisting our moods.

When it comes to Dhamma practice, we don't harbor resentment and enmity but instead let go of all forms of ill will in our actions and thoughts, freeing ourselves from jealousy, aversion, and resentment. Hatred can be overcome only by not harboring resentment or bearing grudges.

Resentment and grudges often lead to reprisals. If we allow a hurtful act to be over and done with, there's no need for us to answer with revenge and hostility. We see that act simply as action (kamma). "Reprisal" *(vera)* means to continue that action further with thoughts of "You did this to me so I'm going to get you back." There's no end to this. It brings about the continual seeking of revenge, and so hatred is never abandoned. As long as we behave like this, the chain remains unbroken and the feuding continues.

That's what the Buddha taught the world, out of compassion for all worldly beings. But the world nevertheless carries on feuding and fighting. The wise should look into this and select those forms of conduct that are of true value. As a prince, the Buddha trained in the various arts of warfare, but he saw that they aren't really useful. They are limited to the world with its fighting and aggression.

Therefore, in training ourselves as those who have left the world—as monks—we must learn to give up all forms of unwholesomeness, all those things that cause enmity. We conquer ourselves, not others. We fight, but we fight only against the defilements: if there is greed, we fight that; if there is aversion, we fight that; if there is delusion, we strive to give it up.

This is called Dhamma fighting. This warfare of the heart is really difficult. In fact, it's the most difficult thing of all. We become monastics in order to contemplate this, to learn the art of fighting greed, aversion, and delusion. This is our prime responsibility. Very few people fight like this. Most people fight with other things; they rarely fight defilements. They rarely even see them.

The Buddha taught us to give up all forms of unwholesomeness and cultivate virtue. This is the right path. Having reached the Path, we must learn, and this means we must be prepared for some hardship, just like students in the world. Students find it difficult enough to obtain the knowledge and learning necessary for them to pursue their careers. So they need endurance. When they feel averse or lazy, they must force themselves to work; only then can they graduate and get a job. The practice for a monk is similar. If we resolve to practice and contemplate, then we will surely see the way.

Diṭṭhimāna is a harmful thing. *Diṭṭhi* means "view" or "opinion." All forms of view are called diṭṭhi: seeing good as evil, seeing evil as good— however we see things. Having views is not the problem. The problem lies with the clinging to those views, which is called *māna:* holding on to those views as if they were the truth. Such clinging leads us to spin around from birth to death, never reaching the end of the Path. So the Buddha urged us to let go of views.

Where many people live together, as monks do in a monastery, they can still practice comfortably if their views are in harmony. But even two or three monks would have difficulty living together if their views were not harmonious. When we humble ourselves and let go of our views, even if there are many of us, we come together in the Buddha, Dhamma, and Sangha.

There need not be disharmony just because many of us live together. Just look at a millipede. A millipede has many legs, doesn't it? You'd think it would have difficulty walking, but actually it doesn't. It has its own order and rhythm. In our practice it's the same. If we practice as the Noble Sangha of the Buddha practiced, then it's easy. That is, *supaṭipanno*—those who practice well; *ujupaṭipanno*—those who practice straightly; *ñāyapaṭi-panno*—those who practice to transcend suffering; and *sāmīcipaṭipanno*—those who practice properly. These four qualities, established within us, will make us true members of the Sangha. Even if we number in the hundreds or thousands, we all travel the same path. We come from different backgrounds, but we are the same. Even though our views may differ, if we practice correctly there will be no friction. Just like all the rivers and streams that flow to the sea, once they enter the sea they all have the same taste and color. When we enter the stream of Dhamma, it's the one Dhamma. Even though we come from different places, we harmonize and merge.

But if there is diṭṭhimāna, disputes and conflict will arise. So the Buddha taught us to let go of views. Don't allow māna to cling to views beyond their relevance.

The Buddha taught the value of constant recollection or mindfulness (sati). Whether we are standing, walking, sitting, or reclining, wherever we are, we should have this power of mindfulness. When we have sati we see ourselves; we see our own minds. We see the "body within the body," "the mind within the mind." If we don't have sati we don't know anything, we aren't aware of what is happening.

So sati is very important. With constant sati we will listen to the Dhamma of the Buddha at all times. This is because "the eye seeing forms" is Dhamma, as is the ear hearing sounds, the nose smelling odors, the tongue tasting flavors, and the body feeling sensations. And when impressions arise in the mind, that is Dhamma also. Therefore one who has constant sati always hears the Buddha's teaching. The Dhamma is always there.

Sati is mindfulness; sampajañña is self-awareness. This awareness is the actual "one who knows," the Buddha. When there is sati-sampajañña, understanding will follow. We know what is going on. When the eye sees forms: Is this proper or improper? When the ear hears sound: Is this appropriate or inappropriate? Is it harmful? Is it wrong? Is it right? And so on with the other senses. If we understand, we hear the Dhamma all the time. So let us all understand that right now we are learning in the midst of Dhamma. Whether we go forward or step back, we meet the Dhamma—it's all Dhamma if we have sati. Watching an animal running around in the forest, we see that animals are the same as us. They run away from suffering and chase after happiness, just as people do. What they don't like they avoid; they are afraid of dying, just like people. If we reflect on this, we see that all beings in the world are the same in their various instincts. Thinking like this is called *bhāvanā,* seeing according to the truth, seeing that all beings are companions in birth, old age, sickness, and death.

Therefore it is said we must have sati. If we have sati we will see the state of our own mind. Whatever we are thinking or feeling, we must know it. This knowing is called *Buddho,* the Buddha, the "one who knows," who knows thoroughly, clearly, and completely. When the mind knows completely, we find the right practice. If you are without sati for five minutes you are crazy for five minutes, heedless for five minutes. To have sati is to know yourself, to know the condition of your mind and your life, to have understanding and discernment, to listen to the Dhamma at all times.

So be sure to practice every day. Whether you're feeling lazy or diligent, just practice. Don't practice only when you're in the mood. If you practice following your moods, it's not Dhamma. Day or night, peaceful mind or not, it doesn't matter. Just practice.

It's like children learning to write. At first they don't write nicely—big, long loops and squiggles. After a while the writing improves. Practicing the Dhamma is like this. At first you feel awkward, sometimes calm, sometimes not—you don't really know what's what. Some people get really discouraged. Don't slacken off! You must persevere with the practice. Keep up the effort, just like the schoolchildren: as they get older they write better and better. They write badly to begin with but soon learn to write beautifully, all because of practice during childhood.

Our practice is like this. Try to have mindfulness at all times: standing, walking, sitting, or reclining. When we perform our various duties smoothly and well, we have peace of mind. When there is peace of mind in our work, it's easy to have peaceful meditation. They go hand in hand. So put effort in your practice. This is training.

CHAPTER 19

JUST DO IT!

Just keep breathing in and out like this. Don't be interested in anything else. It doesn't matter even if someone is standing on their head
with their ass in the air. Don't pay any attention. Just stay with the in-
breath and the out-breath. Concentrate your awareness on the breath. Just
keep doing it.

Don't take up anything else. There's no need to think about gaining
things. Don't take up anything at all. Simply know the in-breath and the
out-breath. The in-breath and the out-breath. *Bud-* on the in-breath; *-dho*
on the out-breath. Just stay with the breath in this way until you are aware
of the in-breath and aware of the out-breath…aware of the in-
breath…aware of the out-breath. Be aware in this way until the mind is
peaceful, without irritation, without agitation, merely the breath going out
and coming in. Let your mind remain in this state. You don't need a goal
yet. This is the first stage of practice.

If the mind is at ease, at peace, then it will naturally be aware. As you
keep staying with it, the breath diminishes, becomes softer. The body
becomes pliable, the mind becomes pliable. It's a natural process. Sitting is
comfortable: you're not dull, you don't nod, you're not sleepy. The mind
has a natural ease with whatever it does. It is still. It is at peace. And then
when you leave the samādhi, you say to yourself, "Wow, what was that?"
You recall the peace that you've just experienced. And you never forget it.

What follows along with us is called sati, the power of mindfulness, and
sampajañña, self-awareness. Whatever we say or do, wherever we go, on

alms round or whatever, while eating a meal, washing our alms bowl, then be aware of what it's all about. Be constantly mindful. Follow the mind.

When you're practicing walking meditation *(cankama)*, select a walking path, say from one tree to another, about fifty feet in length. Walking cankama is the same as sitting meditation. Focus your awareness: "Now, I am going to put forth effort. With strong mindfulness and self-awareness I am going to pacify my mind." The object of concentration depends on the person. Find what suits you. Some people spread mettā to all sentient beings and then, leading off with their right foot, walk at a normal pace, using the mantra *Buddho* in conjunction with the walking. Continually being aware of that object. If the mind becomes agitated then stop, calm the mind, and then resume walking. Be constantly self-aware. Aware at the beginning of the Path, aware at every stage of the Path, the beginning, the middle, and the end. Make this knowing continuous.

Walking cankama means walking to and fro. It's not easy. Some people see us walking up and down and think we're crazy. They don't realize that walking cankama gives rise to great wisdom. Walk to and fro. If you're tired then stand and still your mind. Focus on making the breathing comfortable. When it is reasonably comfortable then switch the attention to walking again.

The postures change by themselves. Standing, walking, sitting, lying down. They change. We can't just sit all the time, stand all the time, or lie down all the time. We have to spend our time with these different postures, so we make all four postures beneficial. We just keep doing it. But it's not easy.

Here's a way to make it easy to visualize it. Take a glass and place it on a table for two minutes. When the time is up, place the glass somewhere else on the table for two minutes. Then put it back where you first had it, again for two minutes. Keep doing that. Do it again and again until you start to suffer, until you doubt, until wisdom arises: "What am I doing, moving a glass back and forth like a madman?" The mind will think in its habitual way. It doesn't matter what anyone says. Just keep moving that glass. Every two minutes, okay?—don't daydream, two minutes not five. As soon as two minutes are up then move it back. Focus on that. This is the matter of action.

Looking at the in-breaths and out-breaths is the same. Sit with your right foot resting on your left leg, sit straight; watch the inhalation to its full extent until it completely disappears in the abdomen. When the inhalation is complete then allow the breath out until the lungs are empty. Don't force it. It doesn't matter how long or short or soft the breath is, let it be just right for you. Sit and watch the inhalation and the exhalation; make yourself comfortable with that. Don't allow your mind to get lost. If it gets lost then stop, look to see where it's got to, why it is not following the breath. Go after it and bring it back. Get it to stay with the breath, and, without doubt, one day you will see the reward. Just keep doing it. Do it as if you won't gain anything, as if nothing will happen, as if you don't know who's doing it, but keep doing it anyway. Like rice in the barn. You take it out and sow it in the fields, as if you were throwing it away; sow it throughout the fields, without being interested in it, and yet it sprouts, rice plants grow up, you transplant it and you've got sweet green rice. That's what it's about.

This is the same. Just sit there. Sometimes you might think, "Why am I watching the breath so intently? Even if I didn't watch it, it would still keep going in and out."

Well, you'll always finds something to think about. That's a view. It is an expression of the mind. Forget it. Keep trying over and over again and make the mind peaceful.

Once the mind is at peace, the breath will diminish, the body will become relaxed, the mind will become subtle. They will be in a state of balance until it will seem as if there's no breath, but nothing happens to you. When you reach this point, don't panic, don't get up and run off because you think you've stopped breathing. It just means that your mind is at peace. You don't have to do anything. Just sit there and look at whatever is present.

Sometimes you may wonder, "Hey, am I breathing?" This is the same mistake. It is the thinking mind. Whatever happens, allow things to take their natural course, no matter what feeling arises. Know it, look at it. But don't be deluded by it. Keep doing it, keep doing it. Do it often. After the meal, air your robe on a line, and get straight out onto the walking meditation path. Keep thinking, *Buddho, Buddho.* Think it all the time that you're walking. Concentrate on *Buddho* as you walk. Wear the path down; wear it down until it's a trench and it's halfway up your calves, or up to your knees. Just keep walking.

It's not just strolling along in a perfunctory way, thinking about this and that for one length of the path, and then going up into your hut and looking at your sleeping mat—how inviting!—and lying down and snoring away like a pig. If you do that you won't get anything from the practice at all.

Keep doing it until you're fed up and then see how far that laziness goes. Keep looking until you come to the end of laziness. Whatever it is you experience, you have to go all the way through it before you overcome it. It's not as if you can just repeat the word *Peace* to yourself and then, as soon as you sit, peace will arise like after flicking a switch, and if it doesn't, you can give up. If that's the case you'll never be peaceful.

It's easy to talk about and hard to do. It's like monks who are thinking of disrobing, saying, "Rice farming doesn't seem so difficult to me. I'd be better off as a rice farmer." They start farming without knowing about cows or buffaloes, harrows or ploughs, nothing at all. They find out that when you talk about farming it sounds easy, but when you actually try it you get to know exactly what the difficulties are.

Everyone would like to search for peace in that way. Actually, peace does lie right there, but you don't know it yet. You can follow after it, you can talk about it as much as you like, but you won't know what it is.

So, do it. Follow it until you know, in step with the breath, concentrating on the breath using the mantra *Buddho*. Just that much. Don't let the mind wander off anywhere else. At this time have this knowing. Do this. Study just this much. Just keep doing it, doing it in this way. If you start thinking that nothing is happening, just carry on anyway. Just carry on regardless and you will get to know the breath.

Okay, so give it a try! If you sit in this way and the mind gets the hang of it, the mind will reach an optimum, a "just right" state. When the mind is peaceful the self-awareness arises naturally. Then if you want to sit right through the night, you feel nothing, because the mind is enjoying itself. When you get this far, when you're good at it, then you might find you want to give Dhamma talks to your friends until the cows come home. That's how it goes sometimes.

It's like the time when Por Sang was still a postulant. One night he'd been walking cankama and then began to sit. His mind became lucid and sharp. He wanted to expound the Dhamma. He couldn't stop. I heard the sound of someone teaching over in that bamboo grove, really belting it out. I thought, "Is that someone giving a Dhamma talk, or is someone complaining about something?" It didn't stop. So I got my flashlight and went over to have a look. I was right. There in the bamboo grove, sitting cross-legged in the light of a lantern, was Por Sang, talking so fast I couldn't keep up.

So I called out to him, "Por Sang, have you gone crazy?"

He said, "I don't know what it is, I just want to talk the Dhamma. I sit down and I've got to talk; I walk and I've got to talk. I've just got to expound the Dhamma all the time. I don't know where it's going to end."

When people practice the Dhamma, I thought to myself, there's no limit to the things that can happen.

So keep doing it, don't stop. Don't follow your moods. Go against the grain. Practice when you feel lazy and practice when you feel diligent. Practice when you're sitting and practice when you're walking. When you lay down, focus on your breathing and tell yourself, "I will not indulge in the pleasure of laying down." Teach your heart in this way. Get up as soon as you awaken, and carry on putting forth effort.

Eating, tell yourself, "I eat this food, not with craving, but as medicine, to sustain my body for a day and a night, only in order that I may continue my practice."

When you lie down, teach your mind. When you eat, teach your mind. Maintain that attitude constantly. If you're going to stand up, then be aware of that. If you're going to lie down, then be aware of that. Whatever you do, be aware. When you lie down, lie on your right side and focus on the breath, using the mantra *Buddho* until you fall asleep. Then when you wake up it's as if *Buddho* has been there all the time; it's not been interrupted. For peace to arise, there needs to be mindfulness there all the time. Don't go looking at other people. Don't be interested in other people's affairs; just be interested in your own.

When you do sitting meditation, sit straight; don't lean your head too far back or too far forward. Keep a balanced "just-right" posture like a Buddha image. Then your mind will be bright and clear.

Endure for as long as you can before changing your posture. If it hurts, let it hurt. Don't be in a hurry to change your position. Don't think to yourself, "Oh! It's too much. I better take a rest." Patiently endure until the pain has reached a peak; then endure some more.

Endure, endure until you can't keep up the mantra *Buddho*. Then take as your object the place where it hurts. "Oh! Pain. Pain. Real pain." You can make the pain your meditation object rather than *Buddho*. Focus on it continuously. Keep sitting. When the pain has reached its limit, see what happens.

The Buddha said that pain arises by itself and disappears by itself. Let it die; don't give up. Sometimes you may break out in a sweat. Big beads, as large as corn kernels, rolling down your chest. But when you've passed through painful feeling once, then you will know all about it. Keep doing it. Don't push yourself too much. Just keep steadily practicing.

Be aware while you're eating. You chew and swallow. Where does the food go to? Know what foods agree with you and what foods disagree. Try gauging the amount of food. As you eat keep looking, and when you think that after another five mouthfuls you'll be full, then stop and drink some water and you will have eaten just the right amount. If you sit or walk afterward, then you won't feel heavy. Your meditation will improve.

Try it. See whether or not you can do it. But that's not the way we usually do it. When we feel full we take another five mouthfuls. That's what the mind tells us. It doesn't know how to teach itself. Craving and defilement lead in a different direction from the teachings of the Buddha. Someone who lacks a genuine wish to train their minds will be unable to do it. Keep watching your mind.

Be vigilant with sleep. Your success will depend on being aware of the skillful means. The amount you sleep may vary—some nights you have an early night and other times a late night. But try practicing like this: whatever time you go to sleep, just sleep at one stretch. As soon as you wake up, get up. Don't go back to sleep. Whether you sleep a lot or a little, just sleep at one stretch. Make a resolution that as soon as you wake up, even if you haven't had enough sleep, you will get up, wash your face, and then start to walk caṅkama or sit in meditation. Know how to train yourself like this. It's not something you can know through listening to someone else. You will know through training yourself, through practice, through doing it. And so I tell you to practice.

This training of the heart is difficult. When you are doing sitting meditation, then let your mind have only one object. Let it stay with the in-breath and the out-breath and your mind will gradually become calm. If your mind is in turmoil, it will have many objects. When you sit, do you think of your home? Some people think of eating Chinese noodles. When you're first ordained as a monk, you feel hungry.[47] You want to eat and drink. You think about all kinds of food. Your mind is going crazy. If that's what's happening, then let it. But as soon as you overcome it, then it will disappear.

Do it! Have you ever walked caṅkama, what was it like? Did your mind wander? If it did, then stop and let it come back. If it wanders off a lot, then don't breathe. Hold your breath until your lungs are about to burst. It will come back by itself. No matter how bad it is, if it's racing around all over the place, then hold your breath. As your lungs are about to burst, your mind will return. You must energize the mind. Training the mind isn't like training animals. The mind is truly hard to train. Don't be easily discouraged. If you hold your breath, you will be unable to think of anything and the mind will run back to you of its own accord.

It's like water in a bottle. When we tip it out slowly, the water drips out—*drip...drip....* But when we tip the bottle more, the water runs out in a continuous stream. Mindfulness is like that. If we accelerate our efforts, practicing in an even, continuous way, our mindfulness will be uninterrupted like a stream of water. No matter whether we are standing, walking, sitting, or lying down, that knowledge is uninterrupted, flowing like a stream.

Our training of the heart is like this. After a moment of mindfulness, it's thinking of this and thinking of that again. It is agitated and mindfulness is not continuous. But whatever it thinks about, never mind, just keep putting forth effort. It will be like the drops of water that become more frequent until they join up and become a stream. Then our knowledge will be encompassing. Standing, sitting, walking, or lying down, whatever you are doing, this knowing will look after you.

Start right now. Give it a try. But don't hurry. If you just sit there watching to see what will happen, you'll be wasting your time. So be careful. If you try too hard, you won't be successful, but if you don't try at all then you won't be successful either.

CHAPTER 20

RIGHT PRACTICE—
STEADY PRACTICE

Bear in mind that this practice is difficult. The mind is the important thing, but training it is hard. Everything within this body-mind system comes together at the mind. The eyes, ears, nose, tongue, and body all receive sensations and send them to the mind, which is the supervisor of all the other sense organs. If the mind is well trained, all problems come to an end. If there are still problems it's because the mind still has doubts; it doesn't know things in accordance with the truth.

Understand that you have come fully prepared for practicing Dhamma. Whether standing, walking, sitting, or reclining, the tools you need with which to practice are well provided, wherever you are. They are there, just like the Dhamma. The Dhamma is something that abounds everywhere. Right here, on land or in water, wherever, the Dhamma is always present. The Dhamma is perfect and complete, but it's our practice that's not yet complete.

The Lord Buddha, fully enlightened, taught a means by which all of us may practice and come to know this Dhamma. It isn't a big thing, but it's the truth of the matter. For example, look at hair. If we know even one strand of hair, then we know every strand, both our own and also that of others. We know that strands of hair are all simply "hair." By knowing one strand of hair we know it all.

Or consider people. If we see the true nature of conditions within ourselves, we know all the other people in the world, because all people are the same. Dhamma is like this. It's a small thing and yet it's big. By seeing the truth of one condition, one sees the truth of them all.

Nevertheless, the training is difficult. It's difficult because of wanting *(taṇhā)*. If you don't "want" then you don't practice. But if you practice out of wanting, you won't see the Dhamma. Think about that. If you don't want to practice, you can't practice. You must first want to practice in order to actually do it. Whether stepping forward or stepping back, you meet desire. This is why the meditators of the past have said that this practice is something that's extremely difficult to do. You don't see Dhamma because of desire. Sometimes the desire is very strong; you want to see the Dhamma immediately, but the Dhamma is not in accord with your mind—your mind is not yet Dhamma.

So the practice is difficult and arduous because of desires. As soon as we sit down to meditate we want to become peaceful. If we didn't want to find peace we wouldn't sit, we wouldn't practice. As soon as we sit down we want peace to be right there, but wanting the mind to be calm makes for confusion, and we feel restless. This is how it goes. So the Buddha says, "Don't speak out of desire, don't sit out of desire, don't walk out of desire. Whatever you do, don't do it with desire." Desire means wanting. If you don't want to do something you won't do it. If our practice reaches this point we can get quite discouraged. How can we practice? As soon as we sit down there is desire in the mind.

Actually, this mind of ours is simply a condition of nature, like a tree in the forest. If you want a board of wood it must come from a tree, but the tree is a tree—not yet a board. Before it can really be of use to us we must take that tree and saw it into boards. Intrinsically it's just a tree, a condition of nature. But in its raw state it isn't yet of much use to those who need timber. Our mind is like this. It is a condition of nature. As such it perceives thoughts; it discriminates into beautiful and ugly, and so on.

This mind of ours must be further trained; we can't just let it be. It's a condition of nature, but we have to train it to realize that it's a condition of nature. We have to improve on nature, so that it's appropriate to our needs, which is Dhamma. Dhamma is something that must be practiced and brought within.

If you don't practice you won't know the Dhamma. You won't know it just by reading or studying. Or if you do know it, your knowledge will be defective. For example, this spittoon here. Everybody knows it's a spittoon, but they don't fully *know* the spittoon. Why don't they fully know it? If I called this spittoon a saucepan, what would you say? Suppose that every time I asked for it I said, "Please bring that saucepan over here," that would confuse you. Why? Because you don't fully know the spittoon. If you did there would be no problem. You would simply pick up that object and hand it to me, because actually there isn't any spittoon. Do you understand? It's a spittoon due to convention. This convention is accepted all over the country, so it's a spittoon. But there isn't any real "spittoon." If somebody wants to call it a saucepan, it can be a saucepan. It can be whatever you call it. Such conventions are called concepts. If we fully know the spittoon, even if somebody calls it a saucepan there's no problem. Whatever others may call it, we are unperturbed because we are not blind to its true nature. One who sees this is one who knows Dhamma.

Now let's come back to ourselves. Suppose somebody tells you that you're crazy or stupid. It may not be true, but you won't feel so good. Everything becomes difficult because of our ambitions to have and to achieve. Because of these desires, and because we don't know according to the truth, we are discontent. If we know the Dhamma, greed, aversion, and delusion will disappear. When we understand the way things are, there is nothing for them to rest on.

If the body and mind are not the self and do not belong to self, then who do they belong to? It's difficult to resolve these things; we must rely on wisdom. The Buddha says we must practice by letting go. It's hard to understand this practice of letting go, isn't it? If we let go, then we don't practice, right? Because we've let go.

Suppose you went to buy some coconuts in the market, and while you were carrying them back someone asked why you bought them.

"I bought them to eat," you say.

"Are you going to eat the shells as well? No? I don't believe you! If you're not going to eat the shells, then why did you buy them too?"

Well, how are you going to answer? We practice with desire. If we didn't have desire, we wouldn't practice. Practicing with desire is taṇhā. Contemplating in this way can give rise to wisdom, you know. As for those coconuts, of course you are not going to eat the shells. Then why do you take them? Because the time hasn't yet come for you to throw them away. They're useful for wrapping up the coconut. If, after eating the coconut, you throw the shells away, there is no problem.

Our practice is like this. When the Buddha instructs us not to act on desire, speak from desire, or walk or sit or eat with desire, he means we should do these things with detachment. It's just like bringing coconuts from the market. We're not going to eat the shells, but it's not yet time to throw them away. The coconut milk, the husk, and the shell all come together; when we buy a coconut we buy the whole package. If somebody wants to accuse us of eating coconut shells that's their business; we know what we're doing. This is how the practice is. Concept and transcendence[48] are coexistent, just like a coconut.

Wisdom is something each of us must find for ourselves. To reach it we must go neither fast nor slow. But we're all in a hurry. As soon as we begin we want to rush to the end. We don't want to be left behind, we want to succeed. When it comes to readying the mind for meditation, some people go too far. They light an incense stick, bow to their shrine, and make a vow: "As long as this incense is not yet completely burnt, I will not rise from my sitting, even if I collapse or die, no matter what. I'll die sitting!" Then they start their sitting, but soon Māra's hordes come rushing at them from all sides. They've only sat for a moment and already they think the incense must be finished. They open their eyes for a peek. "Oh, there's still ages left!"

They grit their teeth and sit some more, feeling hot, flustered, agitated, and confused. Reaching the breaking point, they think, "It must be finished by now." So they take another peek. "Oh no, not even halfway!" Two or three times they peek, and it's still not finished. So they just give up, pack it in, and sit there hating themselves. "I'm so stupid, I'm so hopeless!" This is called the hindrance of ill will. They can't blame others so they blame themselves. And why is this? It's all because of wanting.

Actually, it isn't necessary to go through all that. To concentrate means to concentrate with detachment, not to tighten yourself into knots.

But maybe we read the scriptures, about the life of the Buddha, how he sat under the Bodhi tree and resolved, "As long as I have still not attained supreme enlightenment, I will not rise from this place, even if my blood dries up." Reading this in the books, you may think of trying it yourself. You'll do it like the Buddha. But you haven't considered that your car is only a small one. The Buddha's car was a really big one, so he could make the journey all in one go. With only your tiny little car, how can you possibly get there all at once? It's a different story altogether.

Why do we think like that? Because we're too extreme. Sometimes we go too low; sometimes we go too high. The point of balance is so hard to find.

Now I'm only speaking from experience. In the past my practice was like that. Practicing in order to get beyond wanting.... If we don't want, can we practice? But to practice with wanting is suffering. I was stuck, baffled. Then I realized that steady practice is the important thing. One must practice consistently. They call this the practice that is "consistent in all postures." Keep refining the practice; don't let it become a disaster. Practice is one thing, disaster is another. Most people usually create disaster. When they feel lazy they don't bother to practice; they only practice when they feel energetic. This is how I tended to be.

Is it okay to practice only when you feel like it? Is that in line with the Dhamma? With the teaching? Whether you feel like it or not, you should practice: this is how the Buddha taught. Most people wait till they're in the mood before practicing; when they don't feel like it, they don't bother. This is called disaster, not practice. In the true practice, whether you are happy or depressed, whether it's easy or difficult, whether it's hot or cold, you practice. Standing, walking, sitting, or reclining, you practice steadily, making your sati consistent in all postures.

At first I took the word *consistent* at face value, and thought that you should stand for as long as you walk, walk for as long as you sit, sit for as long as you lie down. I tried this, but I couldn't do it. If a meditator were to make their standing, walking, sitting, and lying down all equal, how long could they keep it up? Stand for five minutes, sit for five minutes, lie down for five minutes.... I couldn't do that for long, so I sat down and thought about it some more. "What does it all mean? People in this world can't practice like this!"

Then I realized, "Oh, that's not right. It can't be right because it's impossible. Making the postures consistent the way they explain it in the books is impossible."

But it is possible to do this: just consider the mind. Have sati (mindfulness), sampajañña (self-awareness), and paññā (all-round wisdom)—this you can do. This is something that's really worth practicing. While standing we have sati, while walking we have sati, while sitting we have sati, and while reclining we have sati—consistently. This is possible. We put awareness into our standing, walking, sitting, and lying down—into all postures.

When the mind has been trained like this it will constantly recollect

Buddho, Buddho, which is knowing. Knowing what? Knowing what is right and what is wrong at all times. Yes, this is possible. This is getting down to the real practice: whether standing, walking, sitting, or lying down, there is continuous sati.

Next you should understand those conditions that should be given up or cultivated. You know happiness, you know unhappiness. When you know happiness and unhappiness, your mind will settle at the point that is free from both. Happiness is the loose path, *kāmasukhallikānuyoga,* or indulgence in sense pleasures. Unhappiness is the tight path, *attakilamathā-nuyoga,* or self-mortification.[49] If we know these two extremes, then even though the mind may incline to one or the other, we pull it back. We know when the mind is inclining toward happiness or unhappiness and we pull it back; we don't allow it to lean over. We adhere to the awareness, not allowing the mind to follow its inclinations.

If you follow your inclinations it's easy, isn't it? But this is the ease that causes suffering, like a farmer who can't be bothered planting and tending his crops. He takes it easy, but when the time comes to eat he hasn't got anything. This is how it goes. I've contended with many aspects of the Buddha's teachings in the past, but I couldn't ever beat them. So I've taken those teachings and used them to train myself and others.

The practice that is important is *paṭipadā.* What is paṭipadā? It is simply all our various activities, standing, walking, sitting, reclining, and everything else. This is the paṭipadā of the body. As for the paṭipadā of the mind: how many times in the course of today have you felt low? How many times have you felt high? Have there been any noticeable feelings? We must know ourselves like this. Having seen those feelings, can we let go? Whatever we can't yet let go of, we must work with. When we see that we can't yet let go of some particular feeling, we must examine it with wisdom. Work with it. This is practice. For example, when you are feeling zealous, practice; and then when you feel lazy, try to continue the practice. If you can't continue at full speed, then at least do half as much. Don't just waste the day away by being lazy and not practicing. Doing that will lead to disaster; it's not the way of a practitioner.

Now I've heard some people say, "Oh, this year I was really in a bad way. I was sick all year. I couldn't practice at all."

Oh? If they don't practice when death is near, when will they? If they're feeling well, do you think they'll practice? No, they get lost in happiness. If they're suffering, they still don't practice; they get lost in that. I don't know when people think they're going to practice! They can only see that they're sick, in pain, almost dead from fever…that's right, heavy stuff, but that's where the practice is. When people are feeling happy, it just goes to their heads and they get vain and conceited.

There was a time in my training, after I had been practicing about five years, when I felt that living with others was a hindrance. I would sit in my kuṭī and try to meditate, and people would keep coming by for a chat and disturbing me. I was fed up, so I went to live in a small, deserted monastery in the forest, near a small village. I stayed there alone, speaking to no one— because there was nobody to speak to.

After I'd been there about fifteen days the thought arose, "Hmm, it would be good to have a novice or *pah kow* here with me. He could help me out with some small jobs." I knew such a thought would come up, and sure enough, there it was!

"Hey! You're a real character!" I said to myself. "You say you're fed up with your friends, fed up with your fellow monks and novices, and now you want a novice. What's this?"

"No," came the reply, "I want a *good* novice."

"Well! Where are all the good people? Can you find one? Where are you going to find him? In the whole monastery there were only no-good people. You must have been the only good person, to have run away like this!"

You have to keep following your thought tracks, until you see—

"Hmm, that's a good question. Where's a good person found? If there aren't any good people, you must find the good person within yourself."

You won't find goodness anywhere else than within yourself. If you are good, wherever you go will be good. Whether others criticize or praise you, you are still good. If you aren't good, then when others criticize you, you get angry, and when they praise you, you're pleased.

I reflected on this and I've always found it true. Goodness must be found within. As soon as I saw this, that feeling of wanting to run away disappeared. Later, whenever that feeling arose, I was aware of it and let it go. Wherever I lived, whenever people condemned or praised me, I would reflect that the point is not whether what they said was good or bad. Good or evil must be seen within ourselves. However other people feel, that's their concern.

Don't go thinking, "It's too hot today," "It's too cold," "It's...." Whatever the day is, that's just the way it is. You are simply blaming your laziness on the weather. We must see the Dhamma within ourselves; then there is a surer kind of peace.

When you experience peace during your meditation, don't be in a hurry to congratulate yourself. Likewise, if there is some confusion, don't blame yourself. If things seem to be good, don't delight in them, and if they're not good, don't be averse. Just look at it all, look at what you have. Don't bother judging. If it's good, don't hold fast to it; if it's bad, don't push it away. Good and bad can both bite, so don't hold fast to them.

The practice is simply to sit and watch it all. Good moods and bad moods come and go according to their nature. Don't only praise your mind or only condemn it. When it's time for congratulations, then congratulate it. But just a little, don't overdo it. Just like teaching a child, sometimes you may have to discipline it a little. Sometimes you may have to punish yourself, but don't punish yourself all the time. If you do that, you'll just give up the practice.

Don't think that sitting with the eyes closed is the only practice. If that's your thinking, change it! Steady practice is having the attitude of practice while standing, walking, sitting, and lying down. When coming out of sitting meditation don't think that you're coming out of meditation. Reflect that you're simply changing postures. If you reflect in this way, you will have peace. Wherever you are, you will have a steady awareness within yourself.

If you indulge in your moods, spending the whole day letting your mind wander where it will, the next time you sit all you'll get is the backwash from the day's aimless thinking. There is no foundation of calm because you've let it go cold all day. If you practice like this, your mind gradually drifts further and further from the practice. Sometimes when I ask my disciples how their meditation is going, they say, "Oh, it's all gone now." You see? They can keep it up for a month or so but in a year or two it's all finished.

Why is this? It's because they don't take this essential point into their practice. When they've finished sitting, they let go of their samādhi. They start to sit for shorter and shorter periods, till they reach the point where as soon as they start to sit they want to finish. Eventually they don't even sit. It's the same with bowing to the Buddha image. At first they make the effort to prostrate every night before going to sleep, but after a while their minds begin to stray. Soon they don't bother to prostrate at all; they just give a cursory nod, till eventually it's all gone. They throw out the practice completely.

Therefore, understand the importance of sati—practice constantly. Right practice is steady practice. Whether standing, walking, sitting, or reclining, the practice must continue. This means that practice, or meditation, is done in the mind, not in the body. If our mind has zeal, is conscientious and ardent, then there will be awareness.

When we understand properly, we practice properly. When we practice properly, we don't go astray. Even if we only do a little, that's still all right. For example, when you finish sitting in meditation, remind yourselves that you are not actually finishing meditation, you are simply changing postures. Your mind is still composed. Whether standing, walking, sitting, or reclining, you have sati with you. If you have this kind of awareness you can maintain your internal practice. In the evening when you sit again, the practice continues uninterrupted. Your effort is unbroken, allowing the mind to attain calm.

When it comes to meditation some people don't get what they hope for, so they just give up, saying they don't yet have sufficient merit to practice. This is the way people are. They side with their defilements.

Whatever happens, don't let your mind stray off the track. Look within yourself and you will see clearly. For the best practice, as I see it, it isn't necessary to read many books. Take all the books and lock them away. Just read your own mind. You have all been burying yourselves in books from the time you entered school. I think that now you have this opportunity and have the time; take the books, put them in a cupboard, and lock the door. Just read your mind. Whenever something arises within the mind, whether you like it or not, whether it seems right or wrong, just cut it off with, "This is not a sure thing." Whatever arises just cut it down: "Not sure, not sure." With just this single axe you can cut it all down. "Not sure" is really an important practice. It develops wisdom. The more you look, the more you will see not-sureness. After you've cut something off with "not sure" it may come circling round and pop up again—but yes, it truly *is* "not sure." Whatever pops up, just stick this one label on it. You will see this same old someone, the desire mind, who's been fooling you, month in, month out, year in, year out, from the day you were born. See this and realize the way things are.

When your practice reaches this point you won't cling to sensations, because they are all uncertain. Have you ever noticed? Maybe you see a clock and think, "How nice." Buy it and watch what happens: in a few days you're bored with it already. "This pen is really beautiful"—so go and buy it. In not many months you tire of it. This is how it is. Where is there any constancy, any certainty?

If we see all these things as uncertain, then their false value fades away. All things become insignificant. Why should we hold on to things that have no value? We keep them only as we might keep an old rag to wipe our feet with. We see all sensations as equal in value because they all have the same nature.

When we understand sensations, we understand the world. If we aren't fooled by sensations, we aren't fooled by the world. If we aren't fooled by the world, we aren't fooled by sensations. The mind that sees this will have a firm foundation of wisdom. Such a mind will not have many problems. Any problems it does have it can solve. When there are no more problems, there are no more doubts. Peace arises instead. If we really practice it must be like this.

CHAPTER 21

SAMMĀ SAMĀDHI—
DETACHMENT WITHIN ACTIVITY

CONSIDER THE BUDDHA. Both in his own practice and in his teaching he was exemplary. The Buddha taught the practice as skillful means for getting rid of conceit; he couldn't do the practice for us. Having heard that teaching, we must teach ourselves, practice for ourselves. The results will arise here, not at the teaching.

The Buddha's teaching can give us an initial understanding of the Dhamma, but that Dhamma is not yet within our hearts. Why not? Because we haven't yet practiced, we haven't yet taught ourselves. The Dhamma arises at the practice. You know it through the practice. If you doubt it, you doubt it at the practice. Teachings from the masters may be true, but they simply point the way. To realize the Dhamma, we must take that teaching into our hearts. That part which is for the body, we apply to the body; that which is for speech, we apply to speech; and that which is for the mind, we apply to the mind. This means that after hearing the teaching we must further teach ourselves to know that Dhamma, to be that Dhamma.

The Buddha said that those who simply believe others are not truly wise. A wise person practices until they are one with the Dhamma, until they have total confidence in themselves, independent of others. Conviction can take various forms. There is conviction according to Dhamma and conviction contrary to the Dhamma. This second way is a heedless, foolhardy understanding: *micchā diṭṭhi*, wrong view.

Take the example of Dīghanakha the brahmin. This brahmin believed only himself. Once when the Buddha was staying at Rājagaha, Dīghanakha went to listen to his teaching. Or you might say that Dīghanakha went to teach the Buddha, because he was intent on expounding his own views.

"I am of the view that nothing suits me," said Dīghanakha.

The Buddha answered, "Brahmin, does this view of yours not suit you either?"

The Buddha's response stumped Dīghanakha. He didn't know what to say. The Buddha explained in many ways, till the brahmin understood: "Hmm, this view of mine isn't right."

On hearing the Buddha's answer the brahmin abandoned his conceited views and immediately saw the truth. He changed right then and there, turning right around, just as one would invert one's hand. He praised the teaching of the Buddha thus:

"Listening to the Blessed One's teaching, my mind was illumined, just as one living in darkness might perceive light. My mind is like an overturned basin which has been turned upright, like a man who has been lost and finds the way."

Now at that time a certain knowledge arose within his mind, within that mind which had been turned upright. Wrong view vanished and Right View took its place. Darkness disappeared and light arose.

The Buddha declared that the brahmin Dīghanakha was one who had opened the Dhamma Eye. Previously Dīghanakha clung to his own views and had no intention of changing them. But when he heard the Buddha's teaching, his mind saw the truth; he saw that his clinging to those views was wrong.

We must change the same way. Before we can give up defilements we must change our perspective. We weren't practicing well, although we thought we were. Now, as soon as we really look into the matter, we turn ourselves upright, just like turning over one's hand. This means that Buddho, the "one who knows," or wisdom, arises in the mind and sees things anew.

Originally the "one who knows" was not there. Our knowledge was unclear, untrue, incomplete. This knowledge was therefore too weak to train the mind. But then the mind changes, or inverts, as a result of this awareness, called wisdom or insight, which exceeds our previous awareness.

The Buddha therefore taught us to look within: *opanayiko*. Don't look outward. Or if you do look outward, *then* look within, to see the cause and effect therein. Look for the truth in all things, because external objects and internal objects are always affecting each other. Our practice is to make our awareness stronger. This causes wisdom and insight to arise, enabling us to know the workings of the mind, the language of the mind, and the ways and means of all the defilements.

When the Buddha first left home in search of liberation, he was probably not really sure what to do, much like us. He tried many ways of developing his wisdom. He sought out teachers, such as Āḷāra Kālāma, and practiced meditation with them…right leg atop the left, right hand on the left…body erect…eyes closed…letting go of everything, until he attained a high level of absorption samādhi.[50] But when he came out of that samādhi his old thinking came up and he would attach to it just as before. Seeing this, he knew that wisdom had not yet arisen. His understanding had not yet penetrated to the truth; it was still incomplete, still lacking. He nonetheless had gained some understanding—that this was not yet the completion of the practice—so he left to look for a new teacher.

The Buddha studied next with Uddaka Rāmaputta and attained an even higher state of samādhi, but when he came out of that state, memories of his former wife, Bimbā,[51] and his son, Rāhula, came back to him. He still had lust and desire. Reflecting, he saw that he still hadn't reached his goal, so he left that teacher also. He had listened to his teachers and had done his best to follow their teachings. But he also continually examined the results of his practice.

After trying ascetic practices, he had realized that starving until one is almost a skeleton is simply a matter of the body. The body doesn't know anything. Attakilamathānuyoga (self-mortification) is like executing an innocent person while ignoring the real thief. Practice, he saw, is not a concern of the body; it is a concern of the mind—all buddhas are enlightened in mind.

States of the body and the mind are transient, imperfect, and ownerless—anicca, dukkha, and anattā. They are simply conditions of nature. They arise depending on supporting factors, exist for a while, and then cease. All beings, including humans, tend to see the arising as themselves, the existence as themselves, and the cessation as themselves. Thus they cling to everything. Having experienced happiness, they don't want suffering. If suffering does arise, they want it to go away as quickly as possible. But it is even better if it doesn't arise at all. This is because they see this body and mind as themselves, or belonging to themselves, and so they demand those things to follow their wishes. The Buddha saw that such thinking is the cause of suffering. Seeing this cause, the Buddha gave it up.

The Noble Truths of suffering, its cause, its cessation, and the way leading to that cessation—people are stuck right here. If people are to overcome their doubts it's right at this point. Seeing that these things are simply *rūpa* and *nāma,* or corporeality and mentality, it becomes obvious that they are not a being, a person, an "I," or a "he" or "she." The constituent qualities simply follow the laws of nature.

Our practice is to know things in this way. We don't have the power to control these things, for we aren't their owners. Trying to control them causes suffering, because they aren't really ours to control. If we know this as it really is then we see clearly. We see the truth; we are at one with it. It's like seeing a lump of red-hot iron that has been heated in a furnace. It's hot all over. Whether we touch it on top, the bottom, or the sides, it's hot. No matter where we touch it, it's hot. This is how you should see things.

Mostly when we start to practice we want to attain, to achieve, to know and to see, but we don't yet know what it is we're going to achieve or know. There was once a disciple of mine whose practice was plagued with confusion and doubts. But he kept practicing, and I kept instructing him, till he began to find some peace. But when he eventually became a bit calm he got caught up in his doubts again. "What do I do next?" he asked me. There! The confusion arises again. He says he wants peace but then when he gets it, he doesn't want it. He asks what he should do next!

So in this practice we must do everything with detachment. We detach by seeing things clearly. Know the characteristics of the body and mind as they are.

When practicing samādhi we fix our attention on the in- and out-breaths at the nose tip or the upper lip. This fixing of attention is called vitakka, or "lifting up." When we have thus "lifted" the mind and are fixed on an object, this is called vicāra, the contemplation of the breath at the nose tip. This quality of vicāra will naturally mingle with other mental sensations, and we may think that our mind is not still, that it won't calm down, but actually this is simply the workings of vicāra as it mingles with those sensations. Now if this goes too far in the wrong direction, our mind will lose its collectedness, so then we must set up the mind afresh, lifting it up to the object of concentration with vitakka. As soon as we have thus established our attention, vicāra takes over, mingling with the various mental sensations.

Now when we see this happening, our lack of understanding may lead us to wonder: "Why has my mind wandered? I wanted it to be still, why isn't it still?" This is practicing with attachment.

Actually the mind is simply following its nature, but we go and add on to that activity by wanting the mind to be still and wondering why it isn't. Aversion arises and so we add that on to everything else, increasing our doubts, increasing our suffering, and increasing our confusion. So if there is vicāra, reflecting on the various happenings within the mind in this way, we should wisely consider: "Ah, the mind is simply like this." There, that's the "one who knows" talking, telling you to see things as they are. The mind is simply like this. We let it go at that, and the mind becomes peaceful. When once again it's no longer centered, we bring up vitakka again, and soon there is calm again. Vitakka and vicāra work together like this. We use vicāra to contemplate the various sensations that arise. When vicāra becomes gradually more scattered, we once again "lift" our attention with vitakka.

The important thing here is that our practice at this point must be done with detachment. Seeing vicāra interacting with mental sensations, we may think that the mind is confused, and we become averse to this. Right here we cause ourselves to suffer. We aren't happy simply because we want the mind to be still. This is wrong view. If we correct our view just a little and see this activity as simply the nature of mind, just this is enough to subdue the confusion. This is called *letting go*.

Now, if we don't attach, if we practice detachment within activity—and activity within detachment—then vicāra will naturally tend to have less to work with. If our mind ceases to be disturbed, the vicāra will incline to contemplating Dhamma, because if we don't contemplate Dhamma the mind returns to distraction.

So there is vitakka then vicāra, vitakka then vicāra, vitakka then vicāra, and so on, until vicāra becomes gradually more subtle. At first vicāra goes all over the place. It's like flowing water. If we get obsessed with it and want to stop the flow, then naturally we suffer. If we understand that the water simply flows because that's its nature, then there's no suffering. Vicāra is like this. There is vitakka, then vicāra, interacting with mental sensations. We can take these sensations as our object of meditation, calming the mind by noting those sensations.

If we know the nature of the mind like this then we let go, just like letting the water flow by. Vicāra becomes more and more subtle. Perhaps the mind inclines to contemplating the body, or death for instance, or some other theme of Dhamma. When the theme of contemplation is right, a feeling of well-being will arise. What is that well-being? It is pīti (rapture), which may manifest as goose pimples, coolness, or lightness. The mind is enrapt. This pīti is accompanied by pleasure, sukha, the coming and going of various sensations, and the state of *ekaggatārammaṇa,* or one-pointedness.

In the first stage of concentration, then, there are vitakka, vicāra, pīti, sukha, and ekaggatā. So what is the second stage like? As the mind becomes progressively more subtle, vitakka and vicāra appear comparatively coarse, so they are discarded, leaving only pīti, sukha, and ekaggatā. This is something that the mind does of itself. We don't have to conjecture about it, we just know things as they are.

As the mind becomes more refined, pīti is eventually thrown off, leaving only sukha and ekaggatā, and so we take note of that. Where does pīti go? It doesn't go anywhere; it's just that the mind becomes increasingly more subtle so that it throws off those qualities that are too coarse for it. Whatever's too coarse it throws out, and it keeps throwing things off like this until it reaches the peak of subtlety, known in the books as the fourth jhāna, the highest level of absorption. Here the mind has progressively discarded whatever has become too coarse for it, until there remain only ekaggatā and *upekkhā,* or equanimity. There's nothing further.

When the mind is developing the stages of samādhi it must proceed in this way, but let us understand the basics of practice. We want to make the mind still, but it won't be still. This is practicing out of the desire for calm. The mind is already disturbed, and then we further disturb things by wanting to make it calm. This very wanting is the cause. We don't see that this wanting to calm the mind is taṇhā. The more we desire calm, the more disturbed the mind becomes. We end up struggling with ourselves, until we just give up.

If we see that the mind is simply behaving according to its nature, that it naturally comes and goes like this, and if we don't get overly interested in it, we can understand its ways, much the same as a child. Children may say all kinds of things. If we understand them, we just let them talk.

Children naturally talk like that because they don't know any better. When we let go, we have no obsession with the child. We can talk to our guests undisturbed, while the child chatters and plays. The mind is like this. It's not harmful unless we grab on to it and get obsessed over it. That's the real cause of trouble.

When pīti arises one feels an indescribable bliss, which only those who have experienced it can appreciate. Sukha (pleasure) arises, and also one-pointedness. There are vitakka, vicāra, pīti, sukha, and ekaggatā. These five qualities all converge at the one place. Even though they are different qualities, they are all collected in the one place, and we can see them all there, just like seeing many different kinds of fruit in the one bowl. Vitakka, vicāra, pīti, sukha, and ekaggatā—we can see them all in the one mind. If one were to ask, "How is there vitakka, how is there vicāra, how are there pīti and sukha?" it would be difficult to answer, but when they converge in the mind we see how it is for ourselves.

At this point our practice becomes somewhat special. We must have mindfulness and self-awareness and not lose ourselves. Know things for what they are. These are stages of meditation, the potential of the mind. Don't doubt anything with regard to the practice. Even if you sink into the earth or fly into the air, or even "die" while sitting, don't allow doubts to arise. Whatever the qualities of the mind are, just stay with the knowing. This is our foundation: to have sati, mindfulness, and sampajañña, self-awareness, whether standing, walking, sitting, or reclining. Whatever arises, just leave it be, don't cling to it. Liking or disliking, happiness or suffering, doubt or certainty—contemplate with vicāra and gauge the results of those qualities. Don't try to label everything; just know it. See that all the things that arise in the mind are simply sensations. They are transient. They arise, exist, and cease. That's all there is to them; they have no self or being. They are not worthy of clinging to, any of them.

When we see all rūpa and nāma in this way with wisdom, then we will see the transiency of the mind, of the body, of happiness and suffering, of love and hate. They are all impermanent. Seeing this, the mind becomes weary; weary of the body and mind, weary of the things that arise and cease and are transient. When the mind becomes disenchanted, it looks for a way out of all those things. It no longer wants to be stuck in things; it sees the inadequacy of this world and the inadequacy of birth.

When the mind sees like this, wherever we go, we see anicca, dukkha, and anattā—transiency, imperfection, and ownerlessness. There's nothing left to hold on to. Whether we go to sit under a tree or on a mountaintop, we can hear the Buddha's teaching. All trees will seem as one; all beings will be as one—nothing special about any of them. They arise, exist for a while, age, and then die, all of them. If we see that body and mind are simply the way they are, no suffering arises, because we don't hold fast to them. Wherever we go we will have wisdom. Even seeing a tree we can consider it with wisdom. Just seeing grass and insects will be food for reflection.

When it comes down to it, they all fall into the same boat. They are all Dhamma. There's nothing more to it than this. If we can see this, then we have finished our journey. This is called lokavidū—knowing the world clearly as it is. The mind knows itself completely and severs the cause of suffering. When there is no longer any cause, the results cannot arise.

The basics that we need to develop are: firstly, to be upright and honest; secondly, to be wary of wrong-doing; thirdly, to have the attribute of humility within one's heart, to be at ease and content with little. If we are content with little in regards to speech and in all other things, we will see ourselves; we won't be drawn into distractions. The mind will have a foundation of sīla, samādhi, and paññā.

Therefore practitioners of the Path should not be careless. Even if you are right, don't be careless. And if you are wrong, don't be careless. If things are going well or you're feeling happy, don't be careless. Why do I say "Don't be careless"? Because all of these things are uncertain. Know them as such. If you get peaceful, just leave the peace be. You may really want to indulge in it, but you should simply know the truth of it; the same as for unpleasant qualities.

This practice is up to you. Nobody else knows your mind as well as you. The practice requires honesty. Do it properly, not halfheartedly. That doesn't mean you have to exhaust yourselves. If you just have sati and sampajañña, you will be able to see right and wrong within you. If you know this then you will know the practice. You don't need a whole lot. Please make an effort with it.

CHAPTER 22

IN THE DEAD OF NIGHT

IT WAS NEARING NIGHTFALL, and there was nothing else for me to do. If I tried to reason with myself, I knew I'd never go, so I grabbed a *pah kow* (a novice) and just went. "It's time to take a look at your fear," I had told myself. "If it's time for me to die, then let me die. If my mind is going to be so stubborn and stupid, then let it die." That's what I thought to myself. Actually, in my heart I didn't really want to go, but I forced myself to. When it comes to things like this, if you wait till everything's just right, you'll end up never going. So I just went.

I'd never stayed in a charnel ground before. When I got there, words can't describe the way I felt. The pah kow wanted to camp right next to me, but I wouldn't have it. I made him stay at some distance. In reality I wanted him to stay close by to keep me company and for support, but I wouldn't have it.

"If it's going to be so afraid, then let it die tonight," I dared myself. I was afraid, but I also had courage. In the end you have to die anyway.

Well, just as it was getting dark I had my chance. In the villagers came carrying a corpse. Just my luck! I couldn't feel my feet touch the ground, so badly did I want to get out of there. They wanted me to do some funeral chants, but I wouldn't get involved; I just walked away. In a few minutes, after they'd left, I walked back and found that they had buried the corpse right next to my spot. With the bamboo used for carrying the corpse, they had made a platform for me to stay on. So now what was I to do? It's not that the village was nearby either. It was a good two or three kilometers away.

"Well, if I'm going to die, I'm going to die"

If you've never dared to do it you'll never know what it's like. It's really an experience.

As it got darker and darker I wondered where I could run to in that charnel ground.

"Oh, let it die. One is born to this life only to die anyway."

As soon as the sun sank, the night told me to get inside my glot. I didn't want to do any walking meditation; I only wanted to get under my mosquito net. Whenever I tried to walk toward the grave, it was as if something was pulling me back, to stop me from walking. It was as if my feelings of fear and courage were having a tug-of-war. But I walked. This is how you must train yourself.

When it was dark I got into my mosquito net, hanging from the glot. It felt as if I had seven layers of walls all around me; seeing my trusty alms bowl there beside me was like having the company of an old friend. Its presence beside me was comforting. Even a bowl can be a friend sometimes!

I sat in my net watching over the body all night. I didn't lie down or even doze off; I just sat quietly. I couldn't be sleepy even if I wanted to, I was so scared. Yes, I was scared, and yet I did it. I sat through the night.

Now, how many of us have the guts to practice like this? Who dares to spend the night in a charnel ground? If you don't actually do it, you don't get the results; you don't really practice.

When day broke I said to myself, "Oh! I've survived!" I was so glad. I had wanted to kill off nighttime and leave only daylight. "Oh, there's nothing to it," I thought. "It's just my own fear, that's all."

After alms round and the meal I felt good. The sunshine came out, leaving me warm and cozy. I had a rest and walked awhile. I thought, "This evening I should have some good, quiet meditation, because I've already been through it all last night. There's probably nothing more to it."

Then, later in the afternoon, wouldn't you know it? In comes another one, a big one this time.[52] This would be worse than the previous night. They brought the corpse in and cremated it right beside my spot, right in front of my glot.

I thought, "That's good. Bringing in this corpse to burn here is going to help my practice." But again I wouldn't perform any rites for the villagers. I waited for them to leave before taking a look.

Sitting and watching that body burning all night, I can't tell you how it was. Words can't describe it. Nothing I say could convey the fear I felt. In the dead of night—the fire from the burning corpse flickered red and green, and the flames crackled softly. I wanted to do walking meditation in front of the body but could hardly bring myself to do it. The stench from the burning flesh lingered in the air. Eventually I got into my net.

As the flames gently flickered, I turned my back on the fire. I forgot about sleep, I couldn't even think of it; my eyes were fixed rigid with fear. And there was nobody to turn to, nowhere to run to in that pitch black night.

"Well, I'll sit and die here. I'm not moving from this spot."

Here, talking of the ordinary mind, would it want to do this? Would that mind take you into such a situation? If you tried to reason it out, you'd never go. Who would want to do such a thing? If you didn't have strong faith in the teaching of the Buddha you'd never do it.

Now, about 10 p.m., I was sitting with my back to the fire. I don't know what it was, but there came a sound of shuffling from the fire behind me. Had the coffin just collapsed? Or maybe a dog was getting at the corpse? But no, it sounded more like a water buffalo walking slowly around.

"Oh, never mind...."

But then it started walking toward me, just a like a person! It walked up behind me, the footsteps heavy, like a buffalo's, and yet not. Leaves crunched underfoot as it made its way round to the front. Well, I could only prepare for the worst; where could I go? But it didn't really come up to me; it just circled around in front and then went off in the direction of the pah kow. Then all was quiet. I don't know what it was, but my fear made me think of many possibilities.

It must have been about half an hour later, I think, when the footsteps started coming back from the direction of the pah kow. Just like a person! It came right up to me this time, heading for me as if to run me over! I closed my eyes and refused to open them.

"I'll die with my eyes closed."

It got closer and closer until it stopped dead in front of me and just stood stock still. I felt as if it were waving its burnt hands back and forth in front of my closed eyes. Oh, this was really it! I threw out everything, forgot all about the mantra words *Buddho, Dhammo,* and *Saṅgho.* I forgot everything else; there was only the fear filling me to the brim. My thoughts couldn't go anywhere else. From the day I was born I had never experienced such fear. *Buddho* and *Dhammo* had disappeared, I don't know where. There was only fear welling up inside my chest until it felt like a tightly stretched drumskin.

"Well, I'll just leave it as it is; there's nothing else to do."

I sat as if I weren't even touching the ground and simply noted what was going on. The fear was so great that it filled me, like a jar completely filled with water. If you pour water until the jar is completely full, and then pour some more, the jar will overflow. Likewise, the fear built up so much within me that it reached its peak and began to overflow.

"What am I so afraid of anyway?" a voice inside me asked.

"I'm afraid of death," another voice answered.

"Well, then, where is this thing 'death'? Why all the panic? Look where death abides. Where is death?"

"Why, death is within me!"

"If death is within you, then where are you going to run to escape it? If you run away, you die; if you stay here, you die. Wherever you go it goes with you, because death lies within you; there's nowhere you can run to. Whether you are afraid or not, you die just the same. There's nowhere to escape death."

As soon as I had thought this, my perception seemed to change right around. All the fear completely disappeared, as easily as turning over one's own hand. It was truly amazing. So much fear, and yet it could disappear just like that! Fearlessness arose in its place. Now my mind rose higher and higher until I felt as if I were in the clouds.

As soon as I had conquered the fear, rain began to fall. I don't know what sort of rain it was, the wind was so strong. But I wasn't afraid of dying now. I wasn't afraid that branches might come crashing down on me. I paid it no mind. The torrential rain came pelting down, really heavy. By the time it had stopped everything was soaking wet.

I sat unmoving.

So what did I do next, soaking wet as I was? I cried! The tears flowed down my cheeks. I cried as I thought to myself, "Why am I sitting here like some sort of orphan or abandoned child, sitting, soaking in the rain like a man who owns nothing, like an exile?"

And then I thought further, "All those people sitting comfortably in their homes right now probably don't suspect that there is a monk sitting here, soaking in the rain all night like this. What's the point of it all?" Thinking like this, I began to feel so thoroughly sorry for myself that the tears came gushing out.

"They're not good things anyway, these tears, let them flow right on out until they're all gone."

This was how I practiced.

Now I don't know how I can describe the things that followed. I sat and listened. After conquering my feelings I just sat and watched as all manner of things arose in me, so many things that were possible to know but impossible to describe. And I thought of the Buddha's words *Paccattaṁ veditabbo viññūhi*[53]—"the wise will know for themselves."

That I had endured such suffering and sat through the rain like this—who was there to experience it with me? Only I could know what it was like. There was so much fear and yet the fear disappeared. Who else could witness this? The people in their homes in the town couldn't know what it was like. Only I could see it. It was a personal experience. Even if I were to tell others they wouldn't really know. It was something each individual has to experience for themselves. The more I contemplated this, the clearer it became. I became stronger and stronger; my conviction became firmer and firmer, until daybreak.

When I opened my eyes at dawn, everything was yellow. I had been wanting to urinate during the night but the feeling had eventually stopped. When I got up from my sitting, everywhere I looked it was yellow, just like the early morning sunlight on some days. When I went to empty my bladder, there was blood in the urine!

"What's this? Is my gut torn or something?" I got a bit of a fright. "Maybe it's really ripped inside there."

"Well, so what? If it's torn, it's torn; who is there to blame?" a voice told me straight away. "If it's torn, it's torn; if I die, I die. I was only sitting here, I wasn't doing any harm. If it's going to burst, let it burst," the voice said.

My mind was as if arguing or fighting with itself. One voice would come from one side, saying, "Hey, this is dangerous!" Another voice would counter it, challenge it, and overrule it.

"Hmm, where am I going to find medicine?" I wondered. But then the thought arose, "I'm not going to bother with that stuff. A monk can't cut plants for medicine anyway. If I die, I die, so what? What else is there to do? If I die while practicing like this, then I'm ready. If I were doing something bad, that's no good; but I'm prepared to die practicing like this."

Don't follow your moods. Train yourself. The practice involves putting your very life at stake. You must have broken down and cried at least two or three times. That's right, that's the practice. If you're sleepy and want to lie down, don't let yourself sleep. Dispel the sleepiness before you lie down.

Sometimes, when you come back from alms round and you're contemplating the food before eating, you can't settle down. Your mind is like a mad dog, saliva flowing, you're so hungry. Sometimes you may not even bother to contemplate, you just dig in. That's a disaster. If the mind won't calm down and be patient, then just push your bowl away and don't eat. Train yourself, drill yourself; that's practice. Don't just keep on following your mind. Push your bowl away, get up and leave. Don't allow yourself to eat. If your mind really wants to eat so much and acts so stubborn, don't let it eat. The saliva will stop flowing. If the defilements know that they won't get anything to eat, they'll get scared. They won't dare bother you the next day; they'll be afraid they won't get anything to eat. Try it out if you don't believe me.

People don't trust the practice; they don't dare to really do it. They're afraid they'll go hungry, afraid they'll die. If you don't try it out, you won't know what it's about. Most of us don't dare to do it, don't dare to try it out, we're so afraid.

Consider: What is the most important thing of all? There's nothing else, just death. Death is the most important thing in the world. Consider, practice, inquire. If you don't have clothing, you won't die. If you don't have betel nut to chew or cigarettes to smoke, you still won't die. But if you don't have rice or water, then you will die. I see only these two things as being essential in this world. You need rice and water to nourish the body. So I wasn't interested in anything else; I just contented myself with whatever was offered. As long as I had rice and water, that was enough to practice with, and I was content.

Is that enough for you? All those other things are extras. Whether you find them or not doesn't matter. The only really important things are rice and water.

"If I live like this can I survive?" I asked myself, "There's enough to get by on, all right. I can probably get at least rice on alms round in just about any village, a mouthful from each house. Water is usually available. Just these two are enough."

This mind has been deluded now for who knows how many lifetimes. Whatever we don't like or love, we want to avoid. We just indulge in our fears, and then we say we're practicing. This can't be called practice. If it's real practice, you'll even risk your life. If you've really made up your mind to practice, why would you take an interest in petty concerns? "I got only a little, you got a lot." "You quarreled with me, so I'm quarreling with you." I had none of these thoughts because I wasn't looking for such things. Whatever others did was their business. When I went to other monasteries I didn't get involved in such things. However high or low others practiced, I wouldn't take any interest; I just looked after my own business. And so I dared to practice, and the practice gave rise to wisdom and insight.

When your practice has really hit the spot, then you truly practice. Day and night you practice. At night, when it's quiet, I'd sit in meditation, then come down to walk, alternating back and forth like this at least two or three times a night. Walk, then sit, then walk some more. I wasn't bored, I enjoyed it.

Sometimes it'd be raining softly, and I'd think of the times I used to work the rice paddies. My trousers would still be wet from the day before but I'd have to get up before dawn and put them on again. Then I'd have to go down to take the buffalo from its stall underneath the house. All I could see of the buffalo was its neck, it was so muddy in there. I'd grab its rope and it would be covered in buffalo shit. Then its tail would swish around and spatter me with shit on top of that. My feet would be sore from infections, and I'd walk along thinking, "Why is life so miserable?" And now here I was doing walking meditation…so what was a little bit of rain to me? Thinking like this, I encouraged myself in the practice.

If the practice has entered the stream, there's nothing to compare it with. There's no suffering like the suffering of a Dhamma practitioner, and there's no happiness like the happiness of one either. There's no zeal to compare with the zeal of the practitioner, and there's no comparable laziness either. Practitioners of the Dhamma are tops. That's why I say, if you really practice, it's a sight to see.

But most of us just talk about practice. We are like the man whose roof is leaking on one side, so he sleeps on the other side of the house. When the sunshine comes in on that side, he rolls over to the other side, thinking, "When will I ever get a decent house like everyone else?" If the whole roof leaks, he just gets up and leaves. This is not the way to do things, but that's how most people are.

This mind of ours, these defilements, if you follow them they'll cause trouble. The more you follow them, the more the practice degenerates. In real practice you sometimes amaze yourself with your zeal. Whether other people practice well or not, don't take any interest; simply do your own practice consistently. Whoever comes or goes, it doesn't matter, just practice.

Wherever you are still inept, wherever you are still lacking, that's where you must apply yourself. If you haven't yet cracked it, don't give up. Having finished with one thing, you get stuck on another, so persist with that till it's finished. Don't be content until then. Put all your attention on that point. While sitting, lying down, or walking, watch right there.

Be like a farmer who hasn't yet finished his fields. Every year he plants rice, but this year he hasn't yet finished the planting. So his mind is stuck on that; he can't rest content. Even when he's with friends he can't relax; he's always nagged by his unfinished business. Or like a mother who leaves her baby upstairs while she goes to feed the animals below: she's always got her baby in mind, concerned that it might fall somewhere. She may be doing other things, but her baby is never far from her thoughts.

It's just the same for us and our practice—we never forget it. Even though we may do other things, our practice is never far from our thoughts. It's constantly with us, day and night. It has to be like this if you are really going to make progress.

In the beginning you must rely on a teacher to instruct and advise you. When the teacher instructs you, follow the instructions. If you understand the practice, you no longer need the teacher to instruct you; just do the work yourself. Whenever heedlessness or unwholesome qualities arise, know for yourself, teach yourself. The mind is the "one who knows," the witness. The mind knows whether you are still very deluded or only a little.

Practice is like that. It's almost like being crazy, or you could even say you are crazy. When you really practice you are crazy, you "flip." You have distorted perception and then you adjust your perception. If you don't adjust it, it's going to be just as troublesome and just as wretched as before.

So there's a lot of suffering in the practice, but if you don't get to know your own suffering, you won't understand the Noble Truth of Suffering. To understand suffering, to kill it off, you first have to encounter it. If you want to shoot a bird but don't go out and find it, how will you ever shoot it? Suffering, that's what the Buddha taught about: the suffering of birth, the suffering of old age. If you refuse to experience suffering, you won't see it. If you don't see suffering, you won't understand it. If you don't understand suffering, you won't be able to get rid of it.

Now, people don't want to see suffering; they don't want to experience it. If they suffer here, they run over there. They drag their suffering around with them, but they never kill it. They don't contemplate or investigate it. As long as you remain ignorant, wherever you go, you'll find suffering. If you board an airplane to fly away from it, it will board the plane with you. If you dive underwater, it will dive in with you. Suffering lies within us, but we don't understand that. If it lies within us, where can we run to escape it?

You must look into this intently until you're beyond doubt. You must dare to practice. Don't shirk it, either in a group or alone. If others are lazy it doesn't matter. Whoever does a lot of walking meditation, a lot of practice…I guarantee results. If you really practice consistently, whether others come or go or whatever, one rains retreat is enough. Do it like I've been telling you here. Practice is also paṭipadā. What is paṭipadā? Practice evenly, consistently. Don't practice like old Venerable Peh. One rains retreat he determined to stop talking. He stopped talking all right, but then he started writing notes: "Tomorrow please toast me some rice." He wanted to eat toasted rice! He stopped talking but ended up writing so many notes that he was even more scattered than before. One minute he'd write one thing, the next another; what a farce!

I don't know why he bothered determining not to talk. He didn't know what practice is.

Actually, our practice is to be content with little, just to be natural. Don't worry whether you feel lazy or diligent. Don't even say, "I'm diligent" or "I'm lazy." Most people practice only when they feel diligent; if they feel lazy, they don't bother. But monastics shouldn't think like that. When you are diligent, practice. When you are lazy, practice. Don't bother with other things. Throw them out, train yourself. Practice consistently, day or night, this year, next year, whatever the time. Don't pay attention to ideas of diligence or laziness; don't worry whether it's hot or cold, just do it. This is called *sammā paṭipadā*—right practice.

Some people really apply themselves to the practice for six or seven days; then, when they don't get the results they wanted, give it up and revert completely, indulging in chatter, socializing, and whatever. Then they remember the practice and go at it for another six or seven days, then give it up again. That's the way some farmers work. At first they throw themselves into their work. Then, when they stop, they don't even bother picking up their tools; they just walk off and leave them there. Later on, when the soil has all caked up, they remember their work and do a bit more, only to leave it again. Working this way, they'll never get a decent garden or paddy field.

Our practice is similar. If you think this paṭipadā is unimportant, you won't get anywhere with the practice. Sammā paṭipadā is unquestionably important. Do it constantly. Don't listen to your moods. So what if your mood is good or not? The Buddha didn't bother with those things. He had experienced all the good things and bad things, the right things and wrong things. That was his practice. Taking only what you like and discarding whatever you don't like isn't practice, it's disaster. Wherever you go, you will never be satisfied; and wherever you stay, there will be suffering.

Some of us practice because we seek to attain something. If we don't get what we want, we don't want to practice. But the Buddha taught that the cultivation of the practice is for giving up, for letting go, for stopping, for uprooting.

There was once an elder who had initially gone forth into the Mahānikai sect. But he found it not strict enough, so he took *Dhammayuttika*[54] ordination. Then he started practicing. Sometimes he would fast for fifteen days, then when he ate he'd eat only leaves and grass. He thought that eating animals was bad karma, that it would be better to eat leaves and grass.

After a while, "Hmm, being a monk is inconvenient. It's hard to maintain my vegetarian practice as a monk. Maybe I'll disrobe and become a pah kow." So he disrobed and became a pah kow. That way he could gather leaves and grass and dig for roots and yams for himself, which as a monk he could not do. He carried on like that for a while till in the end he didn't know what he should be doing. So he gave it all up. He gave up being a monk, gave up being a pah kow, gave up everything. These days I don't know what he's doing. Maybe he's dead; I don't know. But he gave up because he couldn't find anything to suit his mind. He didn't realize that he was simply following defilements. The defilements were leading him on, but he didn't know it.

"Did the Buddha disrobe and become a pah kow? How did the Buddha practice? What did he do?" He didn't consider this. Did the Buddha go and eat leaves and grass like a cow? Sure, if you want to eat like that go ahead, if that's all you can manage; but don't go round criticizing others. Whatever standard of practice you find suitable then persevere with that. "Don't gouge or carve too much, or you won't have a decent handle."[55]

You'll be left with nothing and in the end just give up. Think about what you're practicing for. This practice is taught for shaking off. The mind wants to love this person and hate that person. We are practicing so that we can give up these very things. Even if you attain peace, throw out the peace. If knowledge arises, throw out the knowledge. If you know, then you know; but if you take that knowing to be your own, then you think you know something. You think you are better than others. After a while you can't live anywhere, because wherever you live, problems arise. If you practice wrongly, it's just as if you didn't practice at all.

Practice according to your capacity. Do you sleep a lot? Then try going against the grain. Do you eat a lot? Then try eating less. Take as much practice as you need, using sīla, samādhi, and paññā as your basis. Then throw in the dhutanga practices too. These dhutanga practices are for digging into the defilements. You may find the basic practices still not enough to really uproot the defilements, so you have to incorporate the dhutanga practices as well. Living at the foot of a tree, living in a charnel ground—try it out. What's it like to live in a charnel ground? Is it the same as living in a group?

Dhutanga: This translates as "the practices that are hard to do." These are the practices of the Noble Ones. Whoever wants to be a Noble One must use the dhutanga practices to cut through the defilements. It's difficult to observe them and it's hard to find people with the commitment to practice them, because they go against the grain. They say to limit your robes to just the basic three robes, to eat only what you get on alms round, to eat your alms food directly from the bowl, to refuse any food offered to you afterward.

Keeping this last practice in central Thailand is easy; the food is quite adequate, because there they put a lot of different foods in your bowl. But when you come to the Northeast, here this dhutanga takes on subtle nuances—here you get plain rice! In these parts the tradition is to put only plain rice in the alms bowl. This dhutanga practice then becomes really ascetic. You eat only plain rice; whatever is brought to offer afterward you don't accept. Then there is eating once a day, at one sitting, from only one bowl—when you've finished eating you get up from your seat and don't eat again that day. It's hard these days to find people with enough commitment to do this practice because it is demanding, but that is why it is so beneficial.

What people call practice these days is not really practice. If you really practice it's no easy matter. Most people don't dare to really practice, don't dare to really go against the grain. They don't want to do anything that runs contrary to their feelings. People don't want to resist the defilements; they don't want to dig at them or get rid of them.

In our practice we say not to follow your own moods. We have been fooled for countless lifetimes already into believing that the mind is our own. Actually, it isn't; it's just an impostor. It drags us into greed, aversion, and delusion; into theft, plunder, desire, and hatred. These things aren't ours. Just ask yourself right now: "Do I want to be good?" Everybody wants to be good. Now, doing all these things, is that good? People commit malicious acts, and yet they want to be good. That's why I say these things are tricksters; that's all they are.

The Buddha didn't want us to follow this mind; he wanted us to train it. If it goes one way, then take cover another way. When it goes over there, then take cover back here. To put it simply: Whatever the mind wants, don't let it have it. It's as if we've been friends for years but we finally reach a point where our ideas are no longer the same. We split up and go our separate ways. We no longer understand each other; in fact, we even argue, so we break up. That's right, don't follow your own mind. Whoever follows their own mind follows its likes and desires and everything else; that person hasn't yet practiced at all.

This is why I say that what people call practice is not really practice; it's disaster. To put it straight, in our practice you have to commit your very life. This practice does entail some suffering. Especially in the first year or two, there's a lot of suffering. The young monks and novices really have a hard time.

I've had a lot of difficulties in the past, especially with food. What would you expect? Becoming a monk at twenty when you are just getting into your food and sleep.... Some days I would sit alone and just dream of food. I'd want to eat bananas in syrup, or papaya salad, and my saliva would start to run. This is part of the training. All these things are not easy. This business of food and eating can lead one into a lot of bad karma. Take someone who's just growing up, just getting into his food and sleep, and constrain him in these robes—his feelings run amok. It's like damming a flowing torrent: sometimes the dam just breaks.

My meditation in the first year was nothing else, just food. Sometimes I would sit there, and it was almost as if I were actually popping bananas into my mouth. I could almost feel myself breaking the bananas into pieces and putting them in my mouth. And this is all part of the practice.

So don't be afraid of it. We've all been deluded for countless lifetimes now, so coming to train ourselves, to correct ourselves, is no easy matter. But if it's difficult, it's worth doing.

Why should we bother with easy things? We should train ourselves to do that which is difficult.

It must have been the same for the Buddha. If he had cared only about his family and relatives, his wealth, and his past sensual pleasures, he'd never have become the Buddha. These aren't trifling matters, either; they're just what most people are looking for. So going forth at an early age and giving up these things is just like dying. And yet some people come up and say, "Oh, it's easy for you, Luang Por. You've never had a wife and children to worry about!" I say, "Don't get too close to me when you say that or you'll get a clout over the head!" as if I didn't have a heart or something!

Establish peace within you. In time you will understand. Practice, reflect, contemplate, and the fruits of the practice will be there. The cause and the result are proportional. Don't give in to your moods. In the beginning even finding the right amount of sleep is difficult. You may determine to sleep a certain amount but can't manage it. You must train yourself. Whatever time you decide to get up, then get up as soon as it comes round. Sometimes you can do it, but sometimes as soon as you awake you say to yourself, "Get up!" and it won't budge! You may have to say to yourself, "One...two.... If I reach the count of three and still don't get up may I fall into hell!" You have to teach yourself like this. When you get to three you'll get up immediately; you'll be afraid of falling into hell. The well-trained mind won't dare cause trouble. All Noble Ones have confidence in their own hearts. We should be like this. Some people become monastics simply to find an easy life. But where does ease come from? What are its preconditions? All ease has to be preceded by suffering. You have to work before you get money, isn't that so? You must plough the fields before you get rice. In all things you must first experience difficulty. If you don't study the books, can you expect to be able to read and write? It can't be done.

This is why most people who have studied a lot and become monks never get anywhere. Their knowledge is of a different kind, on a different path. They don't train themselves; they don't look at their minds. They only stir up their minds with confusion, seeking things that are not conducive to calm and restraint. The knowledge of the Buddha is not worldly but supramundane, an altogether different kind of knowing.

This is why whoever goes forth into the Buddhist monkhood must give up whatever status or position they have held previously. Even when a king goes forth he must relinquish his previous status. He can't bring his worldly power into the monkhood and throw his weight around. The practice requires relinquishing, letting go, uprooting, stopping. You must understand this in order to make the practice work.

If you are sick and don't treat the illness with medicine, do you think the illness will cure itself? Wherever you feel fear, go there. If you know of a cemetery or charnel ground that is particularly fearsome, go there. Put on your robes, go there and contemplate: *Aniccā vaṭa saṅkhārā...*[56] Stand there or do walking meditation, look inward, and see where your fear lies. It will be all too obvious. Understand the truth of all conditioned things. Stay there and watch until dusk falls and it gets darker and darker, until you are even able to stay there all night.

The Buddha said, "Whoever sees the Dhamma sees the Tathāgata. Whoever sees the Tathāgata sees nibbāna." If we don't follow his example, how will we see the Dhamma? If we don't see the Dhamma, how will we know the Buddha? If we don't see the Buddha, how will we know the qualities of the Buddha? Only if we practice in the footsteps of the Buddha will we know that what the Buddha taught is utterly certain, that the Buddha's teaching is the supreme truth.

PART 3

Wisdom

CHAPTER 23

WHAT IS CONTEMPLATION?

*The following teaching is taken from a session of questions and answers
that took place at Wat Gor Nork monastery during the Vassa (rains retreat)
of 1979, between Venerable Ajahn Chah and a group of English-speaking disciples.
Some rearrangement of the sequence of conversation has been made for ease
of understanding.*

The knowing that arises is above and beyond the process of
thinking. It leads to not being fooled by thinking anymore.

*Question: When you teach about the value of contemplation, are you speaking
of sitting and thinking over particular themes—the thirty-two parts of the body,
for instance?*

Answer: That is not necessary when the mind is truly still. When tranquillity is properly established the right object of investigation becomes obvious. When contemplation is "true," there is no discrimination into "right" and "wrong," "good" and "bad"; there is nothing even like that. You don't sit there thinking, "Oh, this is like that, and that is like this," etc. That is a coarse form of contemplation. Meditative contemplation is not merely a matter of thinking—rather, it's what we call "contemplation in silence." While going about our daily routine we mindfully consider the real nature of existence through comparisons. This is a coarse kind of investigation but it leads to the real thing.

When you talk about contemplating body and mind, though, do we actually use thinking? Can thinking produce true insight? Is this vipassanā?

In the beginning we need to work using thinking, even though later on we go beyond it. When we are doing true contemplation all dualistic thinking has ceased, although we need to consider dualistically to get started. Eventually, all thinking and pondering come to an end.

You say that there must be sufficient tranquillity (samādhi) to contemplate. Just how tranquil do you mean?

Tranquil enough for there to be presence of mind.

Do you mean staying with the here-and-now, not thinking about the past and future?

Thinking about the past and future is all right if you understand what these things really are, but you must not get caught up in them. Treat them the same as you would anything else—don't get caught up. When you see thinking as just thinking, then that's wisdom. Don't believe in any of it! Recognize that all of it is just something that has arisen and will cease. Simply see everything just as it is—it is what it is—the mind is the mind—it's not anything or anybody in itself. Happiness is just happiness, suffering is just suffering—it is just what it is. When you see this you will be beyond doubt.

Is true contemplating the same as thinking?

We use thinking as a tool, but the knowing that arises because of its use is above and beyond the process of thinking; it leads to our not being fooled by our thinking anymore. You recognize that all thinking is merely the movement of the mind, and also that the knowing is not born and doesn't die. What do you think all this movement called "mind" comes out of? What we talk about as the mind—all the activity—is just the conventional mind. It's not the real mind at all. What is real just *is;* it's not arising and it's not passing away.

Trying to understand these things just by talking about them, though, won't work. We need to really consider impermanence, unsatisfactoriness and impersonality (anicca, dukkha, anattā); that is, we need to use thinking to contemplate the nature of conventional reality. What comes out of this work is wisdom; and if it's real wisdom, everything's completed, finished—we recognize emptiness. Even though there may still be thinking, it's empty—you are not affected by it.

How can we arrive at this stage of the real mind?

You work with the mind you already have, of course! See that all that arises is uncertain, that there is nothing stable or substantial. See it clearly and see that there is really nowhere to take a hold of anything—it's all empty.

When you see the things that arise in the mind for what they are, you won't have to work with thinking anymore. You will have no doubt whatsoever in these matters.

To talk about the "real mind" and so on may have a relative use in helping us understand. We invent names for the sake of study, but, actually, nature just is how it is. For example, sitting here downstairs on the stone floor. The floor is the base—it's not moving or going anywhere. Upstairs, above us, is what has arisen out of this. Upstairs is like everything that we see in our minds: form, feeling, memory, thinking. Really, they don't exist in the way we presume they do. They are merely the conventional mind. As soon as they arise, they pass away again; they don't really exist in themselves.

There is a story in the scriptures about Venerable Sāriputta examining a bhikkhu before allowing him to go off wandering *(dhutanga vatta)*. He asked him how he would reply if he was questioned, "What happens to the Buddha after he dies?" The bhikkhu replied, "When form, feeling, perception, thinking, and consciousness arise, they pass away." Venerable Sāriputta passed him on that.

Practice is not just a matter of talking about arising and passing away, though. You must see it for yourself. When you are sitting, simply see what is actually happening. Don't follow anything. Contemplation doesn't mean being caught up in thinking. The contemplative thinking of one on the Way is not the same as the thinking of the world. Unless you understand properly what is meant by contemplation, the more you think the more confused you will become.

The reason we make such a point of the cultivation of mindfulness is because we need to see clearly what is going on. We must understand the processes of our hearts. When such mindfulness and understanding are present, then everything is taken care of. Why do you think one who knows the Way never acts out of anger or delusion? The causes for these things to arise are simply not there. Where would they come from? Mindfulness has got everything covered.

Is this mind you are talking about called the "Original Mind"?

What do you mean?

It seems as if you are saying there is something else outside the conventional body-mind (the five khandas). Is there something else? What do you call it?

There isn't anything, and we don't call it anything—that's all there is to it! Be finished with all of it. Even the knowing doesn't belong to anybody, so be finished with that, too! Consciousness is not an individual, not a being, not a self, not an other, so finish with it—finish with everything! There is nothing worth wanting! It's all just a load of trouble. When you see clearly like this, then everything is finished.

Could we not call it the "Original Mind"?

You can call it that if you insist. You can call it whatever you like, for the sake of conventional reality. But you must understand this point properly. This is very important. If we didn't make use of conventional reality, we wouldn't have any words or concepts with which to consider actual reality—Dhamma. This is very important to understand.

What degree of tranquillity are you talking about at this stage? And what quality of mindfulness is needed?

You don't need to go thinking like that. If you didn't have the right amount of tranquillity, you wouldn't be able to deal with these questions at all. You

need enough stability and concentration to know what is going on—
enough for clarity and understanding to arise.

Asking questions like this shows that you are still doubting. You need
enough tranquillity of mind to no longer get caught in doubting what you
are doing. If you had done the practice, you would understand these things.
The more you carry on with this sort of questioning, the more confusing
you make it. It's all right to talk if the talking helps contemplation, but it
won't show you the way things actually are. This Dhamma is not understood because somebody else tells you about it; you must see it for yourself—paccattaṁ.

If you *have* the quality of understanding that we have been taking
about, then we say that your duty to *do* anything is over, which means that
you don't do anything. If there is still something to do, then it's your duty
to do it.

Simply keep putting everything down, and know that that is what you
are doing. You don't need to be always checking up on yourself, worrying
about things like "How much samādhi?"—it will always be the right
amount. Whatever arises in your practice, let it go; know it all as uncertain,
impermanent. Remember that! It's all uncertain. Be finished with all of it.
This is the way that will take you to the source—to your Original Mind.

CHAPTER 24

DHAMMA NATURE

SOMETIMES, when a fruit tree is in bloom, a breeze stirs and scatters some of its blossoms. Some buds remain and grow into small, green fruit. A wind blows and some of these fall to the ground. Other fruits ripen, and then they too fall.

And so it is with people. Like flowers and fruit in the wind, they fall at different stages of life. Some people die while still in the womb; others live for only a few days after birth. Yet others die after just a few years, or in their youth or maturity. Still others reach a ripe old age before dying.

When reflecting upon people, we consider the nature of the fruit in the wind: both are very uncertain. Such uncertainty can also be seen in the monastic life. Some people come to the monastery intending to be ordained but change their minds and leave, some with their heads already shaved. Others are already novices; then they decide to leave. Some are ordained for only one rains retreat and then disrobe. Just like fruit in the wind—all very uncertain.

Our minds are also similar. A mental impression arises, draws and pulls at the mind; then the mind falls—just like fruit.

The Buddha understood this uncertain nature of things. He observed the phenomenon of fruit in the wind and reflected upon the monks and novices who were his disciples. He found that they, too, were essentially of the same nature—uncertain! How could it be otherwise? This is just the way of all things.

Thus if you are practicing with awareness, you don't need to have someone to teach you all that much for you to be able to see and understand. An example is the case of the Buddha who, in a previous life, was King Janaka Kumāra. He didn't need to study very much. All he had to do was observe a mango tree.

One day, while visiting a park with his retinue of ministers, from atop his elephant he spied some mango trees heavily laden with ripe fruit. Not being able to stop at that time, he resolved to return later to partake of some. Little did he know, however, that his ministers, who were following, would greedily gather all the fruit, whether by knocking them down with poles or by breaking off whole branches, tearing and scattering the leaves.

Returning in the evening to the mango grove and already imagining the delicious taste of the mangoes, the king discovered that all had been taken. Not only that, but branches and leaves were scattered everywhere.

Disappointed and upset, the king then noticed another mango tree nearby with its leaves and branches still intact. He realized why: this tree had no fruit. If a tree has no fruit, nobody disturbs it, so its leaves and branches are not damaged. This lesson kept him absorbed in thought all the way back to the palace: "It is unpleasant, troublesome, and difficult to be a king. A king must be constantly concerned for all his subjects. What if there are attempts to attack, plunder, and seize parts of his kingdom?" He could not rest peacefully; even in his sleep he was disturbed by bad dreams. He saw in his mind, once again, the mango tree, without fruit but with undamaged leaves and branches. "If we become similar to that mango tree," he thought, "our leaves and branches, too, will not be damaged."

He sat in his chamber and meditated. Finally, he decided to become a monk, having been inspired by this lesson of the mango tree. He compared himself to that mango tree and concluded that if one didn't become involved in the ways of the world, one would be truly independent, free from worries or difficulties. The mind would be untroubled. Reflecting thus, he became a wandering monk.

From then on, wherever he went, when asked who his teacher was, he would answer, "A mango tree." He didn't need to receive that much teaching. A mango tree was the cause of his awakening to the *opanayiko-dhamma*, the teaching leading inward. And with this awakening, he became a monk, one who has few concerns, is content with little, and who delights in solitude. He had given up his royal status, and his mind was finally at peace.

We too, like the Buddha when he was King Janaka Kumāra, should look around us and be observant, for everything in the world is ready to teach us. With even a little intuitive wisdom, we will then be able to see clearly through the ways of the world. We will come to understand that everything in the world is a teacher. Trees and vines, for example, can reveal the true nature of reality. With wisdom there is no need to question anyone, no need to study. From nature we can learn enough to be enlightened, because everything follows the way of truth. It does not diverge from truth.

Associated with wisdom are self-composure and restraint, which, in turn, can lead to further insight into the ways of nature. In this way, we will come to know the ultimate truth of everything being anicca, dukkha, anattā. Take trees, for example; all trees upon the earth are equal, are one, when seen through the reality of anicca-dukkha-anattā. First they come into being, then they grow and mature, constantly changing, until they finally die, as every tree must.

In the same way, people and animals are born, grow, and change during their lifetimes until they eventually die. The multitudinous changes that occur during this transition from birth to death show the way of Dhamma. That is to say, all things are impermanent, having decay and dissolution as their natural condition. If we have awareness and understanding, if we study with wisdom and mindfulness, we will see Dhamma as reality. We will see people as constantly being born, changing, and finally passing away. Everyone is subject to the cycle of birth and death; all of us in the universe are as one. Seeing one person clearly and distinctly is the same as seeing everyone in the world.

In the same way, everything is Dhamma—not only the things we see with our physical eye but also the things we see in our minds. A thought arises, then changes and passes away. It is *nāma-dhamma,* simply a mental impression that arises and passes away. This is the real nature of the mind. Altogether, this is the Noble Truth of Dhamma. If one doesn't look and observe in this way, one doesn't really see! If one does see, one will have the wisdom to listen to the Dhamma as proclaimed by the Buddha.

Where is the Buddha?
The Buddha is in the Dhamma.
Where is the Dhamma?

The Dhamma is in the Buddha.
Right here, now!
Where is the Sangha?
The Sangha is in the Dhamma.

The Buddha, the Dhamma, and the Sangha exist in our minds, but we have to see this clearly. Some people just say casually, "Oh, the Buddha, the Dhamma, and the Sangha exist in my mind." Yet their own practice is not in accord with truth. It is thus not possible that the Buddha, the Dhamma, and the Sangha should be found in their minds, because the mind must first be that mind that knows the Dhamma. Only then will we come to know that truth does exist in the world, and that it is possible for us to practice and thereby realize it.

For instance, nāma-dhamma—feelings, thoughts, imagination, and so forth—are all uncertain. When anger arises, it grows, changes, and finally disappears. Happiness too arises, grows, changes, and finally disappears. They are empty. They are not really any "thing." Internally, there is this body and mind. Externally, there are trees, vines, and all manner of things that display this universal law of uncertainty.

Whether it is a tree, a mountain, or an animal, it's all Dhamma, everything is Dhamma. Where is this Dhamma? Speaking simply, that which is not Dhamma doesn't exist. Dhamma is nature. This is called the *sacca-dhamma*, the true Dhamma. If one sees nature, one sees Dhamma; if one sees Dhamma, one sees nature. Seeing nature, one knows the Dhamma.

And so, what is the use of a lot of study when the ultimate reality of life, in its every moment, in its every act, is just an endless cycle of births and deaths? If we are mindful and clearly aware in any posture (sitting, standing, walking, and lying down), then self-knowledge is ready to be born—that is, the knowing of the truth of Dhamma, right here and now.

Right now the Buddha—the real Buddha—is still living, for he is the Dhamma itself, the sacca-dhamma. And sacca-dhamma, that which enables one to become buddha, still exists. It hasn't fled anywhere! It gives rise to two buddhas: one in body and the other in mind.

"The real Dhamma," the Buddha told Ānanda, "can only be realized through practice." Whoever sees the Dhamma, sees the Buddha. Whoever sees the Buddha, sees the Dhamma. And how is this? Previously no buddha existed; it was only when Siddhatta Gotama realized the Dhamma that he became the Buddha. If we explain it in this way, then he is the same as us. If we realize the Dhamma, then we will likewise be the Buddha. This is called the buddha in mind, or nāma-dhamma.

We must be mindful of everything we do, for we become the inheritors of our own good or evil actions. In doing good, we reap good. In doing evil, we reap evil. All you have to do is look into your everyday lives to know that this is so. Siddhatta Gotama was enlightened to the realization of this truth, and this gave rise to the appearance of a buddha in the world. Likewise, if each and every person practices to attain to this truth, then they, too, will be a buddha.

Thus, the Buddha still exists. On hearing this, some people become very happy, saying, "If the Buddha still exists, then I can practice Dhamma!" That is how you should see it.

The Dhamma that the Buddha realized is the Dhamma that exists permanently in the world. It can be compared to groundwater. When a person wishes to dig a well, they must dig down deep enough to reach groundwater. The groundwater is already there. They do not create it; they just discover it. Similarly, the Buddha did not invent the Dhamma, did not decree the Dhamma. He merely revealed what was already there. Through contemplation, the Buddha saw the Dhamma. So it is said that the Buddha was enlightened, for enlightenment is knowing the Dhamma. The Dhamma is the truth of this world. Because he saw this, Siddhatta Gotama is called "the Buddha." And the Dhamma is that which allows other people to become a buddha: "one who knows," one who knows Dhamma. If beings have good conduct and are devoted to the Buddhadhamma, then those beings will never be short of virtue and goodness. With understanding, we will see that we are really not far from the Buddha, but sitting face to face with him. When we understand the Dhamma, then at that moment we will see the Buddha.

If one really practices, one will hear the Buddhadhamma whether one is sitting underneath a tree, is lying down, or in whatever posture. This is not something merely to think about. It arises from the pure mind. Just remembering these words is not enough, because this depends upon seeing the Dhamma itself, nothing other than this. Thus we must be determined to practice to be able to see this, and then our practice will really be complete.

Wherever we sit, stand, walk, or lie down, we will hear the Buddha's Dhamma.

The Buddha taught us to live in a quiet place so that we can learn to collect and restrain the senses of eye, ear, nose, tongue, body, and mind. This is the foundation for our practice, since these are the places where all things arise, and they arise only in these places. Thus we collect and restrain these six senses in order to know the conditions that arise there. All good and evil arise through these six senses. They are the predominant faculties in the body. The eye is predominant in seeing; the ear in hearing; the nose in smelling; the tongue in tasting; the body in contacting hot, cold, hard, and soft; and the mind in the arising of mental impressions. All that remains for us to do is to build our practice around these points.

This practice is easy because all that is necessary has already been set down by the Buddha. It's as if the Buddha had planted an orchard and invited us to partake of its fruit. We ourselves do not need to plant one. Whether it's virtue, meditation, or wisdom we're concerned with, we don't need to create, decree, or speculate. All we need to do is follow what already exists in the Buddha's teaching.

Therefore, we are beings who have much merit and good fortune in having heard the teachings of the Buddha. The orchard already exists; the fruit is already ripe. Everything is already complete and perfect. All that is lacking is someone to pick the fruit and eat it, someone with faith enough to practice!

We should consider that our merit and good fortune are very valuable. All we need to do is look around and see how other creatures are possessed of ill fortune. Take dogs, pigs, snakes, and other creatures. They have no chance to study Dhamma, no chance to know Dhamma, no chance to practice Dhamma. These are beings possessed of ill fortune who are receiving karmic retribution. When one has no chance to study, to know, and to practice Dhamma, one has no chance to be free from suffering.

As human beings we should not allow ourselves to become victims of ill fortune, deprived of proper manners and discipline. Do not become a victim of ill fortune! Do not become one without hope of attaining the Path of freedom to nibbāna, without hope of developing virtue. Do not think that we are already without hope! By thinking that way, we become possessed of ill fortune like those other creatures.

We are beings who have come within the sphere of influence of the Buddha. Thus we already possess sufficient merit and resources. If we correct and develop our understanding, opinions, and knowledge in the present, then it will lead us to behave and practice in such a way as to see and know Dhamma in this present life.

We are thus different from other creatures. We are beings that have the capacity and opportunity to be enlightened to the Dhamma. The Buddha taught that in this present moment the Dhamma exists here in front of us. The Buddha sits facing us right here and now! At what other time or place are you going to look?

If we don't think rightly, if we don't practice rightly, we will fall back to being animals, creatures in hell, hungry ghosts, or demons.[57] How is this? Just look in your mind. When anger arises, what is it? There it is, just look! When delusion arises, what is it? That's it, right there! When greed arises, what is it? Look at it right there!

When the mind does not recognize and clearly understand these mental states, it ceases to be that of a human being. All conditions are in the state of "becoming." Becoming gives rise to "birth" or existence as determined by the present conditions. Thus we become and exist as our minds condition us.

CHAPTER 25

LIVING WITH THE COBRA

THE TEACHING that we study and practice here at Wat Pah Pong is the practice to be free of suffering in the cycle of birth and death. In order to do this practice, you must regard all the various activities of mind, all those you like and all those you dislike, in the same way as you would regard a cobra. The cobra is an extremely poisonous snake, poisonous enough to kill you if it should bite. And so it is with our moods; the moods that we like are poisonous, the moods that we dislike are also poisonous. Both prevent our minds from being free, and both hinder our understanding of the truth as it was taught by the Buddha.

Thus we must try to maintain our mindfulness throughout the day and night. Whatever you may be doing, be it standing, sitting, lying down, speaking, or whatever, you should do with mindfulness. When you are able to establish this mindfulness, you'll find that there will arise clear comprehension associated with it, and these two conditions will bring about wisdom. Thus mindfulness, clear comprehension, and wisdom will work together, and you'll be like one who is awake both day and night.

These teachings left us by the Buddha are not teachings to be just listened to, or simply absorbed on an intellectual level. They are teachings that through practice can be made to arise and be known in our hearts. Wherever we go, whatever we do, we should have these teachings. And what we mean by "have these teachings" or "have the truth" is that, whatever we do or say, we do and say with wisdom. When we think and contemplate, we do so with wisdom. We say that one who has mindfulness and clear comprehension, combined with wisdom, is one who is close to the Buddha.

When you leave here, you should practice bringing everything back to your own mind. Look at your mind with this mindfulness and clear comprehension and develop this wisdom. With these three conditions a *letting go* will arise. You'll know the constant arising and passing away of all phenomena.

You should know that that which is arising and passing away is only the activity of mind. When something arises, it passes away and is followed by further arising and passing away. In the way of Dhamma we call this arising and passing away "birth and death"; and this is everything—this is all there is. When suffering has arisen, it passes away and, when it has passed away, suffering arises again. There's just suffering arising and passing away. When you see this much, you'll be able to know constantly this arising and passing away; and when your knowing is constant, you'll see that this is really all there is. Everything is just birth and death. It's not as if there is anything that carries on. There's just this arising and passing away as it is—that's all.

This kind of seeing will give rise to a tranquil feeling of dispassion toward the world. Such a feeling arises when we see that actually there is nothing worth wanting; there is only arising and passing away, a being born followed by a dying. This is when the mind arrives at letting go—letting everything go according to its own nature. Things arise and pass away in our mind, and we know this. When happiness arises, we know it; when dissatisfaction arises, we know it. And this "knowing happiness" means that we don't identify with it as being ours. When we no longer identify with and cling to happiness and suffering, we are simply left with the natural way of things.

So we say that mental activity is like the deadly poisonous cobra. If we don't interfere with a cobra, it simply goes its own way. Even though it may be extremely poisonous, we are not affected by it; we don't go near it or take hold of it, and it doesn't bite us. The cobra does what is natural for a cobra to do. That's the way it is. If you are clever you'll leave it alone. And so you let be that which is good. You also let be that which is not good—let it be according to its own nature. Let be your liking and your disliking. Treat them the same way as you treat the cobra. Don't interfere. We don't want evil, but nor do we want good. We want neither heaviness nor lightness, neither happiness nor suffering. When, in this way, our wanting comes to an end, peace is firmly established.

When we have this kind of peace established in our minds, we can depend on it. This peace, we say, has arisen out of confusion. Confusion has ended. The Buddha called the attainment of final enlightenment an "extinguishing," in the same way that fire is extinguished. We extinguish fire at the place where it appears. Wherever it is hot, that's where we can make it cool. And so it is with enlightenment. Nibbāna is found in saṁsāra. Enlightenment and delusion exist in the same place, just as do hot and cold. It's hot where it was cold and cold where it was hot. When heat arises, the coolness disappears, and when there is coolness, there's no more heat. In this way nibbāna and saṁsāra are the same.

We are told to put an end to saṁsāra, which means to stop the ever-turning cycle of confusion. This putting an end to confusion is extinguishing the fire. When external fire is extinguished, there is coolness. When the internal fires of sensual craving, aversion, and delusion are put out, then this is coolness also.

This is the nature of enlightenment; it's the extinguishing of fire, the cooling of that which was hot. This is peace. This is the end of saṁsāra, the cycle of birth and death. When you arrive at enlightenment, this is how it is. It's an ending of the ever turning and ever changing; an ending of greed, aversion, and delusion in our minds. We talk about it in terms of happiness because this is how worldly people understand the ideal to be, but in reality it has gone beyond both happiness and suffering. It is perfect peace.

CHAPTER 26

THE MIDDLE WAY WITHIN

THE TEACHING of Buddhism is about giving up evil and practicing good. Then, when evil is given up and goodness is established, we let go of both. The Middle Way is the path to transcend both of those things.

All the teachings of the Buddha have one aim—to show the way out of suffering to those who have not yet escaped. The teachings give us the Right Understanding. If we don't understand rightly, then we can't arrive at peace.

When all the buddhas became enlightened and gave their first teachings, they spoke of two extremes: indulgence in pleasure and indulgence in pain. These are two types of infatuation, between which those who are caught in the sensory world must fluctuate, never arriving at peace but forever spinning in saṁsāra.

The Enlightened One observed that we are all stuck in these two extremes, never seeing the Middle Way of Dhamma. Such is the way of intoxication, not the way of a meditator, not the way to peace. Indulgence in pleasure and indulgence in pain are, to put it simply, the way of slackness and the way of tension.

If you investigate within, moment by moment, you will see that the way of tension is one of anger, of sorrow. Going this way, you encounter only difficulty and distress. As for the opposite indulgence, in pleasure, if you've transcended this, you've transcended happiness. Neither happiness nor unhappiness is a peaceful state. The Buddha taught to let go of both. This is the right practice. This is the Middle Way.

The Middle Way does not refer to our body and speech; it refers to the mind. When a mental impression we don't like arises, it affects the mind and there is confusion. When the mind is confused, when it's "shaken up," this is not the right way. When a mental impression that we like arises, the mind goes to indulgence in pleasure—that's not the way either.

None of us wants suffering; we all want happiness. But in fact happiness is just a refined form of suffering. You can compare happiness and unhappiness to a snake. The head of the snake is unhappiness, the tail is happiness. The head of the snake is really dangerous, it has the poisonous fangs. If you touch it, the snake will bite straight away. But never mind the head; even if you grab hold of the tail, it'll turn around and bite you just the same, because both the head and the tail belong to the snake.

In the same way, both happiness and unhappiness, or pleasure and sadness, arise from the same source—wanting. So when you're happy, your mind isn't peaceful. It really isn't! For instance, when we get the things we like, such as wealth, prestige, praise, or happiness, we are pleased. But the mind still harbors some uneasiness because we're afraid of losing it. That very fear isn't a peaceful state. Later on we may actually lose that thing and then we really suffer.

Thus, even when you're happy, suffering is imminent if you aren't aware. It's just the same as grabbing the snake's tail—if you don't let go it will bite. So whether it's the snake's tail or its head, that is, wholesome or unwholesome conditions, they're all just characteristics of the Wheel of Existence, of endless change.

The essence of Buddhism is peace, and that peace arises from truly knowing the nature of all things. If we investigate closely, we can see that peace is neither happiness nor unhappiness. Neither of these is the truth.

The human mind, the mind that the Buddha exhorted us to know and investigate, is something we can only know by its activity. The true Original Mind has nothing to measure it by, nothing to know it by. In its natural state it is unshaken, unmoving. When happiness arises, all that happens is that this mind moves: it gets lost in a mental impression. When the mind moves like this, clinging and attachment come into being.

The Buddha has already laid down the path of practice in its entirety, but either we have not yet practiced or we've practiced only in speech. Our minds and our speech are not yet in harmony, we just indulge in empty talk. But the basis of Buddhism is not something that can be talked about or guessed at. The real basis of Buddhism is full knowledge of the truth of reality. If you know this truth, then no teaching is necessary. If you don't know it, then even when you listen to the teaching, you won't really understand. This is why the Buddha said, "The Enlightened One only points the way." He can't do the practice for you, because the truth is something you cannot put into words or give away.

All the teachings are merely similes and comparisons, means to help the mind see the truth. If we haven't seen the truth we must suffer. For example, we commonly use the word *saṅkhāra* when referring to the body. Anybody can utter the word, but in fact we have problems simply because we don't know the truth of these saṅkhāras, and thus cling to them. Because we don't know the truth of the body, we suffer.

Here's an example. Suppose one morning you're walking to work and a man yells abuse and insults at you from across the street. As soon as you hear this abuse, your mind changes from its usual state. You don't feel so good; you feel angry and hurt. That man walks around abusing you night and day. Whenever you hear the abuse, you get angry, and even when you return home, you're still angry because you feel vindictive; you want to get even.

A few days later another man comes to your house and calls out, "Hey! That man who abused you the other day, he's mad, he's crazy! Has been that way for years! He abuses everybody. No one takes any notice of anything he says." As soon as you hear this you are suddenly relieved. That anger and hurt pent up within you all these days melts away completely. Why? Because now you know the truth of the matter. Before, you thought that man was normal, so you were angry with him. Your misunderstanding caused you to suffer. As soon as you found out the truth, everything changed: "Oh, he's mad! That explains everything!"

Now that you understand, you feel fine. Now you can let go. If you don't know the truth, you cling right there. When you still thought that man who abused you was normal, you could have killed him. But when you found out the truth, you felt much better. This is knowledge of the truth.

Someone who sees the Dhamma has a similar experience. When attachment, aversion, and delusion disappear, they disappear in the same way. As long as we don't know these things we think, "What can I do? I have so much greed and aversion." This is not clear knowledge. It's just like when we thought the madman was sane. When we finally see that he was mad all along, we're relieved. No one could show you this. Only when the mind sees for itself can it uproot and relinquish attachment.

It's the same with this body that we call saṅkhāra. Although the Buddha has already explained that it's not substantial or a real being as such, we still don't agree; we stubbornly cling to it. If the body could talk, it would be telling us all day long, "You're not my owner, you know." Actually it's telling us all the time, but it's in Dhamma language, so we're unable to understand it.

For instance, the sense organs of eye, ear, nose, tongue, and body are continually changing, but I've never seen them ask permission from us even once! When we have a headache or a stomachache, the body never asks permission first; it just goes right ahead, following its natural course. This shows that the body doesn't allow anyone to be its owner; it doesn't have an owner. The Buddha described it as an object void of substance.

We don't understand the Dhamma and so we don't understand these saṅkhāras; we take them to be ourselves, as belonging to us or belonging to others. This gives rise to clinging. When clinging arises, "becoming" follows on. Once becoming arises, then there is birth. Once there is birth, then old age, sickness, death—the whole mass of suffering arises.

This is the paṭiccasamuppāda. Ignorance gives rise to volitional activities; these give rise to consciousness, and so on. All these things are simply events in mind. When we come into contact with something we don't like, if we don't have mindfulness, ignorance is there. Suffering arises straight away. But the mind passes through these changes so rapidly that we can't keep up with them. It's the same as when you fall from a tree. Before you know it—*thud!*—you've hit the ground. Actually you passed many branches and twigs as you fell, but you couldn't count them all. You just fall, and...*thud!*

Paṭiccasamuppāda is the same. If we divide it up as it is in the scriptures, we say ignorance gives rise to volitional activities; volitional activities give rise to consciousness; consciousness gives rise to mind and matter; mind and matter give rise to the six sense bases; the sense bases give rise to sense contact; contact gives rise to feeling; feeling gives rise to wanting; wanting gives rise to clinging; clinging gives rise to becoming; becoming gives rise to birth; and birth gives rise to old age, sickness, death, and all forms of sorrow. But in truth, when you come into contact with something you don't like, there's immediate suffering! That feeling of suffering is actually the result of the whole chain of the paṭiccasamuppāda. This is why the Buddha exhorted his disciples to investigate and know fully their own minds.

When people are born into the world they come without names—once they are born, we name them. This is a convention. We give people names for the sake of convenience, to call one another by. The scriptures are the same. We separate everything up with labels to make studying the reality convenient. In the same way, all things are simply saṅkhāras. Their original nature is merely that of compounded things. The Buddha said that they are impermanent, unsatisfactory, and not-self. They are unstable. We don't understand this firmly, our understanding is not straight, and so we have wrong view. This wrong view is that the saṅkhāras *are* us, we *are* the saṅkhāras; or that happiness and unhappiness *are* us, we *are* happiness and unhappiness. Seeing like this is not clear knowledge of the true nature of things. The truth is that we can't force all these things to follow our desires; they follow the way of nature.

Here is a simple comparison: suppose you go and sit in the middle of a freeway with the cars and trucks charging down at you. You can't get angry at the cars, shouting, "Don't drive over here! Don't drive over here!" It's a freeway. You can't tell them that. So what can you do? You get off the road! The road is the place where cars go. If you don't want the cars to be there, you suffer.

It's the same with saṅkhāras. We say they disturb us, like when we sit in meditation and hear a sound. We think, "Oh, that sound's bothering me." If we think that the sound is bothering us, we suffer. If we investigate a little deeper, we will see that it's we who go out and disturb the sound! The sound is simply sound. If we understand like this, then there's nothing more to it, we leave the sound be. We see that the sound is one thing, we are another. Those who believe that the sound comes to disturb them don't see themselves. They really don't! Once you see yourself, then you're at ease. The sound is just sound; why should you go and grab it? You see that actually it was you who went out and disturbed the sound.

This is real knowledge of the truth. You see both sides, so you have peace. If you see only one side, there is suffering. Once you see both sides, then you follow the Middle Way. This is the right practice of the mind. This is what we call "straightening out our understanding."

In the same way, the nature of all saṅkhāras is impermanence and death, but we want to grab them; we carry them about and covet them. We want them to be true. We want to find truth within things that aren't true. Whenever someone sees like this and clings to the saṅkhāras as being themselves, they suffer.

The practice of Dhamma is not dependent on being a monk, a nun, a novice, or a lay person; it depends on straightening out your understanding. If our understanding is correct, we arrive at peace. Whether you are ordained or not, it's the same; everyone has the chance to practice Dhamma, to contemplate it. We all contemplate the same thing. If we attain peace, it's the same peace for each of us; it's the same path, with the same methods.

Therefore the Buddha didn't discriminate between lay people and monastics; he taught all people to practice to find the truth of the saṅkhāras. When we know this truth, we let saṅkhāras go. If we know the truth, there will be no more becoming or birth. There is no way for birth to take place because we fully know the truth of saṅkhāras. If we fully know the truth, then there is peace. Having or not having, it's all the same. Gain and loss are one. The Buddha taught us to know this. This is peace—peace is liberation from both happiness and unhappiness, both gladness and sorrow.

We must see that there is no reason to be born—no reason, for example, to be born into gladness. When we get something we like we are glad. If there is no clinging to that gladness, there is no birth; if there is clinging, this is called "birth." So if we get something, we aren't born into gladness. If we lose, we aren't born into sorrow. This is the birthless and the deathless. Birth and death are both grounded in clinging to and cherishing the saṅkhāras.

So the Buddha said, "There is no more becoming for me, finished is the holy life, this is my last birth." There! He knew the birthless and the deathless. This is what the Buddha constantly exhorted his disciples to know. This is the right practice. If you don't reach it, if you don't reach the Middle Way, then you won't transcend suffering.

CHAPTER 27

THE PEACE BEYOND

I T'S OF GREAT IMPORTANCE that we practice the Dhamma. If we don't practice, then all our knowledge is only superficial, just an outer shell. It's as if we have some sort of fruit but we haven't eaten it yet. Even though we have that fruit in our hand, we get no benefit from it. Only through the actual eating of the fruit will we really know its taste.

The Buddha didn't praise those who merely believe others; he praised those who know within themselves. Just as with that fruit, once we have tasted it, we don't have to ask anyone whether it's sweet or sour. Our problems are over because we see according to the truth. One who has realized the Dhamma is like one who has realized the sweetness or sourness of the fruit. All doubts are ended right there.

When we talk about Dhamma, all we say can usually be brought down to four things: to know suffering, to know the cause of suffering, to know the end of suffering, and to know the path of practice leading to the end of suffering. This is all there is. All that we have experienced on the path of practice so far comes down to these four things. When we know these things, our problems are over.

Where are these four things born? They are born just within the body and the mind, nowhere else. So why is the teaching of the Buddha so detailed and extensive? It is so in order to explain these things in a more refined way, to help us to see them.

When Siddhatta Gotama was born into the world, before he saw the Dhamma, he was an ordinary person just like us. When he knew what he had to know—that is, the truth of suffering, the cause, the end, and the way leading to the end of suffering—he realized the Dhamma and became a perfectly enlightened Buddha.

When we realize the Dhamma wherever we sit, we know Dhamma; wherever we are, we hear the Buddha's teaching. When we understand Dhamma, the Buddha is within our mind, the Dhamma is within our mind, and the practice leading to wisdom is within our mind. Having the Buddha, the Dhamma, and the Sangha within our mind means that whether our actions are good or bad, we know their true nature clearly.

That explains how the Buddha could discard worldly opinions, praise, and criticism. When people praised or criticized him, he just accepted it for what it was. Praise and blame are simply worldly conditions, so he wasn't shaken by them. Why not? Because he knew suffering. He knew that if he believed in that praise or criticism, they would cause him to suffer.

When suffering arises, it agitates us and we feel ill at ease. What is the cause of that suffering? It's that we don't know the truth. When the cause is present, then suffering arises. Once arisen we don't know how to stop it. The more we try to stop it, the more it grows. We say, "Don't criticize me," or "Don't blame me." But if you try to stop it like this, suffering really comes on; it won't stop.

So the Buddha taught that the way leading to the end of suffering is to make the Dhamma arise as a reality within our own minds. We become those who witness the Dhamma for themselves. If someone says we are good, we don't get lost in it; if they say we are no good, again we don't forget ourselves. This way we can be free. "Good" and "evil" are just worldly dhammas, just states of mind. If we follow them our mind becomes the world; we just grope in the darkness and don't know the way out.

If that's the way we are, we haven't yet mastered ourselves. We try to defeat others, but in doing so we only defeat ourselves. If we have mastery over ourselves, however, we have mastery over everything—over all mental formations, sights, sounds, smells, tastes, and bodily feelings.

Now I'm talking about externals, but the outside is reflected inside as well. Some people know only the outside. For example, we say we try to "see the body in the body."[58] Having seen the outer body is not enough; we must know the body within the body. Then, having investigated the mind, we should know the mind within the mind.

Why should we investigate the body? What is this "body in the body"? When we say to know the mind, what is this "mind"? If we don't know the mind, then we don't know the things within the mind. We are someone who doesn't know suffering, doesn't know the cause, doesn't know the end, and doesn't know the way leading to the end of suffering. Things that should help to extinguish suffering don't help, because we get distracted by things that aggravate it. It's just as if we have an itch on our head and we scratch our leg! If it's our head that's itching, scratching our leg obviously won't give us much relief. In the same way, when suffering arises we don't know how to handle it; we don't know the practice leading to the end of suffering.

For instance, take this body, the one that each of us has brought along to this meeting. If we just see the form of the body, there's no way we can escape suffering. Why not? Because we still don't see the inside of the body, we see only the outside. We see it as something beautiful, something substantial. The Buddha said that only this is not enough. We see the outside with our eyes; a child can see it, animals can see it—it's not difficult. But having seen it, we stick to it, we don't know the truth of it. We grab it and it bites us!

So we should investigate the body within the body. Whatever's in the body, go ahead and look at it. If we just see the outside it's not clear. We see hair, fingernails, and so on, and they are just pretty things that entice us, so the Buddha taught to see the inside of the body, to see the body within the body. What is in the body? Look closely within! We will find many surprises, because even though they are within us, we've never seen them. Wherever we walk we carry them with us, sitting in a car we carry them with us, but we still don't know them at all!

It's as if we visit some relatives at their house and they give us a present. We take it and put it in our bag and then leave without opening it to see what is inside. Later we open it—and it's full of poisonous snakes! Our body is like this. If we just see its shell, we say it's fine and beautiful. We forget ourselves. We forget impermanence, suffering, and not-self. If we look within this body it's really repulsive.

When we look realistically, without trying to sugar things over, we see that the body is pitiful and wearisome. Then dispassion will arise. This feeling of disinterest does not mean that we feel aversion; it's simply that our mind is clearing up, letting go. We see that all things are insubstantial or undependable; they are naturally established just as they are. However we want them to be, they just go their own way regardless. Whether we laugh or cry, they simply are the way they are. Things that are unstable are unstable; the unbeautiful is unbeautiful.

So the Buddha said that when we experience sights, sounds, tastes, smells, bodily feelings, or mental states, we should release them. When the ear hears sounds, let them go. When the nose smells an odor, let it go. Just leave it at the nose! When bodily feelings arise, let go of the liking or disliking that follows, let it go back to its birthplace. The same for mental states. All these things, just let them go their way. This is knowing. Whether it's happiness or unhappiness, it's all the same. This is meditation.

We meditate to make the mind peaceful so that wisdom may arise. This requires that we practice with body and mind in order to see and know the sense impressions of form, sound, taste, smell, touch, and mental formations. In short, it's just a matter of happiness and unhappiness. Happiness is a pleasant feeling in the mind; unhappiness is just an unpleasant feeling. The Buddha taught to separate this happiness and unhappiness from the mind. The mind is that which knows. Feeling[59] is the characteristic of happiness or unhappiness, liking or disliking. When the mind indulges in these things, we say that it clings to or takes that happiness and unhappiness to be worthy of holding. That clinging is an action of mind, and that happiness or unhappiness is a feeling.

When the Buddha told us to separate the mind from the feeling, he didn't literally mean to throw them to different places. He meant that the mind must know happiness and know unhappiness. When sitting in samādhi, for example, and peace fills the mind, then happiness arises but doesn't reach us; unhappiness arises but doesn't reach us. This is what separating the feeling from the mind means. We can compare it to oil and water in a bottle. They don't combine. Even if you try to mix them, the oil remains oil and the water remains water, because they are of different densities.

The natural state of the mind is neither happiness nor unhappiness. When feeling enters the mind, happiness or unhappiness is born. If we are mindful, we know pleasant feeling as pleasant feeling. The mind that knows will not pick it up. Happiness is there but it's "outside" the mind, not buried within it. The mind simply knows the feeling clearly.

If we separate unhappiness from the mind, does that mean there is no suffering, that we don't experience it? Yes, we experience it, but we know mind as mind, feeling as feeling. We don't cling to that feeling or carry it around. The Buddha separated these things through knowledge. Did he experience suffering? Yes, he knew the state of suffering, but he didn't cling to it, so we say that he cut suffering off. And there was happiness too, but he knew that happiness; if it's not known, is like a poison. He didn't hold it to be himself. Happiness was there through knowledge, but he didn't cling to it or carry it around in his mind. Thus we say that he separated happiness and unhappiness from his mind.

When we say that the Buddha and the Enlightened Ones killed defilements, it's not that they really killed them off. If they had killed all defilements, we probably wouldn't have any! They didn't actually kill defilements; but because they knew them for what they are, they let them go. Someone who's stupid will grab them, but the Enlightened Ones recognized that the defilements in their minds were a poison, so they swept them out. They swept out the things that caused them to suffer. One who doesn't know this will see some things, such as happiness, as good, and then grab them, but the Buddha just saw them for what they were and simply brushed them away.

The Buddha knew that because both happiness and unhappiness are unsatisfactory, they have the same value. When happiness arose, he let it go. His practice was right, for he saw that both these things have equal values and drawbacks. They come under the law of Dhamma, that is, they are unstable and unsatisfactory. Once born, they die. When he saw this, Right View arose; the right way of practice became clear. No matter what sort of feeling or thinking arose in his mind, he knew it as simply the continuous play of happiness and unhappiness. He didn't cling to them.

When the Buddha was newly enlightened he gave a sermon about indulgence in pleasure and indulgence in pain. "Monks! Indulgence in pleasure is the loose way, indulgence in pain is the tense way." These were the two things that disturbed his practice until the day he was enlightened, because at first he didn't let go of them. When he knew them, he let them go, and so was able to give his first sermon.

So we say that a meditator should not walk the way of happiness or unhappiness; rather, they should know them. Knowing the truth of suffering, they will know the cause of suffering, the end of suffering, and the way leading to the end of suffering. And the way out of suffering is meditation itself. To put it simply, we must be mindful.

Mindfulness is knowing, or presence of mind. What am I thinking right now? What am I doing? What am I carrying around with me? We observe like this, we are aware of how we are living. Practicing like this, wisdom can arise. We consider and investigate at all times, in all postures. When a mental impression arises that we like, we know it as such; we don't hold it to be anything substantial. It's just happiness. When unhappiness arises, we know it too, and we know that indulgence in pain is not the path of a meditator.

This is what we call separating the mind from the feeling. If we are clever we don't attach, we leave things be. We become the "one who knows." The mind and feeling are just like oil and water; they are in the same bottle but they don't mix. Even if we are sick or in pain, we still know the feeling as feeling, the mind as mind. We know the painful or comfortable states but we don't identify with them. We stay only with peace: the peace beyond both comfort and pain.

You must live like this, that is, without happiness and without unhappiness. You stay only with the knowing, you don't carry things around.

As long as we are still unenlightened all this may sound strange, but that doesn't matter; we just set our goal in this direction. The mind is the mind. It meets happiness and unhappiness and we see them as merely that, there's nothing more to it. They are separate, unmixed. If they are all mixed up then we don't know them. It's like living in a house; the house and its occupant are related, but separate. If there's some danger to our house, we are distressed and feel we must protect it. But if the house catches fire, we get out. And so if a painful feeling arises, we get out of it, just like that. When we know it's full of fire, we come running out. The house is one thing, the occupant is another; they are separate things.

We say that we separate mind and feeling in this way, but in fact they are by nature already separate. Our realization is simply to know this natural separateness according to reality. If we hold they are not separate, it's because we're clinging to them through ignorance of the truth.

So the Buddha told us to meditate. This practice of meditation is very important. Merely to know with the intellect is not enough. The knowledge that arises from practice with a peaceful mind and the knowledge that comes from study are really far apart. The knowledge of the mind that comes from study is not real knowledge. We hold on to this knowledge—but why? We just lose it! And when it's lost we cry.

If we really understand, then there's letting go, leaving things be. We know how things are and don't forget ourselves. If it happens that we are sick, we don't get lost in that. Some people say, "This year I was sick the whole time, I couldn't meditate at all." These are the words of a really foolish person. Someone who's sick or dying should really be diligent in their practice. You may say you don't have time to meditate. You're sick, you're suffering, you don't trust your body, and so you feel you can't meditate. If you think like this, things will be difficult for you. The Buddha didn't teach like that. He said that right here is the place to meditate. When we're sick or almost dying, that's when we can really know and see reality.

Other people say they don't have the chance to meditate because they're too busy. Sometimes schoolteachers come to see me. They say they have many responsibilities so there's no time to meditate. I ask them, "When you're teaching do you have time to breathe?" They answer yes. "So how can you have time to breathe if the work is so hectic and confusing? Here you are far from Dhamma."

Actually this practice is just about the mind and its feelings. It's not something that you have to run after or struggle for. Breathing continues while working. Nature takes care of the natural processes—all we have to do is try to be aware. Just to keep trying, going inward to see clearly. Meditation is like this.

If we have that presence of mind then whatever work we do will be the very tool that enables us to know right and wrong continually. There's plenty of time to meditate; we just don't fully understand the practice, that's all. While sleeping we breathe, eating we breathe, don't we? Why don't we have time to meditate? Wherever we are, we breathe. If we think like this then our life has as much value as our breath. Wherever we are, we have time to meditate.

All kinds of thinking are mental conditions, not conditions of body, so we need simply to have presence of mind. Then we will know right and wrong at all times. Standing, walking, sitting, and lying, there's plenty of time. We just don't know how to use it properly. Please consider this.

When we know, we are someone who's skilled with the mind, with mental impressions. When we are skilled with mental impressions, we are skilled with the world. We become a "knower of the world," which is recognized as one of the "nine qualities of the Buddha." The Buddha was someone who clearly knew the world with all its difficulty. He knew the troublesome, and that which was not troublesome, was right there. This world is so confusing—how is it that the Buddha was able to know it? Here we should understand that the Dhamma taught by the Buddha is not beyond our ability. In all postures we should have presence of mind and self-awareness—and when it's time to sit in meditation, we do that.

We sit in meditation to establish peacefulness and cultivate mental energy, not to play around. Insight meditation is sitting in samādhi itself. At some places they say, "Now we are going to sit in samādhi, after that we'll do insight meditation." Don't separate them like this! Tranquillity is the base that gives rise to wisdom; wisdom is the fruit of tranquillity. Saying that now we are going to do calm meditation, later we'll do insight—you can't do that! You can only separate them in speech. Just as with a knife, there's the cutting edge and the back of the blade; you can't divide them. If you pick up one you get the other. Tranquillity gives rise to wisdom like this.

Morality is the father and mother of Dhamma. In the beginning we must have morality. Morality is peace. This means that there are no wrongdoings in body or speech. When we don't do wrong, we don't get agitated; when we don't become agitated, peace and collectedness arise.

So we say that morality, concentration, and wisdom are the Path on which the Noble Ones have walked to enlightenment. The three are in fact one: morality is concentration, and concentration is morality; concentration is wisdom, and wisdom is concentration. It's like a mango. When it's a flower we call it a flower. When it becomes a fruit we call it a mango. When it ripens we call it a ripe mango. It's always one mango but it continually changes. The big mango grows from the small mango, the small mango becomes a big one. You can call them different fruits or all one. The mango, from the moment it first appears as a flower, simply grows to ripeness. This is enough. Whatever others call it doesn't matter. Once it's born it grows to old age, and then where? We should contemplate this.

Some people don't want to be old. When they get old they become depressed. These people shouldn't eat ripe mangoes! Why do we want the mangoes to be ripe? If they're not ripe in time, we ripen them artificially, don't we? But when we grow old we are filled with regrets. Some people cry, they're so afraid of getting old or dying. If they feel that way, they shouldn't eat ripe mangoes. Better just eat the flowers! If we can see this, then we can see the Dhamma. Everything clears up, we are at peace. Just resolve to practice like this.

You should take what I've said and contemplate it. If anything is not right, please excuse me. You'll know whether it's right or wrong only if you practice and see for yourself. Whatever's wrong, throw it out. If it's right, take it and use it. But actually we practice in order to let go of both right and wrong. In the end we just throw everything out. If it's right, throw it out; wrong, throw it out! Usually if it's right, we cling to rightness; if it's wrong, we hold it to be wrong, and then arguments follow. But the Dhamma is the place where there's nothing—nothing at all.

CHAPTER 28

CONVENTION
AND LIBERATION

THE THINGS OF THIS WORLD are merely conventions of our own making. Having established them we get lost in them and refuse to let go, clinging to our personal views and opinions. This clinging never ends, it is saṁsāra, flowing endlessly on. It has no completion. Now, if we know conventional reality, we'll know liberation. If we clearly know liberation, we'll know conventional reality. This is to know the Dhamma. Here there is completion.

I've watched Westerners when they sit in meditation together. When they get up after sitting, men and women together, sometimes they go and touch each other on the head![60] When I saw this I thought, "Hey, if we cling to conventions, that gives rise to defilements right there." If we can let go of conventions, give up our opinions, we are at peace.

Sometimes when generals and colonels, men of rank and position, come to see me, they say, "Oh, please touch my head."[61] If they ask like this, there's nothing wrong with it; they're glad to have their heads touched. But if you tapped their heads in the middle of the street, it'd be a different story! This is because of clinging. So I feel that letting go is really the way to peace. Touching a head is against our customs, but in reality it is nothing. When people agree to it, there's nothing wrong with it, just like touching a cabbage or a potato.

Accepting, giving up, letting go—this is the way of lightness. Wherever you're clinging, there's becoming and birth right there. There's danger right there. The Buddha taught about conventions and about how to undo them in the right way and thereby reach liberation.

This is freedom, not to cling to conventions. All things in this world have a conventional reality. Having established them, we should not be fooled by them, because getting lost in them really leads to suffering. This point concerning rules and conventions is of utmost importance. One who can get beyond them is beyond suffering.

They are, however, characteristic of our world. Take Mr. Boonmah, for instance; he used to be just one of the crowd, but now he's been appointed district commissioner. It's just a convention, but it's a convention we should respect. It's part of the world of people. If you think, "Oh, before we were friends, we used to work at the tailor's together," and then you go and pat him on the head in public, he'll get angry. It's not right; he'll resent it. So we should follow the conventions in order to avoid giving rise to resentment. It's useful to understand conventions; living in the world is just about this. Know the right time and place; know the person.

Why is it wrong to go against conventions? It's wrong because of people! You should be clever, knowing both convention and liberation. Know the right time for each. If we know how to use rules and conventions comfortably, then we are skilled. If we try to behave according to a higher level of reality at an inappropriate time, this is wrong. Where is it wrong? It's wrong with people's defilements, that's where! Everyone has defilements. In one situation we behave one way; in another situation we must behave in another way. We should know the ins and outs because we live within conventions. Problems occur because people cling to them. If we suppose something to be, then it is. It's there because we suppose it to be there. But if you look closely, in the absolute sense, these things don't really exist.

We monks were once laymen. We lived within the convention of "layman," and now we live within the convention of "monk." We are monks by convention, not monks through liberation. In the beginning we establish conventions like this, but if a person is merely ordained, this doesn't mean they overcome defilements. If we take a handful of sand and agree to call it salt, does this make it salt? It is salt only in name, not in reality. You couldn't cook with it. Its only use is within the realm of that agreement, because there's really no salt there, only sand.

This word *liberation* is itself just a convention, but it refers to that which lies beyond convention. Having achieved freedom, having reached liberation, we'll still refer to it conventionally as "liberation." If we didn't have conventions we couldn't communicate, so it does have its uses.

For example, people have different names, but they are all people just the same. If we didn't have names and we wanted to call out to somebody standing in a crowd, we'd have to yell, "Hey, person! person!" and that would be useless. You couldn't indicate who you were calling to because they're all "person." But if you called, "Hey, John!" then John would come. Names fulfill just this need. Through them we can communicate; they provide the basis for social behavior.

So you should know both convention and liberation. Conventions have a use, but in reality there really isn't anything there. Even people are nonexistent. They are merely groups of elements, born of causal conditions, dependent on conditions, existing for a while, and then disappearing in the natural way. No one can oppose or control all this. But without conventions we would have nothing to say; we'd have no names, no practice, no work. Rules and conventions are established to give us a language, to make things convenient, and that's all.

Take money, for example. In olden times there weren't any coins or notes. People used to barter goods, but these goods were difficult to keep, so they created money. Perhaps in the future a king will decree that we don't have to use paper money. Instead we should use wax, melting it down and pressing it into lumps. We'll call this money and use it throughout the country. Forget wax, we might even decide to make chicken shit the local currency—nothing else can be money, just chicken shit! Then people would fight and kill each other over chicken shit!

This is conventional reality, but to get ordinary people to understand liberation is really difficult. Our money, our house, our family, our children and relatives are simply conventions that we have invented, but really, seen in the light of Dhamma, they don't belong to us. Maybe if we hear this we don't feel so good, but reality is like that. These things have value only through the established conventions. If we establish that it doesn't have value, then it doesn't have value. If we establish that it has value, then it has value. This is the way it is; we bring convention into the world to fill a need.

Even this body is not really ours; we just suppose it to be so. It's truly just an assumption on our part. If you try to find a real, substantial self within it, you can't. There are merely elements that are born, continue for a while, and then die. There's no real, true substance to it, but it's proper that we use it. It's like a cup. Sooner or later a cup will break, but while it's there you should use it and look after it well. It's a tool for your use. If it breaks there is trouble, so even though it must break, you should try your utmost to preserve it.

And so we have the four supports,[62] which the Buddha taught us to contemplate repeatedly. They are the supports on which a monk depends in order to continue his practice. As long as you live, you must depend on them, but you should understand them. Don't cling to them, for that will give rise to craving.

Convention and liberation are related like this continually. Even though we use conventional reality, don't place your trust in it as being the truth. If you cling to it, suffering will arise. The case of right and wrong is a good example. Some people see wrong as being right and right as being wrong, but in the end who really knows what is right and what is wrong? We don't know. Different people establish different conventions about what's right and what's wrong, but the Buddha took suffering as his guideline. In truth, we don't know. But at a useful, practical level, we can say that right is not to harm oneself or others. This way fulfills a constructive purpose for us.

After all, both rules and conventions and liberation are simply dhammas. One is higher than the other, but they go hand in hand. There is no way that we can guarantee that anything is definitely like this or like that, so the Buddha said to just leave things be. Leave them be as uncertain. However much you like or dislike them, you should understand them as uncertain.

Regardless of time and place, the whole practice of Dhamma reaches completion at the place where there is nothing. This is the place of surrender, of emptiness, of laying down the burden. This is the finish. It's not like the person who says the flag is fluttering because of the wind, whereas someone else says it's because of the flag. There's no end to this! It's just like the old riddle: Which came first, the chicken or the egg? There's no way to reach a resolution; this is just nature.

All these things we say are merely conventions; we establish them ourselves. If you know these things with wisdom, you'll know impermanence, unsatisfactoriness, and not-self. This is the outlook that leads to enlightenment.

Training and teaching people with varying levels of understanding is really difficult. Some people have certain ideas. You tell them something and they don't believe you. You tell them the truth and they say it's not true. "I'm right, you're wrong...." There's no end to this.

If you don't let go there will be suffering: Four men go into the forest. They hear a chicken crowing, *Kak-ka-dehh!* One of them wonders, "Is that a rooster or a hen?" Three of them say it's a hen, but the fourth disagrees. "How could a hen crow like that?" he asks. They retort, "Well, it has a mouth, hasn't it?" They argue and argue, really getting upset over it, but in the end they're all wrong. Whether you say "hen" or a "rooster," they're only names. We establish these conventions, saying a rooster is like this, a hen is like that; a rooster cries like this, a hen cries like that...and this is how we get stuck in the world! Remember this! If you just know that in reality there's no hen and no rooster, then that's the end of it.

The Buddha taught us not to cling. How do we practice non-clinging? We practice simply by giving up clinging, but this non-clinging is very diffi-cult to understand. It takes keen wisdom to investigate and penetrate this, to really achieve non-clinging.

When you think about it, whether people are happy or sad, content or discontent, doesn't depend on their having little or having much—it depends on wisdom. All distress can be transcended only through wisdom, through seeing the truth of things.

So the Buddha exhorted us to investigate, to contemplate. In this con-templation we simply try to understand these problems correctly. This is our practice. Birth, old age, sickness, and death are the most natural and common of occurrences. The Buddha taught to contemplate these facts, but some people don't understand. "What is there to contemplate?" they say. They're born, but they don't know birth; they'll die, but they don't know death.

A person who investigates these things repeatedly will see their nature. Having seen this, they will gradually solve their problems. Even if they still have clinging, if they have wisdom and see that old age, sickness, and death are the way of nature, then they will be able to relieve their suffering. We study the Dhamma simply for this—to cure suffering.

The basis of Buddhism doesn't include that much; there's just the birth and death of suffering, and this the Buddha called the truth. Birth is suffering, old age is suffering, sickness is suffering, and death is suffering.

People don't see this suffering as the truth. If we know truth, then we know suffering.

This pride in personal opinions, these arguments, they have no end. In order to put our minds at rest, to find peace, we should contemplate our past, the present, and what's in store for us—such as birth, old age, sickness, and death. What can we do to avoid being plagued by these things? Right now we may not be too worried, but we should still keep investigating until we know the truth about them. Then all our suffering will abate, because we will no longer cling.

CHAPTER 29

NO ABIDING

SOME PARTS OF THE TEACHINGS we hear but can't understand. We think they should say something else, so we don't follow them. But really, there's a reason for all the teachings. It may seem that things shouldn't be that way, but they are. At first I didn't even believe in sitting meditation. I couldn't see what use it would be just to sit with your eyes closed. And walking meditation.... Walk from this tree to that tree, turn around, and walk back again? Why bother? What's the use of all that walking? I thought like that, but actually walking and sitting meditation are of great use.

Some people's tendencies lead them to prefer walking meditation; others prefer sitting, but you can't do without either of them. In the scriptures they talk about the four postures: standing, walking, sitting, and lying. We live with these four postures. We may prefer one or another, but we must use all four.

They say to make these four postures *even*, to make the practice even in all postures. At first I couldn't figure out what this meant, to make them even. Did it mean we are to sleep for two hours, then stand for two hours, then walk for two hours.... Is that it? I tried that—couldn't do it, it was impossible! That's not what it means to make the postures even. "Making the postures even" refers to the mind, to our awareness. It has to do with giving rise to wisdom in the mind, illumining the mind. This wisdom of ours must be present in all postures; we must know, or understand, constantly. Standing, walking, sitting, or lying, we know all mental states as impermanent, unsatisfactory, and not self. Making the postures even in this way can be done; it isn't impossible. Whether liking or disliking are present in the mind, we don't forget our practice; we are aware.

If we just focus our attention on the mind constantly, then we have the gist of the practice. Whether we experience mental states that the world knows as good or bad, we don't forget ourselves; we don't get lost in good or bad. We just go straight. Making the postures constant in this way is possible.

If we have constancy in our practice, then when we are praised it's simply praise; if we are blamed it's just blame. We don't get high or low over it, we stay right here. Why? Because we see the danger in all those things, we see their results. We are constantly aware of the danger in both praise and blame. Normally, if we are in a good mood, the mind is good too; we see them as the same thing. If we are in a bad mood, the mind goes bad as well, and we don't like it. This is the way it usually is with us, but it is uneven practice.

If we have enough constancy to know our moods and to know we're clinging to them, this is already better, even though we still can't let go. That is, we have awareness; we know what's going on. We see ourselves clinging to good and bad, and we know it. We cling to good and know it's not the right practice, but we still can't let go. This is fifty percent or seventy percent of the practice already. There still isn't release, but we know that if we could let go that would be the way to peace. We keep seeing the harmful consequences of all our likes and dislikes, of praise and blame, continuously. Whatever the conditions may be, the mind is constant in this way.

But for worldly people, if they get blamed or criticized, they get really upset. If they get praised, it cheers them up. If we know the truth of our various moods—if we know the consequences of clinging to praise and blame, the danger of clinging to anything at all—we will become sensitive to our moods. We will know that clinging to them really does cause suffering. We see this suffering, and we see our very clinging as the cause of that suffering. We begin to see the consequences of grasping and clinging to good and bad. We've grabbed them and seen the results—no real happiness—so now we look for a way to let go.

Where is this "way to let go"? In Buddhism we say, "Don't cling to anything." We never stop hearing about this "don't cling to anything"! This doesn't mean we can't hold things, but we don't cling. Like this flashlight. "What's this?" we wonder, so we pick it up. "Oh, it's a flashlight." Then we put it down again. This is the way we hold things.

If we didn't hold anything at all, what could we do? We couldn't do walking meditation or any other activity. So we do have to hold things. True, this is a kind of wanting, but later on it leads to pārami (virtue or perfection). Like wanting to come here, for instance. Venerable Jagaro[63] came to Wat Pah Pong. He had to want to come first. If he hadn't felt that he wanted to come, he wouldn't have. It's the same with everyone; people come here because of wanting. But when wanting arises, don't cling to it! So you come, and then you go back.... What is this? We pick it up, look at it, and see, "Oh, it's a flashlight," then we put it down. This is called holding but not clinging; we let go. We know and then we let go. To put it simply we say just this, "Know, then let go." Keep looking and letting go. "This, they say is good; this, they say is not good." Know, and then let go. Good and bad, we know it all, but we let it go. We don't foolishly cling to things, but we "hold" them with wisdom. Practicing in this "posture" can be constant. You must be constant like this. Make the mind know in this way, let wisdom arise. When the mind has wisdom, what else is there to look for?

We should reflect on what we are doing here. Why are we living here? What are we working for? In the world they work for this or that reward, but the monks teach something a little deeper than that. Whatever we do, we ask for no return. We work for no reward. Worldly people work because they want this or that, because they want some gain or other, but the Buddha taught to work just in order to work; we don't ask for anything beyond that.

If you do something just to get some return, it'll cause suffering. Try it yourself! You want to make your mind peaceful, so you sit down and try to make it peaceful—you'll suffer! Try it. Our way is more refined. We do something and then let go of it. Do and then let go.

Look at the brahmin who makes a sacrifice: he has some desire in mind, so he makes a sacrifice. Those actions of his won't help him transcend suffering because he's acting on desire. In the beginning we practice with some desire in mind; we continue to practice, but we don't attain our desire. So we practice on and on until we reach a point where we're practicing for no return; we're practicing in order to let go. This is something we must see for ourselves; it's very deep. Maybe we practice because we want to go to nibbāna—right there, you won't go to nibbāna! It's natural to want peace, but it's not really correct. We must practice without wanting anything at all. If we don't want anything at all, what will we get? We don't get anything! Whatever you get is a cause for suffering, so we practice not getting anything.

Just this is called "making the mind empty." It's empty but there is still doing. This emptiness is something people don't usually understand, only those who reach it see the real value of it. It's not the emptiness of not having anything; it's emptiness within the things that are here. Like this flashlight: we should see this flashlight as empty; because of the flashlight there is emptiness. It's not the emptiness where we can't see anything; it's not like that. People who understand like that have got it all wrong. You must understand emptiness within the things that are here.

Those who are still practicing because of some gaining idea are like the brahmin making a sacrifice just to fulfill some wish. Like the people who come to see me to be sprinkled with "holy water." When I ask them, "Why do you want this holy water?" they say, "We want to live happily and comfortably and not get sick." There! They'll never transcend suffering that way.

The worldly way is to do things for a reason, to get some return, but in Buddhism we do things without any gaining idea. The world has to understand things in terms of cause and effect, but the Buddha teaches us to go above and beyond cause and effect. His wisdom was to go above cause, beyond effect; to go above birth and beyond death; to go above happiness and beyond suffering.

Think about it: there's nowhere to stay. We people live in a home. To leave home and go where there is no home—we don't know how to do that, because we've always lived with becoming, with clinging. If we can't cling we don't know what to do.

So most people don't want to go to nibbāna, because there's nothing there; nothing at all. Look at the roof and the floor here. The upper extreme is the roof; that's an "abiding." The lower extreme is the floor, and that's another "abiding." But in the empty space between the floor and the roof there's nowhere to stand. One could stand on the roof, or stand on the floor, but not on that empty space. Where there is no abiding, that's where there's emptiness, and nibbāna is this emptiness.

People hear this and they back up a bit; they don't want to go. They're afraid they won't see their children or relatives. This is why, when we bless the lay people, we say, "May you have long life, beauty, happiness, and strength." This makes them really happy. "Sādhu!" they all say. They like these things. But if you start talking about emptiness, they don't want to hear about it; they're attached to abiding.

Have you ever seen a very old person with a beautiful complexion, with a lot of strength, or a lot of happiness? No. But we say, "Long life, beauty, happiness, and strength," and they're all really pleased. Every single one says, "Sādhu!" This is like the brahmin who makes oblations to achieve some wish.

In our practice we don't make oblations; we don't practice in order to get some return. We don't want anything. If we still want something, then there is still something there. Just make the mind peaceful and have done with it. But if I talk like this you may not be very comfortable, because you want to be "born" again.

All you lay practitioners should get close to the monks and watch their practice. To be close to the monks means to be close to the Buddha, to be close to his Dhamma. The Buddha said, "Ānanda, practice a lot, develop your practice! Whoever sees the Dhamma sees me, and whoever sees me sees the Dhamma."

Where is the Buddha? We may think the Buddha has lived and passed away, but the Buddha is the Dhamma, the truth. Some people like to say, "Oh, if I was born in the time of the Buddha, I would go to nibbāna." Stupid people talk like this here. But the Buddha is still here. The Buddha is truth. Regardless of whoever is born or dies, the truth is still here. The truth never departs from the world; it's here all the time. Whether a Buddha is born or not, whether someone knows it or not, the truth is still here.

So we should get close to the Buddha, we should come within and find the Dhamma. When we reach the Dhamma we will reach the Buddha; seeing the Dhamma, we will see the Buddha, and all doubts will dissolve.

To make a comparison, it's like Teacher Choo. At first he wasn't a teacher, he was just Mr. Choo. When he studied and passed the necessary grades, he became a teacher and became known as Teacher Choo. How did he become a teacher? Through studying the required subjects. When Teacher Choo dies, the study to become a teacher still remains, and whoever studies it will become a teacher. That course of study to become a teacher doesn't disappear anywhere, just like the truth, the knowing of which enabled the Buddha to become the Buddha. So the Buddha is still here. Whoever practices and sees the Dhamma sees the Buddha.

So don't be heedless, even in minor things. Try hard, try to get close to the monastic community; contemplate things and then you'll know. Well, that's enough, huh? It must be getting late now; some people are getting sleepy. The Buddha said not to teach Dhamma to sleepy people.

CHAPTER 30

RIGHT VIEW—
THE PLACE OF COOLNESS

THE PRACTICE of Dhamma goes against our habits; the truth goes against our desires, so we have difficulty with the practice. Some things that we understand as wrong may be right, while the things we take to be right may be wrong. Why is this? Because our minds are in darkness, we don't clearly see the truth. We don't really know anything and so are fooled by people's lies. That which is right they call wrong, and we believe them; that which is wrong they say is right, and we believe them again. This is because we are not yet our own masters. Our moods lie to us constantly. We shouldn't take this mind and its opinions as our guide, because it doesn't know the truth.

Some people don't want to listen to others at all, but this is not the way of the wise. A wise person listens to everything. One who listens to Dhamma must listen just the same, whether they like it or not, and not blindly believe or disbelieve. They must stay at the halfway mark, the midpoint, and not be heedless. They just listen and then contemplate, giving rise to the right results accordingly.

A wise person should contemplate and see the cause and effect for themselves before they believe what they hear. Even if the teacher speaks the truth, don't just believe it, because you don't yet know the truth of it for yourself.

It's the same for all of us. I started practicing long before you, and I've heard many lies. For instance, "This practice is really difficult." Why is the practice difficult? It's hard only because we think wrongly, we have wrong view.

Previously I used to live with other monks, but that didn't feel right. I ran off to the forests and mountains, fleeing the crowd, the monks and novices. I thought that they weren't like me; they didn't practice as hard as I did. They were sloppy. So-and-so was like this or so-and-so was like that. This was something that really put me in turmoil; it was the cause for my continually running away. But whether I lived alone or with others, I still had no peace. On my own I wasn't content; in a large group I wasn't content. I thought this discontent was due to my companions, due to my moods, due to my living place, the food, the weather—due to this and that. I was constantly searching for something to suit my mind.

As a dhutanga monk, I went traveling, but things still weren't right. "What can I do to make things right?" I wondered. "What can I do?" Living with a lot of people, I was dissatisfied; living with just a few, I was dissatisfied. For what reason? I just couldn't see it. Why was I dissatisfied? Because I had wrong view, just that; because I still clung to the wrong Dhamma. Wherever I went, I was discontented, thinking, "Here it's no good, there it's no good," on and on like that. I blamed others. I blamed the weather, the heat and cold, I blamed everything! Just like a mad dog. It bites whatever it meets, because it's mad. When the mind is like this our practice is never settled. Today we feel good, tomorrow no good. It's like that all the time. We don't attain contentment or peace.

The Buddha once saw a jackal, a wild dog, run out of the forest. It stood still for a while, then it ran into the underbrush, lay down awhile, and then ran out. Then it ran into a hollow tree, then out again. Then it went into a cave, only to run out again. One minute it stood quiet, the next moment it ran, then it lay down, then it jumped up…. That jackal had mange. When it stood still it felt the mange itching, so it would run. Running, it was still uncomfortable, so it would stop. Standing was still uncomfortable, so it would lie down. Then it would jump up again, running into the underbrush, the hollow tree, never staying still.

The Buddha said, "Monks, did you see that jackal this afternoon? Standing, it suffered. Running, it suffered. Sitting, it suffered. Lying down, it suffered. In the underbrush, in the hollow tree, or in the cave, it suffered. It blamed standing for its discomfort, it blamed sitting, it blamed running and lying down; it blamed the tree, the underbrush, and the cave. In fact the problem was with none of those things. That jackal had mange. The problem was with the mange."

We monks are just like that jackal. Our discontent is due to wrong view. Because we don't exercise sense restraint we blame our suffering on externals. Whether we live at Wat Pah Pong, in America, or in London, we aren't satisfied. If we go to live at Wat Pah Nanachat or any of the other branch monasteries, we're still not satisfied. Why not? Because we still have wrong view within us. Wherever we go we aren't content.

But just as that jackal will be content wherever it goes once the mange is cured, so it is for us. I reflect on this often, and I teach it often, because it's very important. If we know the truth of our various moods, we arrive at contentment. Whether it's hot or cold, we are satisfied; whether we're with many people or with just a few, we are satisfied. Contentment doesn't depend on how many people we are with, it comes only from Right View.

But most of us have wrong view. It's just like a maggot: a maggot's living place is filthy, its food is filthy, but that suits the maggot fine. If you take a stick and brush it away from its lump of dung, it'll struggle to crawl back in. It's the same when the Ajahn teaches us to see rightly. We resist; it makes us feel uneasy. We run back to our lump of dung, because that's where we feel at home. We're all like this. If we don't see the harmful consequences of all our wrong views, we can't abandon them, and the practice is difficult.

If we have Right View, wherever we go we are content. I have practiced and seen this already. These days many monks, novices, and lay people come to see me. If I still didn't understand, if I still had wrong view, I'd be dead by now! The right abiding place for monks, the place of coolness, is just Right View itself. We shouldn't look for anything else.

So even though you may be unhappy, it doesn't matter; your unhappiness is inconstant. Is that unhappiness your "self"? Is there any substance to it? Is it real? I don't see it as being real at all. Unhappiness is merely a flash of feeling that appears and then vanishes. Happiness is the same. Is there a consistency to happiness? Is it truly an entity? It's simply a feeling that flashes suddenly and is gone. There! It's born and then it dies. Love just flashes up for a moment and then disappears. Where is the consistency in love, hate, or resentment? In truth, there is no substantial entity there; they are merely impressions that flare up in the mind and then die. They deceive us constantly; we find no certainty anywhere. Just as the Buddha said, when unhappiness arises, it stays for a while, then disappears. When unhappiness disappears, happiness arises and lingers for a while and then dies. When happiness disappears, unhappiness arises again…on and on.

In the end we can say only this: apart from the birth, the life, and the death of suffering, there is nothing. There is just this. But we who are ignorant run and grab it constantly. We never see the truth of it, that there's simply this continual change. If we understand this, we won't need to think very much, but we'll have much wisdom. If we don't know it, then we'll have more thinking than wisdom—and maybe no wisdom at all! It's not until we truly see the harmful results of our actions that we can give them up. Likewise, it's not until we see the real benefits of practice that we can follow it, and begin working to make the mind good.

If we cut a log of wood and throw it into the river, and if it doesn't sink or rot, or run aground on the riverbank, it will reach the sea. Our practice is comparable to this. If you practice according to the path laid down by the Buddha, following it straight, you will transcend two things. Which two? Just those two extremes that the Buddha said were not the path of a true meditator—indulgence in pleasure and indulgence in pain. These are the two banks of the river. One is hate; the other is love. Or you can say that one riverbank is happiness, the other unhappiness. The log is this mind. As it flows downriver, it will experience happiness and unhappiness. If the mind doesn't cling to that happiness or unhappiness it will reach the ocean of nibbāna. You should see that there is nothing other than happiness and unhappiness arising and disappearing. If you don't run aground on these things, then you are on the path of a true meditator.

This is the teaching of the Buddha. Happiness and unhappiness, love and hate, are simply established in nature according to its constant law. The wise person doesn't follow or encourage them; they don't cling to them. This is the mind that lets go of indulgence in pleasure and indulgence in pain. It's the right practice. Just as that log of wood will eventually be carried to the sea, so will the mind that doesn't attach to these two extremes inevitably attain peace.

CHAPTER 31

OUR REAL HOME

A talk addressed to an aging lay disciple approaching her death, as well as to her family and caregivers.

Resolve now to listen respectfully to the Dhamma. While I am speaking, be as attentive to my words as if it were the Lord Buddha himself sitting before you. Close your eyes and make yourself comfortable, composing your mind and making it one-pointed. Humbly allow the Triple Gem of wisdom, truth, and purity to abide in your heart as a way of showing respect to the Fully Enlightened One.

Today I have brought nothing of material substance to offer you, only the Dhamma, the teachings of the Lord Buddha. You should understand that even the Buddha himself, with his great store of accumulated virtue, could not avoid physical death. When he reached old age he ceded his body and let go of the heavy burden. Now you too must learn to be satisfied with the many years you've depended on your body. You should feel that it's enough.

Think of household utensils that you've had for a long time—cups, saucers, plates. When you first got them, they were clean and shining, but now after using them for so long, they're starting to wear out. Some are already broken, some have disappeared, and those that are left are wearing out; they have no enduring form. And it's their nature to be that way. Your body is the same, continually changing from the day you were born, through childhood and youth, until now it's reached old age. You must accept this. The Buddha said that conditions, whether internal bodily conditions or external conditions, are not-self; their nature is to change. Contemplate this truth clearly.

This very lump of flesh lying here in decline is reality, sacca-dhamma. The facts of this body are reality; they are the timeless teaching of the Lord Buddha. The Buddha taught us to contemplate this and come to terms with its nature. We must be able to be at peace with the body, no matter what state it is in. The Buddha told us that we should ensure that it's only the body that is locked up in jail, and not to let the mind be imprisoned along with it. Now as your body begins to run down and wear out with age, don't resist, but also don't let your mind deteriorate along with it. Keep the mind separate. Give energy to the mind by realizing the truth of the way things are. The Lord Buddha taught that this is the nature of the body; it can't be any other way. Having been born it gets old and sick and then it dies. This is a great truth that you are presently witnessing. Look at the body with wisdom and realize this.

If your house is flooded or burnt to the ground, allow that threat to affect only the house. If there's a flood, don't let it flood your mind. If there's a fire, don't let it burn your heart. Let it be merely the house—which is outside— that is flooded or burned. Now is the time to allow the mind to let go of attachments.

You've been alive a long time now. Your eyes have seen any number of forms and colors, your ears have heard so many sounds, you've had any number of experiences. And that's all they were—experiences. You've eaten delicious foods, and all those good tastes were just good tastes, nothing more. The bad tastes were just bad tastes, that's all. If the eye sees a beautiful form, that's all it is—a beautiful form. An ugly form is just an ugly form. The ear hears an entrancing, melodious sound, and it's nothing more than that. A grating, discordant sound is simply that.

The Buddha said that rich or poor, young or old, human or animal, no being in this world can maintain itself in any single state for long. Everything experiences change and deprivation. This is a fact of life we cannot remedy. But the Buddha said that what we can do is contemplate the body and mind to see their impersonality, to see that neither of them is "me" nor "mine." They have only a provisional reality. Like your house, it's only nominally yours. You couldn't take it with you anywhere. The same applies to your wealth, your possessions, and your family—they're yours only in name. They don't really belong to you; they belong to nature.

Now this truth doesn't apply to you alone; everyone is in the same boat—even the Lord Buddha and his enlightened disciples. They differed from us only in one respect, and that was their acceptance of the way things are. They saw that it could be no other way.

So the Buddha asked us to probe and examine the body, from the soles of the feet up to the crown of the head, and then back down to the feet again. Just take a look at the body. What sort of things do you see? Is there anything intrinsically clean there? Can you find any abiding essence? This whole body is steadily degenerating. The Buddha taught us to see that it doesn't belong to us. It's natural for the body to be this way, because all conditioned phenomena are subject to change. How else would you have it? In fact there is nothing wrong with the way the body is. It's not the body that causes suffering; it's wrong thinking. When you see things the wrong way, there's bound to be confusion.

It's like a river. Water naturally flows downhill. That's its nature. If a person was to go and stand on the river bank and want the water to flow back uphill, they would be foolish. Wherever they went, their foolish thinking would allow them no peace of mind. They would suffer because of their wrong view, for their thinking goes against the stream. If they had Right View, they would see that the water must inevitably flow downhill, and until they realized and accepted that fact, they would be bewildered and frustrated.

The river that must flow down a slope is like your body. Once young, your body's become old and is meandering toward death. Don't go wishing it were otherwise; it's not something you have the power to remedy. The Buddha told us to see the way things are and then let go of our clinging to them. Take this feeling of letting go as your refuge. Keep meditating even if you feel tired and exhausted. Let your mind be with the breath. Take a few deep breaths and then establish the attention on the breath, using the mantra word *Bud-dho*. Make this practice continual. The more exhausted you feel, the more subtle and focused your concentration must be, so that you can cope with any painful sensations that arise. When you start to feel fatigued, bring all your thinking to a halt, let the mind gather itself together, and then turn to knowing the breath. Just keep up the inner recitation, *Bud-dho, Bud-dho.*

Let go of all externals. Don't go grasping at thoughts of your children and relatives; don't grasp at anything whatsoever. Let go. Let the mind unite in a single point, and let that composed mind dwell with the breath. Let the breath be its sole object of knowledge. Concentrate until the mind becomes increasingly subtle, until feelings are insignificant and there is great inner clarity and wakefulness. Then any painful sensations that arise will gradually cease of their own accord.

Look upon the in- and out-breaths as if they were relatives who come to visit you. When the relatives leave, you follow them out to see them off. You watch until they've walked up the drive and out of sight, and then you go back indoors. We watch the breath in the same way. If the breath is coarse, we know that it's coarse; if it's subtle, we know that. As it becomes increasingly fine we keep following it, at the same time awakening the mind. Eventually the breath disappears altogether and all that remains is that feeling of alertness. This is called meeting the Buddha. We have that clear, wakeful awareness called Buddho, the "one who knows," the awakened one, the radiant one. This is meeting and dwelling with the Buddha, with knowledge and clarity. It was only the historical Buddha who passed away. The true Buddha, the Buddha that is clear, radiant knowing, can still be experienced and attained today. And if we do attain it, the heart is unified.

So let go, put everything down, everything except the knowing. Don't be fooled if visions or sounds arise in your mind during meditation. Lay them all down. Don't take hold of anything at all. Just stay with this unified awareness. Don't worry about the past or the future; just be still and you will reach the place where there's no advancing, no retreating, and no stopping, where there's nothing to grasp at or cling to. Why? Because there's no self, no "me" or "mine." It's all gone. The Buddha taught us to be emptied of everything in this way, not to carry anything around. To know, and having known, let go.

Realizing the Dhamma, the path to freedom from the round of birth and death, is a task that we all have to do alone. So keep trying to let go and understand the teachings. Put effort into your contemplation. Don't worry about your family. At the moment they are as they are; in the future they will be like you. There's no one in the world who can escape this fate. The Buddha taught us to lay down those things that lack a real abiding essence. If you lay everything down you will see the truth; if you don't, you won't. That's the way it is. And it's the same for everyone in the world. So don't grasp at anything.

If you find yourself thinking, well, that's all right too, as long as you think wisely. Don't think foolishly. If you think about your children, think about them with wisdom, not with foolishness. Whatever the mind turns to, think about it with wisdom, be aware of its nature. If you know something with wisdom, you let it go and there's no suffering. The mind is bright, joyful, and at peace. It turns away from distractions and is undivided. Right now what you can look to for help and support is your breath.

This is your own work, no one else's. Leave others to do their own work. You have your own duty and responsibility; you don't have to take on those of your family. Don't take on anything else, let it all go. This letting go will make your mind calm. Your sole responsibility right now is to focus your mind and bring it to peace. Leave everything else to others. Forms, sounds, odors, tastes—leave them to others to attend to. Put everything behind you and do your own work, fulfill your own responsibility. Whatever arises in your mind, be it fear of pain, fear of death, anxiety about others, or whatever, say to it, "Don't disturb me. You're no longer any concern of mine." Just keep saying this to yourself when you see those dhammas arise.

What does the word *dhamma* refer to? Everything is a dhamma; there is nothing that is not a dhamma. And what about the world? The world is the very mental state that is agitating you at the present moment. "What are these others going to do? When I'm gone who will look after them? How will they manage?" This is all just "the world." Even the mere arising of a thought—the fear of death or pain—is the world. Throw the world away! The world is the way it is. If you allow it to dominate consciousness, your mind becomes obscured and can't see itself. So whatever appears in the mind, just say, "This isn't my business. It's impermanent, unsatisfactory, and not-self."

Thinking you'd like to go on living for a long time will make you suffer. But thinking you'd like to die soon or right away isn't right either. It's suffering, isn't it? Conditions don't belong to us, they follow their own natural laws. You can't do anything about the way the body is. You can beautify it a little, make it look attractive and fresh for a while, like the young girls who paint their lips and let their nails grow long, but when old age arrives, everybody's in the same boat. That's the way the body is, you can't make it any other way. But what you can improve and beautify is the mind.

Anyone can build a house of wood and bricks, but that sort of home, the Buddha taught, is not our real home, it's only nominally ours. It's a home in the world and it follows the ways of the world. Our real home is inner peace. An external, material home may well be pretty, but it is not very peaceful—there's this worry and then that—so we say it's not our real home, it's external to us. Sooner or later we'll have to give it up. It's not a place we can live in permanently because it doesn't truly belong to us; it belongs to the world. Our body is the same. We take it to be a self, to be "me" or "mine," but in fact it's not really so at all; it's another worldly home. Your body has followed its natural course from birth, and now it's old and sick. You can't forbid it from doing that. That's the way it is. Wanting it to be any different would be as foolish as wanting a duck to be like a chicken. When you see that that's impossible—that a duck must be a duck and a chicken must be a chicken, and that bodies have to get old and die—you will find courage and energy. However much you want the body to go on lasting, it won't do that.

The Buddha said,

Aniccā vata saṅkhārā	Impermanent are all conditioned things
Uppāda vaya dhammino	Of the nature to arise and pass away
Uppajjitvā nirujjhan'ti	Having been born, they all must cease
Tesaṁ vūpasamo sukho	The calming of conditions is true happiness[64]

The word *saṅkhāra* refers to this body and mind. Saṅkhāras are impermanent and unstable. Having come into being they disappear, having arisen they pass away, and yet everyone wants them to be permanent. This is foolishness. Look at the breath. Having come in, it goes out; that's its nature, that's how it has to be. The inhalations and exhalations have to alternate, there must be change. Conditions exist through change; you can't prevent it. Just think, could you exhale without inhaling? Would it feel good? Or could you just inhale? We want things to be permanent but they can't be; it's impossible. Once the breath has come in, it must go out. When it's out, it comes back in again, and that's natural, isn't it? Having been born we get old and then die, and that's totally natural and normal. It's because conditions have done their job, because the in-breaths and out-breaths have alternated in this way, that the human race is still here today.

As soon as we are born, we are dead. Our birth and our death are just one thing. It's like a tree: when there's a root there must be branches. When there are branches there must be a root. You can't have one without the other. It's a little funny to see how at death people are so grief-stricken and distracted, and at birth how happy and delighted. It's delusion; nobody has ever looked at this clearly. I think if you really want to cry, it would be better to do so when someone's born. Birth is death, death is birth; the branch is the root, the root is the branch. If you must cry, cry at the root; cry at the birth. Look closely: If there were no birth, there would be no death. Can you understand this?

Don't worry about things too much; just think, "This is the way things are." This is your work, your duty. Right now nobody can help you, there's nothing that your family and possessions can do for you. All that can help you now is clear awareness.

So don't waver. Let go. Throw it all away.

Even if you don't let go, everything is starting to leave you anyway. Can you see that, how all the different parts of your body are trying to slip away? Take your hair; when you were young it was thick and black. Now it's falling out. It's leaving. Your eyes used to be good and strong but now they're weak; your sight is unclear. When your organs have had enough they leave, for this isn't their home. When you were a child your teeth were healthy and firm; now they're wobbly, or you've got false ones. Your eyes, ears, nose, tongue—everything is trying to leave because this isn't their home. You can't make a permanent home in conditions; you can only stay for a short time and then you have to go. It's like a tenant watching over his tiny little house with failing eyes. His teeth aren't so good, his eyes aren't so good, his body's not so healthy; everything is leaving.

So you needn't worry about anything, because this isn't your real home; it's only a temporary shelter. Having come into this world, you should contemplate its nature. Everything is preparing to disappear. Look at your body. Is there anything there that's still in its original form? Is your skin as it used to be? Is your hair? They aren't the same, are they? Where has everything gone? This is nature, the way things are. When their time is up, conditions go their way. In this world there is nothing to rely on—it's an endless round of disturbance and trouble, pleasure and pain. There is no peace.

When we have no real home we're like aimless travelers out on the road, going here and there, stopping for a while and then setting off again. Until we return to our real homes we feel uneasy, just like a villager who's left their village. Only when they get home can they really relax and be at peace.

Nowhere in the world is there any real peace to be found. The poor have no peace and neither do the rich; adults have no peace and neither do children; the poorly educated have no peace and neither do the highly educated. There's no peace anywhere; that's the nature of the world. Those who have few possessions suffer, and so do those who have many. Children, adults, the aged, everyone suffers. The suffering of being old, the suffering of being young, the suffering of being wealthy, and the suffering of being poor—it's all nothing but suffering.

When you've contemplated things in this way you'll see anicca, impermanence, and dukkha, unsatisfactoriness. Why are things impermanent and unsatisfactory? Because they are anattā, not-self.

Both your body that is lying sick and in pain, and the mind that is aware of its sickness and pain, are called dhamma. That which is formless—the thoughts, feelings, and perceptions—is called nāma-dhamma. That which is racked with aches and pains is called rūpa-dhamma. The material is dhamma and the immaterial is dhamma. So we live with dhammas, in dhammas, and we are dhammas. In truth, there is no self to be found; there are only dhammas continually arising and passing away. Every single moment we're undergoing birth and death. This is the way things are.

When we think of the Lord Buddha, how truly he spoke, we feel how worthy he is of reverence and respect. Whenever we see the truth of something, we see his teachings, even if we've never actually practiced the Dhamma. But even if we have a knowledge of the teachings and have studied and practiced them, as long as we still haven't seen the truth we are still homeless.

So understand this point. All people, all creatures, are preparing to leave. When beings have lived an appropriate time, they must go on their way. Rich, poor, young, and old must all experience this change.

When you realize that's the way the world is, you'll feel that it's a wearisome place. When you see that there's nothing real or substantial you can rely on, you'll feel weary and disenchanted. Being disenchanted doesn't mean you are averse; the mind is clear. It sees that there's nothing to be done to remedy this state of affairs; it's just the way the world is. Knowing in this way you can let go of attachment, letting go with a mind that is neither happy nor sad, but at peace with conditions through seeing their changing nature with wisdom. *Aniccā vaṭa saṅkhārā*—all conditions are impermanent.

Impermanence is the Buddha. If we truly see an impermanent condition, we see that it's permanent—in the sense that its subjection to change is unchanging. This is the permanence that living beings possess: continual transformation from childhood through to old age, and that very impermanence, that propensity to change, is permanent and fixed. If you look at it like this your heart will be at ease. When you consider things in this way you'll see them as wearisome, and disenchantment will arise. Your delight in the world of sense pleasures will disappear. You'll see that if you have many possessions, you have to leave a lot behind. If you have few, you leave few behind. Wealth is just wealth, long life is just long life. They're nothing special.

What is important is that we should do as the Lord Buddha taught and build our own home, building it by the method that I've been explaining to you. Build your own home. Let go. Let go until the mind reaches the peace that is free from advancing, free from retreating, and free from stopping still. Pleasure is not your home, pain is not your home. Pleasure and pain both decline and pass away.

The Buddha saw that all conditions are impermanent, so he taught us to let go of our attachment to them. When we reach the end of our life we'll have no choice anyway. So wouldn't it be better to put things down before then? They're just a heavy burden to carry around; why not throw off that load now? Let go, relax, and let your family look after you.

Those who nurse the sick grow in goodness and virtue. The patient who is giving others that opportunity shouldn't make things difficult for them. If there's a pain or some problem or other, let them know and keep the mind in a wholesome state. One who is nursing parents should fill his or her mind with warmth and kindness and not get caught up in aversion. This is the one time you can repay your debt to others. From birth throughout childhood and until you grew up, you've been dependent on your parents.

That you are here today is because your mother and father have helped you in so many ways. You owe them an incredible debt of gratitude.

So today, all of you children and relatives gathered together here, observe how your mother has become your child. Before you were her children; now she has become yours. She has become older and older until she has become a child again. Her memory goes, her eyes don't see so well, and her ears aren't so good. Sometimes she garbles her words. Don't let it upset you. You who are nursing the sick must know how to let go also. Don't hold on to things, just let her have her own way. When a young child is disobedient, sometimes the parents let it have its own way just to keep the peace, just to make it happy. Now your mother is just like that child. Her memories and perceptions are confused. Sometimes she muddles up your names, or asks you to bring a cup when she wants a plate. It's normal, don't be upset by it.

Let the patient bear in mind the kindness of those who nurse and patiently endure the painful feelings. Exert yourself mentally; don't let the mind become scattered and confused, and don't make things difficult for those looking after you. Let those who are nursing fill their minds with virtue and kindness. Don't be averse to the unattractive side of the job, cleaning up the mucus and phlegm, urine and excrement. Try your best. Everyone in the family should give a hand.

She is the only mother you have. She gave you life; she has been your teacher, your doctor, and your nurse—she's been everything to you. That she has brought you up, shared her wealth with you, and made you her heir is the great goodness of parents. That is why the Buddha taught the virtues of *kataññū*, knowing our debt of gratitude, and *katavedī*, trying to repay it. These two dhammas are complementary. If our parents are in need, unwell, or in difficulty, then we do our best to help them. This is *kataññū-katavedī*, the virtue that sustains the world. It prevents families from breaking up, and makes them stable and harmonious.

Today I have brought you the gift of Dhamma in this time of illness. I have no material things to offer you; there seem to be plenty of those in this house already. And so I give you the Dhamma, something that has lasting worth, something that you'll never be able to exhaust. Having received it, you can pass it on to as many others as you like and it will never be depleted. That is the nature of truth. I am happy to have been able to give you this gift of Dhamma and hope it will give you the strength to deal with your pain.

CHAPTER 32

THE FOUR NOBLE TRUTHS

H AVING BEEN A TEACHER for many years now, I've been through my share of difficulties. At present there are altogether about forty branch monasteries[65] of my monastery, Wat Nong Pah Pong, but even these days I have followers who are hard to teach. Some know how to practice but don't bother; some don't know how and don't try to find out. I don't know what to do with them. Why do human beings have minds like this? Being ignorant is not so good, but even when I tell them, they don't listen. I don't know what more I can do. People are so full of doubts in their practice; they're always doubting. They all want to go to nibbāna, but they don't want to walk the Path. It's baffling. When I tell them to meditate, they're afraid, or if not afraid, then just plain sleepy. Mostly they like to do the things I don't teach. When I have spoken with other teachers of the Dhamma, they have told me that their followers are just the same. This is the pain of being a teacher.

The teaching I offer you today is a way to solve problems in the present moment, in this present life. Some people say that they have so much work to do they have no time to practice the Dhamma. "What can we do?" they ask. I tell them that practicing meditation is just like breathing. While working we breathe, while sleeping we breathe, while sitting down we breathe. We have time to breathe because we see the importance of the breath. In the same way, if we see the importance of meditation practice, we will find the time to practice.

Have any of you ever suffered? Have you ever been happy? Right here is the truth; this is where you must practice the Dhamma. Who is it who is happy? The mind is happy. Who suffers? The mind suffers. Wherever these things arise, that's where they cease. What is the cause of these things? This is our problem. If we know suffering, the cause of suffering, the end of suffering, and the way leading to the end of suffering, we can solve the problem.

There are two kinds of suffering: ordinary suffering and the extraordinary kind. Ordinary suffering is the suffering that is the inherent nature of conditions: standing is suffering, sitting is suffering, lying down is suffering. Even the Buddha experienced these things. He experienced comfort and pain, but he recognized them as conditions in nature. He knew how to overcome these ordinary, natural feelings of comfort and pain through understanding their true nature. Because he understood this "natural suffering," those feelings didn't upset him.

The important kind of suffering is the second kind, the suffering that creeps in from the outside, the "extraordinary suffering." If we are sick we may have to get an injection from the doctor. When the needle pierces the skin there is some pain, which is only natural. When the needle is withdrawn that pain disappears. This is like the ordinary kind of suffering. It's no problem, everybody experiences it. The extraordinary suffering is the suffering that arises from what we call upādāna, grasping on to things. This is like having an injection with a syringe filled with poison. This is no longer an ordinary kind of pain; it is the pain that ends in death.

Wrong view, not knowing the impermanent nature of all conditioned things, is another kind of problem. Conditioned things are the realm of saṁsāra. Not wanting things to change—if we think like this we must suffer. When we think that the body is ourselves or belongs to us, we are afraid when we see it change. Suppose we lost something. If we thought that object was really ours, we would brood over it. If we couldn't see it as a conditioned thing conforming to the laws of nature, we would experience suffering. But if you breathe in and don't breathe out, or breathe out and don't breathe in, can you live? Conditioned things must naturally change in this way. To see this is to see the Dhamma, to see anicca, change. We live dependent on this change. When we know how things are then we can let go of them.

The practice of Dhamma is to develop an understanding of the way things are so that suffering doesn't arise. If we think mistakenly, we put ourselves at odds with the world, at odds with the Dhamma and with the truth. Suppose you are sick and have to go into hospital. Most people think, "Please don't let me die, I want to get better." This is wrong thinking; it will lead to suffering. You have to think to yourself, "If I recover, I recover. If I die, I die." This is right thinking, because you can't ultimately control conditions. If you think like this, whether you die or recover, you can't go wrong; you don't have to worry. Wanting to get better at all costs and afraid of dying—such is the mind that doesn't understand conditions. You should think, "If I get better, that's fine, and if I don't get better, that's fine too." This way we have tuned ourselves in to the way things are.

The Buddha saw all this clearly. His teaching is always relevant, never outdated. It's still as true as it ever was. By taking this teaching to heart we can gain the reward of peace and well-being.

In the teachings there is the reflection on "not-self": "this is not my self, this does not belong to me." But people don't like this kind of teaching because they are attached to the idea of self. This is the cause of suffering.

A woman asked me about how to deal with anger. I told her that the next time she gets angry, to wind up her alarm clock and put it in front of her. Then to give herself two hours for the anger to go away. If it was really *her* anger, she could probably tell it to go away like this: "In two hours, be gone!" But it isn't really ours to command. Sometimes in two hours it's still here; at other times in less than an hour it's gone. Holding on to anger as a personal possession will cause suffering. If it really belonged to us, it would have to obey us. That it doesn't obey us means it's only a deception. Don't fall for it. Whether the mind is happy or sad, whether it loves or hates, don't fall for it. It's all a deception.

When you are angry, does it feel good or bad? If it feels bad, why don't you throw that feeling away? How can you say that you are wise and intelligent when you hold on to such things? Since the day you were born, how many times has the mind tricked you into anger? Some days the mind can even cause a whole family to quarrel, or cause you to cry all night. And yet we still continue to get angry; we still hold on to things and suffer. If you don't see suffering, you will have to keep on suffering. If you see the suffering of anger, then just throw it away. If you don't throw it away, it'll go on causing suffering indefinitely. The world of saṁsāra is like this. If we know the way it is we can solve the problem.

The Buddha's teaching states that there is no better means to overcome suffering than to see that "this is not my self, this is not mine." This is the greatest method. But we don't usually pay attention to this. When suffering arises we simply cry over it without learning from it. We must take a good hard look at these things, to develop the Buddho, the "one who knows."

Now I'm going to give you some Dhamma that's outside the scriptures. Most people read the scriptures but don't see the Dhamma. They miss the point or don't understand.

Suppose two people are walking together and see a duck and a chicken. One of them says, "Why can't that chicken be like the duck, and why can't the duck be like the chicken?" What they want is impossible. They could wish for the duck to be a chicken and the chicken to be a duck for the rest of their life, and it would not come to pass, because the chicken is a chicken and the duck is a duck. As long as they continued to think like that, they would suffer. The other person sees that the chicken is a chicken and the duck is a duck, and that's all there is to it. No problem.

In the same way, the law of anicca states that all things are impermanent. If you want things to be permanent, you're going to suffer. One who sees that things are naturally impermanent will be at ease and free from conflict. The one who wants things to be permanent is going to have conflict, and maybe even lose sleep over it.

If you want to know the Dhamma, where do you look? You must look within the body and the mind. You won't find it on a bookshelf. To really see the Dhamma you have to look within your own body and mind—there are only these two things. The mind is not visible to the physical eye, it must be seen with the "mind's eye." The Dhamma that is in the body must be seen in the body. And with what do we look at the body? We look at the body with the mind. You won't find the Dhamma by looking anywhere else, because both happiness and suffering arise right here. Or maybe you've seen happiness arising in the trees? Or from the rivers, or the weather? Happiness and suffering are feelings that arise in our own bodies and minds.

Therefore the Buddha tells us to know the Dhamma right here. Someone may tell you to look for the Dhamma in books, but if you think that this is where the Dhamma really is, you'll never find it. If you look in books, then you must reflect on those teachings inwardly. Only then can you understand the Dhamma, for it exists right here in this body and mind of ours.

When we do this, wisdom will arise in our minds. Then no matter where we look, there is Dhamma. We will see anicca, dukkha, and anattā at all times. But we don't see this; we always see things as being our self and belonging to us. This means that we don't see the truth about conventional reality. For example, all of us sitting here have names. Names are a convention. Of course it's useful to have names. Four men, A, B, C, and D, must each have an individual name for convenience in communicating and working together. If we want to speak to Mr. A, we can call out to Mr. A and he will come, not the others. This is the convenience of convention. But when we look deeply into the matter we will see that really there isn't anybody there. We will see transcendence. There is only earth, water, wind, and fire, the four elements. This is all there is to this body of ours.

But we don't see it in this way because of the power of *attavādupādāna,* or clinging to selfhood.[66] If we were to look clearly we would see that there isn't really much to what we call a person. The solid part is the earth element; the fluid part is the water element; the part that consists of air and gas, together with currents of energy coursing through the body, is called the wind element; and the part that provides heat is called the fire element. When earth, water, wind, and fire are brought together they are called a human being. When we break things down and see that there are only these four elements, where is the person to be found?

That's why the Buddha taught that there is no higher practice than to see that "this is not my self and does not belong to me." "Me" and "mine" are simply conventions. If we understand everything clearly in this way we will be at peace. If we realize in the present moment the truth of impermanence, that things are not our self or do not belong to us, then when they disintegrate we are at peace with them. They are merely the elements of earth, water, wind, and fire.

It's difficult to see this, but it's not beyond our ability. If we succeed, we will find contentment; we will have less anger, greed, and delusion. There will always be Dhamma in our hearts. There will be no need for jealousy and spite, because everybody is simply earth, water, wind, and fire. There's nothing more to them than this. When we accept this fact we will see the truth of the Buddha's teaching.

If we could see the truth of the Buddha's teaching, we wouldn't have to use up so many teachers! It wouldn't be necessary to listen to teachings every day. When we understand, we simply do what's required of us. But what makes people so difficult to teach is that they don't accept the teaching and argue with the teachers and the teaching. In front of the teacher they behave all right, but behind his back they become like thieves! People in Thailand are like this, and that's why they need so many teachers.

If you're not careful you won't see the Dhamma. You must be circumspect, taking the teaching and considering it carefully. Is this flower pretty? Do you see the ugliness within it? How long will it stay pretty? How will it look later? Why does it change so? In three or four days, when it loses its beauty, won't you have to throw it out? People are attached to beauty, attached to goodness. If anything is good they just fall for it completely. The Buddha tells us to look at pretty things as just pretty without becoming attached to them. If there is a pleasant feeling we shouldn't fall for it. Goodness is not a sure thing, beauty is not a sure thing. Nothing is certain. This is the truth. Things that aren't true, such as beauty, are things that change. The only truth that beauty has lies in its constant changing. If we believe that things really are beautiful, when their beauty fades our mind loses its beauty too. When things are no longer good our mind loses its goodness too. We "invest" our minds in material things in this way. When they are destroyed or damaged we suffer because we have clung to them as being our own. The Buddha tells us to see that these things are simply constructs of nature. Beauty appears and soon fades. To see this is to have wisdom.

If we think something is pretty, we should tell ourselves it isn't; if we think something is ugly we should tell ourselves it isn't. Try to see things in this way, constantly reflect in this way. We will see the truth within untrue things, see the certainty within the things that are uncertain.

I have been explaining the way to understand suffering, what causes suffering, the cessation of suffering, and the way leading to the cessation of suffering. When you know suffering, you should throw it out. Knowing the cause of suffering, you should throw it out. Practice to see the cessation of suffering. See anicca, dukkha, and anattā and suffering will cease.

What are we practicing for? We are practicing in order to relinquish, not to gain something. A woman told me that she was suffering. When I asked her what she wanted, she said she wanted to be enlightened. "As long as you want to be enlightened," I replied, "you will never become enlightened. Don't want anything."

When we know the truth of suffering, we throw out suffering. When we know the cause of suffering, then we don't create those causes but instead practice to bring suffering to its cessation. The practice leading to the cessation of suffering is to see that "this is not a self, this is not me or mine." Seeing in this way enables suffering to cease. It's like reaching our destination and stopping. That's cessation. That's getting close to nibbāna. To put it another way, going forward is suffering, retreating is suffering, and stopping is suffering. Not going forward, not retreating, and not stopping.... When that happens, is anything left? Body and mind cease here. This is the cessation of suffering. Hard to understand, isn't it? But if we diligently and consistently study this teaching, we will transcend things and reach understanding; there will be cessation. This is the ultimate teaching of the Buddha, the finishing point. The Buddha's teaching finishes at the point of total relinquishment.

Don't be in a hurry to judge whether this teaching is right or wrong. Just listen to it first. If I were to give you a fruit and tell you it's delicious, you should take note of my words but not believe me unquestioningly, because you haven't tasted it yet. If you want to know whether the fruit is sweet or sour, you should cut off a slice and taste it. Then you'll know. The same goes for the teaching I've just given you. Don't throw away this fruit. Keep it and taste it; know its taste for yourself.

The Buddha didn't have a teacher, you know. An ascetic once asked him who his teacher was, and the Buddha answered that he didn't have one. The ascetic just walked off shaking his head. The Buddha was being too honest. He was speaking to one who couldn't know or accept the truth. That's why I tell you not to believe me. The Buddha said that simply to believe others is foolish, because there is no clear knowing within. That's why the Buddha said, "I have no teacher." This is the truth. But you should understand this correctly so as not to disrespect your teacher. Don't go saying, "I have no teacher." You must rely on your teacher to tell you what is right and wrong, and then you must practice accordingly.

In the Buddha's time there were disciples of the Buddha who didn't like him, because the Buddha exhorted them to be diligent, to be heedful. Those who were lazy were afraid of the Buddha and resented him. When he died, one group of disciples cried and were distressed that they would no longer have the Buddha to guide them. Another group of disciples was pleased and relieved that they would no longer have the Buddha on their backs telling them what to do. A third group of disciples was equanimous, having reflected on the truth that what arises passes away as a natural consequence. Which group do you identify with?

These days things aren't much different. All teachers have some followers who resent them. They might not show it outwardly, but it's there in the mind. It's normal for people who still have defilements to feel this way. Even the Buddha had people hating him. I have followers who resent me. I tell them to give up unwholesomeness, but since they cherish their unwholesome actions they hate me. There are plenty of people like this. Those of you who are intelligent will make yourselves firm in the practice of Dhamma.

CHAPTER 33

"TUCCHO POṬHILA"—
VENERABLE EMPTY SCRIPTURE

THERE ARE TWO WAYS to support Buddhism. One is known as *āmisa-pūjā*, supporting through material offerings. These are the four supports of food, clothing, shelter, and medicine. The act of āmisapūjā supports Buddhism by giving material offerings to the Sangha of monks and nuns, enabling them to live in reasonable comfort for the practice of Dhamma. This fosters the direct realization of the Buddha's teaching, in turn bringing continued prosperity to the Buddhist religion.

Buddhism can be likened to a tree. A tree has roots, a trunk, branches, twigs, and leaves. The leaves and branches depend on the roots to absorb nutriment from the soil. The words we speak are like branches and leaves, which depend on a root—the mind—to absorb nutriment and send it out to them. These limbs in turn carry the fruit as our speech and actions. Whatever state the mind is in, skillful or unskillful, it expresses that quality outwardly through our actions and speech.

Therefore the support of Buddhism through the practical application of the teachings is the most important kind of support. For example, in the ceremony of taking the Precepts on observance days, the teacher describes those unskillful actions that should be avoided. But if you simply go through the ceremony of taking the Precepts without reflecting on their meaning, progress is difficult. You will be unable to find the true practice. The real support of Buddhism must therefore be done through *paṭipat-tipūjā*, the "offering" of practice, cultivating true restraint, concentration, and wisdom. Then you will know what Buddhism is all about. If you don't understand through practice, you'll never know, even if you learn the whole Tipiṭaka.

In the time of the Buddha there was a monk known as Tuccho Poṭhila. This monk was one of the Buddha's most learned disciples, thoroughly versed in the scriptures and texts. He was so famous that he was revered by people everywhere and had eighteen monasteries under his care. When people heard the name "Tuccho Poṭhila" they were awestruck, and nobody would dare question anything he taught, so much did they revere his command of the teachings.

One day he went to pay respects to the Buddha. As he was paying his respects, the Buddha said, "Ah, hello, Venerable Empty Scripture!" Just like that! They conversed for a while until it was time to go, and then, as he was taking leave of the Buddha, the Buddha said, "Oh, leaving now, Venerable Empty Scripture?"

That was what the Buddha said. On arriving, "Oh, hello, Venerable Empty Scripture." When it was time to go, "Ah, leaving now, Venerable Empty Scripture?" That was the teaching the Buddha gave. Tuccho Poṭhila was puzzled, "Why did the Buddha say that? What did he mean?" He thought and thought, turning over everything he had learned, until eventually he realized, "It's true! 'Venerable Empty Scripture'—that's me, a monk who studies but doesn't practice." When he looked into his heart he saw that really he was no different from lay people. Whatever they aspired to, he also aspired to; whatever they enjoyed, he also enjoyed. There was no real samaṇa within him, no truly profound quality capable of firmly establishing him in the Noble Way and providing true peace.

So he decided to practice. But there was nowhere for him to go to. All the teachers around were his own students. No one would dare accept him. Usually when people meet their teacher they become timid and deferential, and so no one would dare to become his teacher.

Finally he went to see a certain young novice who was enlightened, and asked to practice under him. The novice said, "Yes, sure you can practice with me, but only if you're sincere. If you're not sincere then I won't accept you." Tuccho Poṭhila pledged himself as a student of the novice.

The novice then told him to put on all his robes. Now there happened to be a muddy bog nearby. When Tuccho Poṭhila had carefully put on all his robes—expensive ones they were, too—the novice said, "Okay, now run down into that bog. If I don't tell you to stop, don't stop. If I don't tell you to come out, don't come out. Okay...run!"

Tuccho Poṭhila, neatly robed, plunged into the bog. The novice didn't tell him to stop until he was completely covered in mud. Finally the novice said, "You can stop now." So he stopped. "Okay, come on up!" And he came out.

Clearly Tuccho Poṭhila had given up his pride. He was ready to accept the teaching. If he hadn't been ready to learn, he wouldn't have run into the bog like that, being such a famous teacher. The young novice, seeing this, knew that Tuccho Poṭhila was sincerely determined to practice. So he gave him a teaching. He taught him to observe sense objects, using the simile of a man catching a lizard hiding in a termite mound. If the mound has six holes in it, how can he catch the lizard? He must seal off five of the holes and leave just one open. Then he simply has to wait and watch, guarding that one hole. When the lizard comes out he can catch it.

Observing the mind is like this. Closing off the eyes, ears, nose, tongue, and body, we leave only the mind. To "close off" the senses means to restrain and compose them. Meditation is like catching the lizard. We use sati to note the breath. Sati is the quality of mindfulness, as in asking yourself, "What am I doing?" Sampajañña is the awareness that "now I am doing such and such." We observe the in and out breathing with sati and sampajañña.

This quality of mindfulness is something that arises from practice. It's not something that can be learned from books. Know the feelings that arise. The mind may be fairly inactive for a while and then a feeling arises. Sati works in conjunction with these feelings, recollecting them. There is sati—the mindfulness that "I will speak," "I will go," "I will sit," and so on—and then there is sampajañña—the awareness that "now I am walking," "I am lying down," "I am experiencing such and such a mood." With these two things, sati and sampajañña, we can know our minds in the present moment. We will know how the mind reacts to sense impressions.

That which is aware of sense objects is called "mind." Sense objects wander into the mind. A sound, for instance, enters through the ear and travels inward to the mind, which acknowledges that it is the sound of a bird, a car, or whatever. Now this mind that acknowledges the sound is still quite basic. It's just the average mind. Perhaps annoyance arises within this one who acknowledges. We must further train "the one who acknowledges" to become "the one who knows in accordance with the truth"—known as Buddho. If we don't clearly know in accordance with the truth, then we get annoyed by the sounds of people, cars, machinery, and so on. The ordinary, untrained mind acknowledges the sound with annoyance. It knows in accordance with its preferences, not in accordance with the truth. We must further train it to know with vision and insight, or *ñāṇadassana*, the power of the refined mind, so that it knows the sound as simply sound. If we don't cling to a sound, there is no annoyance. The sound arises and we simply note it. This is called truly knowing the arising of sense objects. If we develop the Buddho, clearly realizing the sound as sound, then it doesn't annoy us. It arises according to conditions; it is not a being, an individual, a self, an "us" or "them." It's just sound. The mind lets go.

This clear and penetrating knowing is called Buddho. With it we can let the sound simply be sound. It doesn't disturb us unless we disturb it by thinking, "I don't want to hear that sound, it's annoying." Suffering arises because of this attitude. Right here is the cause of suffering: we don't know the truth of this matter, we haven't developed the Buddho. We are not yet clear, not yet awake, not yet aware. Such is the raw, untrained mind, a mind that is not yet truly useful.

We must develop the mind, just as we develop the body. To develop the body we must exercise it, jogging in the morning and evening and so on. Soon the body becomes more agile, stronger; the respiratory and nervous systems become more efficient. Exercising the mind is different. Instead of moving it around, we bring it to a halt, bring it to rest.

For instance, when practicing meditation we take an object such as the in- and out-breaths as our foundation. This becomes the focus of our attention and reflection. We note the breathing, which means that we follow the breathing with awareness, noting its rhythm, its coming and going, and let go of all else. As a result of staying on one object of awareness, our mind becomes refreshed. If we let the mind wander to this or that, however, it cannot unify itself or come to a place of rest.

To say the mind "stops" means that it feels as if it's stopped: it doesn't go running here and there. It's like having a sharp knife. If we use the knife to cut at things indiscriminately, such as stones, bricks, and grass, our knife will quickly become blunt. We should use it for cutting only the things it was meant for. Similarly, if we let the mind wander after thoughts and feelings that have no value or use, the mind becomes tired and weak. If the mind has no energy, wisdom will not arise, because a mind without energy is a mind without samādhi.

If the mind hasn't stopped you can't clearly see the sense objects for what they are. The knowledge that the mind is the mind, sense objects are merely sense objects, is the root from which Buddhism has grown and developed. This is the heart of Buddhism. When we look at ourselves and the way we behave, we are just like little children. A child doesn't know anything. To an adult observing the behavior of a child, the way it plays and jumps around, its actions don't seem to have much purpose. If our mind is untrained, it is like a child. We speak without awareness and act without wisdom. We may fall into ruin or cause untold harm and not even know it.

So we should train this mind. The Buddha taught us to train the mind, to teach it. Even if we support Buddhism with the four requisites, our support is still superficial; it reaches only the bark or sapwood of the tree. The real support, the heartwood, of Buddhism comes through the practice and from nowhere else: from training our actions, speech, and thoughts according to the teachings. This is much more fruitful. If we are straight and honest, possessed of restraint and wisdom, our practice will bring prosperity. There will be no cause for spite and hostility. This is what our religion teaches us.

If we take the Precepts simply out of tradition, then even though our teacher imparts the truth, our practice will be deficient. We may study the teachings and be able to repeat them, but if we really want to understand them we have to practice. Failure to practice may well be an obstacle to our penetrating to the heart of Buddhism for countless lifetimes to come.

Therefore the practice is like the key to a trunk. If we have the right key in hand, the key of meditation, no matter how tightly the lock is closed, when we take the key and turn it, the lock falls open. If we have no key we can't open the lock. We will never know what is in the trunk.

Actually, there are two kinds of knowledge. One who knows the Dhamma doesn't simply speak from memory; he or she speaks the truth. Worldly people usually speak from memory; and what's more, they usually speak with conceit. For example, suppose there are two people who haven't seen each other for a long time. One day they happen to meet on the train. "Oh! What a surprise," says one. "I was just thinking of looking you up!"

Actually it's not true. Really, they hadn't thought of each other at all, but they say so out of excitement. And so it becomes a lie. Yes, it's lying out of heedlessness. This is lying without knowing it. It's a subtle form of defilement, and it happens very often.

So with regard to the mind, Tuccho Poṭhila followed the instructions of the novice: breathing in, breathing out, mindfully aware of each breath, until he saw the liar within him, the lying of his own mind. He saw the defilements as they came up, just like the lizard coming out of the termite mound. He saw them and perceived their true nature as soon as they arose. He noticed how one minute the mind would concoct one thing, the next moment something else.

Thinking is a *sankhata dhamma*, something that is created or concocted from supporting conditions. It's not *asankhata dhamma*, the unconditioned. The well-trained mind, one with perfect awareness, does not concoct mental states. This kind of mind penetrates to the Noble Truths and transcends any need to depend on externals. To know the Noble Truths is to know the truth. The proliferating mind tries to avoid this truth, saying, "That's good" or "This is beautiful"; but if there is Buddho in the mind, it can no longer deceive us, because we know the mind as it is. The mind can no longer create deluded mental states, because there is the clear awareness that all mental states are unstable, imperfect, and a source of suffering to one who clings to them.

Wherever he went, the "one who knows" was constantly in Tuccho Poṭhila's mind. He observed the various creations and proliferations of the mind with understanding. He saw how the mind lied in so many ways. He grasped the essence of the practice: "This lying mind is the one to watch— this is the mind that leads us into extremes of happiness and suffering and causes us to endlessly spin around in the cycle of saṃsāra, with its pleasure and pain, good and evil." Tuccho Poṭhila realized the truth, and grasped the essence of the practice, just like a man grasping the tail of the lizard.

It's the same for us all. Only this mind is important. That's why we train the mind. Now, what are we going to train it with? By having continuous sati and sampajañña we will be able to know the mind. This "one who knows" is a step beyond the mind; it is that which knows the state of the mind. That which knows the mind as simply mind is the "one who knows." The "one who knows" is above the mind, and that is how it is able to look after the mind, to teach the mind to know what is right and what is wrong. In the end everything comes back to this proliferating mind. If the mind is caught up in its proliferations, there is no awareness and the practice is fruitless.

So we must train this mind to hear the Dhamma, to cultivate the Buddho, the clear and radiant awareness, that which exists above and beyond the ordinary mind and knows all that goes on within it. This is why we meditate on the word *Buddho,* so that we can know the mind beyond the mind. Just observe all the mind's movements, whether good or bad, until the "one who knows" realizes that the mind is simply mind, not a self or a person. This is called *cittānupassanā,* contemplation of mind.[67] Seeing in this way we will understand that the mind is transient, imperfect, and ownerless.

We can summarize thus: The mind is that which acknowledges sense objects, which are distinct from the mind; the "one who knows" knows both the mind and the sense objects for what they are. We must use sati to constantly cleanse the mind. Everybody has sati. Even a cat has it when it's going to catch a mouse; a dog has it when it barks at someone. This is a form of sati, but it's not sati according to the Dhamma. Everybody has sati; but there are different levels of it, just as there are different levels of looking at things. For example, when I tell people to contemplate the body, some say, "What is there to contemplate in the body? Anybody can see it— hair, nails, teeth, and skin we can see already. So what?"

This is how people are. They can see the body all right, but their seeing is faulty; they don't see with the Buddho, the "one who knows," the awakened one. They only see the body in the ordinary way; they see it visually. Simply to see the body is not enough. If we only see the body there is trouble. You must see the body within the body; then things become much clearer. Just seeing the body, you get fooled by it, charmed by its appearance. Not seeing transiency, imperfection, and ownerlessness, *kāmachanda* (sense desire) arises. You become fascinated by forms, sounds, odors, flavors, and feelings. Seeing in this way is to see with the mundane eye of the flesh, causing you to love and hate and discriminate into pleasing and unpleasing.

The Buddha taught us that we must see with the "mind's eye." See the body within the body. If you really look into the body...ugh! It's so repulsive. There are today's things and yesterday's things all mixed up in there;

you can't tell what's what. Seeing in this way is much clearer than seeing with the physical eye, with this crazy eye that looks only at things it wants to see. Contemplate with the eye of the mind, with the wisdom eye.

This is the practice that can uproot clinging to the five khandhas—form, feeling, perception, mental formations, and sense consciousness. To uproot attachment is to uproot suffering, because attaching to the five khandhas is the cause of suffering. If suffering arises it is here, at the attachment to the five khandhas. It's not that the five khandhas are in themselves suffering, but the clinging to them as being one's own—that's suffering.

If you clearly see the truth of these things through meditation practice, then suffering becomes unwound, like a screw or a bolt. When a bolt is unscrewed, it withdraws. The mind unwinds in the same way, letting go, withdrawing from the obsession with good and evil, possessions, praise and status, happiness and suffering.

If we don't know the truth of these things it's like tightening the screw all the time. It gets tighter and tighter until it's crushing you and you suffer over everything. When you know how things are, you loosen the screw. In Dhamma language we call this the arising of *nibbidā,* disenchantment. You become weary of things and lay down the fascination with them. If you unwind in this way you will find peace.

People have only one problem—the problem of clinging. Just because of this one thing people will kill each other. All problems, be they individual, family, or social, arise from this one root. Nobody wins; they kill each other but in the end no one gets anything. Gain and loss, praise and criticism, status and loss of status, happiness and suffering—these are the worldly dhammas. These dhammas engulf worldly beings; they are troublemakers. If you don't reflect on their true nature, you will suffer. People even commit murder for the sake of wealth, status, or power. Why? Because they take them too seriously. They get appointed to some position and it goes to their heads, like the man who became headman of the village. After his appointment he became drunk with power. If any of his old friends came to see him he'd say, "Don't come around so often. Things aren't the same anymore."

The Buddha taught us to understand the nature of possessions, status, praise, and happiness. Take these things as they come but let them be. Don't let them go to your head. If you don't really understand these things, you'll be fooled by your power, by your children and relatives...by everything! If you understand them clearly, you know they're all impermanent conditions. If you cling to them they become defiled.

When people are first born there are simply nāma and rūpa, that's all. We add on the business of "Mr. Jones," "Miss Smith," or whatever later on. This is done according to convention. Still later there are the appendages of "Colonel," "Doctor," and so on. If we don't really understand these things we think they are real and carry them around with us. We carry possessions, status, name, and rank around. If you have power, you can call all the tunes. "Take this one and execute him. Take that one and throw him in jail." Rank gives power. This word "rank" here is where clinging takes hold. As soon as people get rank they start giving orders; right or wrong, they just act on their moods. So they go on making the same old mistakes, deviating further and further from the true Path. One who understands the Dhamma won't behave like this. If possessions and status come your way, let them simply be possessions and status. Don't let them become your identity. Just use them to fulfill your obligations and leave it at that. You remain unchanged.

This is how the Buddha wanted us to understand things. No matter what you receive, the mind adds nothing on to it. They appoint you a city councilor: "Okay, so I'm a city councilor…but I'm not." They appoint you head of a committee: "Sure I'm head, but I'm not." Whatever they make of you: "Yes I am, but I'm not." In the end, what are we anyway? We all just die in the end. No matter what they make you, in the end it's all the same. What can you say? If you can see things in this way you will have a solid abiding and true contentment. Nothing is changed.

This is to be not fooled by things. Whatever comes your way, it's just conditions. There's nothing that can entice a mind like this to create or proliferate, to seduce it into greed, aversion, or delusion.

Now this is to be a true supporter of Buddhism. Whether you are among those who are being supported (the Sangha) or those who are supporting (the laity), please consider this thoroughly. Cultivate the sīla-dhamma within you. This is the surest way to support Buddhism. To support Buddhism with the offerings of food, shelter, and medicine is good also, but such offerings only reach the sapwood of Buddhism. A tree has bark, sapwood and heartwood, and these three parts are interdependent. The heartwood relies on the bark and the sapwood; the sapwood relies on the bark and the heartwood. They all exist interdependently, just like the teachings of sīla, samādhi, and paññā—moral discipline, concentration, and wisdom. Moral discipline establishes your speech and actions in rectitude. Concentration firmly fixes the mind. Wisdom thoroughly understands the nature of all conditions. Study this, practice this, and you will understand Buddhism in the most profound way.

If you don't realize these things you will be fooled by possessions, fooled by rank, fooled by anything you come into contact with. We must consider our lives and bring them in line with the teaching. We should reflect that all beings in the world are part of one whole. We are like them, they are like us. They have happiness and suffering just like we do. It's all much the same. If we reflect in this way, peace and understanding will arise. This is the foundation of Buddhism.

CHAPTER 34

"NOT SURE!"—THE STANDARD OF THE NOBLE ONES

THERE WAS ONCE a Western monk, a student of mine. Whenever he saw Thai monks and novices disrobing he would say, "Oh, what a shame! Why do they do that? Why do so many of the Thai monks and novices disrobe?" He was shocked. He would get saddened at the disrobing of the Thai monks and novices, because he had only just come into contact with Buddhism. He was inspired, he was resolute. Going forth as a monk was the only thing to do. He thought he'd never disrobe. But in time some Western monks began to disrobe, and he came to see disrobing as not so important after all.

When people are inspired, it all seems to be so right and good. They have no way to gauge their feelings and don't really understand practice, but they go ahead and form an opinion. Those who do know will have a thoroughly firm foundation within their hearts—but they don't advertise it.

As for myself, when I was first ordained I didn't actually do much practice, but I had a lot of faith. I don't know why, maybe it was there from birth. At the end of the rains retreat the monks and novices who went forth together with me all disrobed. I thought to myself, "What is it with these people?" But I didn't dare say anything to them because I wasn't yet sure of my own feelings, I was too stirred up. But within me I felt that they were all foolish. "It's difficult to go forth, easy to disrobe. These guys don't have much merit. They think that the way of the world is more useful than the way of Dhamma." That's what I thought, but I didn't say anything. I just watched my mind.

I'd see the monks who'd gone forth with me disrobing one after the other. Sometimes they'd dress up and come back to the monastery to show off. I'd see them and think they were crazy, but they thought they looked snappy. I thought they were wrong, but I wouldn't say because I myself was still an uncertain quantity. I still wasn't sure how long my faith would last.

When my friends had all disrobed, I dropped all concern; there was nobody left to concern myself with. I picked up the *Pāṭimokkha* and got stuck into learning that. There was nobody left to distract me and waste my time, so I put my heart into the practice. Still I didn't say anything because I felt that to practice all one's life, maybe seventy, eighty, or even ninety years, and to keep up a persistent effort, without slackening up or losing one's resolve, seemed like an extremely difficult thing to do.

Those who went forth would go forth, those who disrobed would disrobe. I'd just watch it all. I didn't concern myself whether they stayed or went. I'd watch my friends leave, but the feeling I had within me was that these people didn't see clearly. That Western monk probably thought like that. He'd see people become monks for only one rains retreat, and get upset.

Later on he reached a stage we call...*bored;* bored with the holy life. He let go of the practice and eventually disrobed.

"Why are you disrobing?" I asked. "Before, when you saw the Thai monks disrobing you'd say, 'Oh, what a shame! How sad, how pitiful.' Now, when you yourself want to disrobe, why don't you feel sorry now?"

He didn't answer. He just grinned sheepishly.

When it comes to the training of the mind, it isn't easy to find a good standard if you haven't yet developed a "witness" within yourself. In most external matters we can rely on others for feedback. But when it comes to using the Dhamma as a standard, is it within our reach? Do we have the Dhamma yet? Are we thinking rightly? And if it's right, can we let go of rightness or are we still clinging to it?

This is the important thing: you must contemplate until you reach the point where you let go, where there isn't anything left, where there is neither good nor bad. Then you throw it off. This means you throw out everything. If it's all gone, then there's no remainder.

So in regard to this training of the mind, sometimes we may say it's easy. But it's hard to do, very hard. It's hard in that it doesn't conform to our desires: sometimes it seems almost as if the angels were helping us out.

Everything goes right; whatever we think or say seems to be just right. Then we go and attach to that rightness and before long we go wrong and it all turns bad. This is where it's difficult. We don't have a standard to gauge things by.

People who have a lot of faith, who are endowed with confidence and belief but are lacking in wisdom, may be very good at samādhi, but they may not have much insight. They see only one side of everything, and simply follow that. They don't reflect. This is blind faith. In Buddhism we call this *saddhā adhimokkha.* They have faith all right, but it's not born of wisdom. They don't see this yet; they believe they have wisdom, so they don't see where they are wrong.

Therefore they teach about the Five Powers *(bala): saddhā, viriya, sati, samādhi,* and *paññā.* Saddhā is conviction; viriya is diligent effort; sati is mindfulness; samādhi is fixedness of mind; paññā is all-embracing wisdom. Don't say that paññā is simply wisdom—paññā is all-embracing, consummate wisdom.

The wise have given these five steps to us so that we can look at them, first as an object of study, then as a gauge to compare to the state of our own practice as it is. For example, take saddhā: do we have conviction, have we developed it yet? Viriya: do we have diligent effort or not? Is our effort right or wrong? Everybody makes some sort of effort, but is it wise or not? The same goes for sati. Even a cat has sati. When it sees a mouse, sati is there. The cat's eyes stare fixedly at the mouse. Everybody has sati: animals, delinquents, sages—all have it. Samādhi, or fixedness of mind: everybody has this as well. In the sati of the cat, samādhi is also there. Paññā, or wisdom: a cat has this too, but it's not a broad wisdom, like that of human beings. It knows as an animal knows; it has enough wisdom to catch mice for food.

These five things are called Powers. Have these Five Powers arisen from Right View? What is our standard for gauging Right View? We must clearly understand this.

Right View is the understanding that all these things are uncertain. Therefore the Buddha and all the Noble Ones don't hold fast to them. They hold, but not fast. They don't let that holding become an identity. A holding that doesn't lead to becoming is a holding that isn't tainted with desire. Without seeking to become this or that, there is simply the practice itself.

When you hold on to a particular thing is there enjoyment, or is there displeasure? If there is pleasure, do you hold on to that pleasure? If there is dislike, do you hold on to that dislike?

Some views can be used as principles for gauging our practice more accurately. For example, the belief that one is better than others, or equal to others, or more foolish than others, are all wrong views. We may feel these things, but we also know them with wisdom; we know that they simply arise and cease. Seeing that we are better than others is not right; seeing that we are equal to others is not right; seeing that we are inferior to others is not right.

The Right View is the one that cuts through all of this. If we think we are better than others, pride arises. It's there but we don't see it. If we think we are equal to others, we fail to show respect and humility at the proper times. If we think we are inferior to others, we get depressed, believing we are inferior or born under a bad sign and so on. We are still clinging to the five khandhas; it's all simply becoming and birth.

This is one standard for gauging ourselves by. Another one is this: If we encounter a pleasant experience, we feel happy; if we encounter a bad experience, we are unhappy. Are we able to look at both the things we like and the things we dislike as having equal value? Measure yourself against this standard. In our everyday experience, when we hear something we like or dislike, does our mood change? Or is the mind unmoved? Right here we have a gauge.

Just know yourself; this is your witness. Don't make decisions on the strength of your desires. Desires can puff us up into thinking we are something that we're not. We must be very circumspect.

There are so many angles and aspects to consider, but the right way is to follow not your desires but the truth. We should know both the good and the bad, and when we know them, we let go of them. If we don't let go we are still there, we still "exist," we still "have." If we still "are," then there is a remainder; there is becoming and birth in store.

Therefore the Buddha said to judge only yourself, don't judge others, no matter how good or evil they may be. The Buddha merely points out the way, saying, "The truth is like this." Now, is our mind like that or not?

For instance, suppose a monk took some things belonging to another monk, then that other monk accused him, "You stole my things." "I didn't steal them, I only took them." So we ask a third monk to adjudicate. How should he decide? He would have to ask the offending monk to appear before the convened Sangha. "Yes, I took it, but I didn't steal it." Or in regard to other rules, such as pārājika or saṅghādisesa offenses: "Yes, I did it, but I didn't have intention." How can you believe that? It's tricky. If you can't believe it, all you can do is leave the onus with the doer; it rests on him.

But you should know that we can't hide the things that arise in our minds. You can't cover them up, either the wrongs or the good actions. Whether actions are good or evil, you can't dismiss them simply by ignoring them, because these things tend to reveal themselves. They conceal themselves, they reveal themselves, they exist in and of themselves. They are all automatic. This is how things work.

Don't try to guess at or speculate about these things. As long as there is still avijjā (unknowing) they are not finished with. The Chief Privy Councillor once asked me, "Luang Por, is the mind of an anāgāmi pure yet?"[68]

"It's partly pure."

"Eh? An anāgāmi has given up sensual desire; how is his mind not yet pure?"

"He may have let go of sensual desire; but there is still something remaining, isn't there? There is still avijjā. If there is still something left, then there is still something left. It's like the bhikkhus' alms bowls. There are a large-sized large bowl, a medium-sized large bowl, a small-sized large bowl; then a large-sized medium bowl, a medium-sized medium bowl, a small-sized medium bowl; then there are a large-sized small bowl, a medium-sized small bowl, and a small-sized small bowl.... No matter how small it is there is still a bowl there, right? That's how it is with this...sotāpanna, sakadāgāmi, anāgāmi...they have all given up certain defilements, but only to their respective levels. Whatever still remains, those Noble Ones don't see. If they could they would all be arahants. They still can't see all. Avijjā is that which doesn't see. If the mind of the anāgāmi was completely straightened out he wouldn't be an anāgāmi, he would be fully accomplished. But there is still something remaining."

"Is his mind purified?" "Well, it is somewhat, but not one hundred percent." How else could I answer? He said that later on he would come and question me about it further.

Don't be careless. The Lord Buddha exhorted us to be alert. In regard to this training of the heart, I've had my moments of temptation too. I've been tempted to try many things, but they always seemed like they were straying from the Path. They were a sort of swaggering in the mind, a sort of conceit. They were diṭṭhi and māna—views and pride. It's hard enough just to be aware of these two things.

There was once a man who wanted to be ordained as a monk in memory of his late mother. He arrived at this monastery, laid down his robes, and, without so much as paying respects to the monks, started doing walking meditation right in front of the main hall...back and forth, back and forth, really showing his stuff.

I thought, "Oh, so there are people around like this, too!" This is saddhā adhimokkha—blind faith. He must have determined to get enlightened before sundown or something; he thought it would be so easy. He didn't look at anybody else, just put his head down and walked as if his life depended on it. I just let him carry on, but I thought, "Oh, man, you think it's that easy or something?" In the end I don't know how long he stayed; I don't think he was ever ordained.

As soon as the mind thinks of something, we send it out every time. We don't realize that this is simply the habitual proliferation of the mind, which disguises itself as wisdom and waffles on in minute detail. This mental proliferation seems very clever—if we didn't know better we might mistake it for wisdom. But when it comes to the crunch, it's not the real thing. When suffering arises, where is that so-called wisdom then? Is it of any use? It's only proliferation after all.

So stay with the Buddha. In our practice we must turn inward and find the Buddha. The Buddha is still alive to this very day, go in and find him. At anicca, go in and find him there. Go and bow to him: anicca, uncertainty. You can go right there for starters.

If the mind tries to tell you that you are a sotāpanna now, and you were to bring this thought to the Buddha, he'd say, "It's all uncertain." If you were to decide you are a sakadāgāmi, he'd simply say, "Not a sure thing!" If the thought "I'm an anāgāmi" were to arise, the Buddha would tell you only one thing: "Uncertain." If it even comes to the point of thinking you are an arahant, he'd tell you even more firmly, "It's all *very* uncertain."

These are the words of the Noble Ones: "Everything is uncertain, don't cling to anything." Don't just hold on to things foolishly. Don't cling to things, holding fast to them without letting go. Look at things as appearance and then send them on to transcendence. That's how you must be. There must be appearance and there must be transcendence.

So I say, "Go to the Buddha." Where is the Buddha? The Buddha is the Dhamma. All the teachings in this world can be contained in this one teaching: aniccaṁ. Think about it. I've searched for over forty years as a monk and this is all I could find. That and patient endurance. Anicca: it's all uncertain. No matter how sure the mind wants to be, just tell it, "Not sure!" Whenever the mind wants to grab on to something as a sure thing, just say, "It's not sure, it's transient." Just ram it down with this. Using the Dhamma of the Buddha comes down to this. Whether standing, walking, sitting, or lying down, you see everything this way. Whether liking or disliking arises, you see it all the same way. This is getting close to the Buddha, close to the Dhamma.

This is a valuable way to practice. All my practice from the early days up to the present has been like this. I didn't rely on the scriptures, nor did I disregard them. I didn't rely on a teacher, nor did I "go it alone." My practice was always "neither this nor that."

It's a matter of "finishing off"—that is, practicing to the finish, seeing the practice to completion, seeing the apparent and also the transcendent.

If you practice consistently and consider things thoroughly, you will eventually reach this point. At first you hurry to go forward, hurry to come back, and hurry to stop. You continue to practice like this until you reach the point where it seems that going forward is not it, coming back is not it, and stopping is not it either! It's finished. This is the finish. Don't expect anything more than this; it finishes right here. Khīnāsavo—one who is completed. He doesn't go forward, doesn't retreat, and doesn't stop. There's no stopping, no going forward, and no coming back. It's finished. Consider this; realize it clearly in your own mind. Right there you will find that there is really nothing at all.

Whether this is old or new to you depends on you, on your wisdom and discernment. One who has no wisdom or discernment won't be able to figure it out. Just look at mango or jackfruit trees. If they grow up in a clump, one tree may get bigger first and then the others will bend away, growing outward from that bigger one. Who tells them to do that? This is their nature. Nature contains both the good and the bad, the right and the wrong. It can either incline to the right or incline to the wrong. If we plant any kind of trees at all close together, the trees that mature later will branch away from the bigger tree. This is nature, or Dhamma.

Likewise taṇhā, desire, leads us to suffering. But if we contemplate it, it will lead us out of desire, and we will outgrow taṇhā. By investigating taṇhā, we shake it up, making it gradually lighter and lighter until it's all gone. The same as the trees: does anybody order them to grow the way they do? They can't talk or move around, and yet they know how to grow away from obstacles. Wherever they're crowded, they bend outward.

The Dhamma is right here. One who is astute will see it. Trees by nature don't know anything; they act on natural laws, yet they know enough to grow away from danger and to incline toward a suitable place. And so do reflective people. We go forth into the homeless life because we want to transcend suffering. What is it that makes us suffer? If we follow the trail inward, we will find out. That which we like and that which we don't like are unsatisfactory. If they are unsatisfactory, then don't go so close to them. Do you want to fall in love with conditions or hate them? They're all uncertain. When we incline toward the Buddha, all this comes to an end.

I was ordained in an ordinary village temple and lived in village temples for quite a few years. In my mind I conceived the desire to practice, I wanted to be proficient, I wanted to train. There wasn't anybody giving any teaching in those monasteries but the inspiration to practice arose. I traveled and I looked around. I had ears so I listened, I had eyes so I looked. Whatever I heard people say, I'd tell myself, "Not sure." Whatever I saw, I told myself, "Not sure." Even when I smelled an odor, I would tell myself, "Not sure," or when my tongue contacted sweet, sour, salty, pleasant, or unpleasant flavors, or feelings of comfort or pain arose in my body, I'd tell myself, "This is not a sure thing!" And so I lived with Dhamma.

In truth it's all uncertain, but our desires want things to be certain. What can we do? We must be patient. The most important thing is *khanti,* patient endurance. Sometimes I'd go to see old religious sites with ancient monastic buildings, designed by architects, built by craftsmen. In some places they would be cracked. Maybe one of my friends would remark, "Such a shame, isn't it? It's cracked." I'd answer, "If that weren't the case then there'd be no such thing as the Buddha, there'd be no Dhamma. It's cracked like this because it's perfectly in line with the Buddha's teaching." Deep down inside, I was also sad to see those buildings cracked, but I'd throw off my sentimentality and try to say something that would be of use to my friends, and to myself.

"If it wasn't cracked like that, there wouldn't be any Buddha!"

Perhaps my friends weren't listening, but I was. This way of considering things is very, very useful. Suppose someone were to rush in and say, "Luang Por, do you know what so-and-so just said about you?" or, "He said such and such about you." Maybe you even start to get angry. You hear a little criticism, and you're ready for a showdown! Emotion arises. We must know these moods every step of the way. We may get ready to retaliate, but upon looking into the truth of the matter we may find that, well, they had said or meant something else.

And so it's another case of uncertainty. Why should we rush in and believe things? Why should we put our trust so much in what others say? Whatever we hear we should take note, be patient, look into the matter carefully.

Speech that ignores uncertainty is not the speech of a sage. Whenever we dismiss uncertainty, we cease to be wise, and we are no longer practicing. Whatever we see or hear, be it pleasant or sad, just say, "This is not sure!" Say it firmly to yourself. Bring everything into perspective with this. Don't build things up into major issues; bring them all down to this. Here is where defilements die.

If we come to understand the true nature of things like this, lust, infatuation, and attachment fade away. Why do they fade away? Because we understand, we know. We shift from ignorance to understanding. Understanding is born from ignorance, knowing is born from unknowing, purity is born from defilement. It works like this. Not discarding anicca, not discarding the Buddha—that's what "The Buddha is still alive" means. That the Buddha has passed into nibbāna is not necessarily true. In a profound sense the Buddha is still alive. It's much like how we define the word *bhikkhu*. If we define it as "one who asks,"[69] the meaning is very broad. We can define it this way, but to use this definition too much is not so good— we don't know when to stop asking! To define this word in a more profound way, we would say that a bhikkhu is "one who sees the danger of saṁsāra."

Isn't this more profound? The practice of Dhamma is like this. If you don't fully understand the Dhamma, it seems to be one thing, but when you fully understand it, it becomes something else. It becomes priceless; it becomes a source of peace.

When we have sati we are close to the Dhamma. If we have sati we will see anicca, the transiency of all things. We will see the Buddha and transcend the suffering of saṁsāra; if not now then sometime in the future.

If we throw away the attributes of the Noble Ones, the Buddha, or the Dhamma, our practice will become barren and fruitless. We must maintain our practice constantly, whether we are working or sitting or simply lying down. When the eye sees a form, the ear hears a sound, the nose smells an odor, the tongue tastes a flavor, or the body experiences a sensation—in all things, don't throw away the Buddha, don't stray from the Buddha.

This is to be one who has come close to the Buddha, who reveres the Buddha constantly. We have ceremonies for revering the Buddha, such as chanting *Arahaṁ Sammā Sambuddho Bhagavā* in the morning. This is one way of revering the Buddha, but it's not revering the Buddha in the profound way I've just described. Revering the Buddha by merely reciting Pali phrases is comparable to defining *bhikkhu* as "one who asks." If we incline toward anicca, dukkha, and anattā—whenever the eye sees a form, the ear hears a sound, the nose smells an odor, the tongue tastes a flavor, the body experiences a sensation, or the mind cognizes mental impressions—this is comparable to defining the *bhikkhu* as "one who sees the danger of saṁsāra." It's so much more profound and cuts through so many things.

This is called *paṭipadā*. Develop this attitude in the practice and you will be on the right path. If you think and reflect in this way, even though you may live far from your teachers, you will still be close to them. If you live close to the teachers but your mind has not yet met them, you will spend your time either faultfinding or adulating them. If they do something that suits you, you'll say they're good; and if they do something you dislike, you'll say they're bad—and that's as far as your practice goes. You won't achieve anything by wasting your time looking at someone else. But if you understand this teaching, you can become a Noble One in the present moment.

For the newer monks I've already laid down the schedule and rules of the monastery, such as: "Don't talk too much." Don't transgress the existing standards, the path to realization, fruition, and nibbāna. Anyone who transgresses these standards is not a real practitioner, not one who has come with a pure intention to practice. What can such a person ever hope to see? Even if they were near me every day they wouldn't see me. Even if they were near the Buddha they wouldn't see the Buddha, if they didn't practice. So knowing the Dhamma or seeing the Dhamma depends on practice. Have confidence, purify your own heart. If anger or dislike arise just leave them at the mind, but see them clearly! Keep on looking at those things. As long as there is still something there, it means we still have to dig and grind away right there. Some say, "I can't cut it, I can't do it"—if we start saying things like this there will only be a bunch of worthless fools here, because nobody cuts away their defilements.

You must try. If you can't yet cut it, dig in deeper. Dig at the defilements, uproot them. Dig them out even if they seem hard and fast. The Dhamma is not something you reach by following your desires. Your mind may be one way, the truth another. You must watch up front and keep a lookout behind as well. That's why I say, "It's all uncertain, all transient."

This truth of uncertainty—this short and simple truth, so profound and faultless—people tend to ignore. Don't cling to goodness, don't cling to badness. We are practicing to be free of the world, so bring these things to an end. The Buddha taught us to lay them down, to give them up, because they only cause suffering.

CHAPTER 35

STILL, FLOWING WATER

Now please pay attention; don't allow your mind to wander off after other things. Create the feeling that right now you are sitting on a mountain or in a forest somewhere, all by yourself. What do you have sitting here right now? The body and mind, that's all, only these two things. All that is contained within this human frame sitting here now is called *body*. The *mind* is that which is aware and is thinking at this very moment. These two things are also called *nāma* and *rūpa*. *Nāma* refers to that which has no rūpa, or form. All thoughts and feelings, or the four mental khandhas of feeling, perception, mental formation, and consciousness, are nāma; they are all formless. When the eye sees form, that form is called *rūpa*, while the awareness is called *nāma*. Together they are called *nāma* and *rūpa*, or simply body and mind.

Understand that sitting here in this present moment are only body and mind. But we get these two things confused with each other. If you want peace, you must know the truth of them. The mind in its present state is still untrained; it's unclean and unclear. It is not yet the pure mind. We must further train this mind through the practice of meditation.

Some people think that meditation means to sit in some special way, but in actual fact standing, sitting, walking, and reclining are all vehicles for meditation practice. You can practice at all times. Samādhi literally means "the firmly established mind." To develop samādhi you don't have to go bottling the mind up. Some people try to get peaceful by sitting quietly and having nothing disturb them at all, but that's just like being dead. The practice of samādhi is for developing wisdom and understanding.

Samādhi is the firm mind, the one-pointed mind. On which point is it fixed? It's fixed on the point of balance. That's its point. But people practice meditation by trying to silence their minds. They say, "I try to sit in meditation, but my mind won't be still for a minute. One instant it flies off one place, the next instant it flies off somewhere else. How can I make it stop?" You don't have to make it stop, that's not the point. Where there is movement is where understanding can arise. People complain, "It runs off and I pull it back again; then it goes off again and I pull it back once more." So they just sit there pulling back and forth like this.

They think their minds are running all over the place, but actually it only seems like the mind is running around. For example, look at this hall here. "Oh, it's so big!" you say. Actually, it's not big at all. Whether or not it seems big depends on your perception of it. In fact this hall is just the size it is, neither big nor small, but people run around after their feelings all the time. Meditating to find peace of mind: first you must understand what peace is. If you don't understand it, you won't be able to find it. For example, suppose today you brought a very expensive pen with you to the monastery. Now suppose that, on your way here, you put the pen in your front pocket, but at a later time you took it out and put it somewhere else, such as your back pocket. Now you reach into your front pocket.... It's not there! You get a fright. You get a fright because of your misunderstanding, your ignorance of the truth of the matter. Suffering is the result. You can't stop worrying about your lost pen. Your wrong understanding causes you to suffer. "Such a shame! I bought that pen only a few days ago, and now I've lost it."

But then you remember, "Oh, of course! When I went to bathe, I put the pen in my *back* pocket." As soon as you remember this you feel better already, even without seeing your pen. You see that? You're happy already. You can stop worrying about your pen. As you're walking along you run your hand over your back pocket, and there it is. Your mind was deceiving you all along. Now, seeing the pen, your worries are calmed. This sort of peace comes from seeing the cause of the problem, samudaya, or the cause of suffering. As soon as you remember that the pen is in your back pocket, there is nirodha, or the cessation of suffering.

So you must contemplate in order to find peace. What people usually refer to as peace is simply the calming of the mind, not the calming of the defilements. The defilements are simply being temporarily subdued, just like grass you've covered with a rock. If, after three or four days, you take away the rock, the grass grows up again in no long time. The grass didn't die; it was simply suppressed. It's the same as sitting in samādhi: the mind is calmed but the defilements are not. Samādhi brings a kind of peace, but it is like the rock covering the grass. It's only temporary. To find real peace you must develop wisdom. The peace of wisdom is like putting the rock down and not lifting it up, just leaving it where it is. The grass can't possibly grow again. This is real peace, the calming of the defilements.

We speak of wisdom and calm, paññā and samādhi, as separate things, but in essence they are one and the same. Wisdom is the dynamic function of samādhi; samādhi is the passive aspect of wisdom. They arise from the same place but take different directions, different functions. Like this mango here. A small green mango eventually grows larger and larger until it's ripe. It is all the same mango, not different mangoes. The small mango, the larger one, and the ripe one are all the same mango, but its condition changes. In Dhamma practice, one condition is called samādhi; the later condition is called paññā, but in actuality sīla, samādhi, and paññā are all the same thing, just like the mango.

In any case, in our practice, no matter what aspect you refer to, you must always begin with the mind. Do you know what this mind is? What is it? Where is it? Nobody knows. All we know is that we want to go over here or over there, we want this and we want that, we feel good or we feel bad, but the mind itself seems impossible to know. What is the mind? The mind has no form. That which receives impressions, both good and bad, we call "mind." It's like the owner of a house. The owners stay put at home while visitors come to see them. They are the ones who receive the visitors. Who receives sense impressions? What is it that perceives? Who lets go of sense impressions? That is what we call "mind." But people can't see it, so they think themselves around in circles. "What is the mind? Is it the brain?" Don't confuse the issue like this. But what is it that receives impressions? Some impressions it likes and some it doesn't. Who is that? Is there someone who likes and dislikes? Sure there is, but you can't see it. We assume it to be a self, but it's really only nāma-dhamma.

Therefore we begin the practice by calming the mind. Put awareness into the mind. If the mind is aware it will be at peace. Some people don't go for awareness; they just want to have peace, a kind of blanking out. So they never learn anything. If we don't have this "one who knows," what is there to base our practice on?

If there is no long, there is no short. If there is no right, there can be no wrong. People these days keep studying, looking for good and evil. But that which is beyond good and evil they know nothing of. All they know is the right and the wrong—"I'm going to take only what is right. I don't want to know about the wrong. Why should I?" If you try to take only what is right, in a short time it will go wrong again. Right leads to wrong. They study the long and the short, but that which is neither long nor short they know nothing of. A knife has a cutting edge, a blunt edge, and a handle. Can you lift only the cutting edge? Can you lift only the blunt edge of the blade, or the handle? The handle, the blunt edge, and the sharp edge are all parts of the same knife: when you pick up the knife you get all three parts together. In the same way, if you take up goodness, badness follows. If you take up happiness, suffering follows. The practice of clinging to goodness and rejecting badness is the Dhamma of children. It's like a toy. Sure, it's all right, you can take just this much, but if you grab on to goodness, badness will follow. The end of this path is confused; it's not so good. If you don't study this, there can be no completion.

Take a simple example. If you have children, suppose you want only to love them and never harbor aversion. This is the thinking of one who doesn't know human nature. If you hold on to love, aversion will follow. Similarly, people study the Dhamma to develop wisdom, so they study good and evil very closely. Then, having identified good and evil, what do they do? They try to cling to the good, and evil follows. They didn't study that which is beyond good and evil. This is what you should study.

Such people say, "I'm going to be like this," "I'm going to be like that," but they never say, "I'm not going to be anything because there really isn't any *I*." This they haven't studied. All they want is goodness, and if they attain it, they lose themselves in it. Yet when things get too good, they'll start to go bad, and so people end up just swinging back and forth.

Train the mind until it is pure. How pure should you make it? If it's really pure, the mind should be above both good and evil, above even purity. It's finished. That's when the practice is finished. Only when you can make your mind beyond both happiness and suffering will you find true peace. That's the true peace. This is the subject most people never study; they never really see this one. Don't think that training the mind is simply sitting quietly. Some people complain, "I can't meditate, I'm too restless. Whenever I sit down, I think of this and that. I can't do it. I've got too much bad karma. I should use up my bad karma first and then come back and try meditating." Sure, just try it. Try using up your bad karma.

The so-called hindrances are the things we must study. Whenever we sit, the mind immediately goes running off. We follow it and try to bring it back and observe it once more. Then it goes off again. This is what you're supposed to be studying! Most people refuse to learn their lessons from nature—like a naughty schoolboy who refuses to do his homework. They don't want to see the mind changing. But then how are you going to develop wisdom? We have to live with change like this. When we know that the mind is just this way, constantly changing, when we know that this is its nature, we will understand it.

Suppose you have a pet monkey. Monkeys don't stay still for long, they like to jump around and grab things. That's how monkeys are. Now you come to the monastery and see a monkey here. This monkey doesn't stay still either, it jumps around just like your pet monkey at home. But it doesn't bother you, does it? You've raised a monkey before, so you know what they're like. If you know just one monkey, no matter where you go, no matter how many monkeys you see, you won't be bothered by them, will you? That's because you are one who understands monkeys.

If we understand monkeys then we won't become a monkey. If you don't understand monkeys, you may become a monkey yourself! Do you understand? If you see it reaching for this and that and you shout, "Hey, stop!" and you get angry—"That damned monkey!"—then you're one who doesn't know monkeys. One who knows monkeys sees that the monkey at home and the monkey in the monastery are just the same. Why should you get annoyed by them? When you see what monkeys are like, that's enough; you can be at peace.

Peace is like this. We must know sensations. Some sensations are pleasant, some are unpleasant, but that's not important. That's just their business. Just like the monkeys. We should understand sensations and know how to let them go. Sensations are uncertain. They are transient, imperfect, and ownerless. Everything that we perceive is like this. When eyes, ears, nose, tongue, body, and mind receive sensations, we know them, just like knowing the monkeys. Then we can be at peace.

There must be these things. If there were no sensations you could develop no wisdom. For the really earnest student, the more sensations the better. But many meditators shrink away from sensations. They don't want to deal with them. This is like the naughty schoolboy who won't go to school, won't listen to the teacher. These sensations are teaching us. When we know sensations, we are practicing Dhamma. The peace within sensations is just like understanding the monkey here. When you understand what monkeys are like you are no longer troubled by them.

The practice of Dhamma is like this. The Dhamma isn't far away, it's right with us. The Dhamma isn't about the angels on high or anything like that. It's simply about us, about what we are doing right now. Observe yourself. Sometimes there is happiness, sometimes suffering, sometimes comfort, sometimes pain, sometimes love, sometimes hate. This is Dhamma, do you see? You have to read your experiences.

You must know sensations before you can let them go. When you see that sensations are impermanent, they will not trouble you. As soon as a sensation arises, just say to yourself, "Hmm, not a sure thing." When your mood changes, "Hmm, not sure." You can be at peace with these things, just like seeing the monkey and not being bothered. If you know the truth of sensations, that is knowing the Dhamma. You let go of sensations, seeing that they are all invariably uncertain.

What we call uncertainty here is the Buddha. The Buddha is the Dhamma. The Dhamma is the characteristic of uncertainty. Whoever sees the uncertainty of things sees their unchanging reality. That's what the Dhamma is like. And that is the Buddha. If you see the Dhamma, you see the Buddha. Seeing the Buddha, you see the Dhamma. If you know anicca, uncertainty, you will let go of things and not grasp on to them.

You say, "Don't break my glass!" Can you prevent something that's breakable from breaking? It will break sooner or later. If you don't break it, someone else will. If someone else doesn't break it, one of the chickens will! The Buddha says to accept this. Penetrating the truth of these things, he saw that this glass is already broken. The Buddha's understanding was like this.

He saw the broken glass within the unbroken one. Whenever you use this glass, you should reflect that it's already broken. Whenever its time is up, it will break. Use the glass, look after it, until the day when it slips out of your hand and shatters. No problem. Why not? Because you saw its brokenness before it broke!

"I really love this glass," you say, "I hope it never breaks." Later on the dog breaks it. "I'll kill that damn dog!" You hate the dog for breaking your glass. If one of your children breaks it, you'll hate them too. Why is this? Because you've dammed yourself up, and the water has nowhere to flow. You've made a dam without a spillway. The only thing the dam can do is burst, right? When you make a dam, you must make a spillway also. When the water rises up too high, it can flow off safely. You have to have a safety valve like this. Impermanence is the safety valve of the Noble Ones. If you have this "safety valve," you will be at peace.

Standing, walking, sitting, lying down, practice constantly, using sati to watch over and protect the mind. As long as you don't throw out the Buddha you won't suffer. As soon as you throw out the Buddha you will experience suffering. As soon as you throw out the reflections on transiency, imperfection, and ownerlessness, you'll have suffering. If you can practice just this much, it's enough; suffering won't arise, or if it does arise, you can settle it easily, and it will be a cause for suffering not arising in the future. This is the end of our practice, the point where suffering doesn't arise. And why doesn't suffering arise? Because we have sorted out the cause of suffering, samudaya. You don't have to go beyond this point; just this much is enough. Contemplate this in your own mind. Basically you should all have the Five Precepts as a foundation for behavior. It's not necessary to go and study the Tipiṭaka; just concentrate on the Five Precepts first. At first you'll make mistakes. When you realize it, stop, come back, and establish your Precepts again. Maybe you'll go astray and make another mistake. When you realize it, reestablish yourself. If you practice like this, you will have sati at all times, in all postures. When it's time to sit in meditation, then sit. But meditation is not only sitting. You must allow your mind to fully experience things, allow them to flow and consider their nature. How should you consider them? See them as transient, imperfect, and ownerless. It's all uncertain. "This is so beautiful, I really must have it." That's not a sure thing. "I don't like this at all." Tell yourself right there, "Not sure!" Is this true? Absolutely, no mistake. But just try taking things for real: "I'm going to get this thing for sure...." You've gone off the track already. Don't do this. No matter how much you like something, you should reflect that it's uncertain. Some kinds of food seem so delicious, but you should reflect that it's not a sure thing. It may seem so sure, it's so delicious, but still you must tell yourself, "Not sure!" If you want to test out whether it's sure or not, try eating your favorite food every day. Every single day, mind you. Eventually you'll complain, "This doesn't taste so good anymore." Eventually you'll think, "Actually, I prefer that kind of food." That's not a sure thing either!

Some people sit until they fall into a stupor. They might as well be dead; they can't tell north from south. Don't take it to such an extreme. If you feel sleepy then walk, change your posture. Develop wisdom. If you are really tired, then have a rest. As soon as you wake up, then continue the practice; don't let yourself drift into a stupor. You must practice like this. Have reason, wisdom, circumspection.

Start the practice from your own mind and body, seeing them as impermanent. Keep this in mind when you find food delicious. You must tell yourself, "Not a sure thing!" You have to slug it first. Usually it just slugs you first every time, doesn't it? If you don't like anything, you just suffer over it. This is how things slug us. You never get a punch in!

Practice in all postures. Sitting, standing, walking, lying—you can experience anger in any posture, right? You can be angry while walking, while sitting, while lying down. You can experience desire in any posture. So our practice must extend to all postures. It must be consistent. Don't just put on a show, really do it. While sitting in meditation, some incident might arise. Before it's settled, another one comes racing in. Whenever these things come up, just tell yourself, "Not sure, not sure." Slug it before it gets a chance to slug you.

Now this is the important point. If you know that all things are impermanent, all your thinking will gradually unwind. When you reflect on the uncertainty of everything that passes, you'll see that all things go the same way. Whenever anything arises, all you need to say is, "Oh, another one!"

If your mind is peaceful it will be just like still, flowing water. Have you ever seen still, flowing water? Just that! You've seen flowing water and still water, but maybe never still, flowing water. Right there, right where your thinking cannot take you, right in the peacefulness, you can develop wisdom. Your mind will be like flowing water, and yet it's still. Still and yet flowing. So I call it "still, flowing water." Wisdom can arise here.

CHAPTER 36

TRANSCENDENCE

WHEN THE GROUP of five ascetics[70] abandoned the Buddha, he saw it as a stroke of luck, because he would be able to continue his practice unhindered. The five ascetics had abandoned him because they felt that he had slackened his practice and reverted to indulgence. Previously he had been intent on his ascetic practices and self-mortification. In regard to eating, sleeping, and so forth he had tormented himself severely, but he saw that such practices just weren't working. He had been practicing out of pride and clinging. He had been mistaking worldly values and selfhood for the truth.

For example, if one decides to throw oneself into ascetic practices with the intention of gaining praise—this kind of practice is "world inspired": one is practicing for adulation and fame. Practicing with this kind of intention is called mistaking worldly ways for the truth.

Another way to practice is to "mistake one's own views for truth." You only believe in yourself, in your own practice. No matter what others say, you stick to your own preferences. This is called mistaking oneself for the truth.

Whether you take the world or take yourself to be truth, it's all simply blind attachment. The Buddha saw this, and saw that there was no "adhering to the Dhamma," no practicing for the truth. So his practice had been fruitless; he still hadn't given up defilements.

Then he turned around and reconsidered all the work he had put into the practice right from the beginning. What were the results of all that practice?

Looking deeply, he saw that it was full of conceit and full of the world. There was no Dhamma, no insight into anattā, no emptiness or complete letting go.

Looking carefully at the situation, the Buddha saw that even if he were to explain these things to the five ascetics, they wouldn't be able to understand. It wasn't something he could easily convey to them, because they were still firmly entrenched in the old way of practice and seeing things. The Buddha saw that you could practice like that until your dying day, maybe even starve to death, and achieve nothing, because such practice is inspired by worldly values and by pride.

After deep consideration, he understood *sammā paṭipadā,* or right practice: the mind is the mind, the body is the body. The body is not the source of desire or defilement. If you were to destroy the body, you wouldn't destroy defilements. Even fasting and going without sleep until the body was a shriveled wraith wouldn't exhaust the defilements. But the belief that defilements could be dispelled in that way, the teaching of self-mortification, was deeply ingrained in the five ascetics.

The Buddha then began to take more food, eating as normal, practicing in a more natural way. When the five ascetics saw the change in the Buddha's practice they figured that he had given up and reverted to sensual indulgence. The Buddha's understanding had shifted to a higher level, transcending appearances, but the five others saw him as sliding downward, reverting to comfort. Self-mortification was deeply ingrained into the minds of the five ascetics because the Buddha had previously taught and practiced it. But now the Buddha had seen the fault in it and had let it go.

When the five ascetics saw the Buddha acting in a more normal way, they left him. Just as birds fly away from a tree that no longer offers sufficient shade, or fish leave a pool of water that is too small, too dirty, or too warm, just so did the five ascetics abandon the Buddha.

So now the Buddha concentrated on contemplating the Dhamma. He ate more comfortably and lived more naturally. He let the mind be simply the mind, the body be simply the body. He didn't force his practice in excess, just enough to loosen the grip of greed, aversion, and delusion. Previously he had walked the two extremes: When happiness or love arose, he was aroused and became attached to it. He identified with it and wouldn't let go. He would get stuck in it. That was one extreme. The other was when he practiced self-mortification with the five ascetics. These two extremes he called kāmasukhallikānuyoga and attakilamathānuyoga.

The Buddha had been stuck on conditions. He saw clearly that these two ways are not the way for a samaṇa. If he were to flounder in them, constantly running from one extreme to the other, he would never become one who clearly knew the world. Now the Buddha fixed his attention on the mind itself and its training.

All facets of nature proceed according to their supporting conditions. For instance, the body experiences pain, sickness, fever, and colds, and so on. These all naturally occur; they are not problems in themselves. Actually people worry about their bodies too much. Wrong view leads them to worry about and cling to their bodies so much they can't let go.

Look at this hall here. We build the hall and say it's ours, but lizards come and live here, rats and geckoes come and live here, and we are always driving them away, because we hold that the hall belongs to us, not to the rats and lizards.

It's the same with illnesses in the body. We take this body to be our home, something that really belongs to us. If we happen to get a headache or a stomachache, we get upset; we don't want the pain and suffering. These legs are *our* legs, *our* arms, and we don't want them to hurt; this is *our* head, we don't want anything to go wrong with it. We've got to cure all pains and illnesses at all costs.

This is where we are fooled and stray from the truth. We are simply visitors to this body. Just like this hall here, it's not really ours. We are simply temporary tenants, like the rats, lizards, and geckoes. But we don't understand this. Actually the Buddha taught that there is no abiding self within this body, but we go and grasp it as being our self, as being who we are. When the body changes, we don't want it to do so. No matter how much we are told we don't understand. If I say it straight, you get even more fooled. "This isn't yourself," I say, and you go even more astray; you get even more confused and your practice just reinforces the self.

So most people don't really see the self. One who sees the self is one who knows that things neither are the self nor belong to the self. This means investigating saṅkhāras according to their true nature. To know the true nature of saṅkhāras is wisdom. If you don't know the true nature of saṅkhāras, you are at odds with them, always resisting them. Now, is it better to let go of the saṅkhāras or to try to oppose or resist them? And yet we plead with them to comply with our wishes. We look for all sorts of means to organize them or cut a deal with them. If the body gets sick and is in pain we don't want it to be so, so we look for various suttas to chant, such as *Bojjhaṅgo,* the *Dhammacakkappavattana Sutta,* the *Anattālakkhaṇa Sutta,* and so on. We don't want the body to be in pain; we want to protect it, to control it. These suttas can become some form of mystical ceremony, getting us even more entangled in clinging, when we chant them in order to ward off illness, to prolong life, and so on. Actually, the Buddha gave us these teachings to help us see clearly, but we end up chanting them to increase our delusion. *Rūpaṁ aniccaṁ, vedanā aniccā, saññā aniccā, saṅkhāra aniccā, viññāṇaṁ aniccaṁ....*[71] We don't chant these words to increase our delusion. The recollections help us understand the truth of the body, so that we can let it go and give up our clinging.

This is called chanting to cut things down, but we tend to chant in order to extend them all. Or if we feel they're too long, we try chanting to shorten them, to force nature to conform to our wishes. It's all delusion. Everyone sitting here in the hall is deluded. The ones chanting are deluded, the ones listening are deluded, they're all deluded! All they can think is, "How can we avoid suffering?" Where are they ever going to practice?

Whenever illnesses arise, those who know see nothing strange about it. Getting born into this world entails experiencing illness. When the Buddha and the Noble Ones contracted illness, they would treat it with medicine: it was simply a matter of correcting the elements. They didn't blindly cling to the body or to mystical ceremonies and suchlike. They treated illnesses with Right View, not with delusion. "If it heals, it heals. If it doesn't, then it doesn't"—that's how they saw things.

They say that nowadays Buddhism is thriving in Thailand, but it looks to me like it's sunk almost as far as it can. The Dhamma halls are full of attentive ears, but they're attending wrongly—even the senior members of the community. So people just lead one another into more delusion.

How are those people going to transcend suffering? They have chants for realizing the truth, but they turn around and use them to increase their delusion. They turn their backs on the right path. One goes eastward, the other goes west—how are they ever going to meet? They're not even close to each other. They chant, but they chant with foolishness, not with wisdom. They study, but they study with foolishness; they know, but they know foolishly. So they end up going with foolishness, living with foolishness, knowing with foolishness. That's how it is. And the teaching? All they do these days is teach people to be stupid. They say they're teaching people to be clever, to impart knowledge, but when you look at it in terms of truth, you see that they're really teaching people to go astray and grasp at deceptions.

The real foundation of the teaching is in order to see *attā,* the self, as being empty, with no fixed identity, void of intrinsic being. But people come to the study of Dhamma to increase their self-view, so they don't want to experience suffering or difficulty. They want everything to be cozy. They may want to transcend suffering, but if there is still a self how can they ever do so?

Suppose we came to possess a very expensive object. The minute that thing comes into our possession, our mind changes. "Now, where can I keep it? If I leave it there, somebody might steal it." We worry ourselves into a state, trying to find a place to keep it. And when did the mind change? It changed the minute we obtained that object—suffering arose right then. No matter where we leave that object, we can't relax. Whether sitting, walking, or lying down, we are lost in worry.

This is suffering. And when did it arise? It arose as soon as we knew that we had obtained something. Before we had that object there was no suffering. It hadn't yet arisen because there wasn't yet an object for it to cling to.

Attā is the same. If we think in terms of "my self" then everything around us becomes "mine." Confusion follows. The cause of it all is that there is a self. We don't peel off the apparent in order to see the transcendent. You see, the self is only an appearance. You have to peel away the appearances in order to see the heart of the matter, which is transcendence. Overturn the apparent to find the transcendent.

You could compare it to unthreshed rice. Before you can eat rice, you must thresh it. Get rid of the husks and you will find the seed inside.

Now if we don't thresh the rice we won't find the seed. Like a dog sleeping on the pile of unthreshed grain. Its stomach is rumbling, but all it can do is lie there and think, "Where can I get something to eat?" When it's hungry, it bounds off the pile of rice grain and runs off looking for scraps of food. Even though it's sleeping right on top of a pile of food, it knows nothing of it. Why? It can't eat the rice. Dogs can't eat unthreshed rice. The food is there but the dog can't eat it.

We may have learning, but if we don't practice accordingly we'll remain just as oblivious as the dog sleeping on the pile of rice grain. It's a shame, isn't it? Now this is the same: there is rice grain but what is hiding it? The husk hides the grain, so the dog can't eat it. And there is the transcendent—what hides it? The apparent conceals the transcendent. People simply sit on top of the pile of rice, unable to eat it—that is, unable to practice, unable to see the transcendent. They get stuck in appearances time and time again. If you are stuck in appearances, suffering is in store: you will be beset by becoming, birth, old age, sickness, and death.

So there isn't anything else blocking people off; they are blocked right here. People who study the Dhamma without penetrating to its true meaning are just like the dog on the pile of unthreshed rice. No matter how much we study the Dhamma, we won't see it if we don't practice.

This is like some sort of sweet fruit: even though the fruit is sweet we must rely on contact with and experience of that fruit before we will know what the taste is like. Now that fruit, even though no one tastes it, is sweet all the same. But nobody knows of it. The Dhamma of the Buddha is like this. Even though it's the truth it isn't true for those who don't really know it. No matter how excellent or fine it may be it is worthless to them.

Why do people grab after suffering? Nobody wants suffering and yet people keep creating the causes of suffering, almost as if they were wandering around looking for it. Within their hearts, people are looking for happiness, yet the mind creates so much suffering. Just seeing this much is enough. It can only be because we don't know suffering. We don't know suffering, don't know the cause of suffering, don't know the end of suffering, and don't know the way leading to the end of suffering. That's why people behave the way they do.

These people have micchā diṭṭhi—wrong view—but they don't see that it's micchā diṭṭhi. Whatever we say, believe in, or do that results in suffering is all wrong view. If it wasn't wrong view it wouldn't result in suffering. We wouldn't cling to suffering or to happiness or to any condition at all. We would leave things to go their natural way, like a stream of water. We don't have to dam it up; we just let it flow along its natural course.

The flow of Dhamma is like this, but the flow of the ignorant mind tries to resist the Dhamma in the form of wrong view. And yet it flies off, seeing wrong view everywhere else, in other people. But that we ourselves have wrong view, this we don't see. It's worth looking into.

Most people are still stuck in the mass of suffering, still wandering in saṁsāra. If illness or pain arise, all they can do is wonder how they can get rid of it. They want it to stop as fast as possible. They don't consider that this is the normal way of saṅkhāras. The body changes and people can't accept it; they've got to get rid of the pain at all costs. However, in the end, they can't win; they can't beat the truth. It all collapses. This is something people don't want to look at.

Practicing to realize the Dhamma is the most excellent of things. Why did the Buddha develop all the perfections? So that he could realize this and enable others to see the Dhamma, know the Dhamma, practice the Dhamma, and be the Dhamma—so that they could let go and not be burdened.

For either happiness or suffering to arise there must be the attā, the self. There must be the "I" and "mine," there must be this appearance. If when all these things arise the mind goes straight to the transcendent, it removes the appearances. It removes the delight, the aversion, and the clinging from those things. Just as when something that we value gets lost: when we find it again, our worries disappear. When we cultivate Dhamma practice and attain the Dhamma, see the Dhamma, then whenever we encounter a problem we solve the problem instantly, right then and there. It disappears completely, laid down, released.

Why is it we are still unattained, still cannot let go? It's because we still don't see the harm clearly. Our knowledge is faulty. If we knew clearly like the Lord Buddha or his arahant disciples, we would surely let go, and our problems would dissolve completely with no difficulty at all.

When your ears hear sounds, then let them do their job. When your eyes perform their function with forms, then let them do so. When your nose works with smells, let it do its job. When your body experiences sensations, then let it perform its natural function. If we just leave our senses to perform their natural functions where will problems arise? There are no problems.

In the same way, all those things that belong to the apparent, leave them with the apparent. And acknowledge that which is the transcendent. Simply be the "one who knows," knowing without fixation, knowing and letting things be their natural way.

To know Dhamma you must know in this way. That is, to know in such a way as to transcend suffering. This sort of knowledge is important. Knowing about how to make things, to use tools, knowing all the various sciences of the world and so on, all have their place, but they are not the supreme knowledge. The Dhamma must be known as I've explained it here. You don't have to know a whole lot; just this much is enough for the Dhamma practitioner—to know and then let go. It's not that you have to die before you can transcend suffering, you know. You transcend suffering in this very life because you know how to solve problems. You know the apparent, you know the transcendent. Know them in this lifetime, while you are here practicing.

You may wonder, "Why does the Ajahn keep saying this?" How could I teach other than the truth? But even though it's the truth, don't hold fast to it! If you cling to it blindly it becomes a falsehood. It's like grabbing the leg of a dog. If you don't let go the dog will spin around and bite you. Try it. If you don't let go it's got no choice but to bite. The world of the apparent is just the same. We live in accordance with conventions, but if we cling to them hard, they bring us suffering. Just let things pass.

Whenever we feel that we are definitely in the right, so much so that we refuse to open up to anything or anybody else, we've gone wrong. We're into wrong view. When suffering arises, where does it arise from? From wrong view.

So I say, "Allow space, don't cling to things." "Right" is just another supposition, just let it pass. "Wrong" is another apparent condition, just let it be at that. If you feel you are right and others contend that you're wrong, don't argue, just let it go. As soon as you know, let go. This is the straight way.

Usually it's not like this. People don't often give in to each other. That's why some people, even Dhamma practitioners who still don't know themselves, may say things that are utter foolishness and yet think they're being wise. They may say something that's so stupid that others can't even bear to listen, and yet they think they are being cleverer than others. Other people can't even listen to the Dhamma and yet they think they are smart, that they are right. They are simply advertising their own stupidity.

That's why the wise say, "Any speech that disregards anicca is the speech not of a wise person but of a fool. It's the deluded speech of one who doesn't know that suffering is going to arise right there." For example, suppose you had decided to go to Bangkok tomorrow and someone were to ask, "Are you going to Bangkok tomorrow?" You reply, "I hope to go to Bangkok. If there are no obstacles I'll probably go." This is called speaking with the Dhamma in mind, speaking with anicca in mind, taking into account the truth: the transient and uncertain nature of the world. You don't just say, "Yes, I'm definitely going tomorrow."

There's still much more to it. The practice of Dhamma becomes more and more refined. But if you don't see the Dhamma, you may think you are speaking right even when you are not, when you are straying from the true nature of things with every word. To put it simply: anything that we say or do that causes suffering to arise should be known as micchā diṭṭhi. It's delusion and foolishness.

Most practitioners don't reflect in this way. Whatever they like they think is right, and they just go on believing themselves. If they receive a gift, a new title, or a promotion, or even words of praise, they think it's great and get puffed up with pride and conceit. They don't consider, "Who am I? Where is this so-called goodness? Where did it come from? Do others have the same things?"

The Buddha taught that we should behave normally. If we don't really chew over this point, delusion will still be sunk deep within us—we are still sunk in wealth, rank, and praise. Because of them, we become someone else: we think we are better than before, that we are something special.

Actually, in truth, there isn't anything to human beings. Whatever we may be, it's only in the realm of appearances. If we take away the apparent and see the transcendent, we realize that there isn't anything there. There are simply the universal characteristics—birth in the beginning, change in the middle, and cessation in the end. If we see this, problems don't arise, and we have contentment and peace.

Trouble arises when we think like the five ascetic disciples of the Buddha. They followed their teacher's instructions, but when he changed his practice they couldn't understand it. They decided that the Buddha had given up and reverted to indulgence. We'd probably do the same, staying stuck in our old ways and convinced we're right.

So I say: Practice, but also look at the results of your practice. Look especially at places where you refuse to follow the teacher or the teachings, where there is friction. Where there is no friction, things flow. Where there is friction and no flow, you create a self and things become solid, a mass of clinging. This is diṭṭhi māna. If we attach even to what is right, refusing to concede to anybody, then it becomes wrong. To cling fast to rightness is simply the arising of self; there is no letting go.

This point gives people a lot of trouble, except for those Dhamma practitioners who understand. If you understand and are a quick practitioner, your response is instantaneous: you just let go. Clinging arises, and immediately there is letting go; you force the mind to let go right then and there.

You must see these two functions operating: the clinging and the one who resists the clinging. Whenever you experience a mental impression, you should observe these two functions operating. Just watch them both. Reflecting and constantly practicing like this, the clinging gets lighter, becomes less frequent. Right View increases as wrong view gradually wanes. Clinging decreases, non-clinging arises. This is the way it is for everybody. Consider this point. Learn to solve your problems in the present moment.

CHAPTER 37

TOWARD
THE UNCONDITIONED

THE POINT OF LISTENING to the Dhamma is, first, to create some understanding of the things we don't yet understand, to clarify them, and, second, to improve our grasp of the things we understand already. We must rely on Dhamma talks to improve our understanding, and listening is the crucial factor. The mind is the important ingredient. The mind is that which perceives good and bad, right and wrong. If we are lacking in sati for even one minute, we are crazy for that minute; if we are lacking in sati for half an hour, we will be crazy for half an hour. However much our mind is lacking in sati, that's how crazy we are. That's why it's especially important to pay attention when listening to the Dhamma.

All creatures in this world are plagued by nothing other than suffering. The purpose of studying the Dhamma is to utterly destroy this suffering. If suffering arises it's because we don't really know it. No matter how much we try to control it through willpower or through wealth and possessions, it is impossible. Only through clear knowledge and awareness, through knowing the truth of it, can suffering disappear. And this applies not only to homeless ones—monks, nuns, and novices—but also to householders: for anybody who knows the truth of things, suffering automatically ceases.

Now the states of good and bad are constant truths. Dhamma means that which is constant, which maintains itself. Turmoil maintains its turmoil, serenity maintains its serenity. Good and bad maintain their respective conditions, just as hot water maintains its hotness—it doesn't change for anybody: whether you're young or old, whatever your nationality, it's hot. So Dhamma is defined as that which maintains its condition. In our practice we must know heat and coolness, right and wrong, good and bad. If we know unwholesomeness, for example, we will not create causes for it to arise.

This is the practice of Dhamma. But many are those who study the Dhamma, learn it, even practice it, but who are not yet one with the Dhamma, and who have not yet quenched the cause of unwholesomeness and turmoil within their hearts. As long as the cause of heat is still present, we can't possibly prevent heat from being there. In the same way, as long as the cause of confusion is within our minds, we cannot possibly prevent confusion from being there, because it arises from this source. As long as the source is not quenched, confusion will arise again.

Whenever we perform good actions, goodness arises in the mind. It arises from its cause. This is called *kusala,* wholesome or skillful. When we understand causes, we can create them, and the results will naturally follow. But people don't usually create the right causes. They want goodness very much, yet they don't work to bring it about. All they get are bad results, embroiling the mind in suffering. All people want these days is money. They think that if they just get enough money, everything will be all right; so they spend all their time looking for money, they don't look for goodness. This is like wanting meat but not using salt to preserve it: you just leave the meat around the house to rot. Those who want money should know not only how to find it but also how to look after it. If you want meat, you can't expect to buy it and then just leave it lying around. It'll just go rotten.

This kind of thinking is wrong. The result of wrong thinking is turmoil and confusion. The Buddha taught the Dhamma so that people would put it into practice, in order to know it, see it, and be one with it—to make the mind Dhamma. When the mind is Dhamma it will attain happiness and contentment. The restlessness of saṁsāra is in this world, and the cessation of suffering is also in this world.

The practice of Dhamma serves therefore to lead the mind to the transcendence of suffering. The body can't transcend suffering—having been born, it must experience pain and sickness, aging, and death. Only the mind can transcend clinging and grasping. All the teachings of the Buddha, which we call *pariyatti,* are a skillful means to this end. For instance, the Buddha taught about *upādinnaka saṅkhāra* and *anupādinnaka saṅkhāra*—

mind-attended conditions and non-mind-attended conditions. Non-mind-attended conditions are usually defined as such things as trees, mountains, rivers, and so on—inanimate things. Mind-attended conditions are defined as animate things—animals, human beings, and so on. Most students of Dhamma take this definition for granted, but if you consider the matter deeply, if you reflect on how the human mind gets so caught up in sights, sounds, smells, tastes, feelings, and mental states, you might see that really there isn't anything that is not mind-attended. As long as there is craving in the mind everything becomes mind-attended.

Studying the Dhamma without practicing it, we will be unaware of its deeper meanings. For instance, we might think that the pillars of this meeting hall, the tables, benches, and all inanimate things are not mind-attended. We only look at one side of things. But just try getting a hammer and smashing some of these things up, and you'll see whether they're mind-attended or not!

It's our own mind, clinging to the tables, chairs, and all of our possessions, that attends these things. Even when one little cup breaks, it hurts, because our mind is attending that cup. Be they trees, mountains, or whatever, whatever things we feel to be ours, they have a mind attending them—if not their own mind then someone else's. These are all mind-attended conditions.

It's the same for our body. Normally we would say that the body is mind-attended. The state of mind that attends the body is none other than upādāna, clinging, latching on to the body and clinging to it as being "me" and "mine."

Just as a blind person cannot conceive of colors—no matter where they look, they see no colors—just so for the mind blocked by craving and delusion; all objects of consciousness become mind-attended: tables, chairs, animals, everything. If we believe that there is an intrinsic self, the mind will attach to everything. All of nature becomes mind-attended; there is always clinging and attachment.

The Buddha talked about *sankhata dhammas* and *asankhata dhammas*—conditioned and unconditioned things. Conditioned things are innumerable—material or immaterial, big or small—if our mind is under the influence of delusion, it will proliferate about these things, dividing them up into good and bad, short and long, coarse and refined. Why does the mind proliferate like this? Because it doesn't know conventional, determinate reality *(sammuti sacca);* it doesn't know about conditions. Not knowing these things, the mind doesn't see the Dhamma. Not seeing the Dhamma, the mind is full of clinging. As long as the mind is held down by clinging there can be no escape from the conditioned world. As long as there is no escape, there is confusion, birth, old age, sickness, and death, even in the thinking processes. This kind of mind is called a saṅkhata dhamma (conditioned mind).

Asaṅkhata dhamma, the unconditioned, refers to the mind that has seen the Dhamma, the truth, of the five khandhas as they are—as transient, imperfect, and ownerless. All ideas of "me" and "mine," "them" and "theirs," belong to the conventional reality. Really they are all conditions. When we know the truth of conditions we know the truth of conventions. When we know conditions as neither ourselves nor belonging to us, we let go of conditions and conventions. When we let go of conditions we attain the Dhamma, we enter into and realize the Dhamma. When we attain the Dhamma we know clearly. What do we know? We know that there are only conditions and conventions: no self, no "us" or "them." This is knowledge of the way things are.

Seeing things thus, the mind transcends them. The body may age, sicken, and die, but the mind transcends these states. When the mind transcends conditions, it knows the unconditioned. The mind becomes the unconditioned, a state that no longer contains conditioning factors. The mind is no longer conditioned by the concerns of the world; conditions no longer contaminate the mind. Pleasure and pain no longer affect it. Nothing can affect the mind or change it; the mind has escaped all constructions. Seeing the true nature of conditions and determinations, the mind becomes free.

This freed mind is called the unconditioned, that which is beyond the power of constructing influences. If the mind doesn't really know conditions and conventions, it is moved by them. Encountering good, bad, pleasure, or pain, it proliferates about them. It proliferates because there is still a cause. The cause is the belief that the body is one's self or belongs to the self; that feelings are self or belong to self; that perception is self or belongs to self, that conceptual thought is self or belongs to self; that consciousness is self or belongs to self. The tendency to conceive things in terms of self is the source of happiness, suffering, birth, old age, sickness, and death. This is the worldly mind, the conditioned mind, spinning around and changing at the directives of worldly conditions.

If we receive some windfall, our mind is conditioned by it. That object impels our mind into a feeling of pleasure, but when it disappears, our mind is pulled into suffering. The mind becomes a slave of conditions, a slave of desire. No matter what the world presents to it, the mind is moved accordingly. This mind has no refuge; it is not yet assured of itself, not yet free. It still lacks a firm base.

Reflect: Even a child can make you get angry. Even a child can trick you—into crying, into laughing, into all sorts of things. Even old people get duped. Conditions are always shaping the deluded mind into countless reactions, such as love and hate, pleasure and pain. They shape our minds like this because we are enslaved by them. We are slaves of taṇhā, or craving. Craving gives all the orders, and we simply obey.

I hear people complaining, "Oh, I'm so miserable. Night and day I have to work in the fields. I have no time at home. In the middle of the day I have to work in the hot sun with no shade. If it gets cold, I can't stay at home; I have to go to work. I'm so oppressed."

If I ask them, "Why don't you just leave home and become a monk?" they say, "I can't leave, I have responsibilities." Taṇhā pulls them back. Sometimes when you're doing the ploughing you might be bursting to urinate so much you just have to do it while you're ploughing, like the buffaloes! This is how much craving enslaves them.

When I ask, "How are things going? Haven't you got time to come to the monastery?" they say, "Oh, I'm really in deep." I don't know what it is they're stuck in so deeply! These are just conditions, concoctions. The Buddha taught to see appearances as such, to see conditions as they are. This is seeing the Dhamma, seeing things as they really are. If you really see these two things, then you must throw them out, let them go.

No matter what you may receive, it has no real substance. At first it may seem good, but it will eventually go bad. It will make you love or hate, laugh or cry, whichever way it pulls you. Why is this? Because the mind is undeveloped.

In the time of our forefathers, when a person died they would invite the monks to recite the recollection on impermanence: *Aniccā vata saṅkhārā / Uppādavaya dhammino / Uppājjitva nirujjhan'ti / Tesaṁ vūpasamo sukho.* All

conditions are impermanent. The body and the mind are both impermanent; they do not remain fixed and unchanging. What is there that doesn't
change within this body? Hair, nails, teeth, skin—are they now the same as
they used to be? The mind—is it stable? Think about it. How many times
is there arising and ceasing even in one day? So both body and mind are
constantly arising and ceasing, in a state of constant turmoil.

The reason you can't see these things in line with the truth is because you
keep believing the untrue. It's like being guided by a blind man who leads
you into forests and thickets. How can he lead you to safety when he can't
see? In the same way our mind is deluded by conditions, creating suffering
in the search for happiness, creating difficulty in the search for ease. We
want to get rid of suffering and difficulty, but instead we create those very
things. And then all we can do is complain. We create bad causes, and the
reason we do so is because we don't know the truth of appearances and
conditions.

Conditions are impermanent, both the mind-attended ones and the non-
mind-attended. In practice, the non-mind-attended conditions are nonexistent. What is there that is not mind-attended? Even your own toilet,
which you would think would be non-mind-attended—try letting someone
smash it with a sledge hammer! He would probably have to contend with
the authorities. The mind attends everything, even feces and urine. Except
for the person who sees clearly the way things are, there are no such things
as non-mind-attended conditions. Appearances are concocted. Why must
we concoct them? Because they don't intrinsically exist. For example, suppose somebody wanted to create a landmark for his property. He could
take a piece of wood or a rock and place it on the ground, and then call it
a marker. Actually, the thing he uses is not itself a marker. Something
becomes a marker only when we assign it a determined existence. In the
same way we "determine" cities, people, cattle—everything! Why must we
concoct these things? Because intrinsically they do not exist.

Concepts such as "monastic" and "lay person" are also concoctions. We
create them because intrinsically they aren't here. It's like having an empty
dish—you can put anything you like into it because it's empty. This is the
nature of conventional reality. Men and women are simply conventional
concepts, as are all the things around us.

If you understand the truth of conventions, you can be at peace. But if you believe that a person, a being, a "mine," a "theirs," and so on are intrinsic qualities, then you'll inevitably laugh and weep over them. If we take such things to be ours there will always be suffering. This is micchā diṭṭhi, wrong view.

We are all lost in conventional reality. This is why at the funeral ceremonies the monks chant, "Impermanent are all conditioned things / Of the nature to arise and pass away." For that's the truth. What is something that, having arisen, doesn't cease? People are born and then they die. Moods arise and then fade. Have you ever seen anybody cry for three or four years? At the most, you may see people crying a whole night, and then the tears dry up.

"The calming of conditions is true happiness," says the chant. If we understand saṅkhāras, proliferations, and thereby subdue them, this is the greatest happiness. This is true merit, to be calmed of proliferations, calmed of "being," calmed of individuality, of the burden of self. Transcending these things one sees the unconditioned. This means that no matter what happens, the mind doesn't proliferate around it. There's nothing that can throw the mind off its natural balance. What else could you want? This is the end, the finish.

The Buddha taught the way things are. Our making offerings and listening to Dhamma talks and so on is in order to search for and realize this. If we realize this, we don't have to go and study vipassanā (insight meditation), it will happen of itself. Both samatha (calm) and vipassanā come into being through causes, just like other determinate things. The mind that knows, which is beyond such things, is the culmination of the practice.

Our practice, our inquiry, is in order to transcend suffering. When clinging is finished with, states of being are finished with. When states of being are finished with, there is no more birth or death. When things are going well, the mind does not rejoice, and when things are going badly, the mind does not grieve. The mind is not dragged all over the place by the tribulations of the world, and so the practice is finished. This is the basic principle for which the Buddha gave his teachings.

The Buddha taught the Dhamma for us to use. Even when we are dying, there is the teaching *Tesaṁ vūpasamo sukho....* But we don't subdue these conditions; instead we carry them around, as if the monks were telling us to do so. We carry them around and cry over them. This is how we get lost in conditions. Heaven, hell, and nibbāna are all to be found at this point.

People are generally ignorant when it comes to conventional realities; they think things all exist of themselves. When the books tell us that trees, mountains, and rivers are non-mind-attended conditions, this is simplifying things, because there's no reference to suffering—it's as if there were no suffering in the world. This is just the shell of Dhamma. If we were to explain things in terms of ultimate truth, we would see that it's people who go and tie all these things down with their attachments. How can you say that things have no power to shape events, that they are not mind-attended, when people will beat their children even over a single tiny needle? One single plate or cup, a plank of wood—the mind attends all these things. Just watch what happens if someone goes and smashes one of them up and you'll find out. Everything is capable of influencing us in this way. Knowing these things fully is our practice; examining those things that are conditioned and unconditioned, mind-attended and non-mind-attended.

This is part of the "external teachings," as the Buddha once referred to them. Once when the Buddha was staying in a forest, he took a handful of leaves and asked the bhikkhus, "Bhikkhus, which is the greater number, the leaves I hold in my hand or the leaves scattered over the forest floor?"

The bhikkhus answered, "The leaves in the Blessed One's hand are few, but the leaves scattered around the forest floor are far greater in number."

"In the same way, bhikkhus, the entirety of the Tathāgata's knowledge is vast, but many of the things he knows do not pertain to the essence of things; they are not directly related to the way out of suffering. There are so many aspects to the teaching, but what the Tathāgata really wants you to do is to transcend suffering, to inquire into things, and abandon clinging and attachment to the five khandhas of form, feeling, perception, mental formations, and sense consciousness. Stop clinging to these things and you will transcend suffering." These teachings are like the leaves in the Buddha's hand. You don't need so many, just a few teachings are enough. As for the rest of them, you needn't worry yourselves. It is just like the vast earth, abundant with grasses, soil, mountains, forests. There's no shortage of rocks and pebbles, but all those rocks are not as valuable as one single jewel. The Dhamma of the Buddha is like this. You don't need a whole lot. All the external teachings are really about the mind. No matter if you study the Tipiṭaka, the Abhidhamma, or whatever, don't forget where it came from.

When it comes to the practice, the only things you really need to start with are honesty and integrity. You don't need to make a lot of trouble for yourself. You may not have studied the Tipiṭaka, but you are still capable of recognizing greed, anger, and delusion, aren't you? Where did you learn about these things? Did you have to read the Tipiṭaka or the Abhidhamma to know greed, hatred, and delusion? Those things are already there in your mind; you don't have to study books to have them. But the teachings are for inquiring into and abandoning these things.

Let the knowing spread from within you and you will be practicing rightly. If you want to see a train, just go to the central station; you don't have to go travelling all the way up the northern line, the southern line, the eastern line, and the western line to see all the trains. If you want to see trains, every single one of them, you'd be better off waiting at Grand Central Station, that's where they all terminate.

Now some people tell me, "I want to practice but I don't know how. I'm not up to studying the scriptures; I'm getting old now, my memory's not so good." Just look right here, at "central station." Greed arises here, anger arises here, delusion arises here. Just sit here and you can watch as all these things arise. Practice right here, because right here is where you're stuck. Right here is where conventions arise, and right here is where the Dhamma will arise. Dhamma practice can be done anywhere. A long time ago I traveled all over looking for a teacher because I didn't know how to practice. I was always afraid that I was practicing wrong. I'd constantly go from one mountain to another, from one place to another—until I stopped and reflected. Now I understand what I was doing. I must have been quite stupid, for I didn't realize then—while I was wandering around looking for places to practice meditation—that the right place was already here, in my heart. All the meditation you want is right there inside you. There is birth, old age, sickness, and death right here within you. That's why the Buddha said, *"Paccattaṁ veditabbo viññūhi"*: the wise must know for themselves. I'd repeated the words before, but I didn't yet understand their meaning. I traveled all over looking for the right place to meditate, and stopped only when I was about to drop dead from exhaustion—only then did I find what I was looking for, inside of me. So now I can tell you about it.

Some people may say you can't practice at home, that there are too many obstacles. If that's the case, then even eating and drinking are going to be obstacles. If eating is an obstacle to practice, then don't eat! People also say they can't practice as a lay person; the surroundings are too crowded. If you live in a crowded place, then look into crowdedness. You can make it open and wide. The mind has been deluded by crowdedness, so train it to know the truth of crowdedness. The more you neglect the practice, the more you neglect going to the monastery and listening to the teaching, the more your mind will sink down into the bog, like a frog going into a hole. Someone comes along with a hook and the frog's done for; they don't have a chance. All they can do is stretch out their neck and offer it to them. So don't work yourself into a corner—someone may just come along with a hook and scoop you up. At home, being pestered by your children and grandchildren, you are even worse off than the frog! You don't know how to detach from these things. When old age, sickness, and death come along, what will you do? This is the hook that's going to get you. Which way will you turn?

This is the predicament our minds are in: engrossed in the children, the relatives, the possessions, and you don't know how to let them go. Without morality or understanding to free things up there is no way out for you. When feeling, perception, mental formations, and consciousness produce suffering, you always get caught up in it. Why does this suffering arise? If you don't investigate you won't know. If happiness arises you simply get caught up in happiness, delighting in it. You don't ask yourself where this happiness comes from.

So change your understanding. You can practice anywhere, because the mind is with you everywhere. While sitting, if you think good thoughts, be aware of them; if you think bad thoughts, be aware of them too. While lying down, do the same. Just watch your own mind. The Buddha's teaching tells us to watch ourselves, not to run after fads and superstitions. That's why he said, "Moral rectitude (sīla) leads to well-being, leads to wealth, leads to nibbāna. Therefore, maintain your Precepts purely."[72] Sīla refers to our actions. Good actions bring good results; bad actions bring bad results. Don't expect the gods to do things for you, or the angels and guardian deities to protect you, or the auspicious days to help you. These things aren't true, so don't believe in them. If you believe in them you will suffer. You'll always be waiting for the right day, the right month, the right year, or the aid of the angels and guardian deities. You'll only suffer. Look into your own actions and speech, into your own kamma. Doing good, you inherit goodness; doing bad, you inherit badness.

If you understand that good and bad, right and wrong, all lie within you, then you won't have to go looking for those things somewhere else. Just look for these things where they arise. If you lose something here, you must look for it here. Even if you don't find it at first, keep looking where you dropped it. But usually, we lose it here then go looking over there. When will you ever find it? Good and bad actions lie within you. One day you're bound to see it, just keep looking right there. All beings fare according to their kamma. What is kamma? People are too gullible. If you do bad things, they say, Yāma, the king of the underworld, will write it all down in a book. When you go there, he takes out this register and looks you up. You're all afraid of Yāma in the afterlife, but you don't know the Yāma within your own minds. If you do something bad, even if you sneak off and do it by yourself, this Yāma knows and will write it all down. You've probably secretly done bad things that no one else saw. But *you* saw it, didn't you? This Yāma sees it all. There's no escaping it.

Is there anybody here who has ever stolen something? There are probably a few of us who are ex-thieves. We know our own intention. When you do bad actions, badness is there; if you do good actions, goodness is there. There's nowhere you can go to hide. Even if others don't see you, you must see yourself. Even if you go into a deep hole you'll still find yourself there. There's no way you can commit bad actions and get away with it. In the same way, why shouldn't you see your own purity? You see it all—the peaceful, the agitated, the liberation, or the bondage—we see all these for ourselves. In this Buddhist religion you must be aware of all your actions. We don't act like the brahmins, who go into your house and say, "May you be well and strong, may you live long." The Buddha doesn't talk like that. How will the disease go away just with talk? The Buddha's way of treating the sick was to say, "Before you fell ill, what happened? What led up to your sickness?" Then you tell him how it came about. "Oh, it's like that, is it? Take this medicine and try it out." If it's not the right medicine he tries another one. This method is scientifically sound. As for the brahmins, they just tie a string around your wrist and say, "Okay, be well, be strong, and after I leave you just get right on up and eat a hearty meal." No matter how much you pay them, your illness won't go away, because their way has no scientific basis. But this is what people like to believe.

All things are just as they are. They don't cause suffering in themselves.

Just like a thorn, a really sharp thorn, does it make you suffer? No, it's just a thorn, it doesn't bother anybody. But if you go and stand on it, then you'll suffer. Why is there this suffering? Because you stepped on the thorn. The thorn is just minding its own business, it doesn't harm anybody. It's because of we ourselves that there's pain. Form, feeling, perception, mental formations, consciousness—all the things in this world are simply there as they are. It's we who pick fights with them. And if we hit them, they're going to hit us back. If they're left on their own they won't bother anybody; only the swaggering drunkard gives them trouble. If you think "I'm good," "I'm bad," "I'm great," "I'm hopeless," then you are thinking wrongly. If you see all these thoughts as merely determinations and conditions, then when others say "good" or "bad" you can leave it be with them. As long as you still see them as "me" and "you," it's like having hornets come buzzing out to sting you. The hornets come at you from their three nests: *sakkāyadiṭṭhi* (belief in the self), *viccikicchā* (doubt), and *sīlabbataparāmāsa* (attachment to rites and practices).[73]

Once you look into the true nature of conventional realities and conditions, pride can no longer prevail. Other people's fathers are just like our father, their mothers are just like ours, their children are just like ours. We see the happiness and suffering of other beings as just like our own. In this way we can come face to face with the future Buddha—it's not so difficult. Everyone is in the same boat. Then the world will be as smooth as a drumskin. If you want to wait around to meet Phra Sri Ariya Metteya, the future Buddha, then just don't practice—you'll probably be around long enough to see him. But he's not so crazy that he'd take people like that for disciples!

Most people just doubt. If you no longer doubt about the self, then no matter what people may say about you, you aren't concerned, because your mind has let go; it is at peace. Conditions become subdued. Grasping after the forms of practice—that teacher is bad, that place is no good, this is right, that's wrong—no. There's none of these things. All this kind of thinking is all smoothed over. You come face to face with the future Buddha. Those who only hold up their hands and pray will never get there.

So here is the practice. The Buddha leads you only to the beginning of the Path. *Akkhātaro Tathāgata*—the Tathāgata only points the way. In my case, he only taught this much—just what I teach you—and the rest was up to me. I can bring you only to the beginning of the Path. Now it's up to you.

CHAPTER 38

EPILOGUE

D o you know where it will end? Or will you just keep on studying like this? That's okay, but it's not external study but internal study that counts. For the internal study you have to study these eyes, these ears, this nose, this tongue, this body, and this mind. This is the real study. The study of books is just external, and it's really hard to ever finish it.

When the eye sees form, what sort of thing happens? When ear, nose, and tongue experience sounds, smells, and tastes, what takes place? When the body and mind come into contact with tangible objects and mental states, what reactions take place? Are there still greed, aversion, and delusion there? Do we get lost in forms, sounds, smells, tastes, textures, and moods? This is the internal study. It has a point of completion.

If we study but don't practice, we won't get results. It's like a man who raises cows. In the morning he takes the cow out to pasture; in the evening he brings it back to its pen—but he never drinks the cow's milk. Study is all right, but don't let it be like this. You should raise the cow and drink its milk too. To get the best results you must study and practice as well.

I'll explain it another way. It's like a man who raises chickens, but doesn't collect the eggs. All he gets is the chicken shit! This is what I tell the people who raise chickens back home. Watch out that you don't become like that! This means we study the scriptures but we don't know how to let go of defilements, we don't know how to push greed, aversion, and delusion out of our mind. Study without practice, without this giving up of defilements, brings no results. This is why I compare it to someone who raises chickens but doesn't collect the eggs, he just collects the shit. It's the same thing.

The Buddha wanted us to study the scriptures, and then to give up unwholesome actions through body, speech, and mind; to develop goodness in our deeds, speech, and thoughts. The real worth of humankind will come to fruition through our deeds, speech, and thoughts. If we only talk, without acting accordingly, the practice is not yet complete. Or if we do good deeds but the mind is still not good, this is still incomplete. The Buddha taught to develop goodness in body, speech, and mind; to develop fine deeds, fine speech, and fine thoughts. This is the treasure of human life. The study and the practice must both be good.

The eight factors of the Eightfold Path of the Buddha, the path of practice, are nothing other than this very body: two eyes, two ears, two nostrils, one tongue, and one body. This is the Path. And the mind is the one who follows the Path. Therefore both the study and the practice exist in our body, speech, and mind.

Have you ever seen scriptures that teach about anything other than the body, speech, and mind? The scriptures only teach about this, nothing else. Defilements are born right here. If you know them, they die right here. So you should understand that the practice and the study both exist right here. If we study just this much, we can know everything. In speech, speaking one word of truth is better than a lifetime of wrong speech. Do you understand? Here's another way of saying it: One who studies and doesn't practice is like a ladle in a soup pot. It's in the pot every day, but it doesn't know the flavor of the soup.

If you don't practice, you may study till the day you die, but you'll never know the taste of freedom!

GLOSSARY

Abhidhamma	The third of the "Three Baskets" of the Tipiṭaka; a systematized compendium of Buddhist philosophy and psychology.
ādinavakathā	Reflection on the inadequacy and limitation of the conditioned world.
ajahn	Teacher (Thai). (Pali: *acariya*.)
ānāpānasati	Mindfulness of breathing.
anattā	Not-self.
anicca	Impermanence or uncertainty.
anicca-dukkha-anattā	The three characteristics of existence: impermanence, suffering, and not-self.
apāya	The four "lower worlds": the animal world, ghost world, demon world, and the hell realms.
arahant	One who has reached the highest state of enlightenment.
bhava	Becoming; the process of existence.
bhāvanā	Meditation, development or cultivation; often used to refer to *citta-bhāvanā,* mind development, or *paññā-bhāvanā,* wisdom development, or contemplation.
bhikkhu	Buddhist monk.
Buddha	"One who knows"; one who is awakened, who represents the state of enlightenment or awakening; the historical Buddha, Siddhatta Gotama. Also: *Buddho.*
caṅkama	Walking meditation.
dāna	Generosity, giving.

Dhamma	The truth of the way things are; the teachings of the Buddha that reveal that truth and elucidate the means of realizing it as a direct experience. (Skt. *Dharma.*)
dhamma	Phenomenon; mental object. See also: *nāma-dhamma, sacca-dhamma, saṅkhata dhamma, sīla-dhamma,* worldly dhammas. (Skt. *dharma.*)
dhutanga	Ascetic or austere practices. A dhutanga monk is one who keeps some of the thirteen ascetic practices allowed by the Buddha over and above the general disciplinary code. In Thai the word is transliterated as *tudong* and has also acquired the meaning of the extended pilgrimages made on foot by monks who pursue such ascetic practices. These practices aid in the cultivation of contentedness, renunciation, and energetic effort.
dukkha	Suffering, unsatisfactoriness; the inherent insecurity, instability, and imperfection of conditioned phenomena.
Eightfold Path	Eight factors of spiritual practice leading to the extinction of suffering: Right View (or Right Understanding), Right Thought, Right Speech, Right Action, Right Livelihood, Right Effort, Right Mindfulness, Right Concentration.
ekaggatā	One-pointedness; the fifth factor of absorption.
Five Precepts:	The five basic guidelines for training oneself in wholesome actions of body and speech: refraining from killing other beings; refraining from stealing; responsible sexual conduct; refraining from lying and false speech; refraining from the use of intoxicants.
glot	A large umbrella equipped with a mosquito net, used by Thai dhutanga monks for meditation and shelter while staying in the forest.
hiri-ottappa	Sense of shame *(hiri)* and an intelligent fear of consequences *(ottappa);* two positive states of mind that lay a foundation for a clear conscience and moral integrity.
jhāna	Absorption; an advanced state of concentration or *samādhi,* wherein the mind becomes absorbed into its meditation subject. It is divided into four levels, each level progressively more refined than the previous one.

kāmachanda	Sensual desire; one of the Five Hindrances, the other four being ill will, sleepiness, restlessness, and worry and doubt.
kamma	Volitional action by means of body, speech, or mind Sanskrit: *karma,* used in the text to indicate the more common, popular usage, implying both action *and* its results.
kammaṭṭhāna	Meditation object; lit., "basis for action"; usually refers to the forty subjects of meditation (listed in the *Visuddhimagga*); more generally, training in sīla, samādhi, and paññā.
khandha	"Heap" or aggregate; one of the five constituents of human existence: form, feeling, perception, mental formations, and sense consciousness. (Skt. *skandha.*)
kilesa	Defilement; mental quality that defiles or stains the heart or mind, such as greed, hatred, delusion, restless agitation, and so on. (Skt. *klesha.*)
kusala	Wholesome or skillful actions or mental states.
kuṭī	A small dwelling place for a Buddhist monastic; a hut.
lobha	Greed.
Luang Por	Venerable Father, Respected Father; a friendly and reverential term of address used for elderly monks.
magga	Path. See Eightfold Path.
Mahā	Title given to monks who have studied Pali and completed up to the fourth year or higher.
māna	Conceit, pride.
Māra	Evil and temptation personified; a powerful malevolent deity ruling over the highest heaven of the sensual sphere; personification of the defilements, the totality of worldly existence, and death.
mettā	Loving-kindness.
nāma	Nonmaterial (mental) phenomena (Also: *nāmadhamma*).

ñāṇadassana	Knowledge and insight (into the Four Noble Truths).
nibbāna	The state of liberation from all suffering and defilements, the goal of the Buddhist path (Sanskrit: *nirvāna*).
nibbidā	Disenchantment, world-weariness.
"one who knows"	An inner faculty of awareness. Under the influence of ignorance or defilements, it knows things wrongly. Trained through the practice of the Eightfold Path, it is the awakened knowing of a Buddha.
opanayiko	Worthy of inducing in and by one's own mind; worthy of realizing; to be tried by practice; leading inward.
ottappa	See *hiri-ottappa.*
pah kow	An eight-precept postulant who often lives with bhikkhus and, in addition to his own meditation practice, also helps them with certain services that the vinaya forbids bhikkhus to do—for example, clearing brush or carrying food overnight through unpopulated regions.
paññā	Wisdom, discernment, understanding of the nature of existence. (Skt. *prajña.*)
pārami	The ten spiritual perfections: generosity, moral restraint, renunciation, wisdom, effort, patience, truthfulness, determination, kindness, and equanimity. Virtues accumulated over lifetimes manifesting as wholesome dispositions. (Skt. *pāramitā.*)
Parinibbāna	Full, or final *nibbāna.* Often applied to the extinction of the five *khandha*s at the passing away of the Buddha.
pariyatti	The teachings as laid down in the scriptures, or as passed down from one person to another in some form; the "theoretical" aspect of Buddhism. *Pariyatti* is often associated with two other aspects of Buddhism—*paṭipatti*, the practice, and *paṭivedha*, the realization. Thus: study—practice—realization.
Path	See Eightfold Path.
paṭiccasamuppāda	Conditioned arising, dependent origination; one of the central doctrines of the Buddhist teaching.

Pāṭimokkha	The central body of the monastic code, which is recited fortnightly in the Pali language.
paṭipadā	Path of practice; road; progress. *Sammā paṭipadā:* right practice.
pīti	Rapture; the third factor of absorption.
rūpa	Material or physical objects, corporeality (Also: *rūpa-dhamma*).
sacca-dhamma	Ultimate truth.
samādhi	Concentration, one-pointedness of mind, mental stability; state of concentrated calm resulting from meditation practice.
samaṇa	A religious seeker living a renunciant life. Originating from the Sanskrit term for "one who strives," the word signifies someone who has made a profound commitment to spiritual practice. Ajahn Chah usually translates the term as "one who is peaceful."
sāmaṇera	Buddhist novice.
samatha	Calm, tranquillity.
sammuti sacca	Conventional, dualistic, or nominal reality; the reality of names, determinations. For instance, a cup is not intrinsically a cup; it is only determined to be so.
sampajañña	Self-awareness, self-recollection, clear comprehension, alertness.
saṁsāra	Wheel of Existence; lit., "perpetual wandering"; the continuous process of being born, growing old, suffering, and dying again and again; the world of all conditioned phenomena, mental and material.
saṅkhāra	Compounded, or conditioned thing; phenomenon; anything constituted by preexisting causes. In the Thai language the word *sungkahn* is commonly used to refer to the body.
saṅkhata dhamma	Conditioned thing, conventional reality; as contrasted with *asaṅkhata dhamma*, unconditioned reality, i.e., *nibbāna,* the deathless.

sati	Mindfulness, recollection.
Siddhatta Gotama	The original name of the historical Buddha.
sīla	Virtuous conduct, morality; moral discipline.
sīla-dhamma	Another name for the moral teachings of Buddhism. On the personal level: "virtue and (knowledge of) truth."
sukha	Happiness, contentment, ease; the fourth factor of absorption.
sutta	A discourse of the Buddha as recorded in the Pali canon (Sanskrit: *sutra*).
taṇhā	Craving; desires conditioned by ignorance of the way things are.
Tathāgata	Perfect One; lit., the one who has "thus gone" or "thus come"; an epithet of the Buddha.
Tipiṭaka	The Buddhist canon. (Sanskrit: *Tripiṭaka*.)
tudong	See *dhutanga*.
upacāra samādhi	"Neighborhood" or access concentration; a degree of concentration before entering absorption or jhāna.
upādāna	Grasping, clinging, attachment.
upekkhā	Equanimity.
vicāra	Contemplation of a meditation theme.
vinaya	The Buddhist monastic code of discipline; lit., "leading out," because maintenance of these rules "leads out" of unskillful actions and unskillful states of mind; in addition it can be said to "lead out" of the household life and attachment to the world.
vipassanā	Insight.
vitakka	The act of bringing the mind to the theme of contemplation.
worldly dhammas	The eight worldly conditions of gain and loss, praise and criticism, happiness and suffering, fame and disrepute.

NOTES

1 *Jhāna:* profound unification of the mind in meditation. The Buddha taught eight distinct levels.

2 *Sīla:* is a broad term whose meaning includes living an ethical life, following moral precepts, and behaving in a restrained manner that does not harm others or oneself. In this translation, it will be rendered as "virtue."

3 *Samādhi:* the focused energy of the mind in meditative concentration.

4 Five Precepts: the five basic guidelines for training oneself in wholesome actions of body and speech: refraining from killing other beings; refraining from stealing; responsible sexual conduct; refraining from lying and false speech; refraining from the use of intoxicants.

5 These words, and the words referred to in notes 9, 10, and 11, are the opening words of a famous teaching the Buddha delivered to a spontaneous gathering of 1,250 of his enlightened disciples at the Bamboo Grove, near Rājagaha, on the full moon of February. The occasion is celebrated by the annual festival of Māgha Puja. This discourse, the "Ovādapāṭimokka," forms verses 183–85 of the *Dhammapada*.

6 The five khandhas: form, feeling, perception, conceptualization or mental formations, and sense-consciousness. These comprise the psycho-physical experience known as the "self."

7 Considered a delicacy in some parts of Thailand.

8 "Looking for merit" is a commonly used Thai phrase. It refers to the custom in Thailand of going to monasteries, or *wats*, paying respect to venerated teachers, and making offerings.

9 These words *(sabba pāpassa akaraṇaṁ)* are from the "Ovādapāṭimokka," and form verses 183–85 of the *Dhammapada*. See note 5, above.

10 See note 5, above.

11 See note 5, above.

12 There is a play on words here between the Thai words *luuk,* meaning "children," and *luuk peun,* meaning, literally, "a gun's children," that is, bullets.

13 The Buddhist Pali canon.

14 At that time Sāriputta had his first insight into the Dhamma, attaining *sotāpanna,* or "stream enterer."

15 *Dhutanga:* Ascetic or austere practices. A dhutanga monk is one who keeps some of the thirteen ascetic practices allowed by the Buddha over and above the general disciplinary code. In Thai the word is transliterated as *tudong* and has also acquired the meaning of the extended pilgrimages made on foot by monks who pursue such ascetic practices. These practices aid in the cultivation of contentedness, renunciation, and energetic effort.

16 That is, *nibbidā,* disenchantment, disinterest in the lures of the sensual world.

17 The Thai word for *bhava—phop—*would have been a familiar term to Ajahn Chah's audience. It is generally understood to mean "sphere of rebirth." Ajahn Chah's usage of the word here is somewhat unconventional, emphasizing a more practical application of the term.

18 Observance days, held roughly every fortnight on the new and full moon days, on which monks and nuns confess their offenses and recite the disciplinary precepts, the Pāṭimokkha. On these days, and on the half-moon days as well, members of the lay community often come and spend their time in the monastery, taking the Eight Precepts for the twenty-four hours, listening to Dhamma talks, and practicing sitting and walking meditation through the night, then return to their homes at dawn.

19 Forest monks boil down the heartwood from the jackfruit tree and use the resulting liquid to both dye and wash their robes.

20 The seven Factors of Enlightenment *(bojjhaṅga)* are *sati,* mindfulness; *Dhamma-vicaya,* investigation of reality; *viriya,* effort; *pīti,* joy; *passaddhi,* tranquility; *samādhi,* concentration, and *upekkhā,* equanimity.

21 This refers to the Venerable Ajahn's early years in the monkhood, before he had begun to practice in earnest.

22 The second *saṅghādisesa* offense, which deals with touching a woman with lustful intentions.

23 The *pācittiya* offense no. 36, for eating food outside of the allowed time—dawn till noon.

24 *Dukkaṭa:* offenses of "wrongdoing," the lightest class of offenses in the vinaya, of which there are a great number. *Pārājika*—offenses of defeat, of which there are four, are the most serious, involving expulsion from the Bhikkhu-Sangha.

25 *Pubbasikkhā Vaṇṇanā* (The Elementary Training): a Thai commentary on Dhamma-vinaya based on the Pali commentaries, especially on the *Visuddhimagga* (Path to Purity), Ācariya Buddhaghosa's exhaustive commentary on the Dhamma-vinaya.

26 *Āpatti:* the name of the offenses of various classes for a Buddhist monk.

27 A "receiving cloth" is a cloth used by Thai monks for receiving things from women, from whom they do not receive things directly. That Venerable Ajahn Pow lifted his hand from the receiving cloth indicated that he was not actually receiving the money.

28 There are very precise and detailed regulations governing the ordination procedure, which, if not adhered to, may render the ordination invalid.

29 The vinaya forbids bhikkhus from eating raw meat or fish.

30 Although it is an offense for monks to accept money, there are many who do. Some may accept it while appearing not to, which is probably how the lay people in this instance saw the Venerable Ajahn's refusal to accept money. He would accept the money, they may have thought, if they didn't overtly offer it to him but just slipped it into his bag.

31 *Añjali* is the traditional way of making greeting or showing respect, as with the Indian greeting *Namaste* or the Thai *wai.*

32 *Sādhu* is the traditional Pali word used to acknowledge a blessing or Dhamma teaching, or to show appreciation or agreement, etc.; it means "it is well."

33 Another transgression of the precepts, a pācittiya offense.

34 *Navakovāda:* a simplified synopsis of elementary Dhamma-vinaya.

35 Many monks undertake written examinations of their scriptural knowledge, sometimes—as Ajahn Chah points out—to the detriment of their application of the teachings in daily life.

36 There is a play on words in the Thai language here based on the word for family—*khrop khrua*—which literally means "kitchen-frame" or "roasting circle." In the English translation we have opted for a corresponding English word rather than attempting a literal translation of the Thai.

37 Both red ants and their eggs are used for food in the northeast of Thailand. Such raids on their nests were not so unusual.

38 The first line of the traditional Pali words of homage to the Buddha, recited before giving a formal Dhamma talk. *Evaṁ* (meaning "thus it is") is the traditional Pali word for ending a talk.

39 Māra: the Buddhist personification of evil and entrapment in suffering.

40 This is shame based on knowledge of cause and effect rather than emotional guilt.

41 "Outer activity" refers to all manner of sense impressions. It is used in contrast to the "inner inactivity" of absorption samādhi (jhāna), where the mind does not "go out" to external sense impressions.

42 Here "heart" has the same meaning as "mind" in other talks.

43 The play on words here between the Thai *patibat* (practice) and *wibat* (disaster) is lost in the English.

44 The ten *pāramitā* or *pāramis* (perfections): generosity, morality, renunciation, wisdom, effort, patience, truthfulness, resolution, goodwill, and equanimity.

45 *Kilesa:* defilements; mental qualities that defile or stain the heart; sensual or selfish desire, anger, delusion, and any unwholesome state of mind based on them.

46 *Kesā, lomā, nakkha, dantā, taco:* contemplation of these five bodily parts constitutes the first meditation technique taught to a newly ordained monk or nun by his or her preceptor.

47 Monks and nuns in Ajahn Chah's tradition eat one meal a day, after the morning alms round.

48 Concept *(sammuti)* refers to conventional or provisional reality, while transcendence *(vimutti)* refers to the liberation from attachment to or delusion within it.

49 These are the two extremes pointed out as wrong paths by the Buddha in his first discourse.

50 The level of nothingness, one of the "formless absorptions," sometimes called the seventh *jhāna* (absorption).

51 Also known as Princess Yasodharā.

52 The body on the first night had been that of a child; on the second night it was that of an adult.

53 The last line of the traditional Pali verses that list the qualities of the Dhamma.

54 *Mahānikai* and *Dhammayuttika* are the two sects of the Theravāda Sangha in Thailand.

55 A Thai expression meaning "Don't overdo it."

56 Literally, "All conditioned things are impermanent." See p. 328 for a full version of the text.

57 According to Buddhist thought, beings are born in any of six states of existence depending on their karma. These include the heavenly states (where happiness is predominant), the human state, and the four above-mentioned lower states (where suffering is predominant). The Venerable Ajahn always stresses that we should see these states in our own minds in the present moment. Depending on the condition of the mind, we can say that we are continually being born in these different states. For instance, when the mind is on fire with anger, we have fallen from the human state and have been born in hell right here and now.

58 This teaching is found in the Buddha's discourse on the Four Foundations of Mindfulness, M10 and D22.

59 "Feeling" is a translation of the Pali word *vedanā*, and should be understood in the sense Ajahn Chah herein describes it: as the mental states of pleasure and pain.

60 In Thailand, to touch a person's head is usually considered an insult.

61 However, it is considered auspicious in Thailand to have one's head touched by a highly esteemed monk.

62 The "four supports" are robes, alms food, lodging, and medicine.

63 Venerable Jagaro was the abbot of Wat Pah Nanachat at that time. He had brought a party of monks and lay people to see Ajahn Chah.

64 A chant traditionally recited at funeral ceremonies.

65 As of 2002, there are more than two hundred branch monasteries, big and small, of Wat Nong Pah Pong, both in Thailand and around the world.

66 One of the four bases of clinging: *kāmupādāna*, clinging to sense objects; *sīlabbatupādāna*, clinging to rites and rituals; *diṭṭhupādāna*, clinging to views; and *attavādupādāna*, clinging to the idea of self.

67 One of the Four Foundations of Mindfulness: body, feeling, mind, and dhammas.

68 *Anāgāmi* (non-returner): The third "level" of enlightenment, which is reached on the abandonment of the five "lower fetters" (of a total of ten) that bind the mind to worldly existence. The first two "levels" are *sotāpanna* ("stream enterer") and *sakadāgāmi* (once returner), the last being *arahant* ("worthy or accomplished one").

69 That is, one who lives dependent on the generosity of others.

70 Five ascetics followed Siddhatta Gotama when he was cultivating ascetic practices prior to his awakening. They left him when he renounced extreme asceticism for the Middle Way.

71 "Form is impermanent, feeling is impermanent, perception is impermanent, volition is impermanent, consciousness is impermanent." These verses are part of the daily morning chanting.

72 This phrase is spoken in Pali at the end of the traditional giving of the Precepts.

73 These qualities are the first three of the Ten Fetters *(samyojana),* the states of mind that bind the heart to the wheel of birth and death. The abandonment of these three is synonymous with "stream entry"—the first level of enlightenment.

SOURCES OF THE TEXT

AJAHN CHAH'S WONDERFULLY SIMPLE STYLE of teaching can be deceptive. It is often only after we have heard something many times that suddenly our minds are ripe, and somehow the teaching takes on a much deeper meaning. His skillful means in tailoring his explanations of Dhamma to time and place, and to the understanding and sensitivity of his audience, was marvelous to see. Sometimes on paper though, it can make him seem inconsistent or even self-contradictory. At such times the reader should remember that these words are a record of a living experience. Similarly, if the teachings may seem to vary at times from tradition, it should be borne in mind that the Venerable Ajahn speaks always from the heart, from the depths of his own meditative experience.

The reader will appreciate that, since Ajahn Chah's talks were never planned out or aimed at a single theme, each of them tends to cover a broad range of aspects of the Buddha's Path—the elements of virtue, meditation, and wisdom constantly interweaving and supporting each other. Nevertheless, there are themes that stand out in each one, and so they have been roughly grouped here accordingly.

The talks gathered in this anthology were originally printed in six different publications; several of them have also been reprinted as individual items or in combination with one or two others. There are inherent difficulties in translating from Thai into English. Much of the repetition that is the art of oral instruction has been omitted, but hopefully not to the extent that the emphasis of the teacher has been lost. Pali words absorbed into the Thai language have, in the course of time, acquired additional meanings: for example, the Thai *arom* refers to the Pali *arammana,* sense object or mental impression, but its common meaning is "mood" or "emotion." Ajahn Chah uses these words in both ways and it has been translated accordingly. Similarly, the word for "mind" and "heart" is the same in Thai and it has been variously rendered in different contexts. Finding the middle way between a dull, over-literal approach and a more flowing, but less precise rendering isn't always easy. Each of the various translators has compromised in different ways. Hopefully they have managed to bring out both the clear simplicity, the directness, and the humor of these talks, and, at the same time, the profundity that underlies and inspires them. The original collections were as follows:

✦ *Bodhinyana* (the title is taken from Ajahn Chah's honorific name, meaning "enlightened knowledge") was the first collection of talks by Ven. Ajahn Chah to be translated and published by his Western students. Since its first appearance in 1979 it has been reprinted many times. The translations were done by a variety of Ajahn Chah's Western monks and nuns.

Fragments of a Teaching: given to the lay community at Wat Pah Pong in 1972.

A Gift of Dhamma: given to the assembly of Western monks, novices and lay people at Wat Pah Nanachat, Ubon, on 10th October, 1977. This discourse was offered to the parents of one of the monks on the occasion of their visit from France.

Dhamma Nature: given to the Western disciples at Wat Pah Nanachat during the Rains Retreat of 1977, just after one of the senior monks had disrobed and left the monastery.

The Two Faces of Reality: an informal talk given at Ajahn Chah's kuṭi, to some monks and novices after the evening meditation, 1976.

The Training of the Heart: given to a group of Western monks from Wat Bovornives, Bangkok, headed by their teacher Phra Khantipalo, in March 1977.

Living with the Cobra: given as final instruction to an elderly Englishwoman who spent two months under the guidance of Ajahn Chah at the end of 1978 and the beginning of 1979.

Reading the Natural Mind: an informal talk given to a group of newly ordained monks after the evening chanting, middle of the Rains Retreat, 1978.

Just Do It!: a lively talk, in Lao dialect, given to the assembly of newly ordained monks at Wat Pah Pong on the day of entering the Rains Retreat, July 1978.

✦ *A Taste of Freedom* was the effort of a single translator, Bruce Evans, who was Ajahn Puriso at the time this book was composed. It was first published in 1981.

About this Mind...

On Meditation: an informal talk given in the Northeastern dialect, taken from an unidentified tape.

The Path in Harmony: a composite of two talks given in England, in 1979 and 1977 respectively.

The Middle Way Within: given in the Northeastern dialect to an assembly of monastics and lay people in 1970.

The Peace Beyond: a condensed version of a talk given to the Chief Privy Councilor of Thailand, Mr. Sanya Dharmasakti, at Wat Pah Pong, 1978.

Convention and Liberation: an informal talk given in the Northeastern dialect, taken from an unidentified tape. The title derives from the dyad of terms *sammut-vimut* in Thai, *sammuti-vimutti* in Pali (see note 47 above).

No Abiding: given to the monks, novices and lay people of Wat Pah Nanachat, on a visit to Wat Pah Pong during the Rains Retreat of 1980.

Right View—The Place of Coolness: given to the monks, novices, and lay people of Wat Pah Nanachat, on a visit to Wat Pah Pong, 1979

Epilogue: excerpted from a talk given to a sincere and somewhat scholarly lay Buddhist, at Oxford, England, 1979.

✦ *Living Dhamma* is a collection of talks that Ajahn Chah gave to lay people; it is a companion volume to *Food for the Heart* (1993), which is comprised of talks to monastics. All the talks of these two books were also translated by Bruce Evans, they were compiled for the occasion of Ajahn Chah's funeral in 1993.

Making the Heart Good: given on the occasion of a large group of lay people coming to Wat Pah Pong to make offerings to support the monastery.

Why Are We Here?: given at Wat Tum Saeng Pet ("Cave of Diamond Light Monastery") to a group of visiting lay people, during the Rains Retreat 1981 shortly before Ajahn Chah's health broke down.

Our Real Home: given to an elderly lay disciple, approaching her death.

The Four Noble Truths: given at the Manjushri Institute, Cumbria, England, 1977.

Meditation—Samādhi Bhāvanā: given at the Hampstead Vihara, London, 1977.

Living in the World with Dhamma: an informal talk given after an invitation to receive alms-food at a lay person's house in Ubon, the district capital, close to Ajahn Chah's monastery.

"Tuccho Poṭhila"—Venerable Empty Scripture: an informal talk given at Ajahn Chah's kuṭī, to a group of lay people, one night in 1978.

Still, Flowing Water: given at Wat Tum Saeng Pet, during the Rains Retreat, 1981.

Toward the Unconditioned: given on a lunar Observance Night, at Wat Pah Pong, 1976.

✦ *Food for the Heart* (1993) is a smaller volume from which this collection takes its name, comprising:

Dhamma Fighting: excerpted from a talk given to monks and novices at Wat Pah Pong.

Understanding Vinaya: given to the assembly of monks after the recitation of the Pāṭimokkha, at Wat Pah Pong during the Rains Retreat, 1980.

Maintaining the Standard: given at Wat Pah Pong, after the completion of the Dhamma exams, 1978.

Right Practice—Steady Practice: given at Wat Kuean to a group of university students who had taken temporary ordination, during the hot season, 1978.

Samma Samādhi—Detachment Within Activity: given at Wat Pah Pong during the Rains Retreat, 1977.

The Flood of Sensuality: given to the assembly of monks after the recitation of the Pāṭimokkha, at Wat Pah Pong during the Rains Retreat, 1978.

In the Dead of Night: given on a lunar Observance Night, at Wat Pah Pong, in the late 60s.

Sense Contact—the Fount of Wisdom: given to the assembly of monks after the recitation of the Patimokkha, at Wat Pah Pong during the Rains Retreat, 1978.

"Not Sure!"—The Standard of the Noble Ones: an informal talk given at Ajahn Chah's kuṭī, to some monks and novices one night in 1980.

Transcendence: given on a lunar Observance Night, at Wat Pah Pong in 1975.

✦ *The Key to Liberation,* in its original Thai form *(Gunjaer Bhāvanā),* was the very first of Ajahn Chah's teachings to appear in print, sometime in the 1960s. This new translation into English was done in 2002.

The Key to Liberation: given to a former scholar monk and a group of his lay students, at Wat Pah Pong, in the 60s.

✦ *Seeing the Way* is a compendium, made in 1988, of teachings given by Ajahn Chah's senior Western monastic students. The book begins with this dialogue.

What is Contemplation?: excerpted from a session of questions and answers that took place at Wat Gor Nork, during the Rains Retreat of 1979, between Ajahn Chah and a group of Western monks and novices. Some rearrangement of the sequence of conversation has been made for ease of understanding.

INDEX

WISDOM PUBLICATIONS

WISDOM PUBLICATIONS, a not-for-profit publisher, is dedicated to making available authentic Buddhist works for the benefit of all. We publish translations of the sutras and tantras, commentaries and teachings of past and contemporary Buddhist masters, and original works by the world's leading Buddhist scholars. We publish our titles with the appreciation of Buddhism as a living philosophy and with the special commitment to preserve and transmit important works from all the major Buddhist traditions.

To learn more about Wisdom, or to browse books online, visit our website at wisdompubs.org.

You may request a copy of our mail-order catalog online or by writing to:

Wisdom Publications
199 Elm Street, Somerville, Massachusetts 02144 USA
Telephone:(617) 776-7416 ✦ Fax: (617) 776-7841
Email: info@wisdompubs.org ✦ www.wisdompubs.org

THE WISDOM TRUST

As a not-for-profit publisher, Wisdom is dedicated to the publication of fine Dharma books for the benefit of all sentient beings and dependent upon the kindness and generosity of sponsors in order to do so. If you would like to make a donation to Wisdom, please do so through our Somerville office. If you would like to sponsor the publication of a book, please write or email us at the address above.

Thank you.

Wisdom is a nonprofit, charitable 501(c)(3) organization affiliated with the Foundation for the Preservation of the Mahayana Tradition (FPMT).